Praise for *Igniting Creativity in Gifted Learners, K–6*

"There are many books that establish the importance of providing creative, stimulating learning experiences, but here is a book that provides strategies for exactly how that can be done. Joan Smutny has brought together a group of creative and exciting teachers who present in clear, usable ways, ideas and strategies that could and should be used in every classroom. Students fortunate enough to have the learning experiences described in this book are sure to gain the information, but more important, they will remember and be able to use the knowledge and skills presented long after these classroom experiences have ended. The students in these classrooms can't help but become more curious, more creative, and far more involved in the ideas and solutions they are learning.

In the pages of this book, the teachers provide a step-by-step approach to using their ideas, to re-create learning environments and lessons. They do not just talk about their work; they describe it so clearly that the reader can use their strategies for the benefit of the students they teach. While all students will gain from such creative learning experiences, gifted students will thrive and develop lifelong skills they can take with them to establish personal techniques that can feed their curiosity and satisfy their need-to-know.

Smutny has brought into being a means for classroom teachers to accomplish creative, exciting learning experiences, sharing the work of teachers who have such experiences with teachers who want to have them."

—Barbara Clark,
Professor Emeritus,
California State University

"This book has a tremendous number of exciting ideas for developing and enhancing the creativity of gifted learners in kindergarten through sixth grade. Teachers from across the country have contributed to this outstanding volume. The instructional activities are linked to the national curriculum standards. This book is a must for every dedicated teacher."

—Frances A. Karnes,
Professor of Curriculum, Instruction, and Special Education,
Director, The Frances A. Karnes Center for Gifted Studies,
University of Southern Mississippi

"This wonderful book is filled with practical strategies to "ignite creativity" in classrooms. Teachers will discover multiple ways to foster their students' creativity. They will find that there is no need to choose between standards and creativity, for in combination they spark learning at high levels. The strategies are applicable in all content areas, so this book is a valuable resource for all teachers."

—Julia L. Roberts,
Mahurin Professor of Gifted Studies,
Executive Director, The Center for Gifted Studies and
The Carol Martin Gatton Academy of Mathematics and Science,
Western Kentucky University

Igniting Creativity in Gifted Learners, K–6: Strategies for Every Teacher should be read by both teachers and parents, for it will invigorate and stimulate the development of creativity for all of our children. This practical book is in a class by itself being for teachers by teachers."

—Dorothy Sisk,
Conn Chair in Gifted Education
and Director of the Gifted Child Center,
Lamar University

"I have absolute faith and confidence in the powerful effectiveness of teachers coaching each other to constantly improve their already wonderful teaching skills. This marvelous book contains priceless examples of teachers sharing their particular expertise in how to bring creativity and excitement back to our classrooms, where it may have been floundering due to the heavy emphasis on standards-based teaching and learning. Best of all, the strategies are integrated with required standards to bring joy back into our classrooms when this experience is desperately needed in American education. Joan Smutny's collection of hands-on strategies shows us all how this can be done. Bravo!"

—Susan Winebrenner,
Author and Staff Development Specialist,
Education Consulting Service, Inc.

Igniting Creativity

in
GIFTED LEARNERS, K–6

Strategies
for
Every
Teacher

Joan Franklin Smutny • S.E. von Fremd

CORWIN PRESS
A SAGE Company

For information:

Corwin Press
A SAGE Company
2455 Teller Road
Thousand Oaks, California 91320
www.corwinpress.com

SAGE Ltd.
1 Oliver's Yard
55 City Road
London EC1Y 1SP
United Kingdom

SAGE India Pvt. Ltd.
B 1/I 1 Mohan Cooperative
 Industrial Area
Mathura Road, New Delhi 110 044
India

SAGE Asia-Pacific Pte. Ltd.
33 Pekin Street #02-01
Far East Square
Singapore 048763

Printed in the United States of America.

Library of Congress Cataloging-in-Publication Data

Smutny, Joan F.
Igniting creativity in gifted learners, K-6 : strategies for every teacher/edited by Joan Franklin Smutny, S.E. von Fremd.
    p. cm.
Includes bibliographical references and index.
ISBN 978-1-4129-5777-9 (cloth)
ISBN 978-1-4129-5778-6 (pbk.)
    1. Gifted children—Education (Elementary)—United States. I. Von Fremd, S. E. II. Title.

LC3993.22.S477 2009
371.95--dc22   2008027698

This book is printed on acid-free paper.

08   09   10   11   12   13   10 9 8 7 6 5 4 3 2 1

Acquisitions Editor:	David Chao
Editorial Assistants:	Mary Dang, Cassandra Harris
Production Editor:	Libby Larson
Copy Editor:	Jeanette McCoy
Typesetter:	C&M Digitals (P) Ltd.
Proofreader:	Wendy Jo Dymond
Indexer:	Jeanne R. Busemeyer
Cover Designer:	Michael Dubowe
Graphic Designer:	Brian Bello

Two thinkers who taught us the true meaning of creativity:

"Imagination is more important than knowledge."

—Albert Einstein

"Creative thinking is the highest form of mental functioning."

—E. Paul Torrance

Contents

Acknowledgments

We would like to acknowledge the 47 teacher-authors whose generosity and openness in sharing their most creative ideas with us have made this book the rich and practical volume that it is. Their hearts and courage in championing the cause of the "different drummer" in gifted children has been our constant inspiration.

We would also like to thank David Chao and the entire Corwin editorial staff, whose support, guidance, and kind thoughts always came at the right moments.

Corwin Press gratefully acknowledges the contributions of the following reviewers:

Ken Klopack
Art & Gifted Education Consultant
Chicago Public Schools
Chicago, Illinois

Dr. Elaine Powers
Gifted Resource
Kenmore Middle School
Arlington, Virginia

Donovan R. Walling
Senior Consultant for the Center for Civic Education
Bloomington, Indiana

About the Authors

Joan Franklin Smutny is founder and director of the Center for Gifted at National-Louis University and a recipient of the NAGC Distinguished Service Award for outstanding contribution to the field of gifted education. She directs programs for thousands of gifted children in the Chicago area annually. She also teaches creative writing in many of these programs as well as courses on gifted education for graduate students at the university. She is editor of the *Illinois Association for Gifted Children Journal*, contributing editor of *Understanding Our Gifted*, and a regular contributor to the *Gifted Education Communicator, Parenting for High Potential* and the *Gifted Education Press Quarterly*. Smutny has authored, coauthored, and edited many books on gifted education for teachers and parents, including *Acceleration for Gifted Learners, K–5* (Corwin Press, 2007), *Reclaiming the Lives of Gifted Girls and Women* (2007), *Differentiating for the Young Child* (Corwin Press, 2004), and *Designing and Developing Programs for Gifted Children* (Corwin Press, 2003). Other recent credits include *Underserved Gifted Populations* (2003), Gifted *Education: Promising Practices* (2003), and *Stand Up for Your Gifted Child* (2001). In 2005, she received the Presidents' Award from the California Association for the Gifted for significant contributions to gifted education.

S. E. von Fremd is an independent scholar, writer, and editor with a background in education, cultural studies, and dance. She performed with the Never Stop Moving Dance Company in Chicago under the direction of Reynaldo Martinez and taught creative dance and theater to children in the city and surrounding areas. Her interest in creativity and culture eventually led her to do a doctorate in performance studies at Northwestern University. This included a year's research in Uganda, where she focused on the role of popular theater and dance in reviving cultural identity and educating children and young people throughout the country. She has written several book reviews on

African musical traditions, a monograph on the cultural legacy of Kenyan novelist Ngugi wa Thiong'o and Nigerian playwright Wole Soyinka, another monograph on refugees in Africa, and an article on the performing arts as a popular forum for education in Uganda. She has also given presentations on Uganda's creative artists under the reign of Idi Amin and on dance movements throughout Africa. In the field of education, she coauthored (with Joan Smutny), *Differentiating for the Young Child* (2004).

About the Contributors

Keith Arney *(Chapter 7, "Looking at Art With a Critical Eye")*, chair of the Nikki Rowe High School art department for McAllen School District is a distinguished fellow and former president of the Texas Art Education Association. As an advocate for art education, he has served on state and national committees and is recognized for his leadership in the arts. row_arneyk@yahoo.com

Jane Artabasy *(Chapter 1, "A Sense of Belonging: Music as Connection and Community Through Creativity")* studied applied voice, piano, and music education at the undergraduate and postgraduate level. Her professional career has included teaching middle and junior high school vocal and general music in the northern suburbs of Chicago, with a particular focus on popular music performance and revues. A recipient of the Golden Apple Award for Excellence in Teaching, she taught musical comedy to gifted middle and high school students for many summers through the Center for Gifted at National-Louis University.

Paul Bamberger *(Chapter 6, "Creativity in the Classroom")* has extensive knowledge in the field of gifted education. He has served the field as gifted coordinator at the elementary and middle school levels. His enthusiasm for gifted education can be seen in his work with gifted students throughout the year. Paul has taught for the suburban public schools, the Youth Education and Talent Search programs at the College of DuPage, and the Worlds of Wisdom and Wonder program at National-Louis University. pondanderings@gmail.com

Scott T. Barsotti *(Chapter 7, "Strategies for Practical Acting Workshops")* is a playwright, director, and performer working in the Chicago theater scene. He has performed with Curious Theatre Branch (where he is a company member), Collaboration, and Illegal Drama to name a few, and his plays have been seen by audiences in Chicago and New York, including the Rhinoceros Theater Festival and the New York International Fringe Festival.

He has mentored for the Steppenwolf Theatre Company Cross-Town Ensemble and has been a guest artist at Columbia College Chicago, the University of Chicago, and the School of the Art Institute of Chicago. For more information, go to www.barsottiplays.com.

Bev Cheairs (*Chapter 2, "A General Guide to Creative Teaching"*), currently a gifted specialist for Wheaton-Warrenville Community Unit School District 200 in Illinois, works with accelerated students ages 6 to 11 in the subject areas of reading and mathematics. She has worked in the field of gifted education for 10 years in the public schools and has taught gifted children for the Center for Gifted at National-Louis University as well as for the Saturday Enrichment Program for Northwestern University. Most recently, she has begun teaching graduate-level courses on educating the gifted elementary school child through Illinois Benedictine University. bcheairs@sbcglobal.net

Rhonda Clevenson (*Chapter 4, "Primary Source Learning"*) is a veteran classroom teacher who enjoys being an instructor with Harvard's Graduate School of Education's Project Zero Classroom Institute and online courses through WIDE World. Rhonda is the program director for the Library of Congress Teaching with Primary Sources Northern Virginia Partnership and the Executive Director of the nonprofit organization formed by educators, Primary Source Learning. rclevenson@pslearning.org

Frances Collins (*Chapter 3, "Mentor Texts"*) has taught kindergarten for the Evanston School District since 2003. She has taught summer courses for gifted children at the Center for Gifted at National-Louis University as well as for Northwestern University's Center for Talent Development. mrhpotter@sbcglobal.net

Gay Doyle (*Chapter 4, "Creating Plays in Social Studies"*) is a fifth-grade teacher at Medinah Intermediate School in Medinah, Illinois. Her passion is social studies, and she is a member of the National Council for Social Studies. During the summer, she enjoys teaching Chicago area gifted children at Summer Wonders, a program for gifted young children through National-Louis University. Her school e-mail is gdoyle@medinah11.org, and her home e-mail is jazznroots@comcast.net.

Liz Fayer (*Chapter 5, "Making Discoveries in Problem-Based Learning"*), a curriculum and instruction specialist in South Dakota, has presented at conferences for gifted children on topics that include problem-based learning (PBL), "backward design," science inquiry, and differentiated instruction. Additionally, she advises and coaches school districts on the alignment of science curriculum to standards, inquiry, engagement, instructional focus, and materials acquisition. As part of this work, she consults for the Center

for the Advancement in math and science at Black Hills State University (BHSU) in South Dakota. Most recently, she developed a forensics curricular day for gifted high school students in conjunction with the Center for Conservation of Biological Resources at BHSU. Sdliz57@aol.com

Carol Fisher *(Chapter 6, "Calendar Challenge," "A Number by Any Other Name," "How Do YOU Count to Ten?," and "Math Literature Links")* has been involved with gifted children for more than 35 years, teaching, coordinating, and creating curriculum in mathematics for the Chicago Public Schools. She has worked with the Center for the Gifted at National-Louis University for more than 20 years creating math and integrated curriculums for summer and weekend programs. A recipient of the Golden Apple Award for Excellence in Teaching, she is looking forward to new adventures. GldnApl@aol.com

Maurice D. Fisher *(Chapter 3, "Ten Essential Criteria for an Advanced Humanities Curriculum for Gifted Students")* has been the publisher of *Gifted Education Press* of Manassas, Virginia, for the past 27 years and is also a program evaluation and research consultant in the Fairfax County, Virginia Public Schools. As part of his research and program evaluation in the district, he has conducted extensive studies on gifted and talented programs that helped bring needed change for both students and teachers. He can be reached at 703-369-5017 or mfisher345@comcast.net.

Jerry Flack *(Chapter 3, "Creative Explorations of Words"; Chapter 4, "Creative Mapping")* is professor emeritus and a President's Teaching Scholar at the University of Colorado. He developed the first gifted programs for students in the Kalamazoo, Michigan, public schools in the 1970s. In 1980, he was named the Future Problem Solving Program national teacher and coach of the year. He created the first MA degree program in gifted education at the University of Colorado in the early 1980s. He served on the Board of Directors of the National Association for Gifted Children, was chair of its Creativity Division, and received that organization's Early Leader Award, Distinguished Service Award, and the 2003 E. Paul Torrance Creativity Award. He may be reached at jflack@ix.netcom.com.

Christopher M. Freeman *(Chapter 4, "Historic Games of Strategy and Geography"; Chapter 6, "Critical and Creative Thinking Ideas in Math")* has taught mathematics at the University of Chicago Laboratory School for over 25 years. During this time, Chris has also taught enrichment math classes for gifted students in Grades 1 through 10 at the Center for Gifted at National-Louis University. Whether playing NIM games, drawing stars, building four-dimensional triangles, or finding patterns in Pascal's Triangle mod n, his students engage in critical and creative thinking in a mathematical context.

He has published several math books for teachers through Prufrock Press: *NIM: Serious Math With a Simple Game* (2001); *Drawing Stars & Building Polyhedra* (2003); *Compass Constructions: Activities for Using a Compass and Straightedge* (2008).

Courtland Funke *(Chapter 3, "Podcasting for and With Gifted and Talented Students")* has been teaching technology to students and teachers in Buffalo Grove, Illinois, for nine years. He has also been working with gifted students in computers and science in the Chicagoland area for more than 10 years. cfunke@sbcglobal.net

Rosemary Ginko *(Chapter 3, "Combining Language Arts and Social Studies for Gifted/Talented Sixth Graders")* is a language arts and literature teacher for gifted and talented sixth- through eighth-graders at the Jimmy Carter Middle School in Albuquerque, New Mexico. She has focused her work on designing and implementing creative, open-ended tasks and questions that challenge students to delve more deeply into topics, while at the same time developing their own study and research skills. Her background includes painting, dance, music, writing, photography, and drama. ginko@aps.edu

Pam Gish *(Chapter 3, "Literature Circles That Promote Higher Level Discussions")* learned firsthand the challenges of raising children with interests and talents not being met in traditional classrooms as a first- and second-grade teacher for six years as well as an at-home mother for 13 years. She taught at Creative Children's Academy in Palatine, Illinois, a school for gifted children, and later became a gifted coordinator in School District 25. Ten years ago, she stepped back into a regular classroom and has been an advocate for gifted education in District 46, serving on both committees and study groups. During the summers, one of her "treats" for herself is teaching for the Center for Gifted at National-Louis University. pam_gish@hotmail.com

Jeanie Goertz *(Chapter 7, "Looking at Art With a Critical Eye")* is assistant professor at Eastern Kentucky University (EKU), teaching graduate courses in gifted education and coordinating the gifted program at EKU Model Laboratory School. She has worked at universities and school districts as a teacher and coordinator of gifted programs in the Midwest and Southwest. An artist herself, she has focused her research on the visual and performing arts as they relate to gifted children and young people. From 1991 to 1993, she was chair of the Visual and Performing Arts Division of NAGC. MJGoertz@aol.com

Jennifer Golwitzer *(Chapter 2, "General Principles for Creative Teaching"; Chapter 3, "Writing Focus")* has been an elementary school teacher for several years and has found great joy in teaching children of differing ability levels during her years of service. She has been actively involved in developing the curriculum at her school and enhancing the learning experiences of all students. She feels privileged to work closely with gifted children and their parents through her own classroom experiences as well as programs offered through the Center for Gifted at National-Louis University. getafisk@aol.com

Christine Gould *(Chapter 7, "First Start in Art")* is an associate professor of teacher education and the director of the Network for Gifted Education at the University of Wisconsin–Stevens Point (UW–SP). She has coordinated a summer practicum and two outreach programs for gifted children at UW–SP and has published a number of articles on gifted education. cgould@uwsp.edu

Lois Veenhoven Guderian *(Chapter 4, "Combined Disciplinary and Interdisciplinary Collaboration Between General Music and Social Studies Classes"; Chapter 6, "Music Improvisation and Composition")* is a choral conductor, music educator, performer, researcher, clinician, author, and composer. As part of her work at Northwestern University, Lois has researched gifted education with a special emphasis on differentiated teaching strategies as applied to music education. She has taken graduate classes in gifted education offered through National-Louis University (NLU), has taught several programs for the Center for Gifted (at NLU) and has taught, coached, and mentored hundreds of young performers and composers. Lois specializes in designing arts curricula that are both discipline based and interdisciplinary and that incorporate creative work—especially music composition, improvisation, and creative dramatics. She has created and implemented several collaborative arts programs for organizations and is the author of the comprehensive music texts on music learning and recorder playing. A versatile composer and writer, her compositions have been internationally recorded, broadcast, and published. lois@loveeg.com

Joyce Hammer *(Chapter 6, "Math Is so Much More Than Two Times Four")* taught mathematics for many years at the Fairview South School in Skokie, Illinois, where she keeps returning because she loves children and loves teaching. In 1978, she founded a gifted program in mathematics and reading for students in kindergarten through eighth grade, a program that continues to flourish.

Pamela Walker Hart *(Chapter 8, "Winged to Fly")* is an award-winning artist, a published writer, and a creativity consultant. She taught the visual arts in public schools to levels K through 12. While teaching visual arts in Nebraska, Wisconsin, and the New York public schools, she established and implemented a pilot Gifted and Talented Visual Arts Program for elementary students. She also created a high school Unified Arts Curriculum and implemented it into eight different art classes. She is active as a visual arts teacher, exhibiting artist, juror, creativity speaker, multimedia presenter, and writer. For more information, visit her Web sites at www.CreativityInsideOut.com and www.pwalkerhart.com or e-mail her at pamelawalkerhart@gmail.com.

Kathryn P. Haydon *(Chapter 5, "Exploring the Rainforest Through Content-Based Language Instruction")* is an educator and writer living in Ojai, California. She has worked with many gifted children as a second-grade teacher and as a Spanish teacher. She has also taught creative writing classes for gifted students in Ojai and through the Center for Gifted in Evanston, Illinois. Most recently, she developed, wrote, and implemented the curriculum for a prekindergarten and primary-level Spanish program at a local school. khaydon@sbcglobal.net

Patricia Hollingsworth *(Chapter 7, "Creative Arts and Words")* is the director of the University School at the University of Tulsa, a school for gifted students from preschool through eighth grade. In addition to her position as director of the school, she also teaches art and kindergarten. She has served as president of the Oklahoma Association for Gifted, Creative, and Talented and was on the Board of Directors of the National Association for Gifted Children for 12 years. She is a coauthor of *Smart Art*, *Active Learning*, *Kinetic Kaleidoscope*, and the SAILS Humanities Curriculum. Additionally, she has written many chapters in books and articles about issues related to gifted students. patricia-hollingsworth@utulsa.edu

Carol V. Horn *(Chapter 4, "Student Historians")* is coordinator of Gifted and Talented Programs for Fairfax County Public Schools in northern Virginia. She has worked in gifted education for 20 years, and in 1995, she achieved National Board Certification. She then went on to develop a Web-based class to assist other teachers through the process. In 2002, she was a recipient of the Hollingsworth Award from the National Association for Gifted Children for outstanding research study in the field of gifted education. Carol has worked extensively to develop and implement the Young Scholars model—a comprehensive approach to finding and nurturing advanced academic potential in young learners from underrepresented populations—through ongoing professional development, collaboration, and teacher leadership. Carol.Horn@fcps.edu

Carol Sandberg Howe *(Chapter 4, "Mighty Mythology" and "Westward Expansion!"; Chapter 5, "Creative Strategies for Two Solar Science Unites for Primary Grades")* is a classroom teacher in gifted education and differentiated instruction in the Chicago and suburban schools. She has also taught in gifted programs at the Center for Gifted at National-Louis University, assisted in the production of educational programs and publications at WTTW, Channel 11, Chicago, and served as editor/writer for a number of notable magazines.

Mark Jurewicz *(Chapter 5, "Bunny Foo-Foo Flu")* is the science teacher for the prekindergarten through fifth-grade students at Quest Academy in Palatine, Illinois, a school for gifted and talented children. He has worked there for 14 years and has helped foster a love for science through hands-on experiments, probing discussions and the appearance of scams that keep the children guessing and thinking for themselves. He has also taught gifted students during the summer through the Center for Gifted at National-Louis University. mark.jurewicz@questacademy.org

Joe Khatena *(Chapter 7, "Teaching Gifted Children to Use Creative Imagination and Imagery to Produce Pictures in Verbal and Visual Art Forms")* is professor and head emeritus in the Department of Educational Psychology and professor emeritus of psychology at Mississippi State University. He has written many articles and books in the area of creativity and was a longtime associate of E. Paul Torrance, the "Father of Creativity" in this country.

Nelly Khatena *(Chapter 7, "Teaching Gifted Children to Use Creative Imagination and Imagery to Produce Pictures in Verbal and Visual Art Forms")* is a charter member of the National Museum of Women in the Arts and a member of the Mississippi Museum of Art. She has written many articles and books in the area of creativity and art as related to gifted and talented children. An accomplished artist herself, Nelly has participated in many exhibits.

Paula Koomjohn *(Chapter 6, "Multiple Strategies for Encouraging Divergent Thinking in Math")* has spent 17 years in the educational field as a middle school math teacher, a publishing company consultant, and an instructor for gifted and talented children. She especially enjoys teaching math to gifted children in summer programs. DPKoomjohn@aol.com

Nathan Levy *(Chapter 2, "Creativity and Critical Thinking")* is a dynamic educator, author, and speaker. He has been an effective teacher, principal, gifted coordinator, and supervisor of instruction in urban, suburban, and rural school districts. In his role as a consultant, he continues to be a hands-on demonstrator of teaching techniques with hard-to-reach as well as gifted children. He currently tours the world sharing his expertise and knowledge. He has written more than 40 books that are used in thousands of classrooms and homes on six continents. nlevy103@comcast.net

Gina Lewis *(Chapter 4, "Drama in the Social Studies Classroom")* is an administrator and teacher at University School at the University of Tulsa. She has taught gifted students for 12 years and has contributed to the field as a writer, speaker, and teacher. gina-lewis@utulsa.edu

Liz Martinez *(Chapter 5, "Thoughts on Science Education for Middle School Gifted and Talented Students")* has spent 27 years in junior high classrooms in a variety of educational settings (including gifted programs) and has focused most of her energy on her passion for science. These years have afforded her many unique opportunities, ranging from working with the Gorilla Foundation to presenting her expertise in science around the country. She enjoys working with the Center for Gifted at National-Louis University, developing science curricula, and teaching gifted and talented students. lizrmartinez@gmail.com

Marian McNair *(Chapter 7, "Creative Art Strategies for the Gifted")* has taught art to gifted students through the Center for Gifted at National-Louis University for eight years. She specializes in community projects with diverse gifted populations and emphasizes cooperative learning groups, team building, and problem solving. In her classrooms, she utilizes flexible structure in an effort to include every student's ideas, employ group work, and promote brainstorming in an affirming environment. She also teaches group art lessons privately in her studio in Lake Forest, Illinois. mere1956@yahoo.com

Elizabeth A. Meckstroth *(Chapter 8, "You Teach What You Are")* coordinated the development of SENG (Supporting Emotional Needs of the Gifted) and has represented gifted children in the press since 1980. Focusing on assessment and counseling, she has worked in supportive cooperation with families of gifted children, as well as with teachers and related organizations. She coauthored *Guiding the Gifted Child* (Great Potential Press, 1989), *Teaching Young Gifted Children in the Regular Classroom* (Free Spirit Publishing, 2003); *Acceleration for Gifted Learners, K–5* (Corwin Press, 2006) and also wrote numerous other book chapters and articles. She is a Senior Fellow with the Institute for Educational Advancement, developing programs for highly gifted children from preschool age and facilitating Yunasa camp for highly gifted adolescents. betmeck@comcast.net

Nancy Messman *(Chapter 4, "Ideas for Teaching American History Units")* has taught gifted elementary school students at Quest Academy, a school for gifted children, in Palatine, Illinois, for 21 years. She was a recipient of the Kohl Teacher Foundation Award in 1993. Nancy is a writer and speaker in gifted education and was a finalist for the Golden Apple Award for Excellence in Teaching in 1994.

Beth Nicholson *(Chapter 5, "An Eclectic Approach to Science Instruction for Gifted Students")* is a former critical care nurse and department administrator who is enjoying her second career as an educator. She currently teaches eighth-grade science in Chicago's western suburbs. She also teaches science to gifted children at multiple locations in the western and southwestern suburbs. A writer and speaker, she enjoys designing new approaches to the creative teaching of science that work well with bright and talented students. kbcmnich2@comcast.net

Leah Novak *(Chapter 7, "Musical Theater Experience")* enjoyed taking gifted enrichment classes so much as a child that she jumped at the opportunity to teach them when she "grew up." She has been teaching instrumental music and music theory in public schools around the Chicago area and musical theater at summer gifted programs. She also freelances as a vocalist and pianist as often as possible. crysong@aol.com

Linda Phemister *(Chapter 4, "Nurturing In-Depth Thinking")* has spent over 20 years working with gifted and talented children, including teaching social studies and language arts classes for seven years. She regularly prepares educators to teach gifted learners as part of her commitment to providing all gifted and talented with the education best suited to their needs. She works extensively in curriculum development, and she was recognized by the Texas Association for the Gifted and Talented in conjunction with the University of North Texas as the 2006–2007 Texas Outstanding Administrator in Gifted Education. She currently serves as the Gifted/Talented Education Program Coordinator for Garland ISD. LLPhemis@garlandisd.net

Susan Scheibel *(Chapter 8, "Ten Actions for Finding the Song, Dance, Hope, Art, and Magic of Creativity")*, with a background in gifted education, became the facilitator for gifted learners in the public schools and worked as an advocate at the state level. Her passion for creativity was early nurtured in the field of visual arts and later grew as she raised three uniquely talented children. Her advocacy and passion for the gifted, talented, and creative of our world continues. She would enjoy your comments and ideas and can be reached at scheib303@comcast.net.

Drew Shilhanek *(Chapter 3, "Reading Focus"; Chapter 4, "Following the Passion of a Gifted Underachiever")* has taught at Quest Academy, a school for gifted learners, for the past six years, having come to the school with seven years of teaching experience in the Iowa and Missouri public schools. He has also participated in Project, a gifted summer program for Grades 6 through 10 at National-Louis University, and Summer Wonders programs for kindergarten through sixth grade. In addition, he has taught a journalism class that produced a yearbook online, a newspaper, and a 110-page literary magazine of Quest students' work. andrew.shilhanek@questacademy.org

Yolanda Toni *(Chapter 3, "Reaching for Depth Through Free-Verse Poetry")* teaches at Fairview South School in Skokie, Illinois. For the past 10 years, she has been teaching kindergarten through 8 students in the school's reading/language arts gifted program. Daily replacement instruction extends from third to eighth grade, and once/twice per week enrichment runs from kindergarten to second grade. She also sponsors the school's Publishing Club, where students in Grades 5 through 8 write, share, and send out their short stories and poems while also publishing a literary magazine that has been ranked for excellence by the National Council of Teachers of English. luccait@core.com

Sally Y. Walker *(Chapter 2, "Relating Differentiation to Creativity")* is a consultant, educator, and published author in the field of gifted education. Sally is the executive director of the Illinois Association for Gifted Children (IAGC). As executive director, she works throughout the state of Illinois to promote awareness and to advocate for gifted children, their parents, and educators. She is the author of the *Survival Guide for Parents of Gifted Kids* (Free Spirit Publishing, 2002). She has coauthored *Teaching Young Gifted Children in the Regular Classroom* (Free Spirit Publishing, 1997), *Making Memories, A Parent Portfolio* (Pieces of Learning, 1997), *A Guide for Parents: Overseeing Your Gifted Child's Education* (IAGC, 1999) and *Acceleration for Gifted Learners, K–5* (Corwin Press, 2007). sywalker@verizon.net

Michael E. Walters *(Chapter 3, "Ten Essential Criteria for an Advanced Humanities Curriculum for Gifted Students")* is a professor of languages and literature at Touro College in New York City and a former teacher in the New York City Public Schools (30 years). He has studied American and English literature for many years and has applied his knowledge of these fields to teaching and writing about gifted students. He can be reached at michaelw@touro.edu.

Valerie Weeks *(Chapter 7, "First Start in Art")* is the founder and director of Early Childhood Accelerated Program (ECAP) Academy in Wichita, Kansas, a unique school designed to serve the needs of gifted early childhood. She has pioneered in this area of giftedness and is a writer, speaker, teacher and administrator of young gifted learners.

Rachel Whitman *(Chapter 5, "Rain Forest")* has acquired wide exposure to different schools in the urban and the suburban areas of Chicago and has worked with children as an assistant teacher, a librarian, a gifted education teacher, a general education teacher, and an ESL teacher. By combining her diverse areas of expertise and experience, she has developed and implemented effective learning projects for gifted learners. Rachel's teaching has allowed students, especially gifted students, to demonstrate and expand their knowledge through creative thinking. rachelawhitman@hotmail.com

Elaine Wiener *(Chapter 3, "Adventures With 'Poetry Pot'")* is associate editor for book reviews for the *Gifted Education Communicator*, an outstanding journal for teachers, administrators, and parents of gifted children. She has spent 40 years in the Garden Grove Unified School District GATE program. She can be reached at esw.ca@worldnet.att.net.

Introduction

In a recent documentary on the creative work of the legendary teacher Albert Cullum*, live footage of his interactions with young students is enough to forever settle the question of whether or not creativity should become a staple in the classroom. In one class, middle school students earnestly debate the merits of Shakespeare, Sophocles, and Shaw. Although a number of these students are gifted, all possess varying degrees of ability and experience. Cullum's creative approach to teaching accommodates this diversity and enables all students to experience what he called their "success level." What he brought to his students was an invitation to participate in an adventure, to use real materials—real books (not readers), real objects, substances, and textures—and explore real issues in the world. Each child did so with a motivation and enthusiasm rarely seen in public school. Each exceeded performance standards for their grade level.

Among the creative strategies Cullum used, he seemed most at home engaging his students through dramatic techniques that unlocked the imagination. His students traveled to another time (history); drew, designed, touched, and crawled around in space (geography); and participated in simulated debates and campaigns. The children built, constructed, imagined, explored, and lived what they studied. What Albert Cullum discovered 50 years ago was the adaptability of creative work to the individual strengths and needs of students. As he described it in the documentary, the creative approach he adopted allowed the "thoroughbreds" (i.e., the gifted kids) to pull to the front of whatever journey they were on, but at the same time, no one is left behind.

In workshops and seminars, teachers often express a wish to use creative processes more. They know that creativity plays a significant role in the growth of concept building and higher-level thinking. But they are afraid. The fears most commonly cited include the following:

---

*The documentary is called *A Touch of Greatness* (2004), directed by Leslie Sullivan, produced by Aubin Pictures in collaboration with Independent Television Service.

"I don't have expertise in creativity or the arts."

"When I see the kids having such a good time, I wonder if they're really learning anything."

"Creative work is too chaotic; I feel out of control."

"I don't know how to relate creativity to the curriculum I have to cover."

"It's hard to tell if creative projects are really teaching them anything. We're always accountable for that."

This book aims to address these concerns through the voices and experiences of teachers who have successfully used creativity in their classrooms. They come from all kinds of schools—public and private, big and small. They serve different communities: mixed-ability gifted, bilingual, multicultural, suburban, urban. A number of them teach in gifted programs where they have learned the importance of throwing caution to the wind on occasion and where they have found a renewed belief in creativity as a life force in teaching gifted learners. Most also teach in places where the focus on curriculum standards and learning goals can sometimes become a preoccupation that, along with the struggle to find adequate time to plan and do creative work, challenges their most inspired ideas. Yet, they have found ways to do it.

One of the advantages of presenting a book by teachers is that it breaks barriers for the readers to find examples of those who are teaching creatively and doing so in circumstances that don't necessarily encourage it. They have spent years honing their techniques and have found ways to navigate around the obstacles (e.g., school schedules and limited resources). What they have achieved is truly remarkable. The chapters on specific subject areas (Chapters 3–7) clearly show that teachers can use creativity and the arts in any classroom anywhere. Guidelines and descriptions in their own words will be assuring to readers who want to know from other teachers how they plan for creative work, how they decide what strategies work best in their subject area, how they relate these to learning goals, and how they sequence creative processes so as to minimize the chaos that sometimes accompanies creativity.

The teacher-authors explain how links can be made to national curriculum standards as well as to teachers' own learning goals, since without this, creativity quickly loses relevance in the classroom. Teachers who've discovered ways to accommodate the creative needs of the gifted within the context of district curricula, state standards, and learning goals are in a unique position to aid fellow teachers in a similar endeavor. Understanding how to make creativity work in the classroom is a fundamental concern that needs to be addressed if they are to take hold of it as a fundamental resource and to realize the significant benefits—to students of all ability levels—of classrooms alive and energized by a more participatory approach to the curriculum.

In this book, "creativity" has a broad application to the classroom because it has less to do with becoming "creative" in the traditional sense and more to do with how children process the ideas set before them. The content that gifted students master is not more important than the process by which they master it. In fact, the process often determines the extent of their mastery. (Has it stimulated higher-level thinking? Inspired the formation of new concepts and ideas? Enabled learners to create links between different bodies of knowledge?) Instead of receiving information, committing it to memory, applying it to textbook problems (in the case of mathematics), or reading a chapter and answering questions (in a reading assignment), the teacher-authors in this book design activities that require mastery and that ask learners to bring forth something more of themselves—their insight, their observation, their imagination, their experience, their passion.

The first chapter provides the rationale for meeting the creative as well as intellectual needs of gifted learners. The benefits to students are clear, and they extend to their emotional well-being as well as to their intellectual or creative life. The chapter concludes with the firsthand experience of a junior high music teacher, a sensitive piece that shows how the creative process, under the guiding hand of a caring teacher, can bring a healing touch to a gifted child in turmoil.

Chapter 2 addresses some of the stickier problems faced by teachers as they try to structure creativity into their daily teaching in diverse, often mixed-ability classrooms. It explores some of the most common concerns teachers have about making creativity a more integral part of the life of their classrooms and shows, through reports from other teachers, how to address these concerns. Drawing on their experiences and insights, it focuses on strategies and general practices that they have found useful in making creativity a rich resource for meeting the learning needs of all their students, particularly the gifted.

The subject chapters include a chapter each on literacy (reading and writing), social studies, mathematics, science, and the arts (both visual and performing). For readers to quickly grasp the different approaches presented, the book includes work from approximately 6 to 10 teachers in each chapter—some from the K through 3 range and others from Grades 4 to 6. In the majority of cases, the age range doesn't matter because strategies can be adapted to accommodate students in a higher or lower grade. This fact in itself provides insight into the versatility of creative teaching strategies.

Each chapter has a simple, easy-to-use structure. The strategies or creative ideas are defined at the beginning of each teacher's contribution, followed by the approximate grade level, its applicability to different subjects, and a description of the process. In most cases, each contribution includes other resources and suggestions if readers wish to explore their idea further or make adjustments for different student needs.

Chapter 8 concludes the book and focuses on ways teachers can discover their own creativity, as this will only enlarge what they can give to their students. Three teachers share their most helpful ideas on tapping this inner reserve and on finding ways to forge a more creative path in today's educational system.

A fundamental aim of this book is to let the lives of teachers speak directly. The chapters are filled with real case studies and provide candid reporting both on areas of challenge and those of notable achievement. An appendix offers additional material—a list of resources and Web sites recommended by the contributors, compilers, and other teachers whose stories have found their way into this volume.

Among its many benefits, certainly a significant one is that creativity in the classroom means significant learning for all students (regardless of ability). For gifted students, though, the creative dimension can become the critical element that saves them from limiting the direction and extent of their personal journeys as learners. Within a creative context, advanced mathematics becomes a wondrous phenomenon, a scientific process presents hidden possibilities, a paragraph becomes the beginning of a book-length fantasy. Creative teaching also reaches the thousands of neglected gifted populations—those who live in remote rural areas, the deprived urban ones, those who speak different languages, those who lack resources for their talents, and those who have special learning problems. Wherever they attend school, they can find, in the rich context of creative classrooms, a path suited to their feet, adaptable to their strengths, and responsive to their needs.

Creativity

A Gift for the Gifted

THE SILENT CALL

It's not easy to hear a silent call, especially in a lively classroom where everyone is learning at different levels. Often, the gifted students, sprinkled willy-nilly throughout the school, sit quiet and studious, rarely letting on that something is missing. Many couldn't put their fingers on it if we asked them to. The creative world they lived in during their earliest years of learning as they touched, tasted, performed, molded, constructed, expressed, and explored their surroundings has lost its validity. They had to let it go in order to ply the more serious waters of skill acquisition and content mastery. The "sense of wonder" so eloquently expressed by Rachel Carson as the most precious element of learning begins to fade. The child's world becomes subjects in a curriculum rather than a world to discover, and learning requires less of the inner life and more of the ability to comply with prescribed steps and sequences.

Gifted learners who come into the world with an abundance of curiosity and inspiration can become particularly disheartened by this process. Creativity in whatever form—from an open questioning technique in a science class to an imaginative exercise in a drama workshop to an interdisciplinary discovery process in a social studies class—revives unused talents and interests and extends their learning in significant ways. In programs across the country, gifted children compose poems and stories, write compelling speeches for simulated trials, develop unique formulas for difficult math problems, and design complex, multimedia compositions in art and film. Families report that their children are more engaged and alive in their learning than they have been for years.

WHY CREATIVITY MATTERS

The importance of creativity becomes apparent when we examine the situations in which gifted students really thrive. Obviously, a more challenging program of study than exists in the regular classroom responds to their advanced learning abilities in many subjects. But what about creativity? A child in an advanced reading group may be delighted to tackle difficult books, especially poetry and historical novels, and enjoys the guided class discussions debating and analyzing the various texts. But what about her own writing? Her own imaginary endings to stories she's read? Or her etchings of characters in her favorite novel? Or poems she thought of writing after her teacher exposed the group to the nature poems of Mary Oliver?

In our school system, there is an unfortunate tendency to place academics and creativity on separate poles—for example, an intensive, accelerated program of advanced mathematics on one side and, on the other, a less academically rigorous "enrichment" activity. Meanwhile, the students, when left to their own devices, do both—that is, they pursue learning on their own at an advanced level *and* explore its creative edge. In history, they imagine living in the world they're exploring. They wonder what motivated certain actions and what might have happened had historical figures made other choices. In science, they study the discoveries of naturalists and start nature journals with watercolors and sketches. They convert a problem involving fractions into a humorous short story and then solve it in a new way.

Pasteur wisely said, "Chance favors the prepared mind." Possessing an advanced understanding of a field with an openness to the unconventional is the best way to discover something new. Through an education that embraces both academic mastery *and* creativity, gifted learners can move beyond the limits of their knowledge and skill and step out into the unknown. The likelihood of this happening in our current educational system is slim, however, because services for gifted students (when they exist at all) tend to focus more on advancing to higher levels of difficulty than on a challenging creative endeavor.

Contrary to what we might suppose, surprisingly few gifted children become creative adults (Winner, 1996). A high level of intelligence does not, in and of itself, ensure a future of creative productivity. Research has proved that the classroom environment—particularly in its influence on motivation and creative expression—plays a central role in the degree to

which high-ability students can become independent, innovative, imaginative thinkers (see Amabile, 1996; Hennessey, 2004). Increased creativity
among gifted students depends as much on learning situations that support it as on talent (see Feldhusen, 1995; Torrance & Sisk, 1997). The challenge is that the learning environment of the average American school
includes pressures that routinely discourage creativity (Amabile, 1996).
The culture of evaluation and testing, the enticements of external reward
(e.g., high grade, praise, recognition), competition between students, the
tendency toward perfectionism, and the imposition of time constraints all
work against the creative process. Over time, sensitive gifted students tend
to approach their education as a means to an end, undermining both creativity and self-determination (Hennessey, 2004).

Even so, they need times in the classroom when they can step back from
these coercive forces and gain experience *making their own contribution* to
the subjects they're learning. This can happen only if the climate of the
classroom nurtures the *intrinsic motivations* of children—the inner curiosity,
imagination, passion. Integrating creativity into the curriculum awakens
this inner spirit—the inventor, the mad scientist, the storyteller, the artist.

BENEFITS OF CREATIVITY FOR THE GIFTED

Though many of us think of gifted children as highly motivated people,
this is not always the case. In fact, many struggle with motivation (Reis &
McCoach, 2000) in our schools. This is understandable given that high-
ability students tend to perform better in situations where they have some
power over their own learning rather than in ones where they must always
respond to external demands, whether from a teacher, a parent, or the curriculum (Hennessy, 2004).

The creative process—structured within the limits and demands of the
classroom—offers gifted students just the sort of environment that enables
them to become motivated again. A common thread among all the contributors to this book is the conviction that the creative process is of value
to both the emotional well-being and the intellectual growth of gifted
learners. The high motivation, engagement, and initiative it generates are
often the most immediate effects. Beyond that, teachers notice that creative
work stimulates higher-level thinking in a wide range of ways: analysis of
problems; awareness of new questions; flexible thinking across disciplines;
sensitivity to pattern, color, gesture, nuance; heightened sensory awareness; discovery of connections; probing of new mysteries. It also fosters a
richer, more nuanced understanding of an issue or subject rarely achieved
in ordinary ways.

In this book, teacher-authors reveal how academics and creativity can
be naturally woven together. In many of their activities, the process begins
with research. Gifted students first delve into the material. Being gifted,

they do it with zest, examining a wide range of sources, posing questions, and gathering the data they require. "Individuals need knowledge in order to be creative; finding problems of increasing sophistication demands increased understanding of the domains in which the problems are found" (Starko, 1995, p. 126). With the knowledge they need, they launch out into the depths, seeking a path of their own—through a new insight or realization, an artistic response or novel proposition. Often, they discover areas where their understanding or skill falls short, and so they return to their teacher with new questions and new problems. This process goes on—with the creative process testing the limits of knowledge and knowledge feeding and expanding the creative process.

Among the many benefits of creativity for high-ability students are these:

- **Personal connections with content areas.** Because of its demand on *individual* thinking, imagining, and analyzing, gifted students immediately become more engaged. Their feelings, interests, and intuitions play a more central role in the learning process. In the Literacy chapter (Chapter 3), for example, Yolanda Toni explores the use of visual art sources as catalysts to inspire individual responses in the form of free verse poems (p. 65). In the Social Studies chapter (Chapter 4), Jerry Flack demonstrates the value of helping gifted learners make creative and personal connections with geography through the creation of what he calls "autobiography maps" (p. 83).

- **Originality and individuality.** The importance of self-expression for gifted students—discovering their own unique abilities, views, interests, tastes and so forth—can never be overestimated. Gifted children need time and opportunities to explore their individual talent, style, and vision. Frances Collins in the Literacy chapter uses what she calls "mentor texts"—examples of writing by professional authors as catalysts for her students to explore and test out their own unique writer voices and styles (p. 56). In the Arts chapter (Chapter 7), Scott Barsotti discusses strategies in acting workshops that can free the creative self of each child and enable students to work freely together as an ensemble (p. 279).

- **Greater exploration of interdisciplinary connections and sources.** Because of the wide range of processes and materials employed, creativity can more effectively accommodate differences in learning styles as well as socioeconomic and cultural backgrounds. Combining media (e.g., text, art, graphs, drama, design, photography, tools) and subjects (math, art, geography, architecture) provides a far richer, more interconnected world for gifted students to make creative leaps. In the Literacy chapter, Courtland Funke shares his program that involved gifted students creating a monthly podcast about their school–an endeavor that draws on their writing ability, musical talents, technical skills, and many other gifts. Lois Guderian, in the Social Studies chapter, finds rich and meaningful connections for gifted students in an interdisciplinary music–social studies project that focuses on the songs of African American spirituals (p. 104).

- **Discovery.** Discovery can happen in any subject and almost always emerges when children have more choices in how they approach an assignment. Even concepts in math or science units can be learned through a process of exploration and inductive reasoning. The children act on situations that, by experimenting, probing, reasoning, imagining, and so forth enable them to *discover* concepts and ideas that might ordinarily be learned more abstractly. For example, in the Mathematics chapter (Chapter 6), Christopher M. Freeman devises a number of gamelike activities that involve students in discovering useful insights about factorization, fraction, and stars (p. 205). In the Science chapter (Chapter 5), Carol Howe stimulates curiosity and wonder as students embark on creative explorations of the solar system (p. 170).

- **Higher-level thinking and depth of learning.** Creative processes stimulate higher-level thinking naturally. Children have to inquire into a question or issue, explore various approaches, analyze needs, examine sources, test options, evaluate information, apply principles, and so forth. Creating cannot take place unless they make what they have learned their own and then take it to the next level—that is, bring out another interpretation, invent a new option, diverge from a convention, and so forth. In the Social Studies chapter, for example, Carol Horn shares how in giving students the role of actual historians they develop new mastery in both cognitive and skill areas as they wrestle with the challenges of gathering data, sifting through sources and interpreting findings (p. 100). In the Mathematics chapter, Carol Fisher explores strategies for stimulating more creative thinking in mathematics, enabling gifted students to create their own equations, using fractions, exponents, and any operation they choose.

- **Artistry and depth of feeling.** Integrating the arts and the creative process into the daily life of the classroom awakens the keen sensibilities of gifted children. They revel in such phenomena as the beauty of numbers, the dazzling array of intricate patterns in nature, or the richness of imagery and meaning in stories or poems. Many gifted learners who qualify for and participate in accelerated learning programs miss the creative dimension, though they may not know this. Joyce Hammer in the Mathematics chapter, for example, shows how important it is for gifted children to appreciate the beauty of mathematics and explores ways teachers can use art to explore geometry (p. 216). In Chapter 8 (the conclusion), Susan Scheibel shares a range of strategies involving song, dance, music, and art that preserve the vital connections we all need to a sensory world that is rich, stimulating, and inspiring (p. 305).

What the authors in this book bring to the subject of creativity in the classroom is a wider spectrum of creative domains than we often see applied to the curriculum. As Clark (2002) has pointed out, the "cognitive, rational view of creativity" has become the most researched in the literature (p. 78). Certainly, much is lost if we limit our classrooms to this one domain and omit, for example, the role of the arts as a catalyst for learning. The chart below is a visual display of this wider spectrum of creativity and the different paths gifted children can take within and across subject areas. We have separated these domains for the purpose of clarifying distinctions; clearly, they overlap and interrelate in actual creative work.

Creative Paths to the Curriculum

Cognitive Creativity	Intuition & the Senses	Imagination	Artistry
Questioning the conventional Divergent reasoning Flexible thinking Fluency Perceiving connections and relations Testing and experimentation	Heightened sensibilities Depth of feeling Intuiting Creative hunches Observation and discrimination Responsiveness to sound, touch, sights, texture, atmosphere, etc.	Vivid imagery Rich, detailed creation of fictional people, places, things Daydreaming Projection of alternate realities, designs, solutions Invention Otherworldliness	Sensitivity and responsiveness to the arts Unique observation and vision of natural world Individualistic views and ideas Whimsy and humor Kinetic awareness Deep connections to rhythms, patterns, colors, shades, etc.
Examples Discovering math formulas Uncovering mysteries of science Analyzing literary themes Addressing obstacles to cleaning up a local river	**Examples** Imaginative processes using arts Intense observation and responses to natural phenomena (e.g., sketching, constructing, writing, analyzing) Embodying roles in literature	**Examples** Lush artistic creations Composition of stories and poems Dramatizations Divergent production (e.g., fractured fairytales)	**Examples** Painting and drawing in natural science Dramatizations of literature and history Multimedia work combining visual or performing arts with text Arts as catalysts for creative writing Literature as catalyst for visual/performing arts compositions

E. Paul Torrance (1995), the great pathfinder in creative teaching and learning, wrote a book called *Why Fly?* that has become a guiding light for many educators who, like the teachers in this book, want to steer their students to the higher realms of the imagination. The list below combines many of his ideas with those of the compilers as well as those shared by the teacher-authors in this book.*

Preparing the Soil

- Openly share your own creative passions with your students.
- Fill the classroom with art, music, and a rich variety of enticing supplies.
- Design work spaces that beckon the creative muse in your students.
- Applaud originality whenever and wherever expressed.
- Protect students from saboteurs: criticism, censure, premature judgment.
- Celebrate risk taking and bold endeavor.

Planting the Seeds

- Awaken imagination and artistic sensibilities through example and exposure to creative people and their works.
- Create open time for creative exploration.
- Share jewels of wisdom about the creative process.
- Point out the hidden, less traveled paths; warn against set patterns.
- Celebrate the beginning steps of children's own creative process.

Watering and Feeding

- Design activities that engage the whole child: touching, feeling, imagining, listening, sensing, composing, combining, writing, improvising, constructing, molding, shaping.
- Provide for advanced learning in a variety of fields.
- Assign work that requires creative and imaginative thinking.
- Nurture boldness in vision and endeavor.

Weeding and Growing

- Teach strategies for *constructive* criticism and evaluation.
- Impart coping skills to deal with peer judgment, crippling perfectionism, and frustration with the creative process.
- Support students' trust in their own creative power.
- Give them opportunities to correct errors, refine visions, rewrite, re-create, improve, elaborate.
- Find venues for students to show/demonstrate/perform/exhibit for real audiences in the community.

Reviewing this list, we can clearly see the weight Torrance placed on nurturing the tender spirit of our students. Creativity is not merely a matter of following prescribed steps or a structured program. It requires

*Originally published in *Acceleration for Gifted Learners, K–5* by Joan Franklin Smutny, Sally Y. Walker, and Elizabeth A. Meckstroth (2007, Corwin Press). Reprinted with permission.

continuous tending, coaxing, and encouragement. We are to applaud originality, teach coping skills, protect from harsh criticism, instill trust in the creative process, and fill our classrooms with art and music. Bolstering the tentative first steps in creative work enables children to become more rooted in the soil, less vulnerable to wind and frost, and more resilient and steady in their growth as creative beings.

Feeding the Heart and Soul . . .

This leads us to one of the most significant benefits that creativity brings to gifted students: the freedom to be one's self and, just as important, the experience of being accepted by like-minded peers. These "peers" can be other gifted students in a class, or they can be people a child does projects with through a Web site. Creative learning environments tend to make gifted students feel freer as individuals, a little less weird among peers. When they find each other, as they often do in special programs or services, the relief is palpable.

Coming to grips with one's self is not an easy task for gifted children whose sensibilities and feelings seem like an endlessly restless sea. For such children, *creativity is the harbor* they need to discover their worth; to find an accepting, receptive hand to guide them; to gather strength for bolder endeavors in the future.

We conclude this chapter with the experience of an outstanding and intrepid music teacher whose gentle guidance helped a gifted "outsider" discover his worth.

A Sense of Belonging:
Music as Connection and Community Through Creativity

By Jane Artabasy

Music's tag as the universal language is true enough, if a tad trite. Organized sound translates to every clime, country, and culture. Youth also embraces its own, if less celebrated, universality—especially during the preteen and teen years. It involves belonging and acceptance as one of the "tribe." To an ubersensitive adolescent, the cruelest cut is to be implicitly "voted off the island," whether by verbal harassment, physical bullying, or the worst slap of all: being ignored. Although low status is searingly painful, invisibility still trumps it.

However, a good school confronts this adolescent fear of "uncoolness" if it consciously partners cognition with community in its methods and mission. And as a curricular area, music bends effortlessly to this duality of purpose. Its practice inherently nurtures the bonds of sound and psyche. Invariably, when a fine arts curriculum connects the innately communal nature of music to the primal needs of young people for like-minded companionship, the results are, in the adolescent vernacular, downright awesome.

Pedagogues regularly tout group interaction as a viable method of learning. But we rarely claim *interpersonal connection as learning itself*. As the culture of testing has saturated education, we've also come to accept the code of the test, which quantifies or numbers almost every aspect of achievement. This effectively, if inadvertently, isolates both individual and intellect from the social context of life. Once we've surrendered to the expediency of percentiles, to that degree have we unwittingly trivialized the act of thinking itself.

A test-centered school model reflexively restricts thought to the act of interacting with data, whereas the true essence is in the forming and forging of a life, with all the adventure and experience therein implied. When perceived through our most creative impulses, the fabric of learning is a seamless garment, woven from the cloth of our whole selves. Segmenting and measuring the garment does nothing to add either beauty or strength to its design. In truth, an individual's thoughtful evolution in life unfolds as an art as much as a science, and music fills us with the sound of that art, the aural imperatives of soul.

Not all, but many, children struggle with rites of connection during their school experience, straining to conform themselves to the daunting strictures of the intensely social hothouse of contemporary school life. The paradigms of popularity, like the proverbial 800-pound gorilla in the room, are silent but deadly. They are frighteningly arbitrary and cruelly Darwinian for even the sturdiest of students.

But gifted children may face the most difficult challenge of all, and most glaringly so at the middle school age. Their heightened sensitivity frequently becomes an Achilles heel. Young people who shine brighter or more intensely than many of their peers, immediately defy the norm and stand out as the dreaded "different." While this status may secretly torture and embarrass them, the temptation among adults is to assume that their inner lives, full of sparkling ideas and speed-of-light reasoning, must be the ultimate and only fulfillment they need or crave. It is a myth both ill conceived and wrongheaded.

The stereotype of the brilliant loner persists as fertile ground for novels or movies, but it fails the test of real life, which cries out for unbroken bonds of human affection. Even as solitude is our friend, breathing the restorative atmosphere of reflection into life, isolation is a very different animal. If left unattended for too long, it quickly slides into alienation, a dangerous, destructive emotion for any young person, brilliant or otherwise.

We all need, to varying degrees, the secret place of our own minds— that private universe of comfort and unfettered thought at the core of our being. But lines of family, friends, mentors, acquaintances, and even beloved pets must radiate outward from that core of self in a grand panoply of connection. These ties, broadening and deepening our cognition as we interact with other perspectives and modes of consciousness, give our lives meaning and purpose. Whether young or old, brilliant or not so much, the need to belong and to feel the touch of external affirmation is no less compelling, no less important a quest, than the desire to expand and nurture the inner reaches of our imagination and creativity. Whether at home, school, or play, our basic longings exert strong, if elusive, power over our thoughts, actions, and relationships.

That brings us again to music. Consider the dynamics of a fine symphony orchestra. In the best ensembles, the musicians are individually talented, disciplined, devoted disciples of their instruments. Most of them perform regularly in solo settings. But not even the most brilliant virtuoso would claim solo work as the only and ultimate apogee of musicianship. At all levels of accomplishment, performers experience deep and spiritual connections to music while in ensemble with others. The concert of human beings, in focused togetherness, is as central to the magic of an aesthetic moment as is the concert of notes. In that sense, Yo-Yo Ma and the last-chair cellist of the symphony orchestra have more in common than not. This dynamic is no less true for the musical activities of young people in school environments.

It is wise, in teaching vocal music, to take at least as many views of the forest as of the trees. Attention to detail and a slavish devotion to perfection is the musician's stock in trade, the source of our practice and performance. Middle school children—and especially gifted students—respond enthusiastically to exciting challenges and to the demands of excellence. Yet, they need more. They yearn not just to be taught, but to be seen, to be the object of someone's respectful attention. First, they want affirmation as a valued person, and only then, as scholars, singers, dancers, and so on. A good teacher will strive to enhance musical abilities. A great one will mentor and encourage the spiritual arc of those abilities.

The particulars of this approach are simple enough, but they do require patience and commitment. When sculpting the outlines of a middle school vocal performance, include student choice, ownership, and community from the beginning stages. This sharing of power ensures a learning experience not just of excellence but also of depth and reflection. Use theme and point of view as unifying devices, and don't be afraid to let the students, together, help form the vision. From the first moments as a class, involve students in repertoire choices, solo and ensemble possibilities, choreography, and original script. Don't be afraid of discussion and disagreement, but always hold their feet to the fire in terms of reaching eventual consensus.

For example, begin by choosing a title for the show, such as "High Energy," "Shed a Little Light," or "Lighten Up!" Then, solicit song titles and ideas correlative in some way with the theme. Discuss the value and appropriateness of the suggestions and bring them to a vote. Find the scores and arrange and/or transpose them to fit your voices. Teach the music, hone the vocalism, and, later in the process, if appropriate, add student-generated choreography and script (connecting each song to the theme). As the program comes together, assign myriad solo parts—perhaps one verse of a song per person—dance segments, speaking parts, and/or walk-ons.

This philosophy works best when many students have short solos, instead of a few assigned long ones. Of course, some voices are better than others. So what? Comparisons are inevitable but shouldn't be restrictive. This is school, not Broadway. Everyone should use the voice he or she has now. It's the only way to get better.

And never fear spontaneity. It's the spice that livens the stew. When that arm shoots up, in the middle of rehearsal, and you hear, "Ooh, ooh, can we try this?" well, try it. Your rehearsal plan should never preclude the possibility of spontaneous delight and serendipity. In classroom priorities, ideas should always outrank schedules. Discipline, in its highest sense, is important as the glue of forward motion. But in education, our business is thought, not control.

Your students have by now personally invested in the process, because you began by appealing to their musical instincts, aesthetic sense, work ethic, and their awakening sense of music-as-community and community-as-music. And what of the gifted students in the class? Throughout the project, they've exercised their considerable abilities but in tandem with others. Their special talents have been affirmed, but so have the talents of everyone else, without artificially imposed hierarchies injecting jealousy and resentment into the mix. (Fine arts classes are usually scheduled from the broadest forms of inclusion, with the entire spectrum of abilities represented in each class. In this community-based model of teaching, everyone can find a niche, a talent to share, from singing solos, to dancing, to writing, to short speaking parts.)

Of course, this "bottom-up" model of music methodology doesn't preclude moments of frustration or conflict. In fact, it practically invites them. After all, we are speaking of middle school. But even tension and anger can offer gifts of blessed, if unintended, consequences. The salvation, however, is to stay focused on the harmony of both music and oneself, in concert with others. Case in point:

My job of teaching middle school vocal music spanned several decades, and a long career spawns many memories. I especially recall one steamy day of rehearsal in June, a few days before our final show of the year. A cruel taunt, whispered during a dance sequence, ignited a temper tantrum from one of my more volatile eighth-grade boys. (Let's call him Tim, a very gifted and talented "loner.") Extended and foul-mouthed shouting ensued but, fortunately, no physical fallout. It was the end of the period, so I kept Tim after class. He had retreated to a corner of the room and hunched down over a desk. He glared my way, raised his palm, and yelled, "Save it!

Whatever you want, Mrs. A., just forget it. I've heard it all, and I'm not interested. Everybody in this #@%^& place hates me, and I hate them. And this stupid school too. So just leave me alone."

One of my stronger suits as a teacher was a hefty head of steam in a tight pinch and plenty of hot air. But this time, I resisted my preachy tendencies. The moment needed silence. Suddenly, the glare softened, and tears started streaming down Tim's face. He began sobbing uncontrollably. A wrenching sadness welled in his eyes, pouring out of him from that place in all of us where we bury our most secret pain. The hurt of many years, the anguish of being on the outside looking in, came rushing out of that boy in torrents of anger, frustration, and hopelessness.

It was not a moment for platitudes or tiresome bromides, and frankly, it didn't matter. A broken heart craves compassion, not expertise or technique. I spoke as quietly and gently as I could:

"Tim, all that may be true. I wouldn't claim to know what you've been going through. But I do know I don't hate you. In fact, I like you . . . very much. You're an incredibly good and sensitive person, and I'm so grateful to know you and to have you in my class." I paused. "You do belong here, on this earth and in this room, you know, or you wouldn't be here. You just have to learn how not to be so hard on yourself."

Our discussion took a few more moments and a few more turns. Then, at some point, he allowed himself a sort of half smile.

"You aren't lying are you, just to make me feel better? You really like me?"

I nodded enthusiastically. "Of course, doofus!"

"Well," he grinned, "that's not what I really want, but it's better than nothing."

We middle school teachers and students know to interpret those words as more than faint praise. Such a charming and disarming specimen is the American teenager!

Soon after, events moved differently, both musically and emotionally. Tim and I worked out the more glaring behavioral issues with the offending student and generated a cathartic "heart-to-heart" with the class the next day. Our rehearsal dynamic quickly recovered a more generous enthusiasm. The music brought us together, as did the exercise of forgiveness. As we entered the last days of preparation, the students found a flow—in the music, in themselves, and with each other—even as the excitement of "game day" escalated. While we sang, danced, and laughed together, the sounds healed and restored us, as did our collective resolve. The performance itself—ironically entitled, "Get Over It!"—resonated with inspiration and joy. The students had earned a oneness of mind that was central to their learning, not ancillary to it or an afterthought.

This isn't to suggest that Tim's problems disappeared or that his popularity took a dramatic turn upward. If music isn't so simple, neither are the imperatives of metacognition. But undeniably, we had felt the exhilaration of love, incremental, yet irresistible. And a ripple of that love touched our audience, too. It was all so sublime.

And aren't those heavenly moments of surety in who we are and what we are doing the purest echoes of the fine art of learning?

"Blessed be the ties that bind" us—to ourselves, to others, and to music as creativity in action.

REFERENCES

Amabile, T. M. (1996). *Creativity in context.* Boulder, CO: Westview Press.

Clark, B. (2002). *Growing up gifted: Developing the potential of children at home and at school.* Upper Saddle River, NJ: Merrill Prentice Hall.

Feldhusen, J. F. (1995). *Talent identification and development in education (TIDE)* (2nd ed.). Sarasota, FL: Center for Creative Learning.

Hennessey, B. A. (2004). *Developing creativity in gifted children: The central importance of motivation and classroom climate.* Storrs, CT: National Research Center on the Gifted and Talented.

Reis, S. M., & McCoach, D. B. (2000). The underachievement of gifted students: What do we know and where do we go? *Gifted Child Quarterly, 44,* 152–170.

Smutny, S. Y. W., Walker, S. Y., & Meckstroth, E. A. (2007). *Acceleration for gifted learners, K–5.* Thousand Oaks, CA: Corwin Press.

Starko, A. J. (1995). *Creativity in the classroom: Schools of curious delight.* White Plains, NY: Longman.

Torrance, E. P. (1995). *Why fly? A philosophy of creativity.* Norwood, NJ: Ablex.

Torrance, E. P., & Sisk, D.A. (1997). *Gifted and talented in the regular classroom.* Buffalo, NY: Creative Education Foundation Press.

Winner, E. (1996). *Gifted children: Myths and realities.* New York: Basic Books.

2

Making Creativity Work

Practical Suggestions by Classroom Teachers

Introduce the subject of creativity to a group of teachers and many will immediately bring up the practical challenges involved—their accountability, for example, to deliver certain content and achieve curriculum standards, or the pressures of testing that force them to devote more time to skills and knowledge. Most teachers who want to be more creative need strategies for navigating around the pressures of a school system that is not structured for creativity. So how do we make creativity not only work within the constraints we teach but also support fundamental learning goals? And how do we structure it in such a way that gifted students can be challenged to exercise their intellectual and creative powers in substantial ways?

Teachers have had to grapple with these questions and devise strategies for making creativity an inherent part of learning rather than just an enjoyable and sometimes distracting interlude. For creativity to become a vibrant and workable dimension in the daily life of the classroom, certain fundamentals need to be in place. Let's look at the key hurdles teachers often mention when the subject of creativity in the classroom comes up.

"I don't have enough training in creative or artistic work."

- Start from the premise that using creative strategies in your classroom is within your reach.

With the exception of fine or performing arts instruction, many teachers who do creative work in their classrooms do not have special training. So, for instance, you might see students doing dramatic poetry readings as Elaine Weiner's class (see Chapter 3) does or, *doing history* (another creative enterprise)—exploring and evaluating sources and questioning, analyzing, and interpreting data—like the students in Carol Horn's or Rhonda Clevenson's classes (see Chapter 4). Even if you want to embark on a project that demands a real arts background, you can always collaborate with another teacher, as Lois Guderian suggests in an activity involving a social studies and music teacher (see p. 104 in the Social Studies chapter).

"Sometimes I think of a creative approach to something, but then I'm not sure if it's appropriate for my particular kids or for what I've got planned for the next two weeks."

- Focus your creative ideas on the learning goals (what you want your students to understand/achieve) and on the learners (their strengths, weaknesses, learning preferences, interests, etc.).

What skills, concepts, and knowledge do the students need to master and within what period? What are their special interests, strengths, areas of expertise, and learning preferences? What areas of knowledge and understanding do they possess that would contribute to the content at hand? How would creative processes enhance and challenge what these children already have? Creativity builds on what the students themselves bring to the learning table—all their best talents and strengths, including those of character.

"Creativity doesn't integrate well with the curriculum."

- Creative work should not take you away from the curriculum but provide ways to expand and enhance it. For the gifted, creative processes offer the kind of opportunity they need for more open-ended and complex ideas and problems.

Creativity enables gifted students to think analytically, to synthesize and evaluate new concepts as can be readily seen, for example, in creative science classes where students construct models, conduct experiments, create drawings, diagrams, reports, and graphs as they explore and share their latest scientific discoveries. Clearly, this level of learning is superior to amassing facts. At the end of this chapter, Nathan Levy explores how creative and critical (or divergent and convergent) thinking cohere and enhance each other when gifted children have the opportunity to develop both simultaneously.

"It's hard to think about creativity when you have to worry about curriculum standards. Creativity is kind of like a dessert rather than a main meal; who has time for it?"

- Treat curriculum standards as a guide and catalyst for creative work rather than as a hindrance to it.

Those standards that relate to higher-level thinking contain within them the seeds for creativity. Examples abound in the subject chapters. "Podcasting for and With Gifted and Talented Students" by Courtland Funke (Chapter 3) is a multimedia project that embraces different technologies, as well as writing, recording, producing, editing, interviewing, and more. Students make tangible gains in creative thinking as well as in knowledge and skill while they assemble material, conduct interviews, critique their work, and compose original podcasts. All this activity relates to a language arts standard focusing on the use of different information resources for researching, synthesizing, and communicating knowledge.

When you review the curriculum standards and learning outcomes for your gifted children, try to identify where creativity would best serve them. In what instances would creativity enhance learning, and where might it be counterproductive? What kind of creative activity and materials would support learning outcomes? What would provide for gifted learners the greatest challenge and stimulation for their higher-level thinking abilities?

"When I think of creativity, all I think of is the arts."

- Broaden your understanding of the different forms creativity can take.

In some cases, it involves designing activities in such a way that students have to question how they're approaching a topic or problem and think differently about it. Christopher Freeman's (see Chapter 6) collection of math activities enable students to invent their own formulas and solutions; they strengthen their inductive reasoning abilities, but they do so in a process that frees them from old patterns. Liz Fayer's (see Chapter 5) approach to science involves an open inquiry into phenomena, a multifaceted exploration of data and the invention, for example, of weather equipment and cloudscapes.

In many cases, the strengths and learning styles of gifted students suggest the kind of creative process that would work best in particular classes. Think about the different needs of a gifted student with a strong leaning toward the kinetic or a student more at home in a literary activity. Ask yourself: What kind of creative learning experience should my gifted students engage in at this moment—one involving inductive thinking, a sensing/intuiting process, an imagining/feeling process? In what way would creative work be most effective here—as a catalyst in the beginning, as a process throughout the assignment, or as a final project?

"Creative work seems pretty chaotic at times."

- Maintain a focus and order for the class.

A certain amount of chaos in a creative classroom is natural. As gifted learners become animated and inspired, the energy and enthusiasm level in the class often rises. However, as Bev Cheairs reports later in this chapter, gifted students also have a need to know where they're headed and what the schedule will be for the day. They like established routines, learning stations, and organized plans. Maintaining this focus often means, as Jennifer Golwitzer points out (p. 24 of this chapter), planning ahead and being prepared for those who finish assignments early. Having the next step at your fingertips helps gifted learners keep their momentum and continue moving forward in meaningful work.

"I don't have a lot of supplies. It's expensive for me to have to go out and buy a whole lot of stuff that may or may not even work out."

- Begin with what is readily available through your own connections and community.

Most teachers gather materials gradually, often serendipitously. Once people discover what you're doing in the classroom, they begin to donate things. A mother contributes costumes or construction materials. A teacher passes along art materials he no longer needs. A library contributes large stacks of nature magazines and secondhand books. A local art supply store donates items left over from a sale. Items considered useless before (e.g., egg cartons, colored wire, assorted buttons, old hats, string, and Popsicle sticks) become creative aids in a math-oriented construction project or a prop in a simulation. As you explore the materials and other sources that would best challenge advanced students, consider not only objects but also nature exhibits, recordings, videos, software, and Web sites. Learning centers—too often confined to the lower grades—are useful areas for storing and displaying resources for creative work and can provide choices in different talent areas and learning styles.

Making Creativity Work in the Classroom

---

1. **When you begin planning, think first of the learning goals, including those for gifted students.** Identify where creativity is useful to achieving these goals and where it is not. Knowing up front where creativity can enhance your work with the children will enable you to prepare students and manage the process effectively.

2. **The next most important focus is the students themselves.** What are their needs, strengths, weaknesses, skills, interests? What knowledge, experience, and skill do they bring to the table? What will most engage and challenge them? Creativity must build on the strengths of your students.

3. **Use curriculum standards as a guide, not a restriction in the planning process.** In many cases, standards do not apply to the advanced learning needs of the gifted, yet you can still incorporate them in a way that does not limit the creative options of high ability students.

4. **Make sure you have a full range of creative strategies to draw from.** In other words, there will be times when creative problem solving best serves the aims of a science unit. But in other cases, it might be a visual arts process or a divergent thinking task or an exercise for the imagination.

5. **Establish practical routines for creative work that support student responsibility and self-directed learning.** You can minimize the chaos that sometimes accompanies a creative process by giving them experience in designing and arranging the work space, retrieving and storing materials, and working collaboratively in a freer, less teacher-directed mode.

In their own words, the following teacher-authors report the simple practices or arrangements that have made creativity in the classroom work for them. Gifted students, like all students, want to know what they're going to do and why. They want to know how to proceed, what choices they have, and how they can gauge their own progress. Each of the three authors has a different way of addressing the subject of creativity in the classroom. Some have general suggestions with examples; others are more elaborate in their focus on a specific domain.

A General Guide to Creative Teaching

By Bev Cheairs

The words of Robert Maynard Hutchins have become a catalyst for me in teaching the varied and complex child described as gifted. He states, "The object of education is to prepare the young to educate themselves throughout their lives." The next few paragraphs outline what I consider general perspectives that have allowed me to creatively teach gifted learners successfully.

Have a firm model in place.

I must acknowledge, among other educators, Madeline Hunter, whose Seven Step Instructional Model I learned while attending the University of Northern Colorado as an undergraduate. Contrary to some criticisms of the model as too rigid, it has remained, for me, a supportive and yet flexible idea ingrained in the forward regions of my mind. This instructional model is like the keys on the piano. The keys are the vehicles to play scales and to create music. The Seven Step Instructional Model is the vehicle that enables me to employ the essentials of teaching gifted students. I become a creative instructor because I have a keen understanding of the complexities of these seven steps when instructing gifted learners.

Begin with a thought for the week.

When entering my classroom, students find the daily schedule on the board and a "Thought for the Week." The schedule presents an organized plan of lessons for the students to focus upon. In particular, gifted students have emotional needs to visualize the plan. Some gifted students need the ability to process in their mind what will transpire in the classroom they are entering. Other gifted students view the schedule as a routine that they depend upon to release their anxious mind of concerns, which creates the stimulation necessary to think. Such a simple thing as a daily schedule heightens the social and emotional needs of gifted students.

The Thought for the Week provides the student with a guide for weekly lessons. I make reference to this Thought for the Week during daily lessons rather than in math or in reading class. In my weekly lesson plan book, I plan what think I will use during each week. These thoughts may be referenced during lessons, or students may observe these thoughts and consider how they will "play into" the lesson objectives of the week.

A few times, I have purposely omitted writing the "Thought for the Week" on the board only to realize the students depend on the words as a form of motivation for creative thinking and learning. Below are a few of the statements I have sensitively selected.

- "The real voyage of discovery consists not in seeking new landscapes but in having new eyes." *Marcel Proust*
- "Education is helping the child realize his potentialities." *Erich Fromm*
- "Make the most of yourself, for that is all there is of YOU." *Ralph Waldo Emerson*
- "Courage is not the absence of fear, but rather the judgment that something else is more important than fear." *Ambroise Redmoon*
- "Learning is the discovery that something is possible." *Fritz Perls*

Know where you're headed.

The lesson for the day begins with an objective. I state what I want the students to learn, or I write the objective on the board for them to see. By stating the lesson objectives, I remain focused on the skill to be taught. An example of this is reflected in teaching Shakespeare to fifth-grade students. The topic of Shakespeare is expansive; however, the objective is to introduce the students to the playwright in a focused way. My objective for one day: "Who was Shakespeare to Elizabethan England? Who was he at age 12? At age 20?" and so forth. I referred to the book, *The World of Shakespeare* (Claybourne, 1996) as well as many Web sites that present information and pictures to students at their level of understanding.

If the subject of math were fractions, the focus for a class of third-grade students, I would state the objective as follows: learning fractions with chocolate. The author, Jerry Palotta, and illustrator, Rob Bolster, have created a wonderful book titled *The Hershey's Milk Chocolate Fractions Book.* By introducing students to this book, *students* are engaged to further their understanding of fractions with an advanced concept study of twelfths.

Let the standards be a general guide.

Standards can be a real hurdle for teachers sometimes, especially if they're trying to bring something creative to the classroom. When teaching for my district, which is in Illinois, I follow the established guidelines that encompass the Illinois State Learning Standards, but I don't let them become a dictator. I treat them as a map. Taken in this way, teachers can make *procedures and expectations work for them,* by using creativity to achieve learning benchmarks.

REFERENCE

Claybourne, A. (1996). *The world of Shakespeare.* London: Saffron Hill.

General Principles for Creative Teaching

By Jennifer Golwitzer

I have found these principles most helpful in my own creative teaching.

Have high expectations for quality work.

Some gifted children are so bored that they finish assignments quickly just to get to the next thing. They need to know that quality is important. If students come to you with a phrase such as, "I'm done," but you are unable to read anything on the paper, or the paper looks like it has been stepped on, wrinkled, and eaten by the family dog, remind the students that you are looking for their best work and that you would like them to redo it. At first, the children may respond negatively. However, once they realize that turning in quality work will result in more challenging and interesting activities, children will start to take pride in the work and will feel that someone is looking out for their interests and needs.

Teach children to make friends with mistakes.

We have erasers because we make mistakes. Celebrate mistakes in class because we learn the best lessons by making mistakes! Some children are deathly afraid of making a mistake and can be paralyzed by the very thought of being wrong. Call attention to your own mistakes so children can learn that even adults slip up sometimes!

Create a structure that will support creativity in the classroom.

Goals. Setting goals at the beginning of the year is extremely important, but even more important is revisiting those goals every week so students are constantly reminded of what they wish to accomplish during a period. They can also check off goals that they've met and then set new ones. This helps many students focus their attention on productive and positive progress.

Plan ahead and be prepared. These two actions can save time and energy when children finish quicker than anticipated. Having a next step in mind helps the children find security and makes the day go smoothly because the students are always busy doing something productive and meaningful.

Rubrics. Rubrics are helpful to all students in all of the subject areas because they clearly outline what is expected, and gifted students particularly need this.

Integrate

Teaching more than one subject at a time not only saves time in the long run but also helps students form connections between subjects in a way that makes the learning process more meaningful. For example, my class often reads and writes during social studies class to synthesize new information and express new ideas and concepts. In addition, graphs and charts apply to many different areas, which can expand the learning process. Pointing these facts out to students helps them understand that all of the subject areas work in tandem to create a solid foundation for educational goals.

Differentiate

Using different approaches for individual students is one of the most successful tools that can be used. Even in creative endeavors, differentiation helps individual children move forward at a pace and level appropriate for them. Try to be several steps ahead in any curriculum so there is always a plan.

Understand the importance of self-selected projects.

DO NOT assign busy work. That will only frustrate, annoy, and turn off gifted children who finish quickly with accuracy. Once students finish the work assigned correctly, they can embark on a project that reinforces and pulls together skills and knowledge recently learned. However, this project should also be one that transports the children to new territory— new topics, knowledge, concepts, skills; otherwise, it will merely repeat what the children have already learned.

Relating Differentiation to Creativity

By Sally Y. Walker

Differentiation aims to make learning meaningful and engaging for students with a wide range of abilities and learning styles. It's often seen as a method for moving children forward at different levels—compacting the curriculum for a gifted child, for example, while providing more practice time for a struggling student. But differentiation is also an effective system for doing creative work.

Open-Ended Responses

Build in open-ended responses where the child can be as innovative and creative a thinker as possible. With this approach, there are no right or wrong answers, and creativity is the goal. Ideas to keep in mind to support this goal include the following: To what extent do you express *originality* (responding in new and unique ways), *fluency* (able to come up with many responses), *flexibility* (stretching beyond expected answers to new categories), and *elaboration* (extending and adding details)? Group brainstorming, as well as independent work, accomplishes this task. Tie it to the content that you are teaching. These prompts can also be used for fun story starters.

Fluency Tasks: How many . . .

- types of hats
- things come to mind when you think of 100
- words that make you think of fun
- ways to let someone know you love him or her
- uses for sea shells

- ways to save energy
- things can you make with a circle
- things to do with old magazines
- things that make crunchy sounds
- things that are scary
- red things you can find in a grocery store
- ways to lift a heavy object
- uses for a wheel

. . . can you think of?

Flexibility Tasks

- How could you find the width or length of your classroom without using a ruler or yardstick?
- Write five sentences using the word *read* in a different way.
- Think of a way to open a car door without touching it.
- How could you cook a dinner without using a stove, oven, or microwave?
- How is a pencil like a plant?
- If you were a ball, what would recess mean to you?
- What is the color of love? What is the smell of fun? What is the sound of soft?
- Think of at least five ways to use an empty box besides holding something.
- How can you catch a flying insect without using a net?
- What might be some reasons for not wearing shoes?
- If you were an ant, what would small mean to you?
- Name a dozen things to do with popcorn besides eating it.
- Write a letter from one storybook character to another.

Originality Tasks

- Make up new words for a song.
- Make up a new holiday to celebrate something special. (Create a card to go with the holiday, decorations, song, etc.)
- Create a plan for healthy eating.
- Design a hat that could also be used as a purse or wallet.
- Make up a conversation between hot and cold.
- Create a recipe for happiness.
- Create a new kind of ice cream.
- Design an owner's manual for one of your textbooks.
- Design an original award for someone.
- Create a new cartoon character. Write a caption for your character.
- Create a recipe for taking away meanness.

Elaboration Tasks

- Use three letters that are given and make new words (eat, met, cat). You may add letters before, after, or between the given letters.
- Draw a long line. Add details to make it into something special.
- Create a new recipe for a new type of cookie.
- Make your thumbprint. Give it details to make it into something else. Give it a voice. What would it say?
- Illustrate your favorite story or poem.
- What would you do to make the school more beautiful? Design a plan.
- Add words to sentences to make them more interesting.
- Print your first, middle, and last names. Draw details to make them into an interesting design.
- What can you add to a cardboard box to make a fun toy for a small child?

Differentiated instruction has creativity built into it. Teachers who differentiate are already accustomed to making adjustments for children with different learning needs: One needs a more advanced assignment; another wants to try another math problem to be sure he understands the process; another student wants a more hands-on process to match his strong kinesthetic learning style, and so forth.

In such an environment, teachers can easily devise creative activities in their subject areas. By using creativity, you are removing the ceiling from a gifted child's learning process. You are also removing the pressure. Students can be as good as they can without the internal demand to find the "right" answer. Creativity builds interest, investment, and inquiry. Copying stops where creativity begins. All the students begin to realize that everyone views things differently.

The concluding piece by Nathan Levy addresses the important question of how creativity and critical thinking relate to one another. He contends that an overemphasis on the creative mode tends to frustrate students' attempts to find solutions to problems or, in the case of a research project, to reach a hypothesis or at least a tentative conclusion. We need both convergent and divergent thinking, both academic rigor and open-ended thinking.

Certainly, we've seen enough in the field to know that the separation between academics and creativity ultimately leaves gifted students— and *all* students for that matter—with an impoverished education. Alfred North Whitehead put it nicely, "Fools act on imagination without knowledge; pedants act on knowledge without imagination" (quote in Parnes, 1967, p. 7).

REFERENCE

Parnes, S. J. (1967). *Creative behavior guidebook.* New York: Scribner's.

Creativity and Critical Thinking

By Nathan Levy

Most bright people are intuitive thinkers. In fact, if you are reading this, you probably are one of those people. You probably have the ability to see things more quickly than most and need fewer cues to "see the picture." However, thinking intuitively is not the same as thinking critically. Unfortunately, despite the attempts of educators and parents to challenge young people to think critically at high levels, we have not succeeded.

As a teacher of the gifted, a principal, and an educational consultant, I have seen the same consistent patterns in gifted children and adults! They often tackle a problem with eager enthusiasm. If there are not positive results in a very short time, participants begin to put their energies into "reading" cues from the instructor. Most teachers in our current classrooms (thanks to the influence of the "bogus self-esteem" movement) enable their students. Often with body language, verbal cues and/or actual hints, the adults lead the students in the right direction. Gifted students have become masterful at reading adults. Unfortunately, they have not become better critical thinkers. What can we do to improve the status quo?

There are many definitions of critical thinking. It refers to those kinds of mental activities that are clear, precise, and purposeful. It is typically associated with solving complex, real-world problems, generating multiple (or creative) solutions to a problem, drawing inferences, synthesizing and integrating information, distinguishing between fact and opinion, or estimating potential outcomes. Over the years, the debate on how to teach critical thinking best seems to have centered around two points of view:

1. Set up separate programs to teach the components of critical thinking.

2. Integrate critical thinking into all subjects.

Several school programs have been well thought out (De Bono's Just Think is one example) and embraced by its supporters. Several others have been used by teachers in gifted and regular education programs. Several appear to work, but there seems to be minimal transfer to life learning. What do we do?

Let us put this in perspective in a workplace example. When XYZ Company decided there was a need for a new toothpaste, the head of company did not send down the prototype with directions to immediately bring the toothpaste to market. A science-related department worked on the ingredients of the product with a goal of finding a toothpaste that actually cleaned teeth. They had to creatively look at the many possibilities available. After all, there are hundreds of different toothpaste products that can clean teeth. Ultimately, the company had to decide on the final ingredients.

While this was happening, the product and advertising departments were brainstorming and experimenting with the unlimited design possibilities for this new brand. Ultimately, these groups had to "converge" their myriad options into a small number for field-testing. The field-testing would ultimately result in a Crest, Gleem, or Colgate toothpaste product with appealing packaging, taste, and (hopefully) effective teeth-cleaning ability.

Back in the classroom, gifted children have been inundated with activities to get them to look at problems from a variety of perspectives. However, teachers still need to encourage children to open their minds and say, "Ah!" It is the step where learners have to focus back to the best decision, or sometimes the best answer where our students are stymied. In reaction to the drill and recitation of yesteryear, the educational establishment has overreacted. The past several years have been spent inculcating educators to only focus on open-ended thinking. This was needed, but we have gone too far. In all walks of life, the road must be taken in one direction or another (thank you, Robert Frost). The debate on whether gifted programs should focus on getting students to be creative thinkers or pursue more knowledge is not a debate at all. Gifted and talented students need to do both.

Gifted children will have a chance to use better thinking strategies consistently if their teachers and parents understand ways to help them. One major step is to clarify the components of critical thinking in clearer terms. I use a simple blueprint when training teachers, administrators, and parents. It has worked well in providing common language.

When I train teachers, I try to simplify critical thinking into three components. The first component is convergent thinking. This type of thinking refers to problems or questions where there is a definite correct answer. Examples include building a model from directions or asking who is the vice president of the United States. Convergent thinking requires recall and/or looking up information that is "right there." When pupils seek answers, they can find the "correct" ones.

Divergent thinking refers to problems where there are many possibilities. Divergent thinking is often referred to as creative thinking, open-ended thinking, and thinking outside the box. Analogies, brainstorming, and upside down approaches are examples. I once asked an eight-year-old gifted boy to tell me what he saw on his visit to the zoo earlier that day. Twenty minutes later, he was still going on. His "list" included gum wrappers, the wire garbage baskets, and ten types of hats, in addition to the myriad animals (which was all I expected). This fluency was very creative. Many gifted children are instinctively aware of many more things than average children.

The third component is something I call cultural literacy (those things we should know almost without thinking). Examples are addition facts, multiplication facts, writing a simple grammatically correct sentence, and the basic questions in *Nathan Levy's Test Booklet of Basic Knowledge for Every American Over Nine Years Old.* More and more gifted and talented children do not have a base of knowledge at their fingertips. With the advances in technology, it would seem we could find everything we need. However, conversations would be very limited if we did not have a common knowledge base at our fingertips.

Questions such as, "Which is the most beautiful flower?" or "Who is the best football player that ever played?" are interesting to inspire participants to debate—knowing there are many subjective right answers. The ability to know where Texas or California is located or how many years are in a century call for no debate. There are right answers. The abilities to think convergently and divergently are both needed. Add the dire need for a base of cultural literacy, and we may have hope for gifted and talented pupils to be ready for the world.

What strategies and/or materials will help gifted and talented children become better thinkers? My successful critical thinking series, *Nathan Levy's Stories With Holes* (Volumes 1–20) are the materials I use to show educators and parents how most of society's productive work starts with creative thinking and ultimately moves to convergent thinking. Participants have to try to figure out an answer to a "story" by asking questions that can only be answered by "yes" or "no." ("Why?" or "How many?" cannot be asked with this format.) This series can be found on the Web site www.storieswithholes.com/storwithhol5.html.

A sample story follows:

A man lives on the twentieth floor of an apartment building. Every time he leaves, he rides a self-service elevator from the twentieth floor to the street; but every time he returns, he rides the same self-service elevator only to the fifteenth floor, where he leaves the elevator and walks up the remaining five flights of stairs. Why doesn't he go all the way up?

If they think divergently, they will be able to arrive at a kind of unique convergent answer. The trick is to show teachers how this type of thinking is embedded in all school subjects.

Here are examples of questions children might ask:

Question: Does the elevator go all the way up?

Answer: Yes.

Q: Does he want the exercise?

A: No.

Q: Does it have something to do with the elevator not working right?

A: No.

Q: Does he have a girlfriend on the fifteenth floor who he stops to see?

A: No.

Q: Does he have something different about him?

A: Yes.

Q: Is he a robber?

A: No.

Q: Is he a real person?

A: Yes.

Q: A tall person?

A: No.

Q: Is his size important?

A: Yes.

Q: I know! He's too short to reach the button!

A: Right!

REFERENCES

Levy, N. L. (2005). *Nathan Levy's test booklet of basic knowledge for every American over nine years old.* Hightstown, NJ: NL Associates.

Levy, N. L., & Burke, A. (2004). *Thinking & writing activities for the brain–Book 1.* Hightstown, NJ: NL Associates.

Levy, N. L., & Burke, A. (2004). *Thinking & writing activities for the brain–Book 2.* Hightstown, NJ: NL Associates.

Levy, N. L, & Burke, A. (2004). *Write, from the beginning.* Hightstown, NJ: NL Associates.

Levy, N. L., & Burke, A. (2008). *Not just schoolwork.* Hightstown, NJ: NL Associates.

Levy, N. L., Burke, A., Fisher, E. (2004). *Creativity day by day.* Hightstown, NJ: NL Associates.

it's a date...

Pick one famous person whom you would like to invite to lunch.

1- Write a few sentences that tell whom you would pick and why you would like to have lunch with that person.

2- Write two questions that you would like to ask your guest.

3- List two things that you would tell your guest about yourself.

4- Write a menu for your luncheon. Write it on a sheet of paper that looks like this:

~MENU~
PREPARED BY ___(your name)___
FOR ___(your guest's name)___

?

Source: From *Write, From the Beginning* (p. 42) by Nathan Levy & Amy Burke. Hightstown, NJ: NL Associates Inc., www.storieswithholes.com. Used with permission.

directions...

Write <u>ten</u> sentences that begin with the words :

above me...

or

Write <u>ten</u> sentences that begin with the words:

below me...

or

Write <u>ten</u> sentences that begin with the words: 600 mi.

600 miles to the west of me...

or

Write <u>ten</u> sentences that begin with the words:

1000 light-years away from me, out in space...

Use your imagination to think of real <u>or</u> imaginary things... when you complete ten sentences, write one or two sentences summing up how the things you wrote about make you <u>feel</u>. The feeling checklist will help you.

Source: From *Not Just Schoolwork* (p. 103) by Nathan Levy & Amy Burke. Hightstown, NJ: NL Associates Inc., www.storieswithholes.com. Used with permission.

In a Month

◆ **What is your favorite month?**

◆ **What is your least favorite month?**

◆ **Explain why you feel this way about each of these months.**

Source: From *Creativity Day by Day* (p. 72) by Nathan Levy & Amy Burke with Emily Fisher. Hightstown, NJ: NL Associates Inc., www.storieswithholes.com. Used with permission.

Give And Take

Make a collage of gifts you would like to give to other people. Make a "key" to go with it.

Write and illustrate a story called, "The Worst Gift Ever."

_____

_____

_____

_____

_____

_____

_____

Write a thank you note to someone who gave you something special. _Send it._

_____

_____

_____

_____

_____

_____

_____

_____

_____

Source: From _Thinking and Writing Activities for the Brain—Book 1_ by Nathan Levy & Amy Burke. Hightstown, NJ: NL Associates Inc., www.storieswithholes.com. Used with permission.

Inside And Out

Choose one or more of the following:

1) *Write about one of the most significant events in your life (good or bad).*

_____

_____

_____

_____

_____

2) *"Five percent of life is what happens to us.* Ninety-five percent is how we react to it." (Source Unknown) Explain.

_____

_____

_____

_____

_____

3) *Write about how this quote applies to your life.*

_____

_____

_____

_____

_____

_____

Source: From *Thinking and Writing Activities for the Brain—Book 2* by Nathan Levy & Amy Burke. Hightstown, NJ: NL Associates Inc., www.storieswithholes.com. Used with permission.

3

Literacy Strategies

Reading and Writing

Annie Proulx once said that "the reader writes the story," in reference to the process of reading as an inherently active and creative one. For gifted educator and author Jerry Flack (2000), "Reading is the space capsule that allows gifted children to reach for the stars, pursuing their education well beyond the confines of lockstep progression through the traditional curriculum" (p. 22). This chapter presents reading and writing together, as they evolve simultaneously in a child's literate growth. "Good literature" Flack (2000) explains, "should stimulate their own thinking about important ideas and themes and be the catalyst for finding and using their own voice to write about things that matter to them" (p. 25).

When children read, they

- connect what they know with new information,
- question themselves and the texts,
- visualize and make inferences during and after reading,
- distinguish most important ideas in texts,
- synthesize information and ideas from different texts (from Harvey & Goudvis, 2000).

Writing is intimately connected to this process. More than applying the rules of grammar, usage, and composition, writing demands that students

- think on paper;
- organize their thoughts into ideas;
- pose questions to themselves and their ideas;
- create sequences for their ideas in the form of sentences and paragraphs;
- apply the structure of stories, essays, and poems learned from reading to writing;
- experiment with usage, voice, tone, metaphoric language, and related arts activities; and
- synthesize material (images, writing styles, information, concepts, etc.) and express them through writing.

The creative activities shared by the teachers in the following pages address the need for gifted learners to make deep and meaningful connections with texts of all kinds (fiction, nonfiction, poetry) and to develop their cognitive and expressive gifts. The process of exploring questions, engaging the senses (sight, sound, touch, and possibly smell and taste), doing research, learning stories, studying words and sounds, and inventing texts of their own gives students the experiences they need to become thinking readers and writers. They develop the skills to construct meaning, analyze the motives of characters (or the data of research), and interpret the story (or the findings of a study). Two reports from teachers (below) explore ways they've found to advance the literary abilities of their gifted learners.

REFERENCES

Flack, J. (2000). The gifted reader in the regular classroom: Strategies for success. *Illinois Association for Gifted Children Journal.*

Harvey, S., & Goudvis, A. (2000). *Strategies that work: Teaching comprehension to enhance understanding.* Portland, ME: Stenhouse.

Reading Focus

By Drew Shilhanek

I am currently in my sixth year of teaching at Quest Academy, where we strive to differentiate for each individual student in a variety of ways. Once a student has consistently shown a high level of mastery, we look at advancing that student into higher and more creative kinds of challenges.

Words

- Students may work on word-in-word, which is a creative and challenging way to look at word parts to understand their origin. Students look at a number of examples of ways words are combined to form compound words and study the origins of the base words as to what they mean.
- Students then answer a number of questions about the words in different categories of thinking (e.g., analysis, synthesis, comparison, inference, evaluation). These exercises vary from two-to-three sentence answers to paragraph and short-story answers.

Translation

- Because of the strong French language program in the school, students can also choose to translate poetry. This challenges them cognitively (learning how one language relates to another) as well as creatively (exploring images, phrases, subtleties of language and meaning). This allows students to see nuances in the French language and compare them to English. This is a prime example of challenging students to a higher level of application.

Self-Selected Reading

- We have a population that likes to read novels. Each student is required to choose a book from nine different categories, including animal stories, overcoming obstacles, historical fiction, science fiction and fantasy, nonfiction, poetry, short stories, biographies, and autobiographies. They select a book from one of these categories each month to read in conjunction with any novel we are tackling in class. Reading two books simultaneously is a stimulating way to expand a gifted child's experience of language.

Book Projects

- We have developed a series of independent book projects for students to participate in throughout the year. They choose one of three possible projects to complete at the beginning of the next month. They include the following:

  1. Students can create a reading journal where they write four separate times of at least a half a page each. Students then turn in their final reading journal, totaling at least two pages for the month. I always ask students to reflect on a deeper emotional and analytical level in order to tie the novel to something within them. Connecting with the text fosters a lifelong practice of reading.

2. The second project is a book review. This is a challenging project for students because they tend to summarize the events in the book from beginning to end. Instead of a summary, I have students examine the major events and ideas on a personal and analytical level because I want them to explore the author's meaning in more depth. In the end, by connecting to the text personally, creatively, and analytically, they feel as though the book has become part of them.

3. One of our most popular choices is the book talk on the Collaboratory, an online forum Quest uses through Northwestern University. We create a forum on the Collaboratory called Book Talk. Then, we set up a thread with the book title and a little prompt. Students are then required to post their analysis, reflections, and conclusions they have drawn about the reading. The other students in the forum then respond to other posts and add their own thoughts.

All of these projects engage gifted students in critical and creative thinking and provide many opportunities for them to make meaningful links to different kinds of texts. They also create a fruitful mingling of reading, writing, and speaking that gives them a whole and integrated background in literacy. I have to say that I have been utterly amazed at times with the quality and quantity of posts our students have produced in the online forum. Students write more in those posts than they do for many of the rest of their essays combined. I so enjoy the interaction with the students on all these projects.

Writing Focus

By Jennifer Golwitzer

There are certain practices I've found consistently helpful in preparing my classroom for creative writing through the school year.

- **Writer's workshop format.** The workshop format is ideal for creative work. It works well for introducing new concepts and then for giving students the opportunity and time to write pieces they are interested in starting, continuing, or finishing. The workshop format also enables teachers to conference with children throughout the week—an important factor in ensuring that they progress in their written work.
- **Student-generated lists.** I find that students, particularly gifted students, need opportunities to create their own topics for writing assignments. At the beginning of the year, have students start lists

of writing ideas and then share these lists as a way of exchanging and expanding topic ideas for everyone. They can keep them in personal writing folders and add more ideas as they progress throughout the year.

- **Writing center.** A writing center with a rich variety of materials (text, visual, audio, etc.) for students to explore can help stimulate new ideas at various stages in the writing process. Include sources at different levels of difficulty so that advanced students will find challenging materials to spur them on. A book that provides a funny story or poetry starter, an interesting picture or object can often prompt great writing.

- **The senses.** Students rarely have enough opportunities to explore writing through the five senses. In my introduction, I always include texts that use the five senses to create vivid images in the reader's imagination. Share poetry, short stories, song lyrics, excerpts from familiar stories, and so forth to illustrate how the senses enrich written work. Break the students into partnerships or have them work independently to practice using the five senses to describe a common object to the rest of the class. Remind students to describe the object well so that others can guess the object they've chosen.

- **Music.** Have students listen to a piece of music once. Play the song again. This time, have the students write down words to describe the images they see as the music plays. From the list, they can create a short story, a description of the song, a poem, or any other composition. Audio recordings are a powerful influence on the imagination.

- **The natural world.** Take the class outside to experience writing in a new setting. Children love to be outside to write about the natural world around them. I try to take my students outside during each of the seasons throughout the school year. Remind them to focus on each of their five senses, including taste. I ask my students to imagine what different substances (bark, grass, bushes, rock, etc.) in the surrounding area would taste like. This has proven to be an effective way to incorporate "taste" into students' nature writing. The natural world has inspired countless similes and metaphors for published writers, and it can do the same for students.

- **Humor.** Students need to have fun with the writing process sometimes. Occasionally, I introduce them to new and humorous ways of writing. Fractured fairy tales are very popular in my class because they allow children to put a different spin on familiar fairytales. I usually use "The Three Little Pigs" story. I first share the original story and then read several fractured fairy tales that are based on it. I also try to coordinate the student's own "fractured" story to be written around the time they're learning how to draw cartoon characters in art class. The final products are in full color, laminated, and bound with a binding machine.

Never has the need been greater than now for greater challenge for gifted learners in the humanities. According to Maurice Fisher and

Ten Essential Criteria for an Advanced Humanities Curriculum for Gifted Students

By Maurice Fisher and Michael Walters

1. **Emphasis on Identifying the Gifted Student's Sensibility Levels and Teaching to These Levels**—Students' sensibility levels can be assessed through systematic classroom observations in conjunction with a rating scale such as the Fisher Assessment of Giftedness (Gifted Education Press, 1994). What subjects are most stimulating for the gifted student? What ideas and areas of learning stimulate their interests?

2. **Stress Independent Learning and Self-Study**—This learning approach, used by the great thinkers of the humanities and sciences, will enable the gifted to make conceptual leaps within and across different subjects and to study history, mathematics, science, and other humanities subjects in greater depth than usually occurs in a regular structured curriculum.

3. **Provide Opportunities for Gifted Students to Learn Together in Small Cluster/Affinity Groups**—The interaction between students of similar high abilities and common interests helps them increase their own knowledge and social skills. *Positive synergy* will automatically occur in these groups and will lead to productive individual and group projects.

4. **An Advanced Curriculum Must Be Based Upon the Most Significant Nonfiction and Fiction Books**—The use of challenging content is the most important aspect of the advanced curriculum for the gifted. Excellent resources can be found on the Internet with careful teacher supervision. All major thinking and problem-solving processes must emphasize *strong subject matter content*.

5. **Students Should Read and Study the Biographies of Great Achievers in All Areas of the Humanities, Mathematics, and the Sciences**—By reading biographies of great people, gifted students will be able to identify with these people and become inspired by their accomplishments. They need role models and mentors that appeal to their sensibility levels.

6. **A Historical Approach Should Be Used in Instruction and Learning**—Gifted students can develop a better understanding of literature and science if they study the gradual progression of knowledge and writing in these and other subjects. They must learn that all present-day knowledge has strong connections to the past.

7. **Interdisciplinary Learning**—The teacher should help gifted students to see *links and relationships* among different subjects. This approach to learning will result in the amplification of their knowledge beyond artificially distinct subjects. The great thinkers and doers in all fields of endeavor are very skilled in combining their knowledge from many fields to develop new ideas and products.

8. **Differentiation of Instruction and Learning**—The gifted student must receive an advanced curriculum that provides many opportunities for in-depth learning of each subject in the humanities and sciences. Examples of differentiated learning opportunities are: working with a mentor who is an expert in a specific field; involving independent study in advanced library work; utilizing an accelerated pace in math and science; and incorporating one-on-one student and teacher study.

9. **The Teacher Must Be a Mentor, Role Model, and Major Resource Provider**—Self-study by teachers in different areas of the humanities is essential to provide the environment for high levels of student achievement. They must have a love of learning and constantly be engaged in questioning and analysis of problems in order to keep the gifted classroom alive and stimulating. An example of how teachers can simultaneously be a mentor, role model, and resource provider is having teachers with a lifelong interest in American history discuss outstanding history books they have read and explain how they became interested in this subject to gifted students who have similar preferences.

10. **The Teacher Must Understand and Appreciate Unique Learning Styles**—For gifted students to be highly motivated and to maximize their learning of different humanities subjects, instruction must be fitted to their unique learning styles in verbal, auditory, visual, and perceptual-motor areas.

Michael Walters (see chart on page 43), while differentiated instruction has wrought higher standards for gifted children in subjects such as math and science, in the humanities during the past 10 years, the standard has fallen. The 10 essential criteria itemized by Fisher and Walters are a useful frame for exploring the teacher activities in this chapter.

RESOURCE

Fisher, M. (1994). *Fisher comprehensive assessment of giftedness scale.* Manassas, VA: Gifted Education Press.

Eight other teachers have shared their creative strategies within the general field of literacy in some detail. Although designed for different grade levels, most can be easily adapted. For your convenience, the authors and their contributions are listed below, along with the creative strategies used, the grade level, and the curriculum standards established by the National Council of Teachers of English (NCTE). Obviously, you have to follow your own state's standards, but these examples provide insight into how you can link your own creative projects to standards in your district.

Topics & Authors	Creative Strategies	Grade Level	Standards (examples)
Creative Explorations of Words *Jerry Flack* P. 46	Creative explorations with words Brainstorming Invention Integrated arts experiences Creative writing	All grades	Students apply knowledge of language structure, language conventions, media techniques, figurative language, and genre to create, critique, and discuss print and nonprint texts.
Adventures With "Poetry Pot" *Elaine Wiener* P. 48	Sensing (atmosphere, mood, magic) Imagining Feeling the language, artistry, beauty Embodying poems Dramatizing/speaking	Applicable to all ages	Students use spoken, written, and visual language to accomplish their own purposes (e.g., for learning, enjoyment, persuasion, and the exchange of information).
Literature Circles That Promote Higher-Level Discussions *Pam Gish* P. 54	Role-playing Open-ended questioning Collaborative exploration	Middle school, though adjustable to lower and higher grades	Students read a wide range of print and nonpoint texts to build an understanding of texts, of themselves, and of the cultures of the United States and the world. Among these texts are fiction and nonfiction, classic, and contemporary works.

Topics & Authors	Creative Strategies	Grade Level	Standards (examples)
Mentor Texts *Frances Collins* P. 56	Full sensory exposure to literature (to motivate, inspire, guide writing) Divergent thinking	Elementary, intermediate, and up	Students apply a wide range of strategies to comprehend, interpret, evaluate, and appreciate texts. They draw on their prior experience, their interactions with other readers and writers, their knowledge of word meaning and of other texts, and their understanding of textual features.
Podcasting for and With Gifted and Talented Students *Courtland Funke* P. 59	Interactive media Research and script-writing Hosting podcasts Producing Composing (recording music and sound)	Intermediate and up	Students use a variety of technological and information resources (e.g., libraries, databases, computer networks, video) to gather and synthesize information and to create and communicate knowledge.
Combining Language Arts and Social Studies for Gifted/Talented 6th Graders *Rosemary Ginko* P. 61	Interdisciplinary exploration Open questioning Brainstorming Original composition based on synthesis of elements from different sources	Intermediate, adjustable to lower or higher grades	Students conduct research on issues and interests by generating ideas and questions and by posing problems. They gather, evaluate, and synthesize data from a variety of sources to communicate their discoveries in ways that suit their purpose and audience.
Reaching for Depth Through Free-Verse Poetry *Yolanda Toni* P. 65	Use of arts and multimedia as catalysts Exploration of senses to create new imagery Free association Collaborative poetic compositions	Intermediate and up	Students participate as knowledgeable, reflective, creative, and critical members of a variety of literacy communities
Interpreting Literature: Reader's Theater for Gifted Learners *Joan Franklin Smutny* P. 73	Embodying and interpreting literature Exploring elements of story Brainstorming options Translating from written text to live performance	All grades (adjustments required)	Students participate as knowledgeable, reflective, creative, and critical members of a variety of literacy communities.

CREATIVE EXPLORATIONS OF WORDS

By Jerry Flack

The investigation of the meaning of words is the beginning of education.

—Antisthenes

MAIN CONCEPT

Students should learn to experience and fall in love with language in the same manner that they may enjoy a painting by Picasso or music by Mozart. Creative people tend to have vast storehouses of words, but it is equally essential for the development of language-based creativity for gifted youths to develop great appreciation for the richness of language, in general, and very exceptional words, in particular.

LEVEL

All grades.

APPLICATION

Any unit involving reading and writing: literature, history, sociology.

DESCRIPTION

Creative and gifted children are fascinated by words, and often, the bigger the word, the greater the appeal. *Spessartite, stichomythia, stridulation, sublimity, sumptuousness, surreptitiousness, symmetry!*

Brainstorm. Creative explorations with words may begin when students brainstorm words they enjoy and that possess rich connotative value. Ask students to cite their favorite words, or suggest words (e.g., *pride, giftedness, spiritual*) and seek out related student definitions, impressions, and experiences. Sample words that contain rich multiple layers of meaning include *beauty, genius, patriotism, femininity, masculinity, power, nature, talent, creativity, youth, wisdom, honor, enthusiasm*, and *freedom.*

Explore. Encourage students to select a single word, preferably an abstract noun, and begin thorough investigations and interactions with their words of choice. Tell creative students to steer clear of dictionary definitions at the beginning. Invite a more creative and personal approach to each individual's nuanced understanding of a word.

Create. Invite talented students to create a *biography* of a word. The following steps, addressed directly to students, provide fine guidance, but creative teachers should definitely feel free to expand upon these choices.

Teachers will be amazed at the energy gifted students expend in pursuing this creative word quest.

1. Write your own definition of a single, important word. What do you think the word means?

2. Collect several photographs, post cards, news stories, and many diverse materials associated with your chosen word. Use the media you have found to create a visual collage. Give your chosen word a creative artistic appearance.

3. Write about a personal experience in which your word plays a role. For example, recall a time when you demonstrated *bravery*.

4. Write a poem, story, or song that illustrates the connotation or import of your special word. If your favorite word is a season of the year, you might write a haiku such as the following tribute to *spring*.

Spring

Budding leaves on trees,
Birds singing, flowers blooming.
A new year begins.

5. Engage in demographic research. Ask a minimum of five other people what they believe your chosen word means. Try to ask people from different generations as well as class peers. Record all responses in your word *biography* journal.

6. Be inventive. Create an entirely new word that might be included in a dictionary as a synonym for your word choice. "Never stops trying" might well define the word *creativity*.

7. Use a dictionary. After you have explored the personal, emotional, or connotative meaning of a word, finally consult a dictionary to note how scholars have defined your word. The dictionary definition of a word is referred to as its denotative meaning. If many definitions are noted in the dictionary, record two to four of your favorite options in your word journal.

8. Begin a creative word journal. Compile all of the above words and images in a special journal, notebook, or portfolio. Be sure to use media of choice to fashion a highly artistic cover for your very own, creative "biography" of a word. When your word investigation is complete, you will have an inclusive history and meaning of a special word.

Learning more about words is a creative and exciting challenge for gifted children. If they have another favorite word such as *serendipity*, they can use these same steps to create yet another original word "biography." The experience of "playing with words" becomes a joyous, creative, and rewarding encounter.

ADVENTURES WITH "POETRY POT"

By Elaine Weiner

MAIN CONCEPT

This process is a magical, poetic experience. Drawing on Albert Cullum's inspired *Push Back the Desks,* it provides a rich immersion into poetry through combined recitation, drama, and an environment suited to a poetic mood and atmosphere.

LEVEL

Adaptable to all grades.

APPLICATION

Language arts, creative writing, visual and performing arts, social studies.

DESCRIPTION

Set the Stage

Shhh. Darken the room. Light the candle. Chant a mood-setting poem as everyone settles around the Poetry Pot.

It is a timeless ritual that has its own evolution each year because each group of children responds in original ways. I was a young teacher when I first read Albert Cullum's (1967) *Push Back the Desks.* The second I read the chapter called Poetry Pot, I knew I had taken on a lifelong commitment to the art of magic.

Discuss

As the children sit around the pot, year after year, we discuss how we're going to listen to sounds written by people who can make words paint beauty and excitement. We listen for pictures of places, and we listen for feelings that also live in our own minds.

Listen

A chosen child mystically pulls out a pack of thirty-two duplicate poems from the ancient cauldron we call the Poetry Pot. The teacher reads the poem by candlelight. The intonation of the reading is punctuated by flickering shadows. As these years have passed by, the look of six-, seven-, and eight-year-old faces in candlelight never fails to reveal such wonder.

Children need magic. I need magic.

Recite

Lights on! The pack of poems is distributed. Thirty-two voices read together. "Who will dare?" Then one or two or a group of three or four recite. Finally, solo after solo, and then a total group reading is repeated.

Lights out! A new pack of duplicate poems is pulled out of the pot by a new "chosen" small hand. Shy children recite softly; blustering children "act" the recitation. "Who will dare?" provokes even more volunteers.

Respond

Only two or three poems are "discovered" each Friday afternoon. When the last poem is finished, the candlelit room is darkened one last time to reminisce, to think, to talk, and especially to "observe" the look of a magical environment. Our memory will last until we can reexperience Poetry Pot next week. (Learning that one can hold pleasure in the mind is a side goal.)

Recite More

Then partners, small groups, and sometimes a single child cozy up to various corners, outside trees, or a desk or two to recite to each other. The room buzzes with poetry from our folders—this week's poetry and last week's and all the weeks since September. By June, each child has a collection for childhood eternity.

Extend

Some years, when the chemistry is right, we draw, paint, practice, narrate, act out, develop stage presence, and perfect microphone projection—all for a poetry show.

Some years are not performing years. But every year, we read the world's great poets by candlelight, and we believe that poetry is profound and joyful and silly and sad and comical—and especially magical.

Preparation for Visualization

Preparations for lessons like this start long before the magic and the fanciful content. In the case of Poetry Pot, the beginning brewed during literature hour when my students could sit or lie down on the rug to listen to a story. When I was a young teacher, I didn't realize that you have to teach children to be civilized when lying on a rug, especially if they were not read to before. Therefore, before any great literature entered the classroom, we had lessons in civilized behavior.

Now civilized behavior is important in any classroom, but in a gifted classroom, it becomes an absolute necessity, as they are quick to scrutinize the gaps and inconsistencies of adult actions in very precise and sophisticated ways. To this end, I read the first paragraph from a fetching book and told the children that each day, we would practice civilized behavior until they were ready for this adventure. Each day, after lunch, I would offer the children the opportunity to sit or lie on the rug and close their eyes to rest so they could visualize the story. This was so difficult for many of the children that I began to use *Put Your Mother On the Ceiling: Children's Imagination Games* by Robert De Mille (1976) to develop their ability to hold still as well as visualize.

Visualization

The activities were engaging enough to capture their attention. The visualizing was a skill they had never tried. Once it was mastered, it took care of the need to move their bodies incessantly. I cannot stress the importance of accepting children where they are without harsh judgment. Any time the excitement was too much for any reason, one of the calmer children would beg, "Please read *Put Your Mother on the Ceiling.*"

In later discussions about the visualizations, the children described details and patterns that were far more sophisticated than any I imagined. Finally, the day came. The children could visualize, they were civilized, and it was time to read to them every day after lunch. (I'm going to assume that you realize that there are always a few children who have trouble being civilized and that there are days when the whole class needs to be outside running around to find their civilized selves.)

Reading aloud to a class is a dramatic endeavor worthy of an Oscar. Not only can you use voices, you can also repeat a phrase breathlessly, telling the children, "Listen to how the author said this. Listen to the beautiful phrasing. I'm going to read it again so you can hear it even better than the first time." And any time is a good time to say, "What do you think will happen now?"

The result of these examples were children who: (1) read aloud beautifully, (2) had tears in *their* eyes (children being the most sensitive) when reading their own books, and (3) impulsively ran to the teacher, even when the teacher was with another group, read a phrase out loud because it was so magnificent, and then read that phrase to the whole group.

Yes, yes, of course that got out of hand because everyone wanted to do that. And so, we shifted gears and used yellow *stickums* to write down favorite phrases. When that wore off because it was too tedious, especially for those with immature motor skills, they evolved to smiles on faces while reading to themselves. Shifting gears constantly is a strategy that all good teachers use, but I wonder if we realize that it is a strategy!

So! Now we had the ability to visualize, to use civilized behavior on the rug, to experience dramatic reading by the teacher . . . and the day came when Poetry Pot was introduced. A sign was on the door telling them that "TODAY IS the DAY." They suspected that it was going to be Poetry Pot.

The room was dark, but a low light in a lovely little lamp was on nearby so the children could see as they walked in . . . slowly and carefully. On this first Friday, tables one and two were invited to sit around the pot and all others sat close . . . in a civilized way, of course! They were told that in a minute, the candle in the middle of the pot would be lit. They were told that they needed more civilized behavior than they had ever experienced before because a lit candle could be a problem if someone *had* to put a finger *in* the flame. I reminded them that children in this classroom should have second chances for all kinds of lessons—but *never, never* for sitting too close to the candle. And so they were cautioned that if any student just looked as if he or she were going to put a finger in the candle, he or she would have to move back and *forever* sit as part of the group but not in the front row to the Poetry Pot. Shhhh . . . and then it began . . .

Creative Extensions

Other related lessons evolved naturally when the children were comfortable with dramatic poetry readings and developed a love for listening to beautiful literature read to them. There was a podium sitting to the side of the chalkboard. It was always fascinating to see how different groups of children noticed items in the room at different times of the year. Many lessons were motivated by a child's question or observation. Finally, one day a child asked what "that" was. I wrote *podium* on the chalkboard and said, "Who Will Dare?"

The children all yelled out, "That's like Poetry Pot!" And I said, "It (speaking from the podium) *can* be very much like poetry. The poet speaks aloud his or her interests to the world, and you speak aloud about what interests you to your class.

A simple starter for speeches is to allow children to pick an animal or an object and speak as though they were that subject:

"I am a cat.

I purr when I am happy.

I lovvvvvve to be petted.

I like to be picked up,

and I don't like to be let down!"

By the time we started speeches, the children were comfortable expressing themselves, but there were physical mannerisms to practice:

Walking up to the podium with confidence;

Looking at the audience;

Making eye contact;

Looking to the left, middle, and right of the podium;

Projecting one's voice;

Swallowing the *ums* and *ahs* as you speak; and

Returning to one's seat slowly, with poise.

Each of those actions was practiced. We walked up to the podium, looked at the audience, and returned to our desks. That simple accomplishment took days and days of practice. Projecting one's voice took even longer because that is a matter of confidence. A lesson in "faking it" was spliced in here. The children were told to *pretend* they were confident, and it would happen. How to *pretend* involved holding up one's head, making eye contact, and standing straight with shoulders back. Eliminating *ums* and *ahs* was accomplished by making one-minute speeches without the traps of *ums* and *ahs*. The big secret to that was called "Close Your Mouth!" *Ums* and *ahs* are, therefore, swallowed. Of all public speaking skills that were practiced, getting rid of the *ums* and *ahs* was the most difficult.

I was amazed at the lessons *I* learned. There were children who did this with such ease and grace from day one. There were children who did well enough and improved through practice. There were a few who died a thousand deaths and were praised for just getting up there. And all the students always cheered because they were told that whatever they did at the podium was a step closer to doing it better each time. By the end of the year, all the children could think like a public speaker, privately evaluate their own performance, and analyze what they could do to improve.

Language arts lessons that involve drama and action aim to inspire the children's sense of *wonder*. For this reason, they are sometimes seen as lacking academic value or as belonging to a softer world. But the argument for basics versus creativity is a spurious debate. Both points of view have merit, and the only answer is a marriage of the two.

For example, in a grammar lesson, we organized a Grammar Hospital. Each child, dressed as a physician, had eight sentence strips (eight patients). We sutured the nouns, bandaged the verbs, and performed surgery on the adjectives and other parts of speech. Crayons created little "x" stitches. Scissors performed the surgeries. Bandages strips protected the wounds. We stopped for five-minute snack breaks and professional medical talk and returned to our patients.

These ideas may please those who see the world through creative eyes and spurn rigor. But do not be fooled! Do not be deceived! Every lesson had a follow-up lesson that drilled and grilled. However, those rhythmic practices were frequent and brief and fun and used music when possible. When a college student who returned to visit told me that on a grammar test, he mumbled to himself, "*Be, being, been, am, is, are, was, were, may, can, must, might, could, would, should, shall, will, have, has, had, do, does, did,*" I knew those lessons paid off. The *be* verbs prevailed! And yes, of course, pure memory without the understanding of application has no value. On the other hand, understanding with no facts as foundation for the higher-level skills has no depth!

Culmination

The final magnum opus of our year together was called Round Table Heroes. Remember that the prerequisites for this culminating activity were the self-disciplined actions of *Put Your Mother on the Ceiling*, the literature read to the children all year, the Poetry Pot, the public speaking skills that were ongoing, and the grammar that you could cut and stitch and eat! Blended into those lessons were the whole workings of differentiated instruction based on the standards for gifted education.

The Round Table, inspired by Steve Allen's television show *Meeting of the Minds*, evolved from all the children reading biographies of historical figures. By this time of year, they had been trained in note taking and research skills. (Those lessons ran parallel to all others all year long.) Dressed up as their heroes, they marched down the corridor to Clarke's "Trumpet Voluntary" and fanned out to four tables under the trees set with linen, snacks, drinks, and place cards. They sat down with the body language of very important people from history. These little ones, who couldn't sit still on the rug at the beginning of the year, sat at round tables with the demeanor—almost haughty demeanor—of people brought back from history to talk to us.

Their conversations were peppered with phrases from Bloom's taxonomy in the early days and Dr. Sandra Kaplan's (USC) depth and complexity concepts in the later years. The adult guests at the tables had to stifle grins when they heard, "I had a different point of view when I was writing my science theories. People disagreed with me even though I had evidence to prove my theories." One year, I walked by a table and heard, "Well, there are ethical considerations when such inventions are created. Will they be used for profit or for the good of mankind?"

Many times over the years, I have received notes from college students remembering Poetry Pot, the Round Table, and other special lessons. Sometimes the note refers to delivering a speech in college and how easy it was because of their practice at the podium. One year, however, two-and-a-half decades after a student left the comfort of Poetry Pot, a long letter came, which included this paragraph:

Mrs. Wiener, you took the essence of what *you* loved—your favorite authors, your favorite poets, your favorite musicians, and your favorite painters—and you explored them with intensity. Twenty-five years later I've discovered your secret: You were the Pied Piper, and you believed in the "music" you were making. I found a quote by Amiel that reminds me of you and perhaps every other teacher who seeks to make a difference: "Without passion man is a mere latent force and possibility, like the flint which awaits the shock of the iron before it can give forth its spark."

I know that many teachers have received letters from past students. I am not unique. I hope printing this wonderful letter is not immodest. For me, however, this was the ultimate tribute to my whole career.

RESOURCES

Cullum, A. (1967). *Push back the desks.* New York: Citation Press.
De Mille, R. (1976). *Put your mother on the ceiling.* New York: Penguin Books.

LITERATURE CIRCLES THAT PROMOTE HIGHER-LEVEL DISCUSSIONS

By Pam Gish

MAIN CONCEPT

Literature circles are one method of promoting literary independence in capable readers. While all students love to participate in these types of groups, I have found that gifted students especially flourish when given challenging themes and guidance in developing higher-level discussion questions.

LEVEL

Primary, intermediate, and middle school levels (depending on literary ability)

APPLICATION

This strategy applies to any reading assignments in any subject.

DESCRIPTION

When I began using the literature circle structure in my classroom three years ago, I used Harvey Daniels's philosophy and his book *Literature Circles: Voice and Choice in Book Clubs & Reading Groups* (2002). Each year, I have *tweaked* his method to meet the needs of my students and curriculum. The biggest addition that I have made *to raise the bar* for all my students, and especially my gifted ones, was to incorporate Bloom's taxonomy terms and teach the students when and how to use them.

Roles. In the literature circle paradigm, groups are formed either formally by the teacher or informally by the students around a topic or book. Each participant has a specific *role* in the group session, which rotates. The roles that I have used are Connector, Questioner, Word Wizard, Illustrator, and Character Analyzer, and they all write chapter summaries. Students are responsible for reading the given assignment, preparing for that role, and sharing it when the group meets. At the end of the meeting, they make a new reading assignment and meeting time. Groups are meant to be independent, with the teacher being a facilitator and mentor who sits in on groups. This takes a great deal of training and modeling by the teacher and experienced groups.

Preparation. I spend one to two sessions on each *role*, presenting it, reading a short story, and modeling how it works, and then I have the students practice it themselves and share. After the training is finished, I prefer to group my students by reading level to ensure that their book choices are manageable but still challenging. I offer the group a variety of books at that level and let them come to consensus. They then receive a packet that contains a description of each role with examples and specific role pages to complete.

Higher-level thinking. One of the most critical roles to promote higher-level thinking and discussion is that of the Questioner. This is where the terms from Bloom's taxonomy play a crucial role. I explain the different levels and give them examples from each one. They help me to decide whether a question is *skinny* (one-word answers) or *fat* (thought-provoking answers). This list is printed in their packet, and as I rotate between the groups that are meeting, I take time to ask them who has had the *fattest* questions. When they are doing their reading and working, I rotate around the room offering suggestions and encouragement. With my highest groups, I highlight the application, analysis, synthesis, and evaluation words and require them to use at least one when developing their questions. They soon grow to love the lively discussions, and the quality of divergent thinking and creative ideas has astounded me. This spreads to the other groups as well and goes far beyond the standard teacher questions. Of course, they often get carried away and need teacher assistance to get back on task—but the excitement about these reading groups makes it difficult to go back to the standard format.

Self-management. Organizing and managing literature groups is an ongoing process for me, but the resulting development of higher-level questioning and thinking skills far outweighs the extra effort. There was also an unanticipated consequence to the process that has since appeared in several of my higher-level groups: self-management.

An immature boy often disrupted meetings with his behavior, provoking numerous complaints from students and interventions on my part. However, over the course of time, they worked together to develop a chart to track behavior and establish consequences. This young man, and at times others, took the consequences. The chart was modified several times and finally resulted in a cooperative working group. This took group time and angst, but its lesson was invaluable. It also became a discussion for the whole class and strengthened the process of cooperative-group problem solving for everyone.

REFERENCE

Daniels, H. (2002). *Literature circles: Voice and choice in book clubs & reading groups.* Portland, ME: Stenhouse.

MENTOR TEXTS

By Frances Collins

MAIN CONCEPT

A mentor text acts as a vehicle for instruction, gently leading the student by example towards mastery. In the process, students perceive themselves to be writers. Using mentor texts within the workshop helps to establish this paradigm for the young writers within the classroom.

LEVEL

Elementary, intermediate grades, and up.

APPLICATION

Any units in literacy, social studies, and science that require writing; any unit that exposes children to texts with a high literary quality.

DESCRIPTION

Entering my classroom during our writing workshop, a visitor would be struck by the steady working hum that accompanies our writing time each day. Students, engaged in planning, writing, and conferring with me or their peer-writing partner, work at their own level of ability, as writing workshop allows for such differentiation.

A mentor text could be used to highlight any literary device or genre. Lynne R. Dorfman and Rose Cappelli (2007) describe mentor texts as " . . . snapshots into the future that help students envision the kind of writer they can become; they help teachers move the whole writer, rather than each individual piece of writing, forward" (p. 3).

Poems as Mentor Texts

While I use mentor texts in each of the units of study we explore throughout our year together, poetry allows the students to be exposed to many texts as they are brief and often contain a large wallop for a few lines. I have found that using selected poems as mentor texts is a motivating tool for young poets, often inspiring them to create a new poem, based upon an author's example. One example is a poem I received from a five-year-old after I had read *Twilight Comes Twice* by Ralph Fletcher (1997) to the class. After reading one of his lines about dawn at a baseball field, we, as a class, explored the different meanings of "diamond" and the way Fletcher manipulated these meanings in poetic language. The student followed up this discussion with her work titled "Violet Clouds":

Violet clouds are blooming from the tip
  of my finger,
I hope they won't go away.
I hope they stay for the day.

Her use of the color *violet* as something that could bloom, as in flower, illustrated her manipulation of language as Fletcher had in the read-aloud.

Poems for the Gifted

Choosing poems as mentor texts that are not written specifically for children can also entice gifted writers to explore dramatic imagery and metaphors, such as comparing a life without a dream to a broken-winged bird (in Langston Hughes's poem, "Dreams"). This was the mentor text for another young poet as she created a companion poem capturing the essence of Hughes's message, also titled "Dreams":

Keep your dreams saved in your heart.
Keep them fresh and clear.
The dreams that you wish may not come true, but
Keep your dreams saved in your heart.

Synthesis

While both poems may seem simplistic in style, they represent a higher-level of thinking, as the poets use an established example and weave into it their own imaginative sensibility to create an original work of their own. Diverging from the established example is made possible as the example acts as a living mentor holding the young poets' hands and guiding them while still allowing for their own voice as authors to be expressed.

To reinforce this process, I often read aloud from authors such as Fletcher who have written wonderful texts for young writers. While gifted writers at the kindergarten level may not be able to decode his work, they can appreciate how his words apply to their own compositions. His book *Poetry Matters* (Fletcher, 2002) is a treasure trove of passages waiting to inspire young and old poets. Sections discussing imagery, rhythm, and word play provide gems of examples and minimentors waiting to be discovered.

Divergent Thinking

Fractured fairy tales and alternate versions of stories can also provide young poets with inspiration. After reading many runaway food stories, I brought a few gifted writers together during our writing workshop for a strategy lesson. This format allows me to use flexible grouping to pull students together in small groups that may need specific instruction on a skill or who are excelling and ready for a challenge. This group, having discussed Fletcher's description of a poem from his book *Poetry Matters* (2002) the day before as "a word painting in which the writer tries to capture a moment, an image" (p. 60), used Jan Brett's *Gingerbread Baby* as the basis for the following poem entitled "The Reddish Brown Baby":

> *Baby, baby, reddish and brown*
> *gingery and fragrant.*
> *He ran away.*
> *Ran away and never came back.*
> *Many years passed.*
> *Only crumbs were left,*
> *Tears like pouring rain,*
> *The gingerbread baby has gone away.*

Mentor Texts as Guest Teachers

Using mentor texts within my classroom remains a constant, even as curriculum changes and interests of each new group of students pull us in new directions. These texts allow me to bring in authors as guest teachers each and every day. These guests present children with a gift, a glimpse into their work as writers and how they can become apprentices and follow the path of a writer. Mentor texts create an excitement for writing and often elicit work from students that is their best writing. Often, my gifted writers create new mentor texts themselves in response to a text, thereby providing delicious momentum for the cycle to continue and build as we progress through our year together as a community of authors.

REFERENCES

Brett, J. (1999). *The gingerbread baby.* New York: Putnam Juvenile.

Dorfman, L. R., & Cappelli, R. (2007). *Mentor texts: Teaching writing through children's literature, K–6.* Portland: Stenhouse.

Fletcher, R. (1997). *Twilight comes twice.* New York: Clarion Books.

Fletcher, R. (2002). *Poetry matters: Writing a poem from the inside out.* New York: HarperTrophy.

PODCASTING FOR AND WITH GIFTED AND TALENTED STUDENTS

By Courtland Funke

MAIN CONCEPT

Because of its interdisciplinary and multimedia focus, podcasting can enhance curriculum projects, and as new software is being released each year, the possibilities are endless. At Tripp School, we used podcasting software to create a monthly podcast about our school. I designed the project to serve as a vehicle for students needing an extra challenge during the week. I wanted it to touch upon as many subjects as possible and spark the students' creativity. The project was student driven, and I served only as an advisor and moderator, allowing the students to have creative control over the project.

LEVEL

Intermediate level and up.

APPLICATION

Any topics within the fields of literature, media, history, current events, the arts.

DESCRIPTION

In recent years, the availability and popularity of MP3 players and high-speed Internet connections have helped to create a new form of Internet media, the podcast. Think of a podcast as an episodic radio program available for download on the Internet so that users can listen to it whenever and wherever they like. Most podcasts are devoted to a specific theme or topic, and listeners can usually find a number of podcasts devoted to their interests, no matter how obscure.

To get started, I met with our school's gifted instructor to create a list of students who might be interested in the project. I wanted to keep the numbers low so that each student would have plenty to do each month. Then, I invited those students to our first meeting where I explained the project to them and reviewed the commitments they would need to make in order to participate.

Student Commitments

- Students were not required to participate and would be allowed to stop working on the project at any time. Once a student decided to drop, however, he or she would not be allowed to resume.
- Weekly meetings would be held during the students' "Friday Fun Time" at the end of the day each Friday. Participants would be expected to miss that time each week in order to participate.

- Homework would be assigned.
- Rotating jobs would be assigned on a monthly basis, which allowed everyone to work on each part of the podcast at some point during the year.

Roles Identified

At our first meeting, we set up clearly defined jobs for the project. Each episode would feature the following:

Two hosts

Two producers

Four or five writers

A 10-questions interviewer

Composers

We later added a head writer and special reports to the mix.

Writers were assigned stories to research and write up as scripts for the hosts. Hosts would practice reading their scripts and record them for the podcast episode that month. Producers were responsible for recording each episode, editing those recordings, and inserting sound effects and music. Composers were responsible for writing and recording music for each episode (not as hard as it sounds when using certain types of software).

Content

The initial structure for the podcast was set up as a school news program with a short, 10-question interview segment, but students were allowed to create and add content as a group. Over the course of the year, we added a Joke of the Month, student surveys, teacher surveys, special reports, and specials (art, music, gym, etc.) news.

Teacher Role

As the faculty advisor, I tried to stay as hands-off as possible, and let the students guide themselves and generate their own ideas. My job was to give them the time and the place to get their work done and to set limits to keep them focused. On occasion, I would need to exercise my veto power to keep them from doing something too complicated or time-consuming, but for the most part, their ideas were manageable and fun.

Creative Focus

I did try to steer them creatively with some surveys and activities designed to generate ideas and stimulate their imagination. For our 10-questions segment, I had trouble getting them to propose candidates outside of the school or district to interview, so I created a survey asking for their three favorite, authors, actors, musicians, and three people or jobs they found interesting. We then compiled those names into a list, looked up as many contact addresses as we could find, and mailed requests for interviews. One of the students' favorite authors agreed to be interviewed over the phone almost immediately, and their interest in seeking outside interviewees soared dramatically. We received a number of rejection letters as well, but those were equally interesting to the group as many of them contained autographed photos or signed letters of encouragement. They also reinforced the idea that people were reading the letters we sent even if they declined our offers.

Other Talents

The podcasting project gave some of our musically gifted students an outlet to display their talents. One student was an accomplished piano and violin player. A simple midi cable and our music teacher's midi keyboard were all we needed to record some of the music he had learned for inclusion in the podcasts. We also purchased a nice USB microphone to use to record his violin. Other students played the piano, the viola, and the recorder; all fourth-grade students had been learning to play in music class.

Transformations

As the project progressed, I watched students become more confident, more adventurous, and even more nurturing of each other's talents. Students, who didn't think they were good writers, honed their skills writing collaboratively with stronger writers. Students who were usually timid and quiet, learned to be more vocal during meetings to get their ideas heard by the group or to project their voice when recording their parts as a host. I watched students take pride in their work as the months passed and grow excited each time they found a new outlet to promote the show. In the end, the project worked out far better than I could have imagined.

COMBINING LANGUAGE ARTS AND SOCIAL STUDIES FOR GIFTED/TALENTED SIXTH GRADERS

By Rosemary Ginko

MAIN CONCEPT

These activities depend on the cross-fertilization that interdisciplinary work often promises for the gifted learner. Combining language arts and social studies stimulates intellectual curiosity, critical thinking, and creativity. Students connect with themes that they helped select at the beginning of the year. Developing stronger research and study skills occurs in the process of exploring ideas in an open-ended learning environment and in pursuing questions that arise as they delve more deeply into a topic.

LEVEL

Intermediate level; ideas apply to lower and upper grades as well.

APPLICATION

Language arts, social studies, creative writing, the arts.

DESCRIPTION

Combining language arts and social studies in middle school is an effective way to challenge gifted students at a higher level of learning. With the passage of the No Child Left Behind Act and its focus on the low-achieving population, teachers need to find ways to lift the gifted (and all students) to higher levels of thinking, while at the same time meeting state standards and benchmarks. The strategies I use to engage gifted learners accomplish this.

When I asked my students what they liked best about my class, they made the following statements:

> "I liked when we wrote the fictional narrative because fictional writing rocks; but it was sort of hard due to the use of figurative speech. I also like how my teacher teaches in a more difficult but fun way in our learning." *Jordan S.*

> "One thing I like about this class is when we get to write stories, because I like to write, and the stuff she makes us write is fun to write about." *Danny Q.*

> "I like to learn, read, and to write better." *Steven L.*

> "I like our SSR time, and I love having my friends in here also." *Naomi A.*

> "What I like in gifted literature and language arts class is the way the teacher teaches by making every project fun; and putting the word 'fun' in fundamentals. Also, I like the narrative writes and nonfiction writes." *Michael G.*

> "I love this class because it is challenging in a way that is fun! It is the best class period of the day. If I could, I would sleep in this class. We have brain puzzles and writing prompts. These things make us go beyond imagination." *Ceidric P.*

> "In this class, I like when we work on challenging puzzles and writing assignments." *Jordyn B.*

The Children

The above comments have made it clear to me that they are benefiting from my approach to writing. They respond to an approach that is both fun *and* challenging, some particularly enjoying the word puzzles. My students often mention they like to read, but they don't state specifically why. When I questioned them further about this, they said, "I love an interesting book I can relate to; something that captures my attention; I like a book that challenges me to think." Clearly, challenge carries as much weight as interest for gifted learners. When I thought about all of these statements further and reviewed what I was doing to challenge my sixth-grade gifted and talented kids in language arts and social studies, I created the following strategies that are working well in my gifted classroom. I also integrated culture into my curriculum, which is important in my culturally diverse district.

Multicultural Setting

I work at Jimmy Carter Middle School in Albuquerque, New Mexico, that has as its mission the development of every student's special talents and abilities. The gifted program provides differentiated educational opportunities for students identified through a districtwide qualifying process (an IQ score of 130 and above and high A2L's in reading). Most of my students are reading two or more grade levels above their assigned grade, while some have achieved a post–high school level. The students in my program enjoy many opportunities for academic, creative, and social challenges that help them realize their high potential. Most are Hispanic and Native American, and for this reason, I try to provide activities that respond to their cultures and their needs.

Goal

The goal of this program is to stimulate curiosity, critical thinking, and creativity. I connect student experiences with broad intellectual concepts.

- **Themes.** For example, I use themes such as air or water pollution, overpopulation, World War II and the Holocaust, racism and the civil rights movement, Shakespeare, mythology, Native American myths and stories, New Mexican history and Hispanic culture and myths, and nature. These themes evolve from the students who choose what they would like to study at the beginning of the year.
- **Projects.** I also promote the creation of high quality projects and products. Projects/products allow gifted children more freedom in the way they work and provide an opportunity for immersion into a topic, issue, or interest in far greater depth than the school schedule usually allows.
- **Learning groups.** The students develop the skills necessary to make these products in cooperative learning groups and in other team arrangements. While they are working in these groups, they also develop responsible independence in thought and action.

Differentiation

Since my curriculum is differentiated and relates to broad-based themes and issues, I've been able to develop interactive, higher-order thinking skills, and activities. I try to focus on creative, open-ended tasks and questions that challenge students to delve more deeply into a topic and develop their own study and research skills. I assess the students' achievement through their ability to reason, problem solve, and apply skills as well as through high quality projects; progress is gauged through teacher-designed rubrics, portfolios, and tests. I also assess whether the above goals are designed around state power standards and benchmarks for language arts/ literature at an above-grade level standard of 9 through 12.

For the language arts part of my curriculum, I chose to cover advanced vocabulary, spelling, descriptive writing, persuasive writing, narrative writing, and a research paper. For the literature part of my curriculum, I recently chose to cover four books related to the themes: *The Watsons Go to Birmingham, The Diary of Anne Frank, The Merchant of Venice,* and *Native American Myths.* We also covered some of the book *Rio Grande Stories,* which emphasizes Hispanic culture.

Cross-Curriculum Techniques

The historical aspect is combined with language arts and literature through cross-curriculum techniques. For example, when we read *The Watsons Go to Birmingham,* we discussed the setting of the story—specifically, the civil rights movement. This brought up Martin Luther King and other civil rights activists such as Jesse Jackson, Rosa Parks, Malcolm X, and others. I combined this social studies and literature process with vocabulary, spelling, and a writing assignment—a persuasive paper. The students were to write a paper to explain what racism is and to persuade their audience against it. This would include documenting many examples from history, the book we were reading, and any life experiences they have had themselves.

Another cross-curricular approach is using the book *The Diary of Anne Frank.* This book is an excellent choice for combining social studies, literature, and language arts. Other topics tied into it are racism and culture. This book is an excellent choice for children to read when studying about World War II and the history of the Jewish people in Eastern and Western Europe. Since Anne is a young girl, the children can connect with her as a person.

Culture Connections

When I taught *Rio Grande Stories,* I combined the stories with New Mexico history, Hispanic culture, Native American and Hispanic art, Native American history, and geography. The students produced Native American pottery, wrote their own Native American and Hispanic myths, created maps, and wrote historical narratives through the above cross-curriculum approach.

When I introduced the book *Native American Myths*, we discussed the animal symbolism that Native American populations use in their storytelling techniques. For example, many storytelling techniques that have been handed down throughout their history feature animals such as bears, wolves, and owls, and we discussed this symbolism and what it might mean to different Native American peoples. Some of the students in my class who are Native American also shared a few of their own culture's stories with the class. This brought us to the subject of oral storytelling as a traditional way of transmitting myths from generation to generation.

Create a Myth

The students were then asked to create their own myth and to tell it to the class. I usually grade them from a teacher-made rubric as they present. Occasionally, I ask a Native American elder to visit and discuss storytelling from his tribe at a nearby Pueblo. We have also visited a nearby Native American Reservation, which is a great cultural experience for all. This is the positive part of living in such a culturally rich state such as New Mexico where Native American and Hispanic cultures sometimes comingle due to their shared foods, places, and histories.

It is undoubtedly important that gifted learners master bodies of knowledge as well as research skills that enable them to advance both as students and citizens. More than this mastery, however, is the ability—common to all gifted children regardless of culture or background—to navigate a complexity of ideas far beyond their age, and further, to apply these ideas to different situations, often with novel results. This is the creative impulse within the gifted child.

REACHING FOR DEPTH THROUGH FREE-VERSE POETRY

By Yolanda Toni

MAIN CONCEPT

Composing free-verse poetry provides gifted learners with the opportunity to practice their advanced literary abilities. Without the enforcement of a rhyme scheme, they are free to explore and experiment with figurative language and the intricacies of imagery and interpretation.

LEVEL

Intermediate, middle grades, and up.

APPLICATION

Literature, composition, history, art.

DESCRIPTION

One day last year after a poetry writing activity in my class, one of my fifth-grade students clamored, half talking to himself on his way out the door, "Poetry is cool—it's not just girl stuff, you know." Poetry is not just for girls, and it is not just for boys. Poetry exists for everyone—for all learners of all ages. As professionals, teachers have students write poetry to express their ideas in diverse ways and at various levels. In fact, many of these techniques to be described can be used in a variety of classrooms. However, teachers have to adjust their teaching styles to the needs of their students. As for gifted students, they exhibit a unique profundity as they develop and create their own poetry.

Even at an early age, a clear indicator of gifted talent is a child's ability to understand figurative language in reading and to use it in speech or writing. By the time gifted students reach the intermediate grades, fourth through sixth, they are already composing singular work. With this potential at hand, it is important to focus on free-verse poetry. Smutny (2003) affirms that "without the constrictions of a rhyme scheme, they are free to focus on imagery and point of view and to experiment with different writing styles" (pp. 84–85). Although children may enjoy the sound effects of rhyme or the patterns of syllabication, it binds them into thinking too much about completing a format. This knowledge serves a purpose, but it later pales to the complexity of a free-verse poem that conveys a child's deeper thoughts, feelings, and images.

At a level different from the regular classroom, curriculum for the gifted particularly centers on the actual discipline from which a subject originates. When one examines the actual discipline of English or American literature and the practice of actual authors, the majority of poets in the past century wrote free verse. They also did not use patterned or formatted worksheets to create a poem; they used catalysts. Likewise, gifted students truly blossom and develop their own unique skills as they use catalysts to write free-verse poetry. The following process expands from Smutny's (2003) description of writing free-verse poetry.

Finding Catalysts

The first step in creating such poetry activities is to find appropriate catalysts that will inspire students to write. This initiative takes some time and research. However, after one makes connections with subject matter and overall themes, it doesn't take long to realize that there is a plethora of materials to use with students. I have organized some of the various possibilities into the categories below with examples.

Artwork and Photography

In my classroom, I have a file drawer full of calendar pictures pertaining to a multitude of topics. My students cannot believe how many calendars

I own and must think the file a bottomless pit. After the first of January, one can purchase numerous calendars at reduced prices. That is exactly what I do because calendar photos come in quite handy. For instance, as students learn about Victorian Times while reading *Alice's Adventures in Wonderland* and *Through the Looking Glass* by Lewis Carroll, I connect the concept of Victorian gardens and values to the artwork of Claude Monet, a contemporary of that era.

Furthermore, while reading *The Westing Game* by Ellen Raskin, students extend the motif of patriotism to calendar photographs of everyday, yet significant moments of American life. Observing pictures of outer space helps connect students to the science fiction setting of *A Wrinkle in Time* by Madeleine L'Engle. Utilizing calendars is helpful because each one comes with twelve different pictures regarding the same topic. This aspect not only allows students some choice in their topic of writing but also enables them to connect with the setting or major concepts of the literature they are reading.

Music

Music can really enhance the cultural setting of a story. While reading Norse mythology, students reveal their thoughts as they concentrate on Richard Wagner's *Die Walküre*. The tales of *The Ramayana* include a session of listening to Asian-Indian music. Upbeat Italian folksongs really add bounce to Carlo Collodi's *Pinocchio*. In contrast, the wistful blues connect students emotionally to the melancholy setting of the Great Depression in Irene Hunt's *No Promises in the Wind*.

Video

Walt Disney's film *Fantasia*, the original and *Fantasia 2000*, represents the perfect blend of auditory and visual stimulation for writing poetry. The various clips can link to many topics and concepts such as Greek mythology, change, evolution, power, and so forth.

While viewing any film related to a novel being studied in the classroom, students can pick a character or object on which to focus their writing.

Culinary

Have students eat their topic of writing. Very few actually realize the sweet sensations of Turkish Delight from *The Lion, The Witch, and The Wardrobe* by C. S. Lewis. The yellow cornmeal of polenta in *Pinocchio*, or the fruity flavors of spring in Rudyard Kipling's "Spring Running" from *The Jungle Book* can allow students to actually taste a novel.

The Process of Writing

Once you have found the perfect catalyst for a poetry writing activity, then the real work begins. As I teach a gifted language arts/reading class for grades kindergarten through eighth, many of my students have already experienced writing free-verse poetry before fourth grade. Regardless of grade level, the description below gives a general idea of how I present all catalysts to engage students in writing.

Composing a poem can be just as time-consuming as writing a paragraph or essay. In truth, many authors have discussed how they took hours agonizing over one line in their work. Likewise, a thorough poetry writing lesson should take at least two class periods in order to really give students a taste of being a true writer.

Introduce Catalysts

When beginning the activity, I present the sample catalyst to the class. If I am using a series of calendar pictures, I choose one. I raise various questions that try to connect the catalyst to concepts or themes of the novel we are reading. Then, as a group, we create a sample poem that I write on the board. I may pick out an object or a color to get students started. They scrutinize all the details, big and small, of their catalyst while I ask questions to encourage students to articulate what they see and feel during this observation.

Inspire Discovery and Exploration

During this time, you can also incorporate additional learning objectives. For instance, you can introduce point of view by writing the poem in first, second, or third person. If you want to define a form of figurative language or sound device, such as metaphor, personification, or onomatopoeia, you can model it in the class poem. For instance, ask students if any object in the picture reminds them of person. What does that object do like a person? Then, students develop various examples of personification. In general, my fourth graders can already define and create various types of such "poetry language" (as we call it in my class). However, younger elementary students are typically using it naturally in their speech or writing, even though they may not be able to define specific terms.

After writing and discussing elements of the class poem, students select their own picture and start writing their own poems. As previously stated, by the late intermediate grades, gifted students should already have a good understanding of figurative language, sound devices, and perspective. Once they select their catalyst, I again review with the students the elements that they can use in their writing.

Please note that the order of this process may be tweaked if using video, audio, or food as catalysts. I usually present these devices first and then do a class sample. After that, we review the catalyst again and then the students write their own poem. Teachers have to find the steps best suited to their environment and schedule.

Model a Writer's Behavior

As students put pen to paper, it is important to model the behavior of a writer. Therefore, I also write poetry with the students. Students tend to model teacher behavior, and they focus best in a serene, quiet environment. Students do not converse with their neighbors or me unless they need some helpful criticism. We write in quiet serenity. As I write, I model other attributes of good writing such as mulling over my selection of words. I use a thesaurus. I have a variety of thesauri, physical and Internet ones, readily available for students to use. Students develop an appreciation for the beauty of words as they learn to distinguish how certain words flow better together than others depending upon the context of their work.

Sharing Poems

Students finish their writing as the end of class approaches. If there is time to allow students to share their drafts, do so. As students share, have the class select unique elements of their classmate's work that should be praised. At the end of class, collect students' drafts. Make corrections or suggestions as necessary. If I feel that students need to select better words or expand an idea, I usually just circle them and add some notes. I *do not* write specific words or lines to their writing. I jot down questions or comments to guide them in expanding their ideas further.

The next day, students clamor over the thesaurus to work and develop their ideas. They write or type up their final copies. As some finish before others, students usually enjoy creating illustrations on their pages to accentuate their writing. After everyone finishes, we all share (including me the teacher) our poetry. We comment upon each other's writing and describe what really stands out about each other's work. Although some students may be timid, make sure everyone shares. If extremely shy students refuse to share aloud, offer to read their work for them at first. After a while, it is amazing to see how students develop such confidence about sharing their poetry.

Overall Benefits in the End

The following samples of student work truly show how students can connect concepts from the classroom with their own creative expression. The following poems demonstrate the use of a variety of catalysts.

Artwork and Photography

Photography connects with the "America the Beautiful" theme from *The Westing Game.*

Snowboarding in Lolo, Montana

Wide open spaces around me
Sparkling sapphire snow sorbet
Turquoise and magenta colored skies stand above me.
Swoosh! I hit the shining snow below me.
The icy frost bites my nose.
And the chilly air hits my face.
As I finish my backside grab I stare at
The evergreens beside me and wonder how they survive
In this piercing weather.
The clouds look like big, fluffy cotton balls.
I continue for another backside grab.
Flying through the air I kiss the clouds and stop
At the snow's end perfectly.

Summer Brunson
Grade 5

The artwork of Claude Monet connects to a variety of topics such as Victorian literature.

Field of Tulips

Ruby, topaz, and coral petals pervade the vast field,
With emerald creeping up to any open space left
The prodigious windmill spins as the wind blows everywhere,
making the flora undulate and stretch for the warm sky
The solitary building watches over the beautiful garden, scaring off
    any thieves
The great verdure waits and waits, everyday, craving a new life
The impending sunset warns them about another chilly night
The loving tulips huddle up together,
trying to keep warm and upset about the wintry darkness
The frosty night closes in on the helpless flowers,
ending another long and tedious day

Smita Jain
Grade 5

Music

Indian music adds to the cultural setting of *The Ramayana*.

The Ramayana

The wind holds its breath scared to breathe
Not one ripple on the ocean's glassy complexion

Whoosh! Hanuman races towards the shore.
He jumps up like a stone sent to skip across a lake.
GASP! A horrible lizard streams out of the ocean chomping at him.
Hanuman swiftly dodges all the evil serpents in the sea.
If he gets hit, Rama may never see Sita again.

Kelly Kaufman
Grade 5

Blues music adds to the setting of the Great Depression in *No Promises in the Wind*.

Three O'Clock Blues

A man in plaid burgundy
Struggles to get off his lumpy
grey couch while watching TV
He holds a goldenrod bag of
potato chips in his hand, and
an ebony remote control
He lays back and gives up
Lonely and lazy he ponders about
TV and whether to get up or lay down
Unshaved and spread out, he gazes
out of the foggy window pane
and sees gallons of rain
He doesn't care
because he will stay alone on his couch

Candy Alcat
Grade 6

Video

The various musical skits from *Fantasia* can connect to a variety of themes in the classroom.

The Sorcerer's Apprentice

The surf flings the super sorcerer's apprentice into the whirlpool,
while the majestic mop
waltzes towards the source of waving water, a petit puddle.
SPLASH!
The terrible tide engulfs enormous collections of spectacular spell
*   books.*
The amazing awestruck apprentice races rapidly, running to get the
*   dancing mop*

But there are so many steps of stairs, and time itself seems to be running
   backwards
Then the miraculous magician comes and puts an end to the wet
   abyss

Alexander Mitchell
Grade 4

Culinary

Tasty treats such as Turkish Delight allow students to understand its
tempting power in *The Lion, the Witch, and the Wardrobe.*

Turkish Delight

I am in a silver round box, surrounded by green silk ribbon.
I slip like jell-o and the powder on top of me flakes like the snow in
   Narnia.
I am square, squishy, and I taste like marshmallow.
When I sit on the windowsill, all shining and hot,
I feel like gold and silver.
My friends stick side by side and they are all square and squishy.
It makes me feel alone.
I sit there in the corner,
And wait to enchant anyone who eats me.
I am a very nice Turkish Delight,
but sometimes my powdery goodness overwhelms me.
The next time someone sees me,
I will hop up into their mouth.
So they feel my crystal power.

Rachel Sison
Grade 3

The above poems demonstrate how free verse allows gifted students
the freedom to fully unleash their unique perspective about the world
around them. Furthermore, the skills that they develop in writing poetry
transfer to other writing as well. Skills of observation help students to realize the small yet central details that are necessary for good descriptive
writing. As students write essays or journal entries or short stories or even
extended responses to literature questions, I remind them to write with
"poetry language." These unique expressions and descriptions definitely
apply to a person's everyday writing. Even if students want to dabble with
rhyme again or read famous patterned poems, their background with free
verse will help them focus on depth of expression and not just a rhyme
scheme. The autonomy of the free-verse poem can liberate students from
their inhibitions and guide them into the mindset of true authors.

REFERENCES

Disney, W. (Producer). (1940). *Fantasia.* Burbank, CA: Walt Disney.
Ernst, D. W. (Producer). (1999). *Fantasia 2000.* Burbank, CA: Walt Disney.
Gray, J. E. B. (1961). *Tales from India.* Oxford: Oxford University Press.
Hunt, I. (1970). *No promises in the wind.* New York: Berkley Books.
L'Engle, M. (1962). *A wrinkle in time.* New York: Farrar, Straus and Giroux.
Lewis, C. S. (1950). *The lion, the witch, and the wardrobe.* New York: Harper Trophy.
Raskin, E. (1978). *The westing game.* New York: Penguin Group.
Smutny, J. F. (2003). *Gifted education: Promising practices for the 21st century.* Bloomington, IN: Phi Delta Kappa Educational Foundation.

INTERPRETING LITERATURE: READER'S THEATER FOR GIFTED LEARNERS

By Joan Franklin Smutny

MAIN CONCEPT

Reader's theater can significantly enhance students' understanding of literary texts and stimulate inquiry and analysis. This would include a greater mastery of the elements of story—what they are and how they work together to create a compelling narrative. By embodying stories through reader's theater, the children engage in higher-level thinking and become interpreters of the stories that, previously, they may only have read in a passive mode.

LEVEL

This strategy can work with any level—primary grades through high school.

APPLICATION

Language arts, social studies. A reader's theater experience can expand a gifted child's reading and comprehension of texts and is an effective catalyst for writing assignments. It can also work effectively in a research project where children need to probe for more information and consider new questions.

DESCRIPTION

Reader's theater is an effective way to develop a gifted child's understanding of the elements of story—character development, plot, and fictional environments. By embodying segments of a full-length book or shorter story, children acquire insights about the creative process within literature that they might not gain otherwise. For highly creative children, this process is also an excellent foundation for the students' own story inventions—developing full-bodied characters and believable plots, conflicts, and resolutions.

Begin Small

It is always wise to begin small when first orchestrating this process. Either start with a shorter, manageable story or, if you wish to be more ambitious, break a larger book into sections, divide the class into groups, and have each group tackle a section.

Explore the Story

Before a class can embark on this journey, students have to become familiar with the book or story through discussion and analysis. To foster discussion, I always begin with questions that focus on the main elements of the story:

- What is the story about?
- Who are the main characters?
- Where does it take place and when?
- What are the problems that the main characters face?
- How do they go about solving these problems?
- What changes happen in this story?
- What are some of the most exciting parts? Why do you think they're so important to the story?

If you're working with groups, choose a child in each group to record answers to these questions. Then, when you discuss it as a whole class, you can put their responses on the board as a guide for the work that follows.

Through these questions and others you may think of, you're encouraging your students to think analytically about the story and thereby heighten their own awareness of the key elements that hold the story together. This in turn will help them choose passages to dramatize.

Selecting Important Scenes

Choosing the most critical passages can become, especially for gifted students, a wonderful exercise in higher-order thinking. As the children work through the book or story, keep them focused on the important moments in the development of the plot. They could begin by listing the memorable scenes—those that most interested them as readers or listeners. After the group has compiled the list, have them put it in chronological order and review it. Tell students to look at each scene and ask themselves the following:

- Is this an exciting scene? Why?
- Is this scene necessary to understand the plot? Why? Why not?
- How important is it?

- How could we act it out? If we don't do that, is there a way we can retell the scene using mime and narration?
- What will we gain by keeping this scene?
- What will we lose if we don't use it?

Circulate among the different groups and mediate disagreements where they arise. Put a limit on the number of scenes allowed for each group. Otherwise, the process will quickly become complicated and unmanageable.

Each group can choose one child to be the narrator, and then the others can choose the characters they would most like to dramatize, read, or mime. The unique circumstances of your classroom (time constraints, number of children, students' needs and interests) will require you to be flexible with children's roles. If more than one child wants to play a particular part, you can either audition students for the role or have them take turns. If you have more students than roles, consider distributing the role of narrator to several good readers. Another possibility is to expand the enactments by having children briefly mime parts of the plot that will not be dramatized with narrators summarizing what happens in the intervals between dramatized selections. This solves two problems at once: what to do with children who don't yet have parts and how to tell the audience what has occurred between scenes. Some children may also wish to provide the sound effects or work on props.

Narrative and Dialogue

Once you and the students choose the sections, selecting narrative and dialogue becomes easier and creates a structure for the children to practice their scenes. Assure them that no one has to memorize lines. Explain that they will do one of two things:

- Plan a dramatization in which actors read lines or use their own words to reenact the scenes.
- Write narration for scenes that the actors will dramatize as the narrator reads them.

Becoming the Story

Reader's theater production encourages students to take full ownership of a story. A kinesthetic learning process is at work here. To embody the story vividly, students have to become thoroughly familiar with the characters whose lines they deliver. Ask questions about the following:

- Specific characteristics ("Where do you sleep? What do you eat? How do you move around?").
- The emotions that drive the character ("What are you worried about? What do you want more than anything? Why do you want that? If you could be whatever you wanted, what would you be?").

- The character's history ("How long have you been a spider? What do you do every day? What do you enjoy about being a spider?").
- How the character feels about the other characters and what they do ("What do you think about this new pig who has moved in?").

As they probe the characters, children begin to make the story *their* story. By internalizing the story in this way, they gain an inside knowledge. Their discovery becomes an ongoing, dynamic process.

Encourage children to keep their staging clear and to use simple props, costumes, and sound effects. Circulate among the different groups as they work and offer suggestions on staging and the selection of lines as well as on summaries that operate as transitions from scene to scene or chapter to chapter.

Place the narrator to the side of the dramatic action. Also, groups who plan to use any props, costumes, or sound effects should assign someone to keep a list of any items required for the production. Remind the class that the main purpose of props, costumes, and sound is to give the actors and audience a feel for the place and action.

When the class performs, be as informal and relaxed as possible and encourage the children to do the same. This process is not intended to lead to a flawless theater event but to expand students' experience and understanding of the great art of story-making.

Be positive as the students perform. If a child makes a mistake, minimize it and offer encouragement. Before the performance begins, remind children that the dramatic process is a way to make stories come alive. After the performance(s), lead a discussion about how performing the story changed what they felt and thought about it. What is the difference between reading about a character and being that character? How did this change the story for them?

Final Thoughts

The reader's theater experience brings untold benefits to gifted students. They create more developed characters as well as plots that evolve organically from those characters. With performance experience, the children become more interested in issues of character motivation and how this relates to conflict and suspense in a good story. On a personal level, you can also assign roles that can be empowering for a child. I have seen timid, self-doubting children rise and become powerful characters when they have the medium of a fiction character to do this. One of the great gifts of drama is that it enables even very young children to test out and explore different facets of their own being in a way that is safe. A child can be a queen for a day, a scoundrel, a madman, an elephant, or even the wind from the wolf that rattles the homes of the three little pigs.

4

Social Studies Strategies

For many gifted learners, social studies offer vast and enticing explorations to times and places only imagined. Even during their earliest years, they're on a search for distant shores and epochs. We will find them, as one author found a three-year-old once, in Dave's Down-to-Earth Rock Shop calmly explaining to his father what kind of habitat pterodactyls need. Or we might be teaching a class on an event in the Lewis and Clark expeditions, only to be startled by a student who wants to know if the Native Americans spoke an Indo-European language and, if not, to what family of languages do they belong? Or a sixth grader, pondering the drama of a close presidential race, may question the fairness of the winner-takes-all practice and ask if the United States could ever implement instant run-off voting instead?

Equipped with advanced ability in reading and writing and a curiosity about the world around them, gifted students quickly become adept at conducting their own inquiries and constructing vivid representations of what they know. We met a gifted child who designed what he called a "botanical trail map" of his favorite forest preserve; it provided information on the unique plants and trees that hikers could see on the different trails. Another child one author knows, who spent a year with her father in the Middle East, became fascinated by the relationship of architecture to culture and history and announced one day, at the age of 12, that she wanted to become a specialist in "indigenous architecture." In one creative writing class, another child asked if I thought there would ever be a civil rights movement for animals.

How do we tap this natural reservoir of creativity in gifted learners? There are as many ways to ignite creative thinking in the social studies curriculum as a teacher can imagine and design. For teacher Jennifer Golwitzer, creative exploration does not have to be complex. A few well-orchestrated activities inserted into the day at the right time can go far in extending a gifted child's thinking and imagination. Here are some ideas Jennifer uses for social studies:

Collages

Students love to use old magazines to create art. Have them find pictures to illustrate topics being discussed in class and then create either individual, small-group, or whole-class collages. Draw a map of your state, the United States, or the world and then have the students cut out pictures depicting things/phenomena/activities commonly seen in those places.

Posters

Students can design posters for many topics. When studying the coal mines versus the textile mills, for example, students can design a poster to advertise working in the textile mills to the coal miners, or they could simply draw a picture of how the labor unions came to be and how they helped the people working in the mines.

Long-Term Projects

When studying Wisconsin's history, my students choose a historical figure, event, or city to research and present in our "Wisconsin Trade Show." At the end of the research project, the students have created a research paper, PowerPoint presentation, large tri-fold poster display, and an oral presentation that they share with parents, teachers, fellow students in Grades kindergarten through 8, and sometimes even news reporters who visit throughout the day.

Dressed From the Past

Children enjoy dressing up in the clothes of the times they are studying—a process that has an almost magical effect. Allow students to explore clothing designs, hair styles, and other personal accessories that give them a sensory experience of history.

Role-Plays

When studying certain events in history, have students research and then assume the identity of important characters in the story. For instance, when studying George Washington Carver's *invention* of crop rotation, students reenact the events leading up to Mr. Carver's discovery. They also have to show how Carver taught other people about crop rotation.

Whole-School Studies

My school chooses a topic every two years to study. The entire school focuses on that topic for two weeks. Everyone also dresses up, conducts their own research in a wide range of sources and media, has speakers/presenters come in, attends events related to the topic, prepares and samples foods from the time period (where appropriate), and engages in cultural and arts experiences in response to new insights gained.

Jose Ortega y Gasset once said that we must not let ourselves lose touch with history if we expect to build upon it, but "must feel it under our feet because we raised ourselves upon it."

Creative strategies enable us as teachers to help gifted students not just read about history, but "feel it under [their] feet"—enter the worlds studied and do the work of historians and geographers. Creativity removes them from being spectators to becoming participants in the making of histories. If we think about the process, we can see that historians who succeed in bringing another time and place alive for readers actively draw upon their creative, imaginative side. They

- come to the material brimming over with questions;
- delve imaginatively and intuitively into primary sources (letters, diaries, notes, sketches, photos, drawings, journals);
- ponder life in the time and place of their research (clothing, technologies, geography, climate, architectures, customs, beliefs);
- explore different points of view/interpretations/common beliefs and concepts;
- study interpretations of events/issues/ideas as found in the arts—theater, film, painting;
- pose questions of the sources; and
- synthesize ideas from different sources.

When we as teachers have a clear grasp of the core learning at the heart of our social studies unit, we can more easily integrate creative processes to challenge gifted students. For example, does your unit examine cause-and-effect relationships (in history, environmental conditions, politics, economics)? Are you attempting to strengthen and extend research abilities (gathering information, analyzing and evaluating evidence, etc.)? Do you want your gifted learners to explore the concept of point of view in histories, both written and oral? Do you want your students to make connections between geographic features and cultures, historical events, lifestyles, customs, and so forth? When we can clarify what understandings and skills we most want our students (including our gifted students) to master, we can more easily integrate creative activities that will significantly extend this mastery.

Topics and Authors	Creative Strategies	Grade Level	Standards (examples)
Creative Mapping: Autobiography Maps *Jerry Flack* P. 83	Self-exploration Autobiography Visual exploration Expression in visual art Brainstorming Flexible, divergent thinking	Elementary level, adjustable to higher grades	The student understands how to use mental maps to organize information about people, places, and environments in a spatial context.
Historic Games of Strategy and Geography *Christopher M. Freeman* P. 87	Analytical thinking Imagining Inductive and deductive reasoning Improvisation	These games are for elementary students, but historic games apply to intermediate and upper grades as well.	The student engages in historical analysis and interpretation (this would include formulating questions to focus their inquiry and analysis, explaining causes in analyzing historical actions, challenging arguments of historical inevitability, and hypothesizing the influence of the past).
Nurturing In-Depth Thinking *Linda Phemister* P. 92	Higher-order thinking Revised Bloom's Taxonomy Questioning to probe and discover Creative composition	Basis principles apply to all grades	The student comprehends a variety of historical sources. The student engages in historical analysis and interpretation.
Ideas for Teaching American History Units *Nancy Messman* P. 96	Environmental design Role-playing Crafts as part of dramatic reenactments Journal writing responses Inquiry, research	Intermediate grades, but adjustable to other grade levels	The student understands how communities in North America varied long ago. This includes drawing upon written and visual sources and describes the historical development and daily life of a colonial community, such as Plymouth, in order to create a historical narrative, mural, or dramatization of daily life in that place long ago.
Student Historians *Carol V. Horn* P. 100	Open inquiry Focusing on "big ideas" Interviewing Visiting key sites Exploration of perspective and bias Discovery process	Intermediate level, but can be adapted to other grades	The student conducts historical research. This includes formulating historical questions, obtaining and interrogating historical data from a variety of sources, and supporting interpretations with historical evidence.

Topics and Authors	Creative Strategies	Grade Level	Standards (examples)
Combined Disciplinary and Interdisciplinary Collaboration Between General Music and Social Studies Classes *Lois Veenhoven Guderian* P. 104	Interdisciplinary exploration Open questioning Group learning Analysis of musical elements and connections to social/historical realities Creative learning stations Arts responses to a music–social studies collaboration	Intermediate grades, but adjustable to higher and lower grades	From National Standards for Music: Singing, alone and with others, a varied repertoire of music. This includes singing from memory a varied repertoire of songs representing genres and styles from diverse cultures. Understanding music in relation to history and culture. This includes identifying by genre or style aural examples of music from various historical periods and cultures.
Drama in the Social Studies Classroom *Gina Lewis* P. 108	Dramatic reenactment Creative movement Questioning Improvisation Imaginative identification with characters	The process is applicable to any grade.	National Standards for Arts Education Researching by using cultural and historical information to support improvised and scripted scenes. Achievement standard: Students apply research from printed and nonprint sources to script-writing, acting, design, and directing choices.
Creating Plays in Social Studies *Gay Doyle* P. 113	Inquiry and essential questioning Characterization Creative writing for Reader's Theater Imaginative thinking	Intermediate grades, but adjustable for higher grades.	See above.
Stories of Time Past *Joan Franklin Smutny* P. 116	Open questioning Imaginative responses to catalysts "Stepping into" the past Creative writing Oral interpretation Flexible thinking	Primary to inter-mediate and middle grades	The student engages in historical analysis and interpretation. This includes analyzing historical fiction; distinguishing fact and fiction; comparing different stories about a historical figure, era or event; analyzing illustrations in historical stories; and considering multiple perspectives.

(Continued)

(Continued)

Topics and Authors	Creative Strategies	Grade Level	Standards (examples)
Mighty Mythology *Carol Sandberg Howe* P. 119	Exploration Imagining Theater processes Visual arts activities creative problem-solving Games	Intermediate and middle grades	The student comprehends a variety of historical sources. This includes reading historical narratives imaginatively, appreciating historical perspectives, drawing upon visual data presented in photographs, paintings, etc.
Following the Passion of a Gifted Underachiever *Drew Shilhanek* P. 127	Special interests Small group work Resident expert Role-playing Deliberating in simulated conference Creative problem solving	Intermediate grades, but ideas adaptable to other levels	The student thinks chronologically. This includes identifying a temporal structure of a historical narrative and explaining change and continuity over time. The student engages in historical issues analysis and decision making, which includes proposing alternative ways of solving the problem or dilemma and formulating a position or course of action on an issue.
Primary Source Learning: Thinking Through the Puzzles Life Created *Rhonda Clevenson* P. 130	Questioning, reflecting Making connections and discoveries Exploring point of view Interpreting	Intermediate level and up	The student conducts historical research. This includes formulating historical questions, obtaining and interrogating historical data from a variety of sources, and supporting interpretations with historical evidence.
Westward Expansion! *Carol Sandberg Howe* P. 142	Construction of the Conestoga wagon "Stepping into" the past Open questioning Writing journal entries Exploring sources (print, video, etc.) Visual art interpretations Theatrical responses Games	Middle grades, but adjustable to other levels	The student understands the physical and human characteristics of places. The student understands how culture and experience influence peoples' perceptions of places and regions. The student understands the processes, patterns, and functions of human settlement The student understands how the forces of cooperation and conflict among people influence the division and control of Earth's surface.

CREATIVE MAPPING: AUTOBIOGRAPHY MAPS

By Jerry Flack

MAIN CONCEPT

This process immerses young gifted students into the art and science of cartography, while at the same time inviting a process of self-exploration and expression. A special bonus of creative mapping is that classroom teachers, homeschooling parents, and other mentors will experience positive "Aha!" experiences as they devise imaginative ways to introduce mapping, in general, and Autobiography Maps in particular, to their students.

LEVEL

The creative mapping activities discussed in this article may be utilized with students of any age from very young gifted students, who are developing greater maturity and sophistication in their fine motor skills, consciousness of geography, and sense of place and their personal identity, to older students who are more developed. The same activities may be profitably utilized with middle and secondary students during initial class meetings or even among participants in graduate courses in creativity or the education of gifted students.

APPLICATION

Versatility is one of the many values of creative mapping projects. Further, the primary creative mapping activity, Autobiography Maps, described herein may serve either as a onetime creative experience or as the catalyst for entire social studies, literature, and autobiography units that involve maps, globes, and cartography.

DESCRIPTION

Resourceful teachers will have no trouble finding myriad maps and map books to suit all age levels. The American Automobile Association (AAA) is a gold mine for teachers who want to share local, state, national, and even world maps with students. Such materials are generally given freely to members. Countless issues of the *National Geographic* magazine likewise feature maps even beyond earth to outer space. School and community libraries have vertical files plentiful with such resources.

The map-making resources at the end of this section cite several outstanding map books for students of all ages. The most enchanting and child-centered introduction to creating maps is Sara Fanelli's classic *My Map Book*. Youthful, childlike art is used to fashion maps of the central character's face, bedroom, family, typical day, pet dog, tummy, neighborhood, and even her heart. Best of all, the book's dust jacket unfolds to create a blank, poster-size map that young readers can use to fashion an outsized and glorious map of their own lives and favorite things. Fanelli's brilliantly colorful maps serve as terrific models of the kinds of autobiography maps primary school children can easily replicate.

Attention-grabbing facts may additionally capture the interest of early middle-grade gifted learners. For example, archaeologists note that ancient clay maps are older than the first-known examples of writing. It seems that even seven thousand years ago, people in such places as Mesopotamia were more interested in finding their way than recording information.

An additional manner in which teachers can introduce maps and concurrently "prime the pump" for autobiography maps is by giving each student a copy of the U.S. map (Figure 4.1.) either with or without state names and capitals, depending on the maturity and knowledge of students. Provide many colorful instruments such as felt-tip markers, crayons, and colored pencils. Ask students to use these tools to highlight *five* different geographical locations that have positive personal associations. Urge students to use words, icons, and symbols to note such places as their birth, their favorite vacation (e.g., Disney World), the home state(s) of beloved grandparents, or perhaps locations related to particular passions

Figure 4.1   United States Map

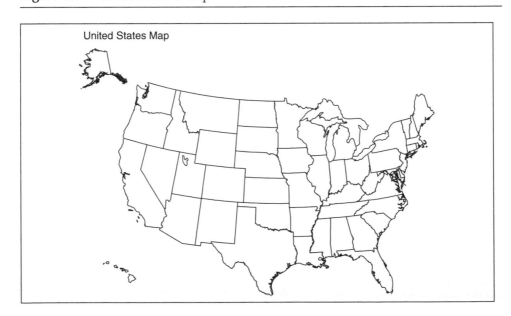

(e.g., Cooperstown, New York, for baseball fans). Students should also note locations that are related to future dreams and aspirations. For example, a third-grade student who hopes to become an astronaut might draw a picture of a space vehicle near the Kennedy Space Center in Florida.

After students have had adequate time to note five special and notable personal map locations, invite them to share their *personalized* United States maps with a partner or within small groups. Since students have created original art work, they should affix their unique artistic signatures to their creations. When this mapping activity is completed early in the school year, an added benefit to the positive student interaction and sharing is that the signed maps may be used to brighten classroom walls and bulletin board displays.

Numerous other warm-up mapping activities can be utilized as motivators for students. Figure 4.2 (p. 86) lists terms familiar to map makers. The list may be shortened or expanded to fit the age or knowledge levels of students. Teachers may want to review terms with students, inviting them to add new mapping vocabulary to the existing list as they go along. Such a list greatly aids younger students in expanding their social studies vocabulary, but most important, the list provides students with language to enrich the creation of their own autobiography maps. They can focus on the artistic, inventive, and personal features of their maps without having to interrupt the flow of creativity to search for map terminology.

One more preliminary step may be a class discussion about the varied information found on maps such as direction indicators. Even very elementary introductions to cartography such as Tish Rabe's (2002) *There's a Map on My Lap!* introduce primary-grade readers to a variety of different kinds of maps, longitude and latitude, scale, map legends, and the compass rose (plus a delightful mnemonic for remembering its purpose: "Never Eat Soggy Wheat" equals the directions north, east, south, and west). A glossary further introduces globes, grids, the equator, and more in simple terms.

Once students have a reasonable grounding in the craft of generating maps, individual creativity takes over in the creation of autobiography maps.

Furnish students with art supplies that include poster paper and colorful marking tools. Students then create autobiography maps. What words, symbols, and pictures highlight the major highways and thoroughfares of students' lives, past, present, and future? Point out to these new kindergarten- through sixth-grade mapmakers that they may use natural phenomena such as mountains, rivers, and clouds or human structures such as roadways, sports facilities, neighborhoods, and even malls.

One clarion call or urgent appeal. It is essential that students' autobiography maps should be optimistic and accentuate the positive. Indeed, a further premapping activity might well be a brainstorming exercise in which students list their most positive traits and assets. Pessimism and self-doubt are creativity "killers." A brainstormed list of highly personal

Figure 4.2   Map Terminology

Map Terms		
Arroyo	Isthmus	River
Bay	Lake	Road
Butte	Mesa	Route
Canyon	Mountain Pass	Savanna
Cataract	Mountain	Sound
City	Mouth	State
Cliff	Oasis	Straight
County	Ocean	Stream
Creek	Pass	Street
Delta	Peak	Swamp
Glacier	Plain	Town
Gulf	Plains	Tributary
Harbor	Plateau	Valley
Highway	Rapids	Village
Hill	Ridge	Volcano
Island		

virtues, dreams, and aspirations will serve students well as they transcribe a list of positive, personal attributes into traditional map-related words, images, and symbols.

Figure 4.3 represents the author's autobiography map. Note that even though the map does reveal a "Procrastination Swamp," this particular personal *location* is intended as self-deprecating humor rather than self-criticism.

The making and sharing of Autobiography maps is a great way to initiate student introspection and prompt student creativity, plus the sharing of these maps will provoke stimulating discussions about similarities and differences in interests, personal experiences, life goals, and future daydreams.

MAP-MAKING RESOURCES

Chancellor, D. (2005). *The Kingfisher first picture atlas* (A. Lewis, Illus.). Boston: Kingfisher.

Fanelli, S. (1995). *My map book.* New York: HarperCollins.

Man, J. (2007). *New traveler's atlas: A global guide to the places you must see in your lifetime.* New York: Barron's Educational Series.

National Geographic Society. (2005). *National Geographic student atlas of the world.* Washington, DC: National Geographic Society.

Rabe, T. (2002). *There's a map on my lap!* (A. Ruiz, Illus.). New York: Random House.

Figure 4.3   Author's Self-Awareness Map

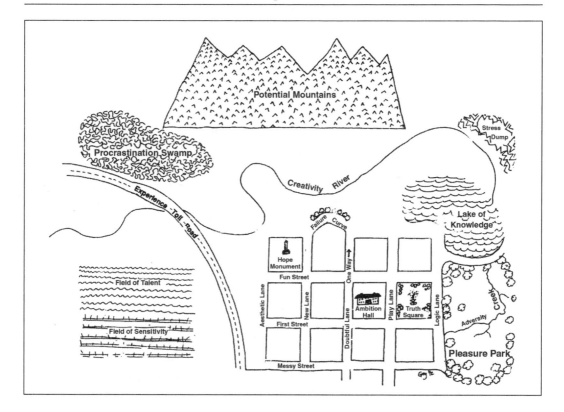

HISTORIC GAMES OF STRATEGY AND GEOGRAPHY

By Christopher M. Freeman

MAIN CONCEPT

Through the use of games, gifted children play roles and become immersed in the decision-making process that underlies history. The process naturally leads to more in-depth understanding of the conditions under which historic decisions were made and allows students to think through the issues themselves as they attempt to weigh consequences and make their own choices.

LEVEL

These games apply primarily to elementary grades, though there are historic games for the higher grades.

APPLICATION

History, geography, economics, politics.

DESCRIPTION

History is the study of choices. Every choice has a consequence, for better or worse. In a democratic society, it is imperative that all citizens make informed decisions, that they not let themselves get carried along with the crowd, and that they consider carefully the consequences of each potential course of action. Students should learn that their own choices determine their own lives, and they influence the progress of mankind.

Historic games involve students in making the decisions that changed history. Through playing these games, students learn why things happened the way they did; they can make mistakes and learn lessons from them, and they become better equipped to make real decisions in the present world.

Geography is the study of the earth's surface and how its features influence human civilization. Where are the resources located? What are the natural trade routes? Which features provide natural defenses from attack? Historic games teach students the strategic importance of geographic features in commerce and in maintaining peace.

I play these games with my own children at home (Grades 3–9). I have organized game classes for the Center for Gifted's Project program (Grades 6–10) and Worlds of Wisdom and Wonder programs (Grades 4–6). And I have organized game activity classes with my sixth graders at the University of Chicago Laboratory Schools. The students have enjoyed playing these games, and they have learned a great deal.

Here are the games I most recommend for elementary school students.

Empire Builder (Mayfair Games, 19th Century, North America)

Players represent railroad companies building networks from New England to California, from Canada to Mexico. The game board is a map of North America, showing the locations of important resources such as copper, timber, oil, corn, and cotton, important cities, and mountains, rivers, and lakes. Players are given possible contracts that promise payment for delivery of certain resources to particular cities that demand them. Students build rail lines by connecting dots on a grid using crayon. It costs twice as much to build across a mountain area, and it costs extra to build a bridge across a river. The winner builds the most economically efficient rail system. I've seen students re-create the Santa Fe, Union Pacific, and Burlington Northern rail lines. Students learn to build trunk lines in central locations and branch lines to remote areas. Kansas City often becomes a major rail hub. Students naturally learn the geography of America and how it influences the economic development of their home state or country.

Variations include *Eurorails,* which is set in Europe and adds the features of ferry transportation and alpine mountains; *Australia Rails,* which is set in Australia and adds the feature of building across desert; *British Rails, Russian Rails, India Rails,* and *Japan Rails.* All these games teach geography in the context of commerce, and all are great fun to play.

Since the rail lines are drawn with crayon, it is easy to put the game away at the end of class and to set it up again the next session. The teacher should supply several small, resealable bags in which to store each player's other equipment. I have found that students work well playing in pairs, with three or four pairs per game board. Sessions can be every day or once a week. A 45-minute class period is a satisfying length for a session. Each game lasts about four or five hours.

History of the World (Avalon Hill, 2100 BC–AD 1920, World)

This game has been out of print, but it is available on the Internet, and it will likely soon be back into production. It is one of the best games ever made.

Forty-nine major empires appear in historical succession in various places around the world. Play occurs in seven epochs of seven empires each. In each epoch, each player is given the location and strength of a new empire, and the player decides how best to expand. As the game progresses, history is reenacted. The Egyptians expand into the Middle East and North Africa; the Persians dominate the Middle East; the Romans take all the coasts of the Mediterranean Sea; the Byzantines counterattack against the Goths; the Mongols ride across Asia into China, India, the Middle East, and Eastern Europe; the Ottoman Turks attack Vienna, and the British use their command of the sea to establish colonies all over the world.

At the beginning of each epoch, the empires are distributed in such a way that leading players tend to receive weaker empires and losing players tend to receive stronger empires, so players' commitment to the game remains high throughout.

When it is time to put the game away at the end of class, you will need to have a list of all 103 lands in the game and to identify what pieces are located where. (I'd be happy to e-mail you my list.) It's nicer, but not necessary, to find a safe place to leave the game board intact between sessions. Twelve students may play in pairs. A full game lasts from six to eight hours.

Age of Empires III (Tropical Games, 16th–18th Century, North & South America)

Players represent European Powers colonizing the New World. Players must choose how to allocate their scarce resources. They may organize voyages of discovery, send colonists overseas, establish trade routes, train missionaries to convert the natives, train professional sea captains to explore more effectively, train merchants to bring in more profit, or train soldiers to defend their empire. As players earn money, they may invest their capital to build monasteries, trading posts, schools, or factories. They may pass laws that encourage emigration, raise tax revenue, or forge alliances with the natives. They even may declare war and try to take control of each other's colonies. Each player makes choices how best to develop and defend his or her own colonies. There are many strategies that lead to success.

Each game board accommodates up to five pairs of students. It is relatively easy to record the position before putting the game away at the end of class. Gallon-size resealable bags can be used to store each team's equipment. This game is probably best played in a double-length class period to minimize setup time. Each game will take about four or five hours.

Axis and Allies (Hasbro, 1942–1945, World War II)

Players represent the United Kingdom, USSR, United States, Germany, and Japan. Players begin with a specified quantity of infantry, tanks, fighters, bombers, submarines, transports, battleships, and aircraft carriers. Each fighting unit has a specified movement capability, cost, and fighting strength (offensive or defensive). Players make decisions what equipment to build and where to attack. The Axis begins with a large amount of equipment but limited production capacity. The United States begins with a large production capacity but limited equipment. To be successful, the Allies must cooperate to preserve Leningrad, Moscow, India, China, and Egypt. The Axis must play quickly and aggressively to take some of these areas with the resources they contain before America can build up its military.

Students learn how the war was fought; they learn why the Americans and British sent so many supplies to Russia, while Russia sent supplies to help defend China; they see why the Allies occupied North Africa and attacked Italy from the south; they learn by experience how control of the sea and air determined victory in the Pacific.

This game requires quite a bit of time at the end of a session to record the position and put it away. It is better to find a safe place to leave the game board intact between sessions. Double-period sessions are needed to maintain continuity. Five pairs of students may play, and trios are possible. The game takes from six to eight hours.

Variations include *Axis and Allies Pacific* and *Axis and Allies Europe*, which focus on one theater of the war or the other.

Kingmaker (Avalon Hill, 15th Century, Britain)

This game is long out of print, but it is still available on the Internet.

Players represent factions of British nobility supporting pretenders to the throne during the Wars of the Roses. The pretenders themselves are just pawns of the nobles, who control their own troops and make all the plans. The game well represents the spirit of the times. And the game is lighthearted because random events ensure that "The best-laid plans o' mice an' men / Gang aft a'gley."

It would be too hard to record a position and put away this game; it needs a separate space where it can be left intact between sessions. The game takes about two to three hours.

Diplomacy (Hasbro, 20th Century, Europe)

Players represent the seven great Powers of Europe prior to and during World War I. Players negotiate alliances and coordinate attacks to eliminate other players until one nation rules more than half the supply centers on the board. Play is highly competitive. There is no element of luck; the players' own decisions determine the outcome.

This game requires an experienced game master because the rules for resolving battle orders are quite complicated and exacting. Each turn allocates 15 minutes for diplomacy, five minutes to write orders, and whatever time is necessary to resolve orders. Therefore, the game fits well into a short class period, during which either one or two turns may be completed. The game includes maps of the game board that are used during diplomatic negotiations and can also be used to record the position. Be aware that, when a nation is eliminated, those players are no longer involved in the game.

Age of Imperialism (Eagle Games, 19th Century, Eastern Hemisphere)

Players represent European Powers forming or expanding colonial empires in Africa, India, Australia, and the Far East. They send out explorers to find resources and befriend the natives; they send out armies to conquer unfriendly natives; they develop resources; they build cities, schools, forts, and railroads; they train engineers to help develop new colonies; they negotiate treaties to cooperate with neighboring powers or the declare war to settle their differences.

The playing board is very large, as are the playing pieces. It's not too hard to record a position after a session. There is a computer DVD version of the game that would be easy to administer if you have the computers available. Otherwise, double-length periods would be best for this game. A full game takes three or four hours.

NURTURING IN-DEPTH THINKING

By Linda Phemister

MAIN CONCEPT

Creating a "thinking classroom" opens up the social studies curriculum for gifted students. In helping them become in-depth, creative thinkers, the teacher's main instructional task is to design activities and environments that stimulate higher-order thought processes. Bloom's revised taxonomy, which includes creativity, helps to guide this process—focusing more on the use of information than on acquiring basic facts and skills.

LEVEL

All ages.

APPLICATION

Higher-order and creative thinking applies to any subject area.

DESCRIPTION

Many of the characteristics and behaviors that are typically associated with gifted learners can be observed in a number of gifted children at an early age. When that is the case, appropriate placement and educational planning is critical. These children have special learning needs including faster pace, greater depth, and different interests than their chronological peers. Consequently, they need exposure to a curriculum that focuses on exploration and manipulation and allows for self-direction and exposure to abstract concepts. According to the National Association for Gifted Children (2000), differentiation of curriculum and instruction for gifted learners should include diverse learning experiences and curricular options (e.g., special seminars, resource rooms, mentorships, independent study, research projects). (Free brochure on gifted program standards available at www.nagc.org/index.aspx?id=546.)

Today's typical classroom may be made up of students from all economic backgrounds and learning-readiness levels. Modifying instruction to match the wide scope of student needs can be a daunting task for most teachers. It requires flexibility of activities and resources.

One way to engage young students in in-depth study is to involve them in higher-order thinking processes. Higher-order thinking means that the students must transform information and ideas. Working with, transforming, or manipulating information and ideas allows students to solve problems, gain greater depth of understanding, and realize new meaning. When students are engaged in the learning process, authentic achievement takes place.

A number of classification systems have been developed to analyze levels of thinking and to direct teacher questions. By far, the most commonly used is the *Taxonomy of Educational Objectives* presented by Benjamin Bloom and his colleagues in 1956. Bloom's taxonomy was a means of expressing qualitatively different kinds of thinking and describes six levels of thought process. Each level includes and builds upon the thinking from the previous level. Bloom's six categories of thinking are as follows:

1. Knowledge/recall

2. Comprehension

3. Application

4. Analysis

5. Synthesis

6. Evaluation

The Revised Bloom's Taxonomy

During the late 1990s, a former student of Benjamin Bloom, Lorin Anderson, assembled a team of cognitive psychologists and curriculum and instructional specialists in order to revisit the taxonomy. Their goal was to examine the relevance of the taxonomy to twenty-first-century teachers and students. Their analysis led to a number of small but significant changes to the original taxonomy. In 2001, the revised taxonomy was published.

The new terms, as defined by Anderson and Krathwohl (2001), are as follows:

- **Remembering:** Retrieving, recognizing, and recalling relevant knowledge from long-term memory
- **Understanding:** Constructing meaning from oral, written, and graphic messages through interpreting, exemplifying, classifying, summarizing, inferring, comparing, and explaining
- **Applying:** Carrying out or using a procedure through executing or implementing
- **Analyzing:** Breaking material into constituent parts, determining how the parts relate to one another and to an overall structure or purpose through differentiating, organizing, and attributing
- **Evaluating:** Making judgments based on criteria and standards through checking and critiquing
- **Creating:** Putting elements together to form a coherent or functional whole; reorganizing elements into a new pattern or structure through generalizing, planning, or producing

The most obvious change in the revised Bloom's is that the names of six major categories were changed from *noun* to *verb* forms. The taxonomy reflects different forms of *thinking* and since thinking is an *active* process, verbs are better descriptors. The major categories were placed in the new order in terms of complexity. The revised taxonomy is intended as a "more authentic tool for curriculum planning, instructional delivery, and assessment" (oz-TeacherNet, quoted in Forehand, 2005).

Creating Thinking Classrooms

The spotlight of a thinking classroom is the Thinking Station. At this station, students engage in creative, in-depth questioning and activity. The content of the questions and activities relates to the subject matter/curriculum introduced by the teacher. The teacher needs to determine how each student will use the Thinking Station. There are different approaches:

- All students work through all levels of Bloom's revised taxonomy at the Thinking Center.
- All students work through the remembering and understanding stages and then select *at least* one question/activity from each other level.
- All children work through remembering and understanding and then select questions/activities from any other level.
  - Teacher may set the number of questions/activities from other levels.
  - Students may choose the number of questions/activities from other levels.
- Some questions/activities are tagged "necessary to complete" while others are "optional to complete."
- All children select questions/activities from any level.
  - Teacher may set minimum number to be addressed.
- Some children work through remembering and understanding and then design their own activities at the higher levels.

The result of the student work at the Thinking Station is a product the students create as they work their way through the assigned questions or activities. For example, during a study of the first Thanksgiving, a teacher may copy for each child the outline of a cornucopia on a Xerox size (or larger) paper.

Materials Needed

- Glue
- Plain paper
- Colored paper (red, green, white, brown, yellow)

- Cutouts of foods for the cornucopia (pumpkins, apples, corn, pota-toes, beans, oranges, etc.) each in a different color with enough for students to have at least four each
- Crayons/markers (if desired)

Steps in the Activity

- Create multiple (2–5) questions for each level of Bloom's revised tax-onomy and write the questions on the food cutouts.
- Make multiple Xerox copies of the food pieces containing the questions.
- Cut out the pieces (students may also cutout the pieces).
- Sort the questions into categories of Bloom's revised taxonomy. For example,
  - o Pumpkin = Remembering/Understanding
  - o Corn = Applying
  - o Beans = Analyzing
  - o Apples = Evaluating/Creating
       (May use up to six foods representing six levels of the taxonomy)
- Students must answer at least one question or complete the activ-ity (teacher determines the number) from each category to fill their cornucopia.
- As students correctly answer the questions on a separate sheet of paper or complete the activity, have them glue the food pieces to the sheet of plain paper containing the cornucopia.
- Once students have responded to all levels of questions required by the teacher, they have a completed cornucopia to display.

Sample Questions/Activities for the Thinking Station

Remembering Questions/Activities

Who were the Pilgrims?
Why did the Pilgrims have a Thanksgiving feast?
Make a list of all the people who were at the first Thanksgiving.

Understanding Questions/Activities

Make a timeline of the events that happened at the first Thanksgiving.
How did Squanto help the Pilgrims survive?
Draw a picture of the first Thanksgiving.

Applying Questions/Activities

Collect pictures from magazines that represent the main characters at the first Thanksgiving.
Describe what could have happened if the Indians did not help the Pilgrims.
Make a diorama of the first Thanksgiving.

Analyzing Questions/Activities

What three questions would you like to ask the Pilgrims?
Why is it important to know about the first Thanksgiving?
Determine why the first Thanksgiving is important to us today.

Evaluating Questions/Activities

From what we know about Squanto, what is the most important thing you can say about him?
Choose your favorite person at the first Thanksgiving and tell why that person is your favorite.
Tell why you would or would not like to be a Pilgrim.

Creating Questions/Activities

Write a poem or song about the first Thanksgiving.
Invent a machine that would have helped the Pilgrims survive.
Create a puppet show about the first Thanksgiving.

REFERENCES

Anderson, L. W. & Krathwohl, D. R. (Eds.). (2001). *A taxonomy of learning, teaching, and assessing: A revision of Bloom's Taxonomy of Educational Objectives.* New York: Longman.

Anderson, L. W., Krathwohl, D. R., Airasian, P. W., Cruikshank, K. A., Mayer, R. E., & Pintrich, P. R., et al. (2000). *A taxonomy for learning, teaching, and assessing: A revision of Bloom's taxonomy of educational objectives.* Boston: Allyn & Bacon.

Forehand, M. (2005). Bloom's taxonomy: Original and revised. In M. Orey (Ed.), *Emerging perspectives on learning, teaching, and technology.* Retrieved July 28, 2008, from http://projects.coe.uga.edu/epltt/

IDEAS FOR TEACHING AMERICAN HISTORY UNITS

By Nancy Messman

MAIN CONCEPT

By creating an imaginative classroom environment and immersing students in the lives of people in a historical period, gifted learners acquire a far more in-depth understanding and analysis of specific events and times. This "living experience" approach ignites students' interest and imagination and enables them to make personal discoveries as they explore and research the historic world around them.

LEVEL

Intermediate and middle school years.

APPLICATION

History, geography, research skills, writing.

DESCRIPTION

Pilgrim Study

To help students understand the Pilgrim story, I begin by setting a tone of authenticity within the classroom environment. As with any story, setting is a vital element; therefore, I begin with how the classroom can take on the shape, feel, and look of the 1620s.

Constructing History

I have built a two-wall log cabin in a corner of my room using stock-ade fencing turned horizontally and joined with L brackets. A cutout door-way allows easy access, and two small windows give a full view into the cabin. Inside, I have built, using two-by-four construction board and one thick board for the mantel, a fireplace covered with cardboard. This was given a base coat of paint. My students then measured the size of a typical brick, and using these measurements, outlined the actual "brick" onto the cardboard. To this, we sponged various paint colors to give an authentic looking brick and filled each line with gray paint for mortar. Actual clay bricks were arranged to form the hearth.

Over the years, I have collected antiques for each of my American history units so that the top of the fireplace also acts as a museum. The children have learned what each piece represents in history and enjoy showing visitors our collection of artifacts.

Math Application

One year, using large pieces of cardboard, the children and I put math to use by building a flat-panel shape to resemble the Mayflower. We examined pictures to cut the correct angles and then painted it using the same colors as the ship. This was attached to one wall of our log cabin and for that unit, the log cabin became the "Captain's Quarters."

Roles

Children were invited to wear Pilgrim clothes on our Pilgrim days in which we reenacted situations both on the ship and upon our arrival in America. Each child took the name of either a *saint* or *stranger* from the voyage, and several children became related to another student. Homemade journals were made, and events were recorded throughout the simulation.

Cuisine

As a culmination to our unit, we cooked dishes similar to ones the Pilgrims would have made for our Thanksgiving feast. Parents were invited to share in the festivities by taking the role of the Native Americans and came dressed in earth-tone clothing. Several fathers played the roles of key Native American figures including Chief Massasoit and Squanto.

Resources

Books and materials from Plimoth Plantation in Massachusetts provide rich resources of information. The Web site is www.plimoth.org. In addition, *Remember Patience Whipple* from the *Dear America* collection gives an engaging account of the Pilgrim story suitable for fourth graders.

Character Education

It is important for the children to realize why the Pilgrims—saints and strangers—wished to make this tremendously difficult journey across the Atlantic Ocean to form their own colony. Freedom of thought and religious expression spurred them to first move to Holland, and then to America. While the saints looked for religious freedom, the strangers were seeking a new way of life. Together, these people formed a compact. Since the students are portraying real characters, they too have an opportunity to write a compact, which can be tied into a character education lesson and can include goals you wish to incorporate into the growth of the students for the school year.

Oregon Trail

Roles

For this unit, each child takes the made-up name of a pioneer that includes a family and livestock. Hand-sewn journals made by each child allow them to keep track of their long, arduous journey.

Mapping

Using an overhead projector and a 1840s map of the United States, we project the map onto a six-foot piece of cloth hung on the wall. Then, we trace the outline of the states and territories onto the cloth. Afterward, we paint the various territories using earth-tone paint colors and use a permanent marker for the rivers and to draw the Oregon Trail.

Actual locations of the trail are also labeled along with physical features of the land. This supports our geography studies and provides a great visual in marking the progress that each wagon train makes on the journey.

I set up my room into three groups consisting of five, six, or seven children representing a wagon train. We outline the actual size of a covered wagon with masking tape and imagine the small space pioneers had to move their essentials across the country. Using tiny wagons of differing colors, the students explore primary sources (books, Web sites, prints, and so forth) as they move their wagons on the map. They keep records of events and sights along the trail as well as situations involving their families; they write poetry and make sketches in their journals. This is a means for charting the progress of individual understanding and acts as a way for each wagon to progress along the trail. Teamwork, responsibility, and good decision-making skills tie in beautifully with our character education program and afford advancement for their wagon as well.

Research

During our pioneer unit, each child selects a topic to research from a list of pioneer skills and/or careers. The goal is for each child to become an expert in one area. A research paper complete with bibliography and visual aids is compiled by each student. The culminating event for the two fifth-grade classes is a Pioneer Day celebration in which we invite everyone in the school along with the fifth-grade parents to visit our pioneer village. The fifth graders come dressed as pioneers, and for a full day, they explain their trade and demonstrate crafts and trades to each visitor who is invited to travel from one area to another. Some areas of study include blacksmithing, general store, schoolhouse, toy maker, spinning, weaving, dyeing, hearth and home, and prairie schooner.

Sources

KC Publications sells a magazine-type picture book on the Oregon Trail that is very useful. The phone number is (800) 626–9673, and the Web site is www.kcpublications.com. Information is given along with journal accounts of pioneers who struggled westward, and beautiful full-page photographs show the countryside and actual sites along the trail. I display the pictures in chronological order, and the writings serve as an important reference in our study.

Throughout our unit, we also use many other sources to gather information about the westward expansion, including some excellent DVDs.

Extensions

In addition to the above learning activities, I also teach the children how to quilt authentic quilt blocks found during this time. They learn how to use a sewing machine and how to hand sew as well. We also cook recipes that the pioneers would have used, and the children learn how to dance the Virginia Reel.

STUDENT HISTORIANS

By Carol V. Horn

MAIN CONCEPT

By assuming the role of historians and actually *creating* history, students gain valuable experience in the research process (primary and secondary sources) and engage in the demanding work of analyzing and interpreting the past. Gifted students enjoy this approach to history because it places them in a more active position, where instead of assimilating facts, they decide which concepts and information to present, analyze their discoveries, and explore the different ways of telling *their histories.*

LEVEL

This process can adjust to almost any grade.

APPLICATION

History, geography, language arts, writing, research, analysis, interpretation.

DESCRIPTION

Working with gifted learners presents unique challenges that require a different way of thinking about student engagement, progress, and achievement. We know that gifted learners obtain the facts quickly and that they integrate knowledge and skills on a more complex and abstract level. Therefore the question becomes, "How do we keep them challenged and engaged in continuous intellectual growth?" A critical piece of the answer lies in the notion of progress and how that is demonstrated by a gifted learner. For these students, learning should be a journey that leads them toward expertise. Such a journey requires multiple opportunities to learn and practice the knowledge, skills, and understandings that are used by experts in the field.

Progress on this journey may be measured through complex tasks that allow students to demonstrate the knowledge, skills, and understandings that they acquire as they replicate the work of a professional in the field.

One of the key elements of instruction that is designed to challenge and engage gifted learners as they travel along this journey from novice toward expert is concept-based instruction with a focus on *big ideas*.

Concepts and Big Ideas

When *big ideas* are woven throughout the curriculum, students have multiple opportunities to make connections and integrate knowledge in a way that is not possible when the focus is purely on the content. For example, a study of the Revolutionary War through the concept of *perspective* provides a better understanding of the many different perspectives the colonists had toward the British depending on their role in life, where they lived, and their connections to England. Students learn that knowledge can change perspective, and they become aware of the fact that their own perspective changes through reading, reflection, and discussion.

The concept of perspective applies to other subjects as well. In a fourth-grade seminar discussion of *Through My Eyes* by Ruby Bridges, the students gained a unique perspective on the Civil Rights movement as shared through the memory of an adult who had first-hand experience with it. As students discussed the challenges and hardships that Ruby Bridges endured as the first black child to enroll and attend an all-white school, the exchange of ideas broadened their own perspective, and the phrase "equal opportunity for all citizens" took on new meaning. They realized that if it had not been for people like Ruby, the racial and ethnic makeup of their class would be different today.

Discovery and Revision

In order for students to understand the role of a historian as a scholar who investigates, interprets, and re-creates the past, they need to focus on two unifying concepts: discovery and revision. Discovery is selected because historians are continually searching for and discovering new clues to help them analyze and interpret the past. As the past is uncovered, a focus on revision emphasizes that as new interpretations and information are discovered, our understanding of the past is continually revised. This is a creative enterprise where new data provide new views of a time or event and, therefore, new possibilities for understanding and expressing it.

Introducing Primary Sources

For gifted learners in fourth through sixth grade, this historian's journey begins with an opportunity to practice historical interpretation and analysis through a research project that focuses on a person whom they know or someone whom they would like to learn more about. Ralph Waldo Emerson once said, "All history becomes subjective; in other words, there is properly no history, only biography" (*Collected Works of Ralph Waldo Emerson—Volume II—Essays: First Series*, 2007)

A Person's Life

The study of a person's life that reaches beyond biographies and trade books may be used to launch students on the historian's journey. By selecting and researching the life of a person (may be a family member) whom they know and would like to learn more about, students gain first-hand experience of the skills a historian needs. They learn about the person using multiple sources of evidence with the following guidelines:

- **Interview.** Conduct an interview either in person, via e-mail, or on the telephone. Prepare questions ahead of time and record what you learn and what you think about the information in your journal. A copy of the interview questions, the name of the interviewee, and the date of your interview should be placed in the pocket of your research folder. Use the same process and interview at least one or more additional individuals who know this person well.
- **Visit.** Plan a site visitation to a place where your person lives and/ or works. Record what you learn along with a response in your research journal. Include photographs, postcards, or drawings of what you saw and learned. Often, a site visitation can be combined with a personal interview.

A Focus

Students are encouraged to choose one aspect of this person's life that they find especially interesting (childhood experiences, schooling, family event, personal success and struggle, unusual interests and pursuits) and write a short historical narrative for a class magazine based on the evidence that has been collected. They are also encouraged to share their first draft with the person that they are writing about in order to check for accuracy.

The following questions are posted to guide their thinking as they conduct their research:

1. Were there any ideas that were revised after you reviewed your findings that might initiate further inquiry and lead to new discoveries?

2. How might your own biases have influenced your understanding of this person's life?

Doing History

By "doing history" through a personal research, students encounter a variety of primary and secondary sources of information and begin to understand the knowledge and skills needed to discover and revise our understanding of the past. Entries in a research journal allow students to document their reflections in response to journal prompts and guiding questions provided by the teacher. Frequent and continuous opportunities to engage in metacognition enable students to develop an appreciation for the power of reflection and revision as they recreate the past.

Historical Sleuthing

Learning to think like a historian becomes an ongoing journey that requires the student to search for clues that lead to a better understanding of people and events from the past. Creativity is critical as they begin to replicate the historian's work and create their own interpretations of past events. By reading and reflecting on primary and secondary sources of information, students gain an understanding of the importance of considering where the evidence originates and how bias and perspective influence interpretation. In the words of sixth-grade students, when you study history through secondary sources

- you gain more background information,
- you read and evaluate what others think,
- the information may be old and you should check the date of publication,
- you learn other people's solutions, and it is harder to imagine what it was really like.

The same students noted that with primary sources

- the information may be limited; you decide what it means,
- it may be more accurate,
- the learning is more powerful,
- you are the problem solver, and it is like being there—it is easier to imagine.

By engaging in the intellectual struggles of historians, gifted learners are able to explore and make sense of the past through systematic, intellectual inquiry. They gain a new appreciation for a historian's work and are excited to learn that historical interpretation is ongoing, dynamic, and evolving through the dual processes of discovery and revision. History is a puzzle to be solved, and the clues lead to new and better understandings of the present.

REFERENCE

Emerson, R. W. (2007). *Collected works of Ralph Waldo Emerson—Volume II—Essays: First Series.* (J. Slater & A. R. Ferguson, eds.). Cambridge, MA: Harvard University Press.

COMBINED DISCIPLINARY AND INTERDISCIPLINARY COLLABORATION BETWEEN GENERAL MUSIC AND SOCIAL STUDIES CLASSES

By Lois Veenhoven Guderian

MAIN CONCEPT

For music teachers and social studies teachers to maintain curriculum goals yet offer students opportunities for rich, interdisciplinary learning experiences, teachers should work together to choose materials and examples that support both interdisciplinary and disciplinary learning. Collaborations between social studies and general music classrooms are often natural as there can be several interdisciplinary possibilities—of historical and social significance—embedded in the songs and pieces of music from any given period. Likewise, all social-cultural and historical periods under study have yielded music and other works of art. In-depth examination of musical compositions can give teachers direction and ideas for designing learning experiences that not only allow students to discover the social and historical meaning of particular works but also allow for students' continued growth in development of musicianship skills, musical understanding, and applied creative work.

LEVEL

Intermediate grades and up.

APPLICATION

Language arts, history, sociology, theater, visual arts, performing arts.

DESCRIPTION

As an example, I present the following scenario. Fifth graders are currently studying causes of the Civil War. In their many classroom discussions on slavery as one of the causes, the classroom and music teacher collaborate in teaching the children a few spirituals. Simply learning how to sing the songs does not provide meaningful learning for the children, nor does it necessarily build on students' knowledge and help to move their learning forward in either subject. Both teachers must look into the songs for ways to design learning experiences that are appropriate for students' current levels of understanding and skill and hold potential for whole group and differentiated learning experiences in support of curriculum goals.

Questioning and Inquiry

The teachers choose to collaborate on the learning *of, in,* and *about,* two African American spirituals. Questions about the songs can guide the direction of teachers' preparations of materials and design of the learning environment. If separate classrooms are to be maintained during the collaboration, questions relating to the music can be examined in the music class. Questions relating to social, cultural, or historical significance can be examined in the social studies class. Each teacher can use the learning from the other area as constant reference. Another way is to combine the studies during both social studies and music class. Teachers can team teach using methods of philosophical inquiry to engage students in thinking and discovery. Work and research stations that appeal to students' interests can provide students with opportunities to pursue topics of interest and learn at their various levels of disciplinary sophistication and talent development.

The many strategies of differentiated teaching as well as teacher-scaffolding strategies are especially useful in designing and carrying out small group and individualized learning. Alternating between whole-class *benchmark* lessons (including hands-on musical experience through playing, singing, creating, or listening), followed by opportunities for small-group and individual research, gives variety and movement to learning experiences. The following questions can serve as a starting point in examining a musical work and springboard for multiple kinds of learning in both the music classroom and the social studies classroom as well as other subject areas of the school. These questions, in general form, can be applied to the study of any work of art, however, are applied specifically to the example under discussion.

Using the Example of the Two African American Spirituals

Questions for Teachers and Students

- How, where, and when did the songs originate?
- Who wrote them and for what purpose? (The creation of songs that were used for secret messages during the time of the Underground Railroad is just one of several purposes—a rich vein of learning to pursue.)
- What are the musical properties—what is the tonal or atonal quality of the songs; what are the characteristic rhythms, harmony, phrasing, articulation?
- What other *music* is similar and in what ways?
- What is the musical form, and what are the musical concepts, signs, or symbols, both new and formerly learned, that the children can discover and learn in these pieces?
- What is the expressive quality?
- What is the meaning of the text? As is often the case with African American spirituals, is there a symbolic meaning?

Questions for Teachers in Preparing Initial Musical Experiences of the Pieces

- In what ways can the children engage *in* the musical experience of the pieces before engaging in the *about, why, when, what,* and *how* of the pieces?
- In what ways can the children learn to sing and play the pieces—classroom instruments, vocally (in unison, choral arrangements)? In these music-making experiences, what musicianship skills can be reinforced or developed? Are there various recorded examples that would open up opportunities for the study of style, the study of the life of particular performers, and aesthetically, musically rich listening experiences?
- What current styles of music have evolved from the African American spirituals, and chronologically, what has been that evolution? How can I engage children in musical experience to acquire this awareness?
- What opportunities for students' creative work are present in songs?

Questions for Teachers and Students

- In what creative products, displays, presentations, or performances can the study of these pieces, in sociocultural and historical contexts as well as current contexts, be shared with the school, community, or others?

Teachers' Roles

The social studies teacher can design learning centers where children can choose various topics to research in relation to the spirituals: African and European origins, life on plantations, Christianizing of the slaves, Underground Railroad, studies of slaves of historical significance, and so on. *The music teacher* can give students participatory experiences (making/performing, creating music, and listening) that help students to understand the musical origins and synthesis of styles from which the spirituals evolved; the relation of these to present styles—popular, art music and, in some cases, world music.

New Learning

For example, embedded in the familiar African American spirituals "Swing Low Sweet Chariot" and "Nobody Knows the Trouble I've Seen" are many possibilities for learning both inside and outside of music. The pieces are written in pentatonic. When F pentatonic is used for the learning and singing of the pieces, many music-making opportunities are available for teachers and students. F pentatonic is not only a good singing key for these pieces in consideration of the young voice, it is also a perfect key for creating ostinato accompaniments to the songs as well as an excellent key for improvisation and composing experiences on all barred instruments. Many additions of student-improvised ostinatos can be added to the playing and singing of "Swing Low Sweet Chariot" and "Nobody Knows the Trouble I've Seen."

Extensions

The songs can also work as partner songs, which are sung at the same time and are an excellent way to help students develop ability in part-singing. Students can learn to play the melody on recorder or on barred instruments, while those with more sophisticated levels of music ability, perhaps in piano or other instruments, can play the accompaniment. Vocal technique, unison, and part singing can be incorporated into the learning of the pieces. In the area of music theory, children can learn the theoretical difference between the five-note scale and the eight-note major and/or minor scales. This can lead to ear training and explorations in harmonizing with I, IV, V, I.

Improvisation

In the pentatonic scale, the tonal arrangement is such that it works beautifully for improvisation. Both simple and complex student-created parts can be combined in layers of sound for rich ensemble experience. Pentatonic question-and-answer phrasing on instruments (teacher initiates a musical question, and students copy the answer exactly or improvise an answer) help to build musicianship and nurture creative response and confidence in students for playing and creating music.

Interconnections

The cultural and historical contexts of the songs are profound. Other than the links to history and social studies, the links to art, literature, poetry, and drama, are endless as are the links to areas within music. Just in music alone, the study of spirituals can lead to musical concepts and historical elements of African music—instruments, rhythms, syncopation, call and response, and cultural and social uses. Learning European styles of music is also embedded in the spirituals: Western scales, melodies, and harmonies; hymns and sacred music as part of the musical synthesis and evolution of spirituals; and other musical forms and expressions.

These links emerge through researching additional literature and through countless listening experiences of these pieces—from students' own singing/playing/performing to the many professional choral and instrumental versions (for contrast and comparison, consider the operatic renditions of the spirituals such as those of Jesse Norman and Kathleen Battle as well as the choral and instrumental arrangements available). Musical links as well as historical links between African American spirituals and just about all modern styles of popular music offer more possibilities for research, exploration, comparison, discovery, creation, and performance. In-depth learning *about, in,* and *through* music is endless while students explore the sociocultural and historical significance of various areas of study in music and social studies.

Composition

Last, but not in any way least, in addition to improvising in pentatonic, students can work alone or in groups to compose their own melodies or songs in pentatonic followed by performances, recording, and evaluation (self, teacher, group) of both learned materials and students' creative work. Further sharing and celebration of students' efforts can be offered to the other age groups in the school, the parents, and public in assemblies, concerts, or by other means. Creative drama, art, dance, movement, and creative writing can also go hand in hand with music and social studies in various collaborations. For example, creations of poetry, song lyrics, dramatic readings, scripts or plays, scenery, murals, choreography, and movement can all be outgrowths of studying the songs. This kind of comprehensive approach can be applied to the study of any work of art. The work itself serves as a nucleus, a point of departure and a framework for more learning experiences and creative work.

DRAMA IN THE SOCIAL STUDIES CLASSROOM

By Gina Lewis

MAIN CONCEPT

The goal of the following creative activity is to bring social studies alive by experiencing a historical event through drama. Drama in the classroom is an excellent device for incorporating the arts into the regular curriculum as well as engaging students in higher-level thinking. Not only is it a huge component of the arts, drama is a teaching device that fully encompasses the active learning of history, which makes it irreplaceable as a learning model.

LEVEL

These ideas can apply to all grade levels, depending on content selected.

APPLICATION

Language arts, creative writing, history, the arts.

DESCRIPTION

This strategy for teaching history integrates reading, writing, and historical research. Participating in drama requires higher-level thinking skills as the students take their knowledge of the subject matter and apply it creatively. This creative application requires analyzing and synthesizing the information they have learned. Self-evaluation can also be explored by giving a pretest and then retesting again at the end of the unit. Students are always amazed at the level of understanding they've acquired through researching the subject matter, creating the play, and then experiencing multiple rehearsals. An accurate time line of the historical event becomes embedded in their minds as well as the events that led up to it. Names and dates become an integral part of their knowledge because they are crucial to the creation of the play. Successfully passing the final test is a given.

The students are truly experiencing creative thinking because the imagination is required to visualize and reenact events. Working cooperatively puts the students into a zone of convergent thinking, and divergent thinking is engaged because each one has personal responsibility and a role to fulfill. To be actively involved in costume, setting, and dialogue results in the stories of history coming alive, thus creating retention in long-term memory.

This process can be made as simple or as complex as warranted. A simple description of the process is included here because it is usually better to begin simply and make additions once mastery has been gained.

Sequence

1. **Story.** First, find a short story or play already in existence that fits the required curriculum. The examples used in this description are from "Ulysses and the Trojan Horse" from the SAILS curriculum *Ancient Greece* workbook and "Active Learning: Increasing Flow in the Classroom." Read the chosen story or play aloud to the students as a guideline to give them an idea of its sequence and flow.

2. **Learning objectives.** The measurable learning objectives involved in this specific drama are that the students become familiar with a historical event by hearing and reading the story of the Trojan Horse. They will write and memorize lines to fit the story as well as invent acting and movement to fit the story. The students will create masks, costumes, and settings to fit the story. Finally, the students will be evaluated with a pretest and posttest over the significant historical facts.

3. **Materials.** Materials needed are appropriate costumes, which can be very simple and improvised by adding a clothing item such as a

hat or jacket to the student's own clothes. The students in this play wore either red or blue sweatshirts and carried props. Masks are fun and easy to make in the classroom, requiring only tag board and markers. Pencil and paper to write down the dialogue of the characters as it evolves is essential, as is a poster board for recording the scene sequence. Recycled cardboard or poster board works well for the setting and props. Painting the various costumes, masks, or setting is an option. Musical instruments that are simple and easy to manipulate such as chimes and a small drum add variation to the sound effects. Student voices used as sound effects are another option. Students in this play created battle sounds, ocean sounds, and the sound of horses running to name a few.

Helpful Suggestions

The students should have as much of the responsibility of creating costume, props, and dialogue as possible to give them ownership and create excitement about the topic. Let them know that creating a play requires many different talents and abilities and that a successful play needs narrators, actors, and set managers.

Roles. Tryouts are optional and can become stressful and time-consuming. An alternative is to ask the students to think of the areas they would like to work in and write their top three selections on a sheet of paper. Organize these (keeping in mind the student's abilities) and give each student at least one of their three selections. Narrators should be able to memorize many lines and project their voices. Actors need to be students who will not get stage fright easily but who like to *ham it up* in front of an audience. Set managers are very important because they have to follow the play and know all their cues. Creative artistic students are great set managers. Remind the students that if they do not get the part that they really wanted, there will be other opportunities.

Guided practice and rehearsal. Always begin with some guided practice after the students are familiar with the story and have received their parts. The scenes have been discussed (or voted on) and are on the sequence board. Everyone has a job to do. Actors and narrators are writing and memorizing their lines while set managers are creating the sets. Set a time limit for the narrator(s) and actors to produce their lines and for the set managers produce their sketches for the setting. Discuss them as a class and do a run through. Rehearsals are imperative but should be kept short. A lot of short rehearsals are better than a few grueling, long ones. Keeping the play short and simple makes rehearsals hassle free. The play should be no longer than 30 minutes maximum.

In the play "The Trojan Horse," some strategies that worked well included the following:

- Helen of Troy had lots of handmaids to fill extra parts.
- Lots of soldiers on both sides provided extra parts.
- One side of the stage held the Greeks wearing one color, and the other side of the stage held the Trojans in another color rather than having students entering and exiting excessively.
- Achilles limped across the stage with an arrow taped to his heel, which was comical.
- When the soldiers were fighting they used very slow, very exaggerated fighting movements without actually touching one another.
- The horse was cardboard (can be cloth) that the students stood behind.
- When the Trojans believed the Greeks had left, it was fun for them to begin partying and singing, "The Greeks are gone! The Greeks are gone! And that's the way, uh huh, uh huh, we like it, uh huh, uh huh!"

Closure. Ideas for closure may include creating a classroom scrapbook or bulletin board of pictures and souvenirs from the play. Students can write a summary of their experience and the important things they learned during the play. A beneficial evaluation method is a pretest and posttest. An example of this from the "The Trojan Horse" play is included.

Extensions. Other contexts where this process can be applied are extension activities such as performing for the parents, other classes, or the entire school. Performing the play for nursing homes or retirement centers benefit the community and teach the students about community service. Read other books, study maps, or find movies about the event.

The most important thing to remember in teaching history through drama is to be flexible and to let the play evolve. Plays can be adjusted to fit almost any grade level, and the students are much more interested when they know that their ideas and contributions will be considered and developed into the play.

Benefits. The benefits observed from participating in historical drama range from experiences in interpretive dance, to creative writing of dialogue and prose, musical composition, and the visual arts (painting and/or drawing of props). Costuming is always optional but is another splendid art form that could be explored. Drama is truly an area where a compendium of the arts can be explored with as much or as little depth as time, student's maturity levels, available resources, and teacher energy allow.

RESOURCES

Hollingsworth, P. (Ed.). (2000). *SAILS Student interdisciplinary learning series.* Tulsa, OK: University School at the University of Tulsa.

SAILS also online www.clickandlearn.com and www.uschool.utulsa.edu

Hollingsworth, P., & Hollingsworth, L. G. (2006). *Active learning: Increasing flow in the classroom.* Wales: Crown House.

Sequence of Events for the Sequence Board

SCENE 1: HELEN IS STOLEN BY PARIS

ULYSSES, ACHILLES, AND GREEK SOLDIERS FOLLOW AFTER

SCENE 2: WAR BETWEEN THE GREEKS AND TROJANS

ACHILLES IS SHOT IN THE HEEL

ULYSSES DECIDES TO BUILD THE HORSE

SCENE 3: GREEKS BUILD THE HORSE

GREEKS ENTER THE HORSE

HORSE IS PUSHED UP TO THE CITY GATES

SCENE 4: TROJANS SEE GREEKS SAILING AWAY AND CELEBRATE

SCENE 5: TROJANS FIND THE HORSE

SCENE 6: LAOCOON THROWS SPEAR AT HORSE

SCENE 7: SINON IS CAPTURED AND TELLS ABOUT THE HORSE

SCENE 8: TROJANS TEAR DOWN THEIR WALL AND CELEBRATE

SCENE 9: GREEKS SNEAK OUT OF HORSE, CAPTURE THE CITY, AND RETRIEVE HELEN

The Trojan Horse Evaluation

1. Who was the Greek queen? _____

2. What was the name of the Greek general? _____

3. What was the name of the Trojan general? _____

4. Who was the great Greek soldier that was shot in the heel? _____

5. The two groups fighting were_____ and_____ _____

6. The Greeks built a _____to trick the Trojans.

7. The Greeks traveled to Troy on _____

8. _____ warned the Trojans not to accept the gift of the horse.

9. _____ was left behind by the Greeks to help trick the Trojans.

10. Who was the goddess that was mentioned in the play? _____

Put the following events in order from numbers 1–9:

_____SINON IS CAPTURED AND TELLS ABOUT THE HORSE.

_____ACHILLES IS SHOT IN THE HEEL.

_____THE TROJANS FIND THE HORSE.

_____HELEN IS STOLEN BY PARIS.

_____THE GREEKS SNEAK OUT OF THE HORSE AND CAPTURE THE CITY OF TROY AND HELEN.

_____THE TROJANS SEE THE GREEKS SAILING AWAY.

_____THE HORSE IS PUSHED UP TO THE CITY GATES.

_____THE TROJANS TEAR DOWN THEIR WALL AND CELEBRATE.

_____LAOCOON THROWS HIS SPEAR AT THE HORSE.

On another sheet of paper, draw and label a scene from the play.
Extra Credit: Who was the author of the original story about the Trojan Horse?

Answer Sheet

1. Helen
2. Ulysses/Odysseus
3. Paris
4. Achilles
5. Greeks and Trojans
6. a wooden horse
7. ships
8. Laocoon
9. Sinon
10. Minerva or Athena

Put the following events in order from numbers 1–9:

__7___SINON IS CAPTURED AND TELLS ABOUT THE HORSE.

__2___ACHILLES IS SHOT IN THE HEEL.

__5___THE TROJANS FIND THE HORSE.

__1___HELEN IS STOLEN BY PARIS.

__9___THE GREEKS SNEAK OUT OF THE HORSE AND CAPTURE THE CITY OF TROY AND HELEN.

__4___THE TROJANS SEE THE GREEKS SAILING AWAY.

__3___THE HORSE IS PUSHED UP TO THE CITY GATES.

__8___THE TROJANS TEAR DOWN THEIR WALL AND CELEBRATE.

__6___LAOCOON THROWS HIS SPEAR AT THE HORSE.

PART 3: ANSWERS WILL VARY.

PART 4: HOMER

CREATING PLAYS IN SOCIAL STUDIES

By Gay Doyle

MAIN CONCEPT

This activity enables students to advance far beyond the knowledge level of a social studies curriculum, because they have to conduct research, explore essential questions (often in different media), and write their own material. The process engages higher-level thinking in gifted students and provides a creative outlet for their imagination and originality.

LEVEL

Intermediate grades and beyond.

APPLICATION

Language arts, social studies, arts and media.

DESCRIPTION

My fifth-grade classroom contains a cluster of gifted children within the regular education setting. I use Reader's Theatre and also put on published plays, using other fifth-grade classes as an audience. However, I challenge the gifted students to create their own plays by providing guidelines to help them bring out the best of their thinking, research, and writing abilities.

Broad Ideas

To start this project, I give students broad ideas about topics to research within a given time frame, such as the Gold Rush, the Oregon Trail, Lewis & Clark, and others. I try to plan this research so it coincides with the post–Revolutionary/pre–Civil War era, but you could use any time period. To begin, I ask students to write an essential question that one might need to think about while learning this information. An essential question might be something like the following: "What qualities does it take to be an explorer at this time period?" "What forces drive a person to make such changes in their lives?" "How have the people of this time period changed the way people live today?" We use essential questions in our class, so this is not a new concept. Students at this age, however, often still need guidance choosing a thoughtful essential question if they have not had much practice creating their own questions. In addition, I ask them to complete a KWL chart (i.e., "what I *know*, what I *want* to know, and what I *learned*"). They research the topic and report back to me so that I can help them check their facts. A time line is presented to the students so they stay on track, use their time wisely, and keep the pace I need.

Structure

After students have their information, I ask them to work on the play itself. I ask students to think of a basic outline for their play and then divide them into smaller groups to write individual scenes. Sometimes groups of students act out a scene before writing it down; other groups have written it down first. Students must also consider the use of costumes and props. In my class, students do not perform on a stage, so the plays do not get too complicated. However, I expect high-quality writing and accurate information/characterization.

Student-Created Quiz

To help all students focus on the essential concepts in the play, the gifted students also write a quiz for the rest of the class to complete after they have viewed the play. I usually ask them to write multiple-choice questions, but the *dummy* answers must be reasonable. They can't be complete giveaways. The quiz must also have an answer key and cover the main ideas presented in the play. The students who write the quiz also take the quiz! Part of the challenge for students is to create a play that presents information in such a way that the rest of the class can answer questions about the key concepts after one performance.

Rubric

I create a rubric to grade the play. It varies based on the topic but usually includes how well the students answered the essential question, how accurate the information is, what was the quality of the miniquiz questions, and how much effort it took in making a seamless performance. I will also be adding quality of writing skill, ideas, organization, and voice to the rubric this year. In addition, students may have points deducted if they do not get their play completed on time.

As a teacher, these are my main roles:

- Choose a content area
- Help students write an essential question to help them focus their research
- Review information for accuracy
- Help guide students' learning by asking probing questions
- Create a time line to keep students and parents informed about time expectations
- Create a grading rubric to keep students and parents informed about content expectations
- Provide time for research, writing, and practice
- Grade the plays
- Guide students through conflict resolution when they have different ideas and cannot seem to resolve them on their own

Finding the time to help students accomplish this task can seem complicated. Students who complete this play start their research before the rest of the class starts to read their plays. They do a portion of the research outside the regular class period, although sometimes students also work independently during class while I teach the prewritten plays to the rest of the class. I am often fortunate to have an aide or a parent volunteer to help supervise students in the library and have laptops available for classroom use. When lack of time is a factor, I ask the students to write Reader's Theatre plays. Students can usually complete these projects in a shorter amount of time. They do not need to worry about costumes and props, and the plays are much shorter.

More often than not, students exceed my expectations in what they learn. They incorporate so much detail that goes beyond the main ideas, and their creative juices transform them into the historic people in the plays! Students who perform a prewritten play are equally expected to learn the fifth-grade content. Since everyone is involved, usually there are no *jealousy* factors between students. Centering the plays on essential questions gives them focus and enables the students to use higher-level thinking skills. Each year that I have had gifted students write their own plays, they become eager learners who truly shine when they have the pressure to dig deeper, the flexibility to be creative, and the guidelines to be successful.

STORIES OF TIME PAST

By Joan Franklin Smutny

MAIN CONCEPT

The primary goal of this strategy is to provide gifted learners with an in-depth understanding of another time and/or historic figure by stepping into the shoes of another person and imaginatively recreating his/her world.

LEVEL

All grades. Even primary students enjoy writing stories from another time, provided they receive sufficient source material (multimedia; multidimensional) and support through the writing process.

APPLICATION

Writing, reading, history, geography.

DESCRIPTION

One of the most successful strategies I have found for igniting the imagination of gifted learners and stimulating new insight into the study of history is to have them write their own biographies and histories (as well as fictional pieces that emerge from this). Gifted students with highly developed but often underutilized imaginations relish the opportunity to step into another time and into the shoes of someone living back then. When structured properly, it can significantly enhance the research and inquiry process in social studies and can enable students to make personal connections with a topic.

Principles to Follow

- Always begin with *students'* questions and interests in learning about this person/historical event. The more connected they are to their own curiosity (what draws them to the subject), the easier it will be for them to do the research. "What do I want to know about this?" should be the driving question in their minds. They should approach this assignment as detectives uncovering clues.

- Provide examples of different kinds of biographies/histories. Students will see from this that not every story starts at the beginning or follows a prescribed chronology. Brainstorm with the children all the different ways people might design their biographies/histories.
- Let students investigate both primary and secondary sources. Give examples of both and explore which ones most connect them to the subject. In addition, provide materials from other media—such as sketches, portraits, documentaries, films, and so forth.
- "What have you discovered?" Have students keep notes of their discoveries as they read and research. The discoveries are the most important to record. They can always jot down pages or places to find facts. But discoveries are the lights that guide their writing.

Point of View

The process of putting themselves into the history they're studying, engages gifted children in higher-level thinking naturally. The very act of identifying with someone else creates shifts in point of view and outlook that might not happen otherwise. Here are a couple of comments from students I know:

> [unit on immigration] "My parents came here from Bosnia when I was little. I always heard their stories of how bad it was before they got out. But writing my own story made me think about how everyone who comes here has something in their past that haunts them—something that pushed them out of their old countries. And sometimes now I think about the old Bosnia before all the fighting and I wonder, do all immigrants dream about their countries?" Sixth Grader.

> [unit on rainforests] "I was a lizard who needs the forest around me. But my friend was a coffee farmer who cuts down trees to make money for his family. We had different stories. He had to grow more coffee plants to feed his family, and there aren't a lot of other jobs. But the trees coming down made me sad. I like being a lizard because lizard's eyes can move in different directions at the same time and see different things. It would be sad if I disappeared with the trees." Third Grader.

For the process to extend in-depth learning, students need access to sources that match their ability levels. Gifted readers need to tackle more challenging texts, not only histories but also biographies, primary writings (diaries, letters, journals), historical novels or short stories, and online sources. Prints, pictures, maps, videos, and other media can then add another dimension to the preparation process. They also need questions to ponder, problems to solve, issues to explore. "What was it like to live back then?" isn't enough to draw them into the material.

The process I give my students in biography/history is as follows:

Sequence

1. Become an expert in your subject (person/ historical event).
   - Find primary sources (diaries, letters, photos, notes, recordings)
   - Find secondary sources (books, stories, documentaries, articles)
   - Explore media representations (feature films, audio, video, art)

2. Think of the qualities you most admire and what enabled this person to achieve; in the case of history, choose anecdotes that seem most important.

3. Write down one or two questions you have—more than anything else—that you want to answer about this person's life/historical event. (Example: What kept Rachel Carson going in her fight against DDT when no one took her seriously? Or why did the Founding Fathers create the electoral college?)

4. Write a biography focusing on the qualities and questions you've chosen, or write history using the same to guide you. Draw on primary and secondary sources and on any other media you have access to (film, photos, sketches, etc.).

5. Orally interpret the person/event in your writing. You can dress up, use sound effects or props, or anything else that will aid you. If you are focusing on an event in history, you could assume the identity of a witness or participant.

6. Write biographical/historical fiction. In the case of biography, for example, choose an object belonging to a person to tell stories that may not be known about the person (e.g., the story of Lincoln writing the Gettysburg address from the point of view of his pen; the story of a Civil War event from the point of view of two brothers, one fighting on the North and the other on the South).

Extension to Fiction

Historical fiction can apply to any grade level and topic. Younger students who may not yet be writing as well can still dictate their stories and sketch events from their imaginations. Writing historical fiction is an ideal extension within a social studies unit and often leads gifted students to appreciate the complexities that arise, for example, from the consideration of multiple points of view. As one exasperated student said to me, "What is a historical fact? A happening combined with a point of view combined with a writer's idea of what happened!" Exploring this aspect of history is ideal for students who've already immersed themselves in a topic and want to address their study in a more creative, explorative way. They can be easily guided to new, more advanced sources and to a creative writing experience that allows them to speculate about what *might* have happened. I know gifted students who leap at this opportunity every time it's offered.

Benefits

Historical and biographical writing engages gifted learners in a process of independent, in-depth inquiry, information-gathering, higher-level thinking, and imagination. It is an ideal way to integrate the academic and creative so as to enhance discovery and invention while at the same time increasing the depth of understanding they bring to the study of history.

MIGHTY MYTHOLOGY

By Carol Sandberg Howe

MAIN CONCEPT

This unit re-creates the world of Greek mythology for gifted students by drawing upon a wide range of disciplines (history, geography, reading, writing, visual art, drama, etc.) and thinking modalities (problem solving, inferring, imagining, categorizing, comparing, analyzing). Through well-orchestrated sequences of activities and assignments (both in groups and independently), students acquire vast amounts of knowledge while at the same time putting their understanding to creative use through projects and performances.

LEVEL

Intermediate and middle school grades, but adaptable to higher and lower grades.

APPLICATION

Because of its interdisciplinary nature, this unit—or portions of it—can be adapted so that it more thoroughly addresses a specific subject or skill area. It is also structured in such a way that teachers can easily extract activities or ideas and use them in their current curriculum with minor changes.

DESCRIPTION

Introduction (Recurring Themes for Teachers)

The myths of Greek/Roman gods, heroes, and monsters have been famous throughout the centuries, and much of our modern morals, language, science, literature/poetry, theatre, art, architecture, and love of sports (the Olympics) are descended from these Greek/Roman civilizations. The Romans conquered the Greeks (197 BC), but eventually adopted much of their culture and their gods. So, *who* was the *real* conqueror?

Whether using Greek or Roman names, who hasn't heard the names of some of the major gods or goddesses: Zeus/Jupiter, Athena/Minerva, Apollo/Apollo, Artemis/Diana, Aphrodite/Venus, and Poseidon/Neptune? Unlike the Egyptians, the Greeks/Romans envisioned their gods in their own human image, subject to the same emotions and faults shared by their mortal subjects: love, happiness, sacrifice, anger, jealously, revenge, and so on.

The Greeks/Romans also created *heroes* with special powers to interact with the gods. What is a hero? The list of Greek/Roman heroes reads like a veritable "who's who," for their famous deeds including Hercules, Odysseus, Perseus, and Jason, all who, in some way, *strived to develop their best qualities and talents, faced their problems and tried to solve them, and strived to help others, usually through great personal sacrifice to themselves.* Children are naturally drawn to these epic tales because they are truly such engaging and exciting stories.

Do today's young men and women have any *real* heroes they can look up to? Who are they? Sports personalities? Movie and television personalities? Fashion models? Rock stars? Are these the personalities to truly admire and emulate for their moral character and good deeds? Or are they admired simply because they are *popular?* Our students need to consider the characteristics of true heroes, those who are making a contribution to society. Perhaps our scientists, astronauts, firemen, policemen, teachers, service men and women, Red Cross volunteers, Nobel Peace Prize winners, or Olympic champions can fill the bill.

Throughout the centuries, these famous Greek myths have continued to inspire us to set goals and make important contributions in our lives.

Take the story of The Trojan War. In 1835, a young man was fascinated by the Greek myths, especially the famous story where the Greeks waged war on the city of Troy in order to get Helen back and devised the clever Trojan Horse to gain entry into the fortress.

The young man wanted to prove that the city of Troy and some of the events were not a fictional *myth* but more likely to be a *legend*, stories partially anchored in fact rather than fiction.

Studying the ancient stories of the *Iliad* and the *Odyssey,* this young man, Heinrich Schliemann, pursued his passionate search until, in 1870, he discovered the real location of the city of Troy and proved to the world that it really existed!

The Ancient Greeks left us a legacy of creativity, determination, and ethics as the foundation for our modern civilization that we can never repay. These gifted people demonstrated that our individual ability to *dream,* to ask *why?* and the courage to pursue "an idea whose time has come" still belongs to each and every one of us.

Overview for Students

For thousands of years, people all over the world have been intrigued by the exciting tales of Greek and Roman mythologies. People of ancient times created myths to explain things they did not understand: the changing seasons, thunder echoes, volcanoes, and the creation of the earth. They reasoned that superhuman powers must be responsible. These imaginative stories of brave heroes, savage monsters, and powerful gods have taught us a great deal about these cultures and how they perceived their world. Although the gods were immortal, they possessed the same human emotions and frailties of the common man. Thus, the gods and the challenges of their mythical adventures gave people the wisdom to handle their everyday problems and shaped powerful moral values that have endured through the ages into the twenty-first century.

Note: This mythology unit was originally structured as a one-week, six-hour-a-day course conducted during gifted summer sessions. During the regular school year, this unit can easily be adapted into segments for a three- or four-week course with a spectacular culminating event showcasing all the special projects.

Daily Morning Activities

The following is a profile of the summer sessions that last for five days, six hours in length, divided into morning and afternoon activities:

At the beginning of the five-day session, the morning class is divided into four Olympic teams, with chosen names such as the famous Gods and Goddesses, the famous Olympic Heroes, famous Enchanted Creatures, and famous Greek Monsters. Daily, each team selects two different Greek stories from a list of 24 famous Greek/Roman myths to read and critique. Myth choices include the following:

How the World Came to Be (the Creation Myth)

Prometheus Gives Fire to Mankind

Pandora's Box

Persephone and Demeter

Theseus and the Minotaur

Pyramus and Thisbe

Phaethon Flies the Horses of the Sun

Diana, Huntress, and Goddess of the Moon

Pygmalion and Galatea

Cupid and Psyche

King Midas and the Golden Touch

Narcissus and Echo

Icarus and Daedalus

The Twelve Labors of Hercules

Perseus and Medusa

Oedipus and the Sphinx

Bellerophon and Pegasus

Jason and the Golden Fleece

The Trojan War

The Illiad

The Odyssey

The Beginning of Rome (Romulus and Remus)

A questionnaire is provided for each myth to assist each team in listing the greatest number of heroic deeds/quests, the slaying of evil creatures or monsters, important moral lessons learned from the story, or immortals performing a deed of mercy or kindness for mortals that can be found in that story. (Each detail is worth 10 points.)

Each myth questionnaire must also include a short profile of the main Greek/Roman god and Olympian hero that appears in the story, which includes a description of each character's origin and unique powers.

Each team will also daily submit four *the answer is . . .* and *matching questions* from their myths to insert into a computerized *Mighty Mythology Jeopardy Game grid* to be played by the entire class on the last day of class.

Daily Afternoon Activities

For the first afternoon, students and teacher *brainstorm* a list of individual, special projects that would complement their daily study of the Greek myths and give each project a *point value,* based on complexity. During each three-hour afternoon session, students choose from these activities to complete as many special mythology projects for extra credit as time permits. Students may take their special project home if they need additional time to complete it. Each student also maintains a *journal* of daily activities, including notes and photographs documenting progress on their afternoon extra credit Greek projects.

At the end of the weeklong contest, members of the team with the most combined questionnaire points, *plus* points for completion of *individual* afternoon projects are awarded a coveted Greek Laurel Wreath during the Friday celebration.

Course Objectives

Knowledge

- Introductory background to Greek history and culture as found in Greek mythology
- Familiarity with the most popular Greek myths
- Observing how the key elements of great literature are interwoven into these famous Greek myths, including characterization, plot, satire, tone, antonyms/synonyms, point of view, setting

Attitudes

The Ancient Greeks developed these myths to explain the mysteries of the world around them and give meaning to their lives. Students will gain and appreciation of the following:

- How myths affect our beliefs
- How beliefs affect our behavior
- How the use of imagination makes life more interesting

Critical Thinking Skills

- Imagining
- Categorizing
- Problem solving
- Comparing/contrasting
- Making inferences

Cooperative Learning Skills

- Participating in group projects
- Making decisions in a group
- Helping one another succeed through peer teaching (jigsaw activities)

Materials Required for Mighty Mythology

- Need a VCR and a tape recorder/player for all five mornings
- *Clash of the Titans,* movie in VCR or DVD format presented to class in selected segments throughout the week
- Library books for further mythology reference (see Resources on p. 126)
- Pull-down world maps to show locations of Greece and Italy
- Twenty sets of reproduced 20 teacher handouts for course syllabus, Greek, Roman myths, Climbing Mt. Olympus activities, and certificates, and bibliography
- Regular lead and colored pencils
- One presentation board for each student; or foam board and thumbtacks, or something similar
- Two packs of white construction paper; two packs of colored construction paper
- Brown butcher paper tracing paper; two packs of lined notebook paper
- One colored folder for each student's work (20)
- Rulers, markers, glue, crayons, tempera paints, brushes
- Twenty pairs of scissors stapler, staples, string, cord, five rolls of Scotch tape
- Styrofoam heads, colored yarn (brown, yellow, red-orange, black)
- Scraps of cloth or felt, old white sheets for togas
- Gold spray paint and six artificial leaf branches for laurel awards
- Newspaper and wheat paste for papier-mâché
- Popsicle sticks for stick or hand puppets
- Box of manila file folders

Monday:

Morning:	Afternoon:
Students watch first segment of *Clash of the Titans* movie **Opening Discussion:** • **What is a myth?** Overview of **Recurring themes** from around the world. • **Greek/Roman Creation Theories** • **Day 1 "Choosing 4 Teams"** • **Explain Contest Rules** At the beginning of the five-day session, the morning class is divided into four Olympic teams, with chosen names such as the famous Gods and Goddesses, the famous Olympic Heroes, famous Enchanted Creatures, and famous Greek Monsters. Daily, each team selects two different Greek stories from a list of 24 famous Greek/Roman myths to read and critique. • See **Overview** for list of Greek myths to choose from. • Each team chooses first two myths to work on.	**Preliminary discussion Questions:** • **Who were the Ancient Greeks?** • **What was Ancient Greece?** **Individual Activity Choices:** **Students choose from the following activities to complete as many "special" mythology projects as class time permits:** • Dioramas, paintings or drawings of a favorite Greek or Roman myths; the Trojan War (Trojan Horse); scenes/models of everyday Greek or Roman life, dress; construct a Greek or Roman ship or temple • Reader's Theatre in "Greek costume" or puppet theatre performances, discovering Greek origins for everyday words • Head busts of your favorite Greek god, goddess, hero, heroine, or monster; or papier-mâché figures • Greek/Roman fresco painting • Stories and pictures of the constellations and planets and how they received Greek/Roman names

Tuesday:

Morning:	Afternoon:
Students watch Second segment of *Clash of the Titans* movie **Opening Discussion:** • **The Greek/Roman gods: Olympians and others** • **Day 2: Explaining Part 1 of the mythology/questionnaire** • Teams choose their next **two** myths • A questionnaire is provided for each myth that assists each team in listing the greatest number of heroic deeds/quests, the slaying of evil creatures or monsters, important moral lessons learned from the story, or immortals performing a deed of mercy or kindness for mortals, that can be found in that story. (Each detail is worth 10 points). Students add handouts to their Mythology Notebook.	Preliminary discussion Questions: • **Where was Ancient Greece?** • **When was Ancient Greece?** **Individual Activity Choices:** Students choose from the following activities to complete as many special mythology projects as class time permits: • Dioramas, pictures and stories of favorite Greek, Roman myths; the Trojan War (Trojan Horse); scenes/models of everyday Greek/ Roman life; construct a Greek or Roman ship or temple • Readers' Theatre in Greek/Roman costume or puppet theatre performances; discovering Greek origins for everyday words • Head busts of favorite Greek/Roman god, goddess, hero, heroine, monster; papier-mâché figures • Greek/Roman fresco painting • Stories, pictures of constellations, planets; how they received Greek/Roman names

Wednesday:

Morning:	Afternoon:
Students watch third segment of _Clash of the Titans_, movie **Opening Discussion:** Famous Greek/Roman Monsters • **Day 3: "Explaining Part 2 of the Mythology/Questionnaire"** • Teams select their 3rd set of myths to review • Each "myth questionnaire" must also include a short profile of the main Greek/Roman god and Olympian hero that appears in the story and include a description of each character's origin and unique powers. • Students add handouts to their Mythology Notebook.	**Preliminary discussion Questions:** • **Give examples of how** language, science, literature/poetry, theatre are descended from these Greek/Roman civilizations. **Individual Activity Choices:** Students choose from the following activities to complete as many mythology projects as class time permits: • Dioramas, pictures and stories of favorite Greek/ Roman myths; the Trojan War (Trojan Horse); scenes of everyday Greek, Roman life and dress; construction of a Greek/Roman ship or temple • Readers' Theatre in Greek costume or Puppet Theatre performances • Research into Greek origins for everyday words • Head busts of favorite Greek god, goddess, hero, heroine, or monster; or papier-mâché figures • Greek/Roman Fresco painting • Stories and pictures of the constellations and planets and how they received Greek/Roman names

Thursday:

Morning:	Afternoon:
Students watch fourth segment of _Clash of the Titans_ movie **Opening Discussion:** **Greek and Roman History, Geography (maps) and Culture** **Day 4: "Explaining Part 4 of the Mythology/Questionnaire"** • Each team will also daily submit four _"the answer island matching "questions"_ from their myths to insert into a computerized Mighty Mythology _Jeopardy_ game grid, to be played by the entire class on the last day of class. • Students add myth handouts to their Mythology Notebook. **Planning for Day 5 Banquet** • Each team plans authentic Greek and Roman foods of the era that they will bring to the Friday afternoon banquet celebration	**Preliminary discussion Questions:** **Give examples of how art, architecture, and love of sports (the Olympics) are descended from these Greek/Roman civilizations.** **Individual Activity Choices:** **Students choose from following activities to complete as many special mythology projects as class time permits:** • Dioramas, pictures and stories of favorite Greek or Roman Myths; the Trojan War (Trojan Horse); scenes of everyday Greek, Roman, or Norse life and dress; construction of a Greek/ Roman Ship or temple • Readers' Theatre in Greek costume or Puppet Theatre performances • Research into Greek origins for everyday words • Head busts of favorite Greek god, goddess, hero, heroine, or monster; papier-mâché figures

(Continued)

Thursday: (Continued)

Morning:	Afternoon:
• Students devote time to designing their Greek or Roman costume for the Friday afternoon culminating banquet and presentation of projects.	• Greek/Roman fresco painting • Stories and pictures of the constellations and planets and how they received Greek/Roman names

Friday:

Morning:	Afternoon:
Students watch final segment of *Clash of the Titans* movie **Opening Discussion:** **What are the recurring themes within the myths?** **finale Culmination activities"** • Teams submit their final point totals for contest and determine the "winning team." • Students add final myth handouts to complete their Mythology Notebook. • Students assemble all the answer/question squares for Mythology Jeopardy Game contest to conducted by the four teams in the afternoon. • Students complete final planning for the afternoon presentations and banquet.	**Culminating activity:** (Parents and students from other home rooms attending) • Students arrange their presentation booths, the banquet tables, Greek/Roman decorations, and food. • Students and parents attend the banquet celebration dressed in student-made Greek and Roman costumes. • Students conduct presentations of all the special projects that they have completed during this Mighty Mythology week. • Students vote on their favorite myth of the entire week. **Presentation of Final Awards for "Mighty Mythology Contest"** • Members of winning team are awarded Greek Laurel Wreath. • All four teams play Mythology *Jeopardy* Game!

REFERENCES AND RESOURCES FOR MIGHTY MYTHOLOGY

Adams, E. (1999). *Ancient Greece.* Ft. Atkinson, WI: Edupress.

Connolly, P. (1999). *The ancient Greece of Odysseus.* New York: Oxford University Press.

Connolly, P., & Solway, A. (2001). *Ancient Rome.* New York: Oxford University Press.

Edgar, F. (1994). *Greek and Roman mythology.* Greensboro, NC: Carson-Dellosa.

Hamilton, E. (1999). *Mythology.* New York: Grand Central.

Keenan, S. (2000). *Gods, goddesses, and monsters, an encyclopedia of world mythology.* New York: Scholastic.

Keller, M. J. (1995). *Ancient Greece activity book.* Ft. Atkinson, WI: Edupress.

Keller, M. J. (1995). *Ancient Rome activity book.* Ft. Atkinson, WI: Edupress.

Tames, R. (2002). *Find out about ancient Greece.* London: Anness.

Peach, S., Millard, A., & Tingay, P. (2004). *Greeks.* London: Usborne.

Posner, P. (2003). *Gods and goddesses from Greek myths.* Grand Rapids, MI: School Speciality Children's.

Schneer, C. H., Harryhausen, R., & Palmer, J. (Producers), & Davis, D. (Director). (1981). *Clash of the Titans* [Motion picture]. United States: United Artists Films.

Thompson, C. E. (1999). *Glow in the dark constellations: A field guide for young stargazers.* New York: Penguin Young Readers Group.

FOLLOWING THE PASSION OF A GIFTED UNDERACHIEVER

By Drew Shilhanek

MAIN CONCEPT

This unit emerged from the need of an underachieving gifted child. By designing a course of study around the advanced knowledge and interests of one gifted student, teachers can extend the learning of the whole class and give that student experience in sharing expertise and determining the direction of her or his own learning. The process described here takes place in the context of an imaginary world conference after World War II. Students explore significant technological advancements in the military and assume the roles of different countries as they explore, debate, and propose strategies for safeguarding the world from future large-scale threats.

LEVEL

This content works best for intermediate through upper grades, but the concept applies to any level.

APPLICATION

History, geography, politics, government, literacy (reading, writing), research.

DESCRIPTION

I teach at a school for the gifted called Quest Academy (see Chapter 3). One of my most successful units came during the 2006–2007 school year. I had a very bright student who didn't seem able to produce quality homework on a consistent basis. I knew the talent and desire were there, but there was a disconnect between working on projects and producing quality finished projects.

Finding the Passion

I approached this student with an idea about a unit on World War II. This student was an expert in military history, especially during the World War II period. I asked him if he wanted to create a unit with me, and he agreed. It looked as if this student was quite excited, but I was a little apprehensive. After all, he had not shown a propensity to follow through, even when the excitement seemed to be there. The next morning, he showed me notes that he had scratched out on paper, and I loved it.

Simple Approach

I structured the unit to be as simple and straightforward as possible. We wanted to look at the technological advancements of six different categories of war in order to call a world conference to discuss, examine, and propose a way to prevent another war like World War II. The assessment was going to look as if we were trying to create something like the United Nations, but we wanted to create an organization with the best technology to diminish the possibility of another world war from breaking out.

Research and Deliberation

This student proposed different advancements in military technology in six different areas. Students were to gather as countries to research these advancements in infantry, tank warfare, air warfare, submarine warfare, D-Day, and the Japanese front in terms of the technology used to defeat the opponent. Students presented their findings as they gathered in countries like the United States, France, Russia, Great Britain, Italy, and France, and shared what they suffered through the most during the war.

Proposals

We then took a student from each country and gathered them with delegates from the other countries and formed six different treaty groups. Groups then wrote proposals to create an organization that would attempt to prevent another world war from happening. This was an end-of-the-year project with eighth graders who were ready to graduate. Grades had already been assigned, but these students were so invested in the process that they continued to be highly productive to the end. The gifted student with whom I had created this unit had such a look of pride and joy on his face as he helped shepherd the class through the deliberation process.

From this experience I have become convinced that we as teachers should engage students in any fashion we can find to motivate and inspire them. This student was more inspired than I had ever seen him, and he ably led the other students. He was our reference point if students didn't know some of the information. He moderated the conference and kept it moving quickly. This was such a high note for this student to end his time at Quest Academy. I hope that he can draw upon the experience and become equally successful in high school.

For those interested, I have included an outline of the unit:

Project: World War II Postwar Summit

Objective: To research major battles and the different means of military uses that fueled World War II in order to proceed into the future in order to prevent another world war of this magnitude.

Students will understand the following:

1. Key battles, strategies, and technologies that changed the face of war

2. The cost of fighting in terms of lives and the economic aspect

3. How America pushed itself to advance technologies, improve weaponry, and use industries at home to become more of a superpower and prove that it could change the course of the war and the world

Goal: Six of the major players in World War II will analyze different aspects of World War II from airpower, naval power, tank warfare, infantry, and two battles on different fronts. These countries will present their findings at a World Summit in order to find a way to maintain peace throughout the world for many years to come.

Countries: United States, France, Russia, Great Britain, Italy, and France.

1. Countries will analyze the different aspects of World War II and will present their findings to the World Summit.

2. After countries present their findings, representatives from each country will form six different groups to write a proposal for the world to move into the future relatively assured of peace.

Research Topics:

Group 1: Air Power

United States versus Germany

Bombing fortress in Europe

Compare fighter power

United States versus Japan

Fighter power

Kamikaze

Little Boy (Nuke)

Group 2: Naval Power

Pearl Harbor

United States versus Japan Aircraft Carriers

German U-boat Wolf Packs

United States versus German naval numbers/power

United States versus Japan naval numbers/power

Group 3: Tank Warfare

German tank power/numbers

Panzers versus Tigers

Blitzkrieg

American tanks

Japanese Tanks

Russian tank hordes

Antitank technology

Group 4: Infantry

German infantry numbers/power

United States infantry numbers/power

Japanese infantry numbers/power

Weapons technology

Machine gun strategy

Improvement from WWI strategy

Group 5: D-Day

Omaha Beach

Casualties/numbers

Importance/plan/events

Strategies

Utah Beach

Casualties/numbers

Importance of strategy/events

Airborne landings

Initial landing numbers

St. Mere Eglise

Other important events

Group 6: Japanese Front

Midway

Naval fight

Ground fight

Iwo Jima

Initial landing

Lasting through the battle

Japanese surrender

Evaluation:

1. Countries will research different aspects of war and will present their findings to the World Summit.
   a. Each person will have his/her written research.
   b. Each country will present its findings.
   c. Each student will hand in his/her research and note card from the presentation.

2. Each country will create an original proposal in order to provide an environment of peace.

PRIMARY SOURCE LEARNING: THINKING THROUGH THE PUZZLES LIFE CREATED

By Rhonda Clevenson

MAIN CONCEPT

Millions of digital primary sources available on the Internet invite students to become historians who use these resources to articulate history through new discoveries instead of merely memorizing someone else's story of the past. These digital resources afford students the opportunity to work like professionals who examine real historical documents. This task demands a high level of literacy and critical thinking skills to construct an interpretation within the historical context.

LEVEL

Intermediate to upper grades.

APPLICATION

History, geography, literacy, higher-level thinking, research skills.

DESCRIPTION

Primary sources are particularly useful for challenging students because each source is both a puzzle by itself and one piece of the topic under study—a much larger puzzle. Multiple correct answers, misleading or incomplete information, and creator bias make primary source learning messy and complex in the classroom, much like the real problems we experience in our daily lives. Thinking through the primary source puzzles that life has created is particularly suited to gifted learners, offering an opportunity to seek novel solutions that lead to unknown questions.

However, obstacles affecting teacher use of this treasure trove of digital historical documents often prevent efficient and effective use of these resources in the classroom. Problems include finding the time to sift through the millions of available digital resources, arranging the items into meaningful groups related to the required curriculum standards, and leading students through a complex inquiry process given the small amount of time allocated for each topic in the school day. These obstacles of search time, resource organization, and efficient inquiry routines are being addressed through a Web site, http://www.PrimarySourceLearning.org, created by classroom teachers and sponsored by the Library of Congress Teaching With Primary Sources Northern Virginia Partnership. The Web site enables teachers to build on searches for digital primary sources started by other classroom teachers, create matrix groupings of primary sources based on curriculum standards, and find instructional materials that use thinking routines to guide student inquiry.

The strategies outlined in this contribution—developed by classroom teachers—are designed to effectively use primary sources to deepen student understanding of the curriculum, particularly with gifted learners. It will also focus on using a matrix to group primary sources for student exploration and leading students through an inquiry process to interpret the primary source.

Organizing Primary Sources Into a Matrix

Students are asked to compare two primary sources or use a small group of primary sources to corroborate ideas presented in a textbook or discovered through research in the classroom. These useful strategies can be even more effective when the teacher asks students to organize the sources into a matrix or table. The horizontal rows might represent different types of facts or concepts that students must know for standardized tests, and the vertical rows might represent themes, persons, places, or periods. The matrix as a whole, considering both the vertical columns and the horizontal columns, challenges students to consider a large-scale idea that is central to the discipline.

Consider the example matrix for explorers where students investigate the question, "What are patterns of exploration including the preparation, process, and consequences?" Throughout the lesson, the teacher asks students to use their developing ideas about exploration patterns from working with the historical sources to support or challenge the understanding goal, "Exploration leads to change."

Organizing the historical documents into a matrix of vertical and horizontal themes creates grouping opportunities for learners such as a small group becoming an expert in a vertical column (individual explorers like Columbus or Ponce de Leon) and then regrouping students by horizontal rows that represent large-scale themes (motivation, obstacles, or achievements considering several different explorers). In a discussion, students use evidence from the primary sources to support their ideas about exploration and change.

Given the complete set of primary sources from the matrix in small four-by-six postcard-type print outs, students can use Robert Marzano's (2001) *Strategies That Work* idea of sorting the primary sources. Students identify similarities and differences to group and then regroup the primary sources using different criteria. Student observations of the items and creative ways to connect new ideas increase with each sort. They apply knowledge and use critical thinking skills through the process of generating labels and describing the criteria for the sorts. The matrix of primary sources may also be used to structure the process of writing research papers by asking students to support their thesis with evidence from the images in a row or column. The teacher differentiates by organizing particular rows or columns to have sources more abstractly related to the topic under study or sources that require more or less academic vocabulary and background knowledge to interpret.

Placing primary sources in a matrix adds dimension to the topic under study. The resources are put in a context of connections where patterns and relationships begin to emerge. When students build a matrix instead of putting resources in a group, they are required to use creative thinking, apply knowledge, and practice media literacy skills to determine which source is the best fit considering not only the topic but also specific relationships between aspects of the topic identified by the vertical and horizontal columns.

Inquiry Routines

Students may choose one resource from the matrix to examine carefully through an inquiry process. *The inquiry process of learning with primary*

Explorers Chart

**Exploration leads to change. What are patterns of exploration
including the preparation, process, and the consequences?**

Themes	Christopher Columbus	Juan Ponce de Leon	Jacques Cartier	Christopher Newport
Point of departure	1	2	3	4
Motivation	5	6	7	8
Obstacles 1	9	10	11	12
Obstacles 2		14	15	16
Accomplishments	17	18	19	20
Consequences	21	22	23	24

sources involves both literacy and understanding. Students use media literacy strategies to evaluate primary sources with regard to the research question, considering their relevance and reliability. Literacy skills help students comprehend the primary sources, while understanding and knowledge enable them to interpret. An inquiry process teaches students to resist the impulse to draw hasty conclusions and to allow more time for thoughtful exploration. There are many published tools available to support students in analyzing primary sources. Often, these handouts begin by asking students to record objective observations of the primary source, and then they guide students in making inferences or subjective observations. Examples might be for students to describe the composition, content, bibliographic information, and possible purpose of the primary sources and then use background knowledge to connect this information to their historical context.

Thinking routines (Tishman, Perkins, & Jay, 1995) differ from analysis tools in that three memorable student actions guide inquiry with or without a handout. These routines help students observe and think about all types of media sources before drawing conclusions and are very practical as students encounter primary sources both in the classroom and in their daily life. The three verbs used in a routine may vary to encourage different types of thinking and different viewpoints. An example three-step routine might be called *Making Connections.* The three-step process for students would be *look, ask,* and *use.* For more advanced students, the vocabulary *examine, question,* and *apply* can be used. The following description and example show how a thinking routine might be used in a classroom.

Step 1: Look Carefully and Connect to Personal Experiences.

The first impulse that learners have when looking at primary sources is to connect what they see to their previous experiences. Learners can relate to primary sources in many different ways. Perhaps the relationship is as simple as the learner has experience with the media type. For example, having taken a picture or written a letter in his or her own life, the learner may have visited the location where the primary source was created, or the learner may be able to connect background knowledge about the subject or period to the source. This process of making connections to previous knowledge and experiences is one of the most important factors in building understanding. So the first action in the thinking routine students take is, "Look carefully to determine how I connect with this source."

Step 2: Ask Questions and Connect to Knowledge

In this step, learners examine the source closely and refer to evidence in the source to support observations. Digital primary sources can be enlarged or cropped to look closely at one section at a time. The second action is to ask questions including "What do I know about this source?" "What don't I know about this source?" and "How can I find out more about this source?" Students may conduct research and/or read a textbook and then return to the primary source to use their new learning to see more details in the source.

Step 3: Use Thinking and Connect to Understanding

Now that some questions have been asked and answered about the source, students extend their thinking to determine how the source might be useful in their study of a topic. The final student actions include considering "What might this source tell me about the topic under study?" "How might this source confirm, challenge, or change my thinking about the topic under study?" "How might this exploration connect to other subjects that I am studying?" and "How can I use my thinking about this source to pursue these questions in my next research project?"

An example. After sorting the images into categories of Civil War and American Revolution, students select one image to examine. The teacher practices the strategy of *look, question, ask* with students as a large group. The students look for connections among their own knowledge and experiences and the image. They pose questions for thinking and further research. Finally, they use this thinking to determine how their knowledge about war has been confirmed, challenged, and/or changed by exploring historical sources, and they raise research questions that they would like to pursue in the future. The thinking routine can be short, taking only a few minutes using learner background knowledge, or it can be extended to include research at the library or on the Internet. Most important, students can be encouraged to *look, ask, use* whenever they see media sources both in school and at home.

Primary sources are fragments of life that survived. Whether the source is a picture, letter, map, sound recording, or oral history, the source does not come with a single correct interpretation. Primary sources inspire questions such as "What is this?" "Why was it made?" and "What might this tell me?" Primary sources are real mysteries from life that learners with all levels of expertise can solve. For gifted learners, the benefits of teaching with primary sources include raising curiosity, relating learning experiences and problem solving to real life, and promoting the habits of questioning, reflecting, and making connections.

Just one quick glance at a primary source won't be enough for any learner. New discoveries can be found each time a learner refers to the source. The sorting of sources into a matrix and using a thinking routine to guide exploration will help learners make connections between their knowledge and experiences to build understanding of a topic. Most important, the past is in a constant process of being interpreted in new ways. Because there are undiscovered and multiple correct answers, when

American Revolution or Civil War

Wars demonstrate both continuity and change.

Compare and contrast aspects of the Civil War and American Revolution.

	Civil War		Revolution	
Motivations	1	2	3	4
Leaders	5	6	7	8
Maps/places	9	10	11	12
Technology	13	14	15	16
Consequences	17	18	19	20

interpreting primary sources, gifted learners are presented with an opportunity to justify their thinking and to use their own knowledge and experiences to develop unique interpretations that can contribute to our understanding of history. The challenge of solving the mysteries that life created will inspire all learners and teachers too.

REFERENCES

Marzano, R., Pickering, D., & Pollock, J. (2001). *Classroom instruction that works: Research-based strategies for increasing student achievement.* Alexandria, VA: Association of Supervision and Curriculum Development.

Tishman, S., Perkins, D. W., & Jay, E. (1995). *The thinking classroom: Learning and teaching in a culture of thinking.* Boston: Allyn & Bacon.

Image Credits Explorers

All images from the Library of Congress Web site (LOC.gov)

Central Intelligence Agency. (1988). United Kingdom, administrative divisions. Library of Congress: American Memory, Map Collections: 1500–2004.

Central Intelligence Agency. (1974). Spain. 4–74. Library of Congress: American Memory, Map Collections: 1500–2004.

Cooley, S. A . (1861–1869). St. Augustine, Florida. Catholic Church. Library of Congress: Prints & Photographs, Civil War Photographs.

Delano, J. (1941). A field of tobacco in the area being taken over by the Army in Caroline County, Virginia. Library of Congress: American Memory, America from the Great Depression to World War II: Photographs from the FSA and OWI, ca. 1935–1945.

Frank and Frances Carpenter Collection. (1900–1923). An iceberg near head of Trinity Bay, Newfoundland. Library of Congress: Prints & Photographs, Carpenter (Frank and Frances) Collection.

Gutiérrez, D. (1562). Americae sive qvartae orbis partis nova et exactissima descriptio/avtore Diego Gvtiero Philippi Regis Hisp. etc. Cosmographo; Hiero. Cock excvde 1562; Hieronymus Cock excude cum gratia et priuilegio 1562. Library of Congress: American Memory, Map Collections: 1500–2004.

Jefferson, T. (1606–1737). Virginia, 1606–92, Charters of the Virginia Company of London; Laws; Abstracts of Rolls in the Offices of State. Library of Congress: American Memory, The Thomas Jefferson Papers at the Library of Congress.

Jefferys, T. (1775). A new map of Nova Scotia, and Cape Breton Island with the adjacent parts of New England and Canada, composed from a great number of actual surveys; and other materials regulated by many new astronomical observations of the longitude as well as latitude; by Thomas Jefferys, geographer to the King. Library of Congress: American Memory, Map Collections: 1500–2004.

Keystone View Company. (c1899). Laliberte's fur parlor—the finest in the world, Quebec, Canada. Library of Congress: Prints & Photographs, Sterograph Cards.

L. Prang & Co. (1893). The First voyage. Library of Congress: Prints & Photographs, Popular Graphic Arts.

Le Moyne de Morgues, J. (1591). Floridae Americae provinciae recens & exactissima descriptio auctorè Iacobo le Moyne cui cognomen de Morgues, qui Laudonierum, altera Gallorum in eam prouinciam nauigatione comitat est, atque adhibitis aliquot militibus ob pericula, regionis illius interiora & maritima diligentissimè lustrauit, & exactissimè dimensus est, obseruata etiam singulorum fluminum inter se distantia, ut ipsemet redux Carolo. IX. Galliarum regi, demonstrauit. Library of Congress: American Memory, Map Collections: 1500–2004.

Maraldi, J. D. (1744). Nouvelle carte qui comprend les principaux triangles qui servent de fondement à la description géometrique de la France: levée par ordre du Roy/par Messrs. Maraldi & Cassini de Thury, de l'Academie Royale des Sciences; trace d'après les Mesures, et gravé par Dheulland; Aubin scripsit. Library of Congress: American Memory, Map Collections: 1500–2004.

Smith, J. (1606). Virginia/discovered and described by Captayn John Smith, 1606; graven by William Hole. Library of Congress: American Memory, Map Collections: 1500–2004.

Unknown. Columbus sneered at in the council of Salamanca. Library of Congress: Prints & Photographs, Popular Graphic Arts.

Unknown. (1910–1930). [European man in metal helmet firing on Indians while other Indians watch]. Library of Congress: Prints & Photographs, Detroit Publishing Company Collection.

Unknown. (c1502). In [Christopher Columbus] [Códice Diplomatico Columbo-Americano] Vellum. [Seville, ca. 1502]. Library of Congress: Exhibitions, 1492: An Ongoing Voyage.

 Unknown. (1502). Columbus' Coat of Arms. Library of Congress: Exhibitions, 1492: An Ongoing Voyage.

 Unknown. (1629). How they took him prisoner in the Oaze, 1607. Library of Congress: America's Library, Meet Amazing Americans.

 Unknown. (1768). A view of Miramichi, a French settlement in the Gulf of St. Laurence, destroyed by Brigadier Murray detached by General Wolfe for that purpose, from the Bay of Gaspe Vue de Miramichi establissement Francois dans le Golfe de St. Laurent, détruit par le Brigadier Murray, détaché a cet effet de la Baye de Gaspé, par le Général Wolfe/ drawn on the spot by Capt. Hervey Smyth; etch'd by Paul Sandby; retouched by P. Benazech. Library of Congress: Prints & Photographs.

 Unknown. (c1850). Jacques Cartier, his first interview with the Indians at Hochelaga now Montreal in 1535. Library of Congress: Prints & Photographs, Popular Graphic Arts.

 Unknown. (c1893). Statue of Columbus [and] the Cathedral. Library of Congress: Prints & Photographs.

 Waldseemuller, M. (1513). American Geographical Sites In Martin Waldseemuller. [Ptolemaeus] Geographiae Opus Novissima Traductione. Library of congress: Exhibitions, 1492: An Ongoing Voyage.

 Wolcott, M. P. (1939). Orange grove near Lakeland, Florida. Library of Congress: Prints & Photographs.

Image Credits Civil War Versus the American Revolution

All items from the Library of Congress Web site (LOC.gov)

Bamberger, S. (1861). Map of battles on Bull Run near Manassas, 21st of July 1861: on the line of Fairfax & Prince William Co[unti]es in Virginia, fought between the forces of the Confederate States and of the United States of America/made from observation by Solomon Bamberger. Library of Congress: American Memory, Map Collections: 1500–2004.

Berger, D. (1784). 1. General Washington's reitende leibgarde 2. die independent company, chef general Washington/D. Chodowiecki id; D. Berger sc. Library of Congress: Prints & Photographs.

Bernard, E. (1783). "View of the Attack on Bunker's Hill with the Burning of Charlestown." Library of Congress: Exhibitions, John Bull & Uncle Sam: Four Centuries of British-American Relations.

Bonne, R. (1788). Les États Unis de l'Amérique septentrionale, partie occidentale. Par M. Bonne, ingenieur hydrographe de la marine. André, sculp. Library of Congress: American Memory, The American Revolution and Its Era: Maps and Charts of North America and the West Indies, 1750–1789.

Claypoole and Dunlap. (1787). Broadside report of the Committee of Style. Library of Congress: Exhibitions, American Treasures of the Library of Congress.

Currier & Ives. (1861). Bombardment of Fort Sumter, Charleston Harbor: 12th & 13th of April, 1861. Library of Congress: Prints & Photographs, Popular Graphic Arts.

Leizalt, B. F. (1780). Combat memorable entre le Pearson et Paul Jones. Augsburg: 1779 1780. Library of Congress: Exhibitions, John Bull & Uncle Sam: Four Centuries of British-American Relations.

Mahon, C. (1861). Map of the alluvial region of the Mississippi Prepared to accompany the report of Capt. A. A. Humphreys and Lieut H. L. Abbot, Corps. of Top'l. Engrs. U.S.A. to the Bureau of Topl. Engrs., War Dept. Drawn by Chs. Mahon. Library of Congress: American Memory, Civil War Maps.

Mitchell, J. (1782). A Map of the British Colonies in North America with the Roads, Distances, Limits and Extent of the Settlements. Library of Congress: Exhibitions, John Bull & Uncle Sam: Four Centuries of British-American Relations.

Mondhare. (1781). Reddition de l'Armee angloises commandee par Mylord Comte de Cornwallis aux armees combinees des Etats Unis de l' Amerique et de France aux ordres des Generaux Washingtonb et de Rochambeau a Yorck Touwn et Glocester dans la Virginie, le 19 October 1781. Library of Congress: American Memory, Map Collections: 1500–2004.

Ned, O. (n.d.). Rally round the cause boys. Air- Battle cry of Freedom. Library of Congress: American Memory, America Singing: Nineteenth-Century Song Sheets.

Newberry, E. (1789). "Boston Tea Party." Library of Congress: Exhibitions, John Bull & Uncle Sam: Four Centuries of British-American Relations.

Paris, Esnauts et Rapilly. (1781). Carte de la partie de la Virginie ou l'armée combinée de France & des États-Unis de l'Amérique a fait prisonnière l'Armée anglaise commandée par Lord Cornwallis le 19 October. 1781, avec le plan de l'attaque d'York-town & de Glocester. Levée et dessinée sur les lieux par ordre des officiers genx. de l'Armée française & américaine. Library of Congress: American Memory, Map Collections: 1500–2004.

Revere, P. (1770). The bloody massacre perpetrated in King Street Boston on March 5th 1770 by a party of the 29th Regt. Library of Congress: Prints & Photographs, Cartoon Prints, American.

Reynolds, W.C. (c.1856). Reynolds's political map of the United States, designed to exhibit the comparative area of the free and slave states and the territory open to slavery or freedom by the repeal of the Missouri Compromise. Library of Congress: American Memory, Map Collections: 1500–2004.

Unknown. (1889). Battle of the Monitor and Merrimac. Library of Congress: Prints & Photographs, Popular Graphic Arts.

Unknown. (1880–1890). Ho for Kansas! Brethren, Friends, & Fellow Citizens: I feel thankful to inform you that the real estate and Homestead Association, will leave here the 15th of April, 1878, In pursuit of Homes in the Southwestern Lands of America. . . . Library of Congress: American Memory, African American Odyssey.

Unknown. (Between 1865–1867). Thirty-Six Star United States Flag. Library of Congress: Exhibitions, American Treasures of the Library of Congress.

Unknown. (c1880). [Ulysses S. Grant, head-and-shoulders portrait, facing left]. Library of Congress: Prints & Photographs.

Unknown. (c1904). Lee and his general. Library of Congress: Prints & Photographs, Popular Graphic Arts.

WESTWARD EXPANSION!

By Carol Sandberg Howe

MAIN CONCEPT

Students research diagrams to build their own three-dimensional Conestoga wagon and create a large, three-dimensional United States *floor* map with key landmarks to mark the progress of their wagons along the Oregon Trail. As students travel westward along the Oregon Trail in their *simulated* wagon train family, they learn to keep a *diary* of what it was like to leave family, home, friends, and familiar surroundings back east, and the lessons they learn while crossing the Western Great Plains toward a new life. Each student family learns to make *life and death* decisions about how to outfit (pack) their Conestoga wagons and how choose the best trail west. Along the trail, they face food shortages, disease, floods, droughts, blocked trails, broken wheels, the challenge of crossing turbulent rivers, and the high Sierra mountains— and Native Americans.

As students learn to make these survival decisions, they earn valuable *travel point* (miles) that determine which wagon train will be the first to reach Oregon and California. Students learn that sometimes pioneer dreams and plans ended in failure, and for the Native Americans (who already inhabited the West), the coming of the pioneers meant the end of their way of life.

LEVEL

Intermediate grades, but adaptable to other levels.

APPLICATION

History, geography, literacy, higher-level thinking, research skills, art, theater.

DESCRIPTION

Adventure! Excitement! Land! Freedom! The story of Westward Expansion during the mid-1800s is justly celebrated in story and song as the greatest adventure in our nation's history.

Can you imagine walking thousands of miles across the prairie, sometimes barefoot? Seeing grasshoppers eat an entire field of your corn after you've worked all summer on this crop and depend on it for your food supply for the winter? Crossing the Rocky Mountains without a map or a winter coat? Personal frontier diaries of the pioneers tell us that you had to do it on foot, not in a comfortable air-conditioned car. Life for boys and girls in the pioneer days was so different from our life today that it is hard to imagine how they survived. But with courage and determination, hundreds of thousands of these pioneers did. Through research, stories, and hands-on projects and role-play simulations, students will relive their remarkable true story.

Westward Expansion Key Events

As the pioneers travel farther and farther West, this unit addresses the Westward Expansion time line of (1840–1890) that covers key periods in American history, including the California Gold Rush (i.e., boomtowns and miners); the Homestead Act and prairie settlers (i.e., pioneer way of life, dress, and how to build a sod house); alternate means of travel west (i.e., the Pony Express, steamboat, stagecoach); the building of the Transcontinental Railroad (the Iron Horse); the Great Plains Indian Wars and Indian removal (i.e., famous Indians and the Plains Indians' threatened way of life versus advancing settlers and the U.S. Cavalry); cowboys, cattle drives, and ranch life (i.e., cowboy dress, care of horses, equipment); frontier towns and the era of famous lawmen and outlaws.

Westward Expansion!

Overview: Daily Activities

Throughout the unit, students will participate in a sequential activity of a simulated wagon train journey to Oregon and California (i.e., construct his or her own covered wagon and model passengers; determine which supplies are best to pack for the trip in a limited amount of wagon space; join one of four wagons departing from Independence, Missouri; establish a set of trail laws; and elect a wagon master to lead the train and enforce the laws. Students will daily calculate the number of travel miles earned by completed afternoon project points to determine the daily progress of each wagon train during the journey of some 2,000 miles. Students will maintain a personal journal diary of thoughts, feelings, and drawings to document their daily experiences and feelings, while on the trail.

Overview: Individual Projects

Students will choose from among the following Wild West projects to prepare as exhibits and class presentations as time permits during the course of the unit.

Note: Each of the following topics has been assigned an appropriate number of points:

the Gold Rush and miners

the Homestead Act and settlers

the building of the Transcontinental Railroad

Native American culture

the Great Plains Native American wars and Native American removal

the western prairie habitat with native plants and animals

cowboy/cowgirl culture

frontier towns

famous characters

lawmen and outlaws.

Students will record their progress on each project of their choice (with appropriate point value) in their Westward Ho! journal.

Course Objectives

Students in the "Westward Expansion" unit will learn the following:

Content/Knowledge

- **The Conestoga Wagon Train and the Oregon Trail**
  - Supplies that early pioneers took west
  - Reasons people risked everything to travel west
  - The effect of nature on pioneer life
  - Obstacles that pioneers faced
  - Possible fates that awaited early homesteaders along the trail
  - Impact upon indigenous Native Americans as pioneers pushed farther and farther west

- **Westward Movement Milestones**
  - Key innovations, inventions, and progress in travel and communication modes created by the westward movement
  - Key policies and historical events during the westward expansion timeline of 1840 to 1890 (the official closing of the American Frontier)

Attitudes (Analyses)

- Understanding the importance of the great migration west (i.e., the pioneers built much of the United States as we know it today)
- Appreciating the settlers' rugged way of life
- Valuing teamwork
- Understanding the role played by the government in creating such incentives as the Homestead Act, the Transcontinental Railroad, and so on
- Examining ethical questions on the impact of the pioneer push westward at the expense of Native Americans
- Valuing the impact of the human spirit (i.e., students discover the "true spirit of the American frontier" and the potential of creativity, loyalty, individual choice, individual responsibility and teamwork that made this country great is alive and well inside them today)

Critical Thinking Skills

- Imagining
- Categorizing
- Problem solving
- Decision making
- Comparing/contrasting
- Making inferences

Cooperative Learning Skills

- Participating in group projects
- Making decisions in a group
- Helping a group succeed by completing their part of the project
- Helping one another succeed through peer teaching

Creative Individual Project Skills (Comprehension/Application)
(refer to following pages for suggested activities)

Group and Individual Activities

Skills: Knowledge, Comprehension, Application	Skills: Application, Analysis, and Creative and Critical Thinking
Present first installment of film, *How the West Was Won!* (1962) Group discussion and research Week 1: Students research and record journals: • What is a pioneer? • Why did the pioneers want to "move West"? • Why did they call the Great Plains the "Great American Desert"? • How far away was Oregon and California; how long did the trip take? • Note: Student teams continue to daily contribute five question/answers "choices" from the above list to the "Westward Ho!" *Jeopardy* grid on computer. *Jeopardy* game to be played on last day of class. Group Activities: Week 1 • Build and paint your own covered wagon; make models of "family" members. • Join one of four wagon trains • Elect wagon master; discuss and establish trail laws. • Research/create a 3-D floor map with key "milestones" along the trail (Independence, Missouri (starting point); Platte River (rough crossing); Courthouse Rock; Chimney Rock; Scott's Bluff; Fort Laramie; Independence Rock; Sweetwater River (need to cross); Fort Bridger; Fort Hall; Snake River (need to cross); Fort Boise; Wind River Mountains; South Pass; Rocky Mountains (Continental Divide) (need to cross); Emigrant Hill; the Dalles; and final destinations of Oregon City and on to California. • Place covered wagons on 3-D floor map to move along during journey. Outfitting your wagon • Present second installment of film *How the West Was Won!* (1962) Week 2: Prompt: When covered wagons left their Independence, Missouri, starting point, every bit of space inside and outside of the 5 ft.-by-10 ft. wagon was used. Alas! Many favorite possessions still had to be left behind. • What is a "Conestoga or covered wagon"? Why were they called "prairie schooners?"	Individual Projects; Presentations Weeks 1–4 (Students have three weeks to complete projects of their choice.) Students may choose to write reports, journals, make costumes and "role-play" events or activities and/or design dioramas, papier-mâché, clay models, or drawings/paintings on the following topics of student choice: • California Gold Rush: Students research and simulate a miner's claim, explain how to record a claim, how to measure what gold was worth, demonstrate how to pan for gold, and allow classmates to try their luck. • Homestead Act: Students re-create the excitement of racing for land by creating a board game. • Prairie Settlers' Way of Life: Students may create dioramas, models, drawings/paintings, or role-play pioneer dress, pioneer food and cooking, and work and life on the prairie (e.g., building a sod house, making children's games, learning to square dance, and presenting famous prairie folk songs). • Pony Express, Stagecoach Travel Research/Create: models of each mode of travel and overland trail maps traveled by these modes of transportation; plot the shortest times and distances from one destination to another; develop a board game/race. Individual Projects, Presentations Weeks 1–4 continued (Students have three weeks to complete projects of their choice) • Building of the Transcontinental Railroad • Research/Analysis: (Student reports and class presentations) • What issues led to the building of the Transcontinental Railroad?

Skills: Knowledge, Comprehension, Application	Skills: Application, Analysis, Creative and Critical Thinking
<ul><li>What is a "Wagon Train?" A "Wagon Master"? "A Scout"?</li><li>What did pioneers use as a "guide" for materials and supplies needed for the trip and for what lay ahead on the trail?</li><li>Compare and Discuss the Oregon Trail, Santa Fe Trail, Old Spanish Trail as possible alternate routes. Which trail was the most direct route?</li><li>Note: Student teams continue to daily contribute five question/answers to the "Westward Ho!" *Jeopardy* grid on computer. *Jeopardy* game to be played on last day of class.</li></ul>Outfitting Your Wagon!<ul><li>Journal Page: *To be completed as an Individual or Group Exercise with the rest of your wagon train members as needed* Step 1: Shopping for Supplies: Read Directions and Fill in the Journal Chart provided with your food and supply choices for the trip. Remember: Your wagon can only hold about 2,500 lbs. of food, equipment, and supplies and your Pa's total budget for the entire trip is only $700.00. Step 2: Total Weight and Cost: Determine the total weight and cost of the food and supply items you have chosen for the trip and see how close you came to staying within budget while providing for the long-term needs of your family on the trip. Step 3: Pack your wagon: As time permits, color, cut out and paste small cardboard models of some of the food and supply items you have selected and place them in your covered wagon.</li><li>Journal Page: List some of your favorite things in your room. Then select one item from your special toys, books, records, etc. and tell why you chose that "one special item" to take with you.</li></ul>Week 3: present third installment of film, *How the West Was Won!* (1962) the Wagon Train Journey Students will begin reading some of their "Westward Ho!" Journal pages aloud to the class. Class Discussion Questions:	<ul><li>Who were the two companies that competed in the race to connect the railroad from East to West?</li><li>What routes did each company take? Describe the difficulties encountered in each route. Which route do you consider more difficult?</li><li>What nationalities and cultures came to help build the railroads? Were they treated fairly?</li><li>Why did Native Americans oppose and attack the Transcontinental Railroad project?</li><li>Create: (3-D diorama: simulate workers laying tracks)</li><li>Great Plains Wars and Native American Removal Research/Analysis:</li><li>What issues prompted the Native Americans to declare war on settlers?</li><li>What were some of the Native American tribes and their cultures?</li><li>What was the U.S. Cavalry?</li><li>What part did they play in the Great Plains Wars?</li><li>Who was George Armstrong Custer?</li><li>Who was Crazy Horse? What led up to Custer's Last Stand?</li><li>What political issues led to the policy of Native American Removal?</li><li>Do you think these issues were fair? Support your answers. Create: Students may create dioramas, models, drawings/ paintings, or role-play Native American culture in costume; famous Indians, all about the buffalo, and the Plains Indians' threatened way of life vs. advancing settlers and the U.S. Cavalry.</li></ul>Individual Projects; Presentations Weeks 1–4 continued (Students have four weeks to complete projects of their choice.)<ul><li>Cowboys, Cattle Drives, and Ranch Life</li></ul>

(Continued)

(Continued)

Skills: Knowledge, Comprehension, Application	Skills: Application, Analysis, Creative and Critical Thinking
• What item was used for an *alarm clock* on the western trail? • What were some of the pioneers' favorite *fast foods* on the trail? • What prairie *item* was commonly used for fuel? • What was the greatest danger to pioneers traveling on the westward movement trails? • What was the greatest danger to pioneers traveling on the westward movement trails? • Note: Student Teams contribute five of the above question/answers to the "Westward Ho!" *Jeopardy* grid on computer. *Jeopardy* game to be played on last day of class.	• Research Question: Where or in what country did cowboys originate? • Product Choices: Create dioramas, paintings, models or role-play; explore cowboy dress in costume; learn about equipment, horses; cowboy sayings, songs, and musical instruments; ranch and cattle drive duties (barbed wire, branding, etc.).

Friday: Present final installment of film, *How the West Was Won!* (1962)

Morning:	Afternoon:
Week 4: End of the Trail Opening Discussion: Students will continue reading some of their "Westward Ho!" Journal pages aloud to the class. Student Team Critique: • Students write a short definition describing each of the Westward Movement Groups. • Students use ballot to vote on their favorite "Wild West" time period and favorite Western that contributed the most to the Westward Expansion Movement. Choices include: • Pioneers/homesteaders/settlers • Gold Rush miners • Transcontinental Railroad builders • Native Americans • Cowboys • Native Americans • Lawmen/gunfighters • Teacher/moderator to determine the winning wagon train team based on points earned for the afternoon projects completed and award prizes. • Student teams play "Westward Ho!" Jeopardy Game. *(NOTE: The Jeopardy question grid was created daily on a computer grid with the answers to Westward Movement questions students were contributing all week.)*	Friday afternoon: Class Discussion/music/videos Topics: Frontier towns and famous lawmen and outlaws; and a history of American folk songs written during the westward expansion period. • Role-play/create dioramas/paintings for frontier towns and dress as and assume identity of famous frontier characters, lawmen and outlaws (e.g., Wild Bill Hickok, Jesse James, Wyatt Earp, Bat Masterson, The Cole Younger Gang, Gunfight at the OK Corral.) • Afternoon reserved for presentations of all the special projects that students have completed during this "Westward Ho!" week.

List of Materials Provided for "Westward Expansion!"

- Need a VCR and a tape recorder/player for all five mornings to present film, *How the West Was Won!* (1962)
- Library books, videos, magazine articles for further Westward Ho! reference
- Large U.S. map depicting Oregon Trail route
- Twenty sets of reproduced 20 teacher handouts for course syllabus
- Twenty project handouts for six Wild West activity areas (i.e., the Gold Rush, the Homestead Act and settlers; the Pony Express; the steamboat and stagecoach travel; the building of the Intercontinental Railroad, the Great Plains Indian wars and Indian removal; cowboys, cattle drives and ranches, frontier towns and famous lawmen and outlaws; and folk songs written during key periods of western expansion; and a bibliography)
- Twenty shoeboxes with lids, wire, muslin cloth, tape, brads, clothespins, cloth swatches, and paint for building/painting individual covered wagons
- Shoeboxes for student dioramas of the above topics
- Sand and pyrite for "panning for gold" experience
- Regular lead and colored pencils
- One presentation board for each student; or foam board and thumb tacks, or something similar
- Two packs of white construction paper, two packs of colored construction paper
- Brown butcher paper, tracing paper for making pioneer or Indian costumes
- Two packs of lined notebook paper for journal work
- One colored folder with folder tabs for each student's work (20)
- Rulers, markers, glue, crayons, tempera paints, brushes
- Modeling clay, Velcro, wall tack
- Large buttons and string
- Twenty pairs of scissors; stapler, staples
- String, cord, three Scotch Tape
- Newspaper, wheat paste for papier-mâché
- Popsicle sticks for stick or hand puppets

Resources for Westward Expansion! Unit

Baicker, K. (2002). *Primary sources teaching kit: The westward movement.* New York: Scholastic.

Connors, M. (1997). *Native American arts and cultures.* Huntington Beach, CA: Teacher Created Materials.

Erickson, P. (1997). *Daily life in a covered wagon.* New York: Penguin.

Ingoglia, G. (1991). *The big golden book of the Wild West: American Indians, cowboys, and the settling of the West.* New York: Western.

Johmann, C., & Rieth, E. (2000). *Going West! Journey on a wagon train to settle a frontier town.* Charlotte, VT: Williamson.

Kalman, B. (1998). *The wagon train (Life in the old west).* New York: Crabtree.

Levine, E. (1999). *If you traveled west in a covered wagon.* New York: Scholastic.

Lybarger, D., Fry, R., & Larsen, L. (1996). *Cowboys: Thematic unit.* Huntington Beach, CA: Teacher Created Materials.

Milliken, L. (1990). *Frontier American activity book.* Ft. Atkinson, WI: Edupress.

Milliken, L. (1990). *Native American activity book.* Ft Atkinson, WI: Edupress.

Murray, S. (2002). *Wild West (Eyewitness guides).* New York: Dorling Kindersley.

Newark, P. (1985). *Illustrated encyclopedia of the old west.* London: Carlton Books.

Oregon Trail. (2002). New York: Scholastic.

Pony Express: Grades 4–8. (2002), New York: Scholastic.

Stanley, D. (2001). *Roughing it on the Oregon Trail.* New York: HarperCollins.

Sterling, M. E. (1992). *Westward ho.* Huntington Beach, CA: Teacher Created Materials.

Stotter, M. (1999). *The wild west.* New York: Kingfisher Chambers Inc.

5

Science Strategies

For many gifted children, an interest in science begins with the natural world. As young children, they feel the rough texture of an oak tree and the smooth surface of the birch. They gather leaves from the maple, linden, apple, the mulberry, and elm and wonder how these differences came to be. On trips by the sea, they ask about the tides, examine mussel beds, and sketch seagulls hanging on the railing of a lobster boat. Parents frequently report the endless barrage of questions their children have about the natural world and how this has sent them traipsing to ecology centers, museums, and observatories to learn more.

As gifted children get older, they hold onto these early explorations as their first forays into science. Anything less than a process of active discovery and exploration is a disappointment and often the cause of gifted children losing interest in science. A highly gifted college student once confided that she had originally wanted to study zoology but later remembered "all those science classes I had to suffer through" and thought the better of it. She later regretted her decision, saying that she wished she hadn't let her early exposure to science turn her away from a field that, even in postgraduate years, still beckoned to her. She wrote,

> When I see zoologists work and when I look at how amateur scientists have developed their knowledge and expertise, I see such a great gulf between the science you get in dry textbook learning and the edge-of-your-seat science you have when there's this constant flow of learning from book to field to microscope to hypothesis to more research to more experiments—all leading to fundamental questions about how things work and why. That's the science I love.

Before examining the possibilities of creativity in the field of science, it's useful to review some of the processes involved. Gifted children in a hands-on science class

- observe (distinguishing characteristics, behaviors, patterns)
- question (what, why, where, how),
- explore relationships, interconnections (e.g., between planets, elements, species),
- hypothesize about cause and effect in phenomena through inductive reasoning,
- follow hunches and clues (by further observation, reading, experimenting, asking, imagining),
- analyze findings,
- synthesize data and formulate hypotheses (through a report, essay, art piece, science fiction story.

Now if we bring creativity into science, these processes expand as students

- observe one aspect of a species (e.g., feet, beaks, claws, leaves, rocks, mosses) that includes a rich diversity of individuals and do a sketch/painting/collage that expresses observations and insights;
- brainstorm new, creative ways to explore a question or find an answer (visualize a range of solutions; question assumptions that may not be valid in every circumstance; try methods used by pioneer scientists of the past);
- experiment with ideas, sources, and materials from other disciplines that bear on a topic or scientific mystery (e.g., interdisciplinary focus on birds and flying; explore interrelationships between planets through bodily movement that demonstrates actual planetary movement);
- test ideas through sketching and constructing models from different angles and perspectives;
- imagine being other species (a lizard, an insect, a bird) and explore the most notable characteristics through scientific inquiry, art, writing (e.g., write a creative writing piece describing the experience of having two eyes on opposite sides of the head that work independently of each other);
- assume the identity of Sherlock Holmes as a way of *detecting* and solving science puzzles. (What tools will you need for your investigation? What thinking strategies did Sherlock use to work through his problems? How can you differentiate between a clue and a detail of no consequence?);
- dramatize a scientific process as accurately as possible with breaks for each phase (the birth of a cloud, the eruption of a volcano, the orbit of the earth around the sun);

- design a flying machine based on the principles of lift and drag and on the experiences and sketches of former inventors (e.g., Leonardo da Vinci, Otto Lilienthal, Clement Ader, Wilbur and Orville Wright).

As explored in Chapter 2, creative processes need to be anchored in learning goals to ensure that students are continuing to grow in fundamental skill and concept areas of science. What are the skills and concepts you want to develop from unit to unit? For example, a major part of science is observation, but do students get enough opportunity to carefully observe flora, fauna, and various phenomena in settings that excite their curiosity? Students of all ability levels need many opportunities to develop their observation skills—to distinguish between species, perceive subtle variations in behavior, and note unique patterns and the circumstances attending them.

As you read the activities shared by the teachers in the following pages and make decisions about how to integrate creativity into science units, consider the following questions:

- What competencies in science will prepare my students for a lifetime of study and discovery?
- What is science really about for my kindergarteners, fifth graders, seventh graders?
- What *big-picture* processes are implied in the standards and curriculum for my grade, and how can creative activities tap into these?

Middle school science teacher Liz Martinez offers some useful general suggestions on how to put creativity to the best use in the science curriculum.

Thoughts on Science Education for Intermediate and Middle School Gifted and Talented Students

By Liz Martinez

Interest

Students have often told me that science is the most difficult yet at the same time one of the most interesting subjects they study in school—even if they don't like science. When asked why, most adolescents have responded to me with something similar to this:

It is a different way of thinking. You can't just memorize the information. Everything is related to each other. There are lots of ways to apply what has been learned. You have to work with other people who might not think the same way that you do. As soon as I think I have it figured out, I think of new questions. Science is all around in everything I do.

In this complex response lies the challenge, thrill, thirst, and need to offer our children quality science experiences.

Misconceptions

Perhaps one of the educator's primary responsibilities, which cannot be measured with standardized testing, is to help put the skip in the step of studying science. This can be done through employing a variety of creative methods. Many students, including gifted and talented, walk in with misconceptions about science. Understanding and locating where misconceptions exist allows the teacher to focus on appropriate content to begin teaching various concepts. This information can also help guide educators' decisions on how to help students apply the content in ways that engage interest, inspire the imagination, and create a hunger to know more.

Real Life

Threading a unit around current or real-life events that exist in the community lends relevance to the topic and hooks the students. For example, some areas were formerly a migration stop for geese, and instead have become a year-round habitat, creating conflict with humans. Another environmental issue is the amount of fertilizer used in suburban areas that eventually ends up in the Mississippi River or the TCE (trichloroethylene) that ends up in some communities' water supply. Other topics of interest can be where to build an amusement park, how to design a new ride, or whether or not a new medication should be tried. Any topic, regardless of its discipline (physics, chemistry, or biology), can become a starting point for engaging students.

Problem-Based Learning and Inquiry

Once a topic is identified, the next step is to create a problem that needs to be solved. Using a combination of PBL and inquiry allows students to gain not only the content but also the process skills that are so critical to their personal and educational futures. By presenting a question or problem to solve in the beginning, students see that they have a chance to make their own decision, based on the facts. They cherish this opportunity since according to them, "We are almost always told what to think in school."

This process also helps them start to decipher and hone the skill of what is pertinent and what is irrelevant. It is important to realize that with this process can come great frustration too, since the path is not always clear-cut, and they may run into dead ends.

Developmentally Appropriate

While developing activities and investigations to support and provide the hands-on portion of the learning, it is good to keep in mind that while these students may be gifted and talented, they are first children. Make sure to start with developmentally appropriate labs, moving from concrete to more abstract. Hold them accountable for their results and sharing these results. Avoid falling back on what I call the constant *wow factor*. (How many times should we ask students to put vinegar and baking soda together?)

Social Discipline

Science is a social discipline. Data need to be shared, analyzed, and interpreted by many. Again, this collaboration can sometimes be frustrating to the gifted child for many reasons. Often, they have been given different work to complete independently and have not had to work closely with others, or they have been unwillingly leaned on as group leaders since other students know the gifted students will do the work and want to do well. In this case, gifted learners should be grouped together to give them the stimulating experience of creative collaboration—sharing and debating hypotheses while they also search, test, reason, adapt, and innovate. A new scientific discovery, after all, may be just outside the door.

Varied Sources

Get students up and out of their seats. Push them past their comfort levels. Provide them a wide variety of materials to read on the topic, even ones with dissenting viewpoints. When teaching about nuclear technology, try starting with *Hiroshima* by John Hersey (1966), which shows the negative and dark side of this technology. Have students listen and draw and write words while you read the first chapter. Divide the rest of the book by chapters to groups of students and let them share. Then, lead students to understand what nuclear energy is, what the intent of the early scientists was, how nuclear technology is used in their everyday lives (from energy to medicine), and what some of the current issues are.

Projects

For a culminating project, provide a large array of choices. Perhaps they write a social action letter regarding funding or research or legislation.

Perhaps the teacher shares a song with students such as "Russians" by Sting or they read Rachel Carson's *Silent Spring*. Students could write a song or a poem. It may be of interest to them to research Yucca Mountain in Nevada as the nuclear waste repository or explore how and why other countries, such as France, tend to have such a different viewpoint of nuclear energy. Creating political cartoons is another suggestion. Interviews with people in related fields of work are enlightening. Doing activities like these allows students to take their knowledge a step further, apply those higher-level thinking skills from Bloom's taxonomy, pursue their interests, and have a say in their education. Choice provides ownership, which in turn generates interest and understanding.

Programs and Resources

No longer are middle school students stuck in a holding pattern until high school. Several wonderful supporting materials exist specifically for middle school science. Many universities and colleges have programs for students and/or education outreach for teachers. Included is a list, by no means exhaustive, of programs and resources that I have found invaluable in reaching the spectrum of students who have crossed my threshold.

- *Conceptual Physics* by Paul G. Hewitt (Great explanation of physics concepts that middle schoolers can grasp.)
- *The Far Side* by Gary Larson (Humor helps!)
- GEMS (*Great Explorations in Math & Science*) guides developed at the Lawrence Hall of Science, University of California, Berkeley (Several science topics and units at www.lhsgems.org)
- The Gorilla Foundation (Information about interspecies communication, conservation, behaviors, language, and intelligence. Teacher materials available at Koko.org or e-mail education@koko.org)
- National Science Foundation (Supports development of outstanding science programs. Become involved in a panel if possible. www.nsf.gov)
- National Science Teacher's Association (Journals, conferences, Web site with accurate content. Excellent staff development and networking opportunities! nsta.org)
- SEPUP (Science Education for Public Understanding Program) developed at the Lawrence Hall of Science, University of California Berkeley, Produced by Lab-Aids (Hands-on, inquiry, literacy based programs. Opportunities for staff development and field-testing exist. Students love this material! www.sepup.org)
- *Teaching Gifted Kids in the Regular Classroom* by Susan Weinbrenner (2003) (Ideas for providing higher-level thinking choices)

Here are some parting thoughts on our mutual passions of science education and gifted and talented students. First of all, remember they are children. Often, they come with some unique characteristics. Put the skip

...cult, and irrelevant subject. My first priority, therefore, is to ...relevant. The next priority is to prepare my students for ...education.

...er, I believe that education is a continuous process in which ...ning experiences should be relevant to their experiences at ...educators as those who must accommodate the diverse ...s of their students to facilitate learning. Varying instructional ...d methods are key components to provide for students' ...y allowing them to create true understanding of the subject. ...er in ability and need different tasks and assessments pre- ...riety of ways to maximize their potential.

...dvocate for using numerous strategies and approaches to ...e classroom, which I believe allows students to make sense ...aught and (hopefully) learned. My teaching methods span ...instruction, physical activities, peer teaching, and games for ...g. I have employed many of the strategies listed below to ...s of advanced learners.

...very

...e science with a student's imagination. Read *Bartholomew* ...*Oobleck* by Dr. Seuss. Divide students into groups. Let ...s discover the properties of Oobleck (cornstarch and water) ...zing numerous utensils (strainers, ice, pot and hot plate, ...rolling pin). After students have explored its properties, tell ...s to write an ending to the story *Bartholomew and the Oobleck* ...n the properties and laws of how they observed Oobleck ...How would they clean up the Kingdom of Didd? ...dents learn from one other. For example, allow students to ...the many explosive facets of soda, which include carbona- ...adspace, and nucleation sites, with physical activities. As ...s apply the scientific process to the activities, tell students to ...eir theories. Invite them to provide the class with their inter- ...n through written and visual representation of what they ...is the scientific cause of the phenomenon they observed. ...w two concepts of the scientific process—observations and ...ons—cut out pictures from a magazine that relate to a ...For example, I have used *objects that are yellow.* Divide ...s into teams. Give each team five numbered pictures. ...brainstorm three observations and a conclusion to support ...ure. They write their responses on a sheet of paper for each ...Review each team's observations and conclusion as a class. ...n that has the most correct observations and conclusions ...ore one point for each correct observation and two points for ...rect conclusion.

into their step so they will continue to take more than the required number of science courses that each state regulates. Teach them to question. Remaining neutral on issues can be difficult, but keep your opinion out of the mix. Make them back up their decisions with evidence. Provide them with the process skills they will use throughout life. Allow students' choices. Provide a variety of experiences. Remember that most will not enter a science related field, but all are scientists. Whether it is knowing what to ask the pharmacist before taking a medicine or deciding which new artificial sweetener to buy at the grocery store, all students will need their science skills so they can be informed citizens. But most of all . . . enjoy!

As in previous chapters, this chart is offecred as an aid to inspire some of your own ideas on the planning process.

Topics & Authors	Creative Strategies	Grade Level	Standards (examples)
An Eclectic Approach to Science Instruction for Gifted Students Beth Nicholson P. 158	Integration of arts and games Design of science models Use of story, cartoon, rap Creative movement and drama to explore science concepts	Intermediate, middle school, and up	As a result of activities in Grades 5–8, all students should develop abilities necessary to do scientific inquiry. This includes posing key questions, designing an investigation, gathering evidence, and formulating a hypothesis.
Making Discoveries in Problem-Based Learning Liz Fayer P. 162	Inquiry Creative reasoning Exploration of data Inventing (e.g., weather equipment, cloudscapes) Open questioning Inductive thinking	Intermediate, middle grades, and up	See above.
Bunny Foo-Foo Flu Mark Jurewicz P. 168	Experiential learning Improvisation Discovery Playing a game Flexible reasoning	Primary to intermediate and middle grades	As a result of their activities in Grades K–4 all students should develop an understanding of the characteristics of organisms, the life cycles of organisms, and organisms and environments. In Grades 5–8 all students should develop understanding of structure and function in living systems, diversity and adaptations of organisms.
Creative Strategies for Two Solar Science Units for Primary and Intermediate Grades Carol Sandberg Howe P. 170 Unit 1, p. 172	Open questioning Creative exploration w/range of materials Observing, sensing Use of multimedia Invention	Primary and intermediate grades	Science and technology: As a result of activities in Grades K–4 all students should develop abilities of technological design and understanding about science and technology.

(Continued)

(Continued)

Topics & Authors	Creative Strategies	Grade Level	Standards (examples)
Creative Strategies for Two Solar Science Units for Primary and Intermediate Grades *Carol Sandberg Howe* Unit 2, p. 178	Open questioning Designing charts Constructing models Experimenting Gathering data Hypothesizing Simulations	Primary and intermediate grades	Science as inquiry: As a result of activities in Grades K–4 all students should develop abilities necessary to do scientific inquiry and an understanding of scientific inquiry.
Rain Forest *Rachel Whitman* P. 184	Open inquiry and research Environmental design of a rainforest in classroom Crafts Exploration of flora and fauna in rain forest	Primary grades	Earth and space science: As a result of activities in Grades K–4 all students should develop an understanding of properties of earth materials. Life science: All students should develop an understanding of the characteristics of organisms, the life cycles of organisms, and organisms and environments.
Imagining Trees *Joan Franklin Smutny* P. 187	Integration of visual art and writing Design/drawing of elements that feed and sustain trees Identification with trees Autobiography as trees (poems, stories)	Primary to intermediate grades	Earth and space science: As a result of activities in Grades K–4 all students should develop an understanding of properties of earth materials and changes in earth and sky.
Exploring the Rainforest Through Content Based-Foreign Language Instruction *Kathryn P. Haydon* P. 191	Immersion in Spanish Environmental design of a rainforest Kinesthetic learning (gesture, dance, mime) Song Imaginative travel Identification of animals in the forest (in Spanish)	Primary school	Life science: All students should develop an understanding of the characteristics of organisms, the life cycles of organisms, and organisms and environments.

AN ECLECTIC APPROACH TO SCIENCE INSTRUCTION FOR GIFTED STUDENTS

By Beth Nicholson

MAIN CONCEPT

Through the use of multiple creative strategies, gifted students become more engaged in the work of science—exploring, observing, questioning,

reasoning, testing, and so forth. D
different times also makes studer
science more deeply.

LEVEL

Intermediate grades and up.

APPLICATION

Science, math, logical reasoning, a

DESCRIPTION

I am an eighth-grade science tea
through sixth-grade gifted studen
ferent roles and careers. I was a
ment administrator, a project ana
wife, and a companion to four res
to fulfill another passion in life.

Many factors inspired me to te
methods and strategies for learni
a daily basis, and the personal a
felt that as a nurse, while I was
I could affect the lives of thousar

Teaching became a personal
be an educator who would allc
standing of the subject they stuc
students make connections from
instruction delivered to them in a

I remember that when I was
ing, especially math. I can recall
board and thinking, "What do a
that I would understand three-di
that when I was in third grade,
sense. Why? Because math had a
ing shopkeeper in school while
add and subtract. I recall makir
multiplication facts. The differen
the board for me to memorize or
a futile pursuit of wisdom left m
mented. Why? *I couldn't make co*
They didn't make sense.

Need for Relevance

As an eighth-grade science t
the beginning of the year with a

abstract, diff
make scienc
future highe

As a teac
students' lea
home. I view
learning styl
strategies ar
needs, therel
Learners dif
sented in a v

I am an
teaching in t
of concepts
differentiatec
active learni
meet the nee

Group Disc

- Combi
  and the
  studen
  by util
  spoon,
  studen
  based
  behave
- Let stu
  explore
  tion, h
  studen
  share t
  pretatic
  believe
- To revi
  conclus
  theme.
  studen
  Studen
  the pic
  picture
  The tea
  wins. S
  each co

Arts

- Let students create a story, cartoon, or rap song while portraying matter changing from one state to another.
- Go outside and use a parachute. Let students act as molecules to reinforce the concepts of density and the kinetic theory of molecular motion.
- Encourage students to represent concepts artistically. I let students draw molecules as they observe matter changing from one state to another as well as draw pictures that reinforce the concepts of molecular movement and cohesion.
- After students learn about changing states of matter and molecular movement, let them act out a dramatization of matter changing states as heat is applied or taken away. Encourage students to coordinate movements with one another or create movements of their own.
- Let students use their imagination and creativity to design their own atom model from an element on the periodic table. For example, students can use various materials to create a nucleus, to identify protons, neutrons, and electrons. Students can also construct subatomic particles, orbital shells, and an electron configuration table.
- Instead of asking students to label the parts of a eukaryotic and prokaryotic cell, let them create puzzles for each type of cell and their organelles. Let students put together other students' puzzles for an assessment.

Games

- Play *The Dating Game* as you reinforce the concepts of covalent bonds by using elements on the periodic table to explain why some elements form bonds with other elements more readily.
- Engage in a game of tug of war as students physically experience how covalent bonds are formed.
- Use games to help students make connections from one idea to another. I like to use vocabulary words to reinforce old concepts while students make connections to new concepts. Let students know that they are going to play a game that has both components of *Pictionary* and charades. Write vocabulary words on separate colored index cards. Introduce new vocabulary words as well. Divide students into groups of four. Tell students that each group of four will be divided into two teams. Each team will play against each other. To play, each team will alternate turns as one team member picks up a vocabulary index card and either draws a picture on a sheet of paper or acts out the vocabulary word to the other team member. If the other team member guesses the correct vocabulary term within one minute or within three guesses, award a point. If not, the opposing

team has the opportunity to steal the point by one member of the team enacting or drawing a picture of the vocabulary term to that student's team member. If that member's answer is correct, the point is stolen. Either way, the card is placed at the bottom of the vocabulary word pile. It is now the opposing team's turn. I played this game with advanced students for a chemistry unit. Students not only reinforced vocabulary concepts to one another, but also taught one another new concepts by making connections from one term to another. For example, a student who drew a picture to enable another to guess the vocabulary term *element* also aided the same student to understand the meaning of a new concept *compound.*

An eclectic approach to science instruction for gifted students enables a teacher to reach children with different strengths and learning styles. Integrating the arts, games, and other creative elements also provides an in-depth science experience, opening up the students' minds to the possibility of discovery and adventure before them.

MAKING DISCOVERIES IN PROBLEM-BASED LEARNING

By Liz Fayer

MAIN CONCEPT

Problem-based learning (PBL) is a highly effective way for gifted students to experience the creative dimension of science and to engage in the heart of scientific processes: observation, exploration, examination of data, inductive and deductive thinking, analysis, and creative and open-minded reasoning.

LEVEL

All grades.

APPLICATION

Science, research and inquiry, math, literacy.

DESCRIPTION

Science, as a discipline, lends itself well to the needs of the gifted. Due to the inquiring nature and the allowance for creative thinking and exploration, science can take gifted students to a high level of critical thinking and processing. One effective way to stimulate interest and ideas is to use PBL in the science classroom. Shelagh A. Gallagher discusses the use of PBL as a vehicle for student ". . . authentic problem solving, hands-on learning, and self-directed learning . . ." adding, ". . . PBL is perfect for gifted students" (Karnes & Bean, 2001). Additionally, the Illinois Math and Science Academy, an internationally recognized pioneering education institution, has a large PBL curriculum component as a means to create real-world problem-solving situations for gifted math and science students. PBL is a part of their mission to help students work through complex issues and find relevance in learning. With the power of PBL in mind, teachers can utilize this type of learning to improve science classroom experiences for their gifted students.

Sequence

Determining knowledge level. PBL was used in a fifth-grade classroom with a weather unit. The teacher, after preassessing the students, realized that the students required additional knowledge to make informed decisions during the beginning of the PBL experience. Therefore, students were first exposed to several demonstrations, experiments, research, and newscasts about weather to add to their background knowledge.

Leadership. Once the teacher felt that these needs were adequately addressed, she began the PBL by addressing the question of leadership. PBL demands that students use positive leadership characteristics as they will be leading the problem-solving experience. Student volunteers read a picture book about a world leader, and then the class discussed the characteristics of a positive leader. Once students were clear about these characteristics and that they would be assuming more leadership over their own learning, they were ready to begin the PBL experience.

The teacher then discussed with students the schedule for the outdoor education day held at the end of the year. Although weather predictions can be found on the Internet for their suburb, they cannot be found for their school. The teacher explored with the students how they could predict the weather for that very important outdoor education day.

As the brainstorming ensued, students came up with the ill-structured question, "How can we predict the weather for our school for outdoor education day?"

The question. Establishing the question set the PBL in motion. Students took turns leading the classroom and small groups toward the goal of weather prediction. The teacher facilitated the learning by questioning, offering options if the students needed that support, and guiding the management of groups (again, only as needed).

Authentic outcome. In these actual experiences, students studied the weather in their area by exploring cloudscapes, creating weather stations, inventing and building weather equipment, collecting and analyzing data, predicting, and then evaluating how well their predictions worked with respect to the actual outdoor education day. All levels of Bloom's taxonomy were utilized, and the level of self-directedness and critical thinking were extremely high as an authentic outcome was part of the educational experience.

Student invention. One interesting point to share is that while the gifted students may have used the Internet to research weather equipment, and they could have chosen to build it the way the directions dictated, they often chose their own route. A fascinating piece of equipment that was built by gifted students was an anemometer or an instrument for measuring wind speed. Although there are many interesting designs on the Internet, this group chose not to look at the Internet and designed their own. They used a tube that was one meter long, a timer, and cotton balls.

When they went outside to measure the wind, they held the cotton ball at one end, and as they let it go in the direction the wind was blowing, they started the timer. They were able to determine that the wind speed was X number of meters per second: Incredibly simple and incredibly inventive!

Needless to say, the engagement was extremely high throughout the PBL, and students were excited to see how their predictions turned out on the final day. The day after outdoor education, as the students walked in the classroom, one said to the teacher, "Are we going to have fun in science again today?" I think that says it all!

Although PBL is highly engaging, not every science experience lends itself to it. When there are topics that need to be addressed that may not lend themselves to PBL, other means to engage gifted students can be employed.

Scientific models. One means is by the use of scientific models. Models are important to understanding science and have been used by scientists for centuries. When something is too big or too small to actually study, scientists use models to explain their observations. A terrific use of models is employed by Great Explorations in Math and Science (GEMS). At the beginning of their unit called *Earth, Moon, and Stars* (Sneider, see www.lhsgems.org/GEM250.html 2008) they use Ancient Models of the World as their hook. A picture of the model used by ancient peoples of India to describe their world invites students to a cosmos where the Earth—surrounded by ocean—has, at its center, a great mountain around which the Sun travels. It slips behind the western side of the mountain at dusk and reappears on the eastern side at dawn.

In the text of the *GEMS* unit, teachers are instructed to lead a discussion about why ancient India peoples would have thought that this explanation or model described their world. Students can use a globe and Google Earth to support their explanations. Once they have determined a reasonable answer, they move on to Greece, Egypt, and China. Students then pair up and discuss, draw, and describe how they think the peoples of ancient time would have understood the places where the students currently live. What model would they have had?

Student models. Students create these models and present them to the class. The creativity and higher-order thinking used by gifted students in this invitation to an astronomy unit were incredible. They have drawn and described models that were highly creative, explanatory, and engaging to their listeners.

Relationships. Relationships are also important to the understanding of science. How is one variable dependent on another? Students can explore relationships in many creative ways including giving students a choice of equipment and a question. What if a science teacher had matchbox cars, rulers, timers, ramps, and blocks and asked students to determine a relationship that describes motion? This type of open-ended inquiry is highly engaging to gifted students, and it is always surprising to see how inventive they can be.

Evidence. Evidence is a key to understanding science: Follow the evidence! One way that this has been used by Physics for Elementary Teachers (PET) is to supply students with all kinds of magnets and magnetic and nonmagnetic materials. Students make predictions and then must follow the evidence that they collect to determine what magnetism is. With every new magnetic experience, students are moved from an initial understanding of magnetism to one that explains the evidence. Where they end up in their understanding is dependent on their level of thinking at the time.

Data. Data collection, observation, and measurement are also key to understanding the heart of the science discipline. Wiggins and McTighe (2001) examine the importance of students understanding what is at the heart of a discipline in their book *Understanding by Design.* What if students are given all sorts of measurement tools including beakers, rulers, scales, and graduated cylinders, plus other materials such as funnels, aluminum foil, wax paper, eyedroppers, and ice cubes? They have a chance to look at all the equipment and are then asked, "How can we measure a phase change?"

Equipment. Students can be completely inventive and involved in spirited learning conversations as they determine the best way to use this equipment (and they may ask for additional materials if the teacher has them or they have them at home) to design an experiment that answers that question. One of the most inventive designs that a gifted student created was letting the ice melt on a piece of aluminum foil. Although this sounds simple, it is actually very complex. The student etched the area (not exactly circular) onto the foil at specific time intervals. Once the ice had melted for the class period, the student took that foil to a math teacher and had the math teacher work with him or her on finding the area of imperfect circles. This gifted sixth-grader created a personal subject integration and an opportunity to learn math at a higher level for the purpose of this application. There was a reason for math after all!

Science reading. The last area that will be discussed here is using reading in science. In her article "Reading Instruction for the Primary Gifted Learner," Bertie Kingore (2002) states, ". . . gifted readers demonstrate a voracious appetite for nonfiction" (p. 12). Therefore, it is imperative that gifted science students have access to many levels of science information on whatever topic is being addressed in the classroom. Additionally, as an alternative to science texts that may be uninteresting to gifted students, teachers can create stories that not only allow science to unfold but also have embedded thinking prompts for gifted students. Here is a short example of such a story:

What Makes Up the Atmosphere?

A Story

Abigail's excitement rose as she saw that there were neat pieces of science equipment on the table at the side of the room. She saw a tall glass with markings on it, a candle, modeling clay, a pie pan, colored water, and matches. All day long, she thought about how those materials were going to be used in science.

Finally, science time came again, and Mr. Garcia was back. He asked everyone to take out a piece of paper and write their names at the top. Next, he asked students to look at the equipment and try to figure out what the experiment's purpose might be. The class had a long discussion, and the students' brains hurt by the end of it, but it seemed that they had gotten the idea. Therefore, on their papers, they wrote down the purpose that they had come up with together. Mr. Garcia wrote the purpose the board. Of course, it was in the form of a question!

Purpose: How can these materials be used to learn about the atmosphere?

The class was beaming with pride, when all of a sudden he asked everyone to now come up with the hypothesis.

If _____ then _____ because

This was all the information he would give the class, and once again they began to work their minds and discuss their ideas. Abigail could tell that Mr. Garcia was not only a good science teacher but also a nice person. Even if it seemed that an idea was way off, he never answered with anything other than positive comments and would try to use questions to elicit more information from students. They knew they were getting close when Mr. Garcia said, "OK, now we are close, we know that if the lit candle is placed under the glass then it will go out—terrific—now who has a because? Why would the candle go out? What is under there that is changing? What will happen to the colored water in the pan?" The students had to think, and someone raised a hand boldly.

Mr. Garcia said, "I think we are all close enough to create our own 'if, then, because' statement. So, please write your statement down on your lab sheet, and then we'll see how our predictions turn out."

After they wrote them down, Mr. Garcia reminded the class that MOST all hypotheses are incorrect and that incorrect ones lead to new ideas. Abigail wondered what new ideas hers might lead to, but before she could get very far with her thoughts—Mr. Garcia placed the candle on top of a piece of clay in the middle of the pie pan, poured the colored water in the pie pan, lit the candle, and placed the glass with markings on it over the candle.

It seemed that no one breathed as they watched the experiment. The candle burned brightly for a while and then dimmed. As it began to dim, colored water seemed to rise in the glass . . . the candle went out. Mr. Garcia asked us to note about how high up the colored water had gone as a percentage. Abigail knew that is was around 20 percent to 25 percent. Before she even realized what she was doing, she raised her hand and answered, "Around 20 to 25 percent."

"Well, that is interesting," said Mr. Garcia. "I know that Ms. Madison has been reading with you about what makes up our atmosphere . . ."

ABIGAIL HEARD NO MORE! Her mouth made an O shape. The candle had used up the oxygen, which is about 21 percent of the atmosphere, and the colored water had taken its place. She could not believe her own thoughts—this was really too cool. She could repeat the experiment at home that night with her family . . .

"Abigail," said Mr. Garcia. That brought her back to the room in a hurry. "Yes," she answered. "What do you think that means?" he asked.

"I think it means that the candle used up the oxygen that was under the glass, and that oxygen takes up 21 percent of our atmosphere, and that's why the colored water rose about the same percentage. It seemed to take the place of the oxygen."

Interesting," said Mr. Garcia. "Now how do we know it wasn't nitrogen that was used by the candle, Jose?"

Jose looked down at his atmosphere sheet. "Because then the colored water would have gone to about 78 percent!"

"Excellent, class! I think we've got it!" shouted Mr. Garcia.

Cognitive and social benefits. Obviously, this could be read to the class and the thinking prompts discussed by the actual science class just as Abigail encounters them. Not only does this provide the teacher with text that encourages thinking, explaining, observing, and discussing, but it also supports a few additional aspects of social-emotional giftedness. It allows girls to be gifted and love science; it allows people of different cultures to be gifted and love science; and it allows for discovery learning as the teacher can stop the reading to actually demonstrate the experiment and then draw students back in with the text. Lastly, as this type of story is teacher-created, it allows the teacher the choice of gender, culture, and outcome and therefore the power to address the social-emotional issues of the gifted children in that particular classroom. What a great way for a teacher to encourage science and provide a welcoming atmosphere for the giftedness of her or his students!

Gifted children become excited throughout these processes due to the opportunity for them to make their own discoveries and to learn science by doing it. In the process of field-testing their ideas, forming theories, examining data, creating new adjustments, and so forth, they begin to experience science as an ever-evolving field they can contribute to rather than a body of knowledge they have to acquire.

RESOURCES

Fayer, L. (2007). *Abigail loves science.* Unpublished manuscript.

Karnes, F. A., & Bean, S. M. (2001). *Methods and materials for teaching the gifted.* Waco, TX: Prufrock Press.

Kingore, B. (Fall 2002). Reading instruction for the primary gifted learner. *Understanding Our Gifted. 15*, 12–15. Retrieved September 20, 2007 http://www.bertieking ore.com/readinginstruction.htm

Physics and Everyday Thinking (formerly Physics for Elementary Teachers). (2007). Retrieved July 15, 2006, from http://petproject.sdsu.edu/

Wiggins, G., & McTighe, J. (2001). *Understanding by design.* Alexandria, VA: ASCD.

Bunny Foo-Foo Flu

By Mark Jurewicz

MAIN CONCEPT

This activity uses a gamelike strategy that enables students to explore the biological processes behind the contraction of a flu.

LEVEL

Primary through intermediate and middle school grades.

APPLICATION

Science, visual thinking, some math.

DESCRIPTION

Science can be one of the most exciting topics to teach with so many fascinating things to introduce children to. There are always great "discoveries" for students to make and ponder. Having them just read about topics in a book is not enough. Some concepts are hard to visualize. It is far better for them to experience or experiment to fully grasp the concept.

The Process

We study Louis Pasteur and his work with vaccines and immunizations. Simply put, it works like this. When a new virus or bacteria establishes itself inside of you, your antibodies try many different ways to destroy it. They actually continue changing tactics until they find a way to destroy the foreign invaders. Once they find a successful defense, they "remember" how to destroy that virus or bacteria quickly the next time it may invade your body.

I thought about how I could make this process of immunization visual and concrete so that my students could see and understand how this happens. I came up with and developed the "Bunny Foo-Foo Flu" activity.

Solving a Puzzle

The simple basis of the activity had to be the solving of a puzzle. I found a pattern for a rabbit that could be made using tangrams. I made several copies of the shape. I divided the class into groups of three to five students and gave each group a copy of the rabbit pattern and each child a set of tangrams. I explained that each small group is a different human body and that each child is an antibody out to destroy the infectious

Bunny Foo-Foo Flu. To do this, they must create the rabbit pattern exactly using their tangrams.

Once someone builds the rabbit, one Bunny Foo-Foo Flu is destroyed. The faster this is done, the less sick students will become and the better off they will be.

To begin the activity, I sneeze to "infect" the class. I then begin to walk around the room dropping onto each groups table a Popsicle stick. (You can use pennies, beads, buttons, or anything you have a lot of.) Each Popsicle stick represents the Bunny Foo-Foo Flu dividing and multiplying. Tell them, "If your table gets five sticks, you begin twitching your nose. If you get ten sticks, then you grow a fluffy tail. At fifteen, you grow long ears, and at twenty you begin hopping around, and you become a Bunny Foo-Foo, and there is no return!"

This gives the student "antibodies" 10 minutes to figure out how to construct the rabbit shape correctly and remove all of the sticks from the center of the table. Each time students within a group (antibody) complete the puzzle, they remove a stick. Then they must scramble their pieces and begin to rebuild it again. If they remove all of the sticks from the center of the table, they survive. If they receive twenty sticks, they have failed to defeat the Bunny Foo-Foo Flu, and they become a Bunny Foo-Foo!

Now, real antibodies are capable of "communicating" with each other. When a solution to destroying an invasive foreign cell is found, all of your antibodies somehow begin to repeat the same tactic until all of the foreign cells are removed. So with that in mind, your students can and *should* also teach each other how to build the rabbit so that they can team up on the flu and remove all of the Popsicle sticks. However, only antibodies from the same body can communicate with each other. So, groups should not help other groups.

The groups that survived and defeated the Bunny Foo-Foo Flu probably had collected quite a few Popsicle sticks and had to work feverishly to get rid of the pile of sticks in the center of the table. But the good news is they are now immune to the Bunny Foo-Foo Flu! To prove it, do the activity again. This time around you will probably have a hard time giving out a second or third stick before they have built the rabbit shape and removed the stick. They, like your antibodies, have remembered how to attack and destroy the invading cells. So, foreign cells don't have a chance to divide and multiply in your body.

This is why we give children immunizations, weakened germs that their bodies can defeat and "learn" to fend off so that if and when they are exposed to the stronger more dangerous ones, their antibodies will remember how to attack and defeat it before they become very sick.

This has been a favorite activity for many groups. I have played this with kindergarteners as well as fourth graders. They have come away with a much better understanding of why they sometimes get a shot from the doctor when they are not even sick! And they always want to do another round. I have also done this with a parent group, and they too were quite engrossed in the whole activity.

Variations

If you have great puzzle solvers, you can vary the game. Hand out the sticks every ten or fifteen seconds. If you have very young ones, hand them out every 45 seconds to one minute. If they already know how to build the rabbit, I have also used a ship shape and called it the "Tug Boat Bloat." Get creative.

Gifted children enjoy the visual, hands-on process as a way of conceptualizing the science. Particularly when they repeat the process, they experience the same learning that the antibodies do after immunization.

CREATIVE STRATEGIES FOR TWO SOLAR SCIENCE UNITS FOR PRIMARY AND INTERMEDIATE GRADES

ALIAS: THERE'S ALWAYS SOMETHING "NEW" UNDER THE SUN!

By Carol Sandberg Howe

Unit 1: Solar Power As an Alternative Energy Solution to Global Warming

Unit 2: Exploring the Sun and Properties of Sunlight

MAIN CONCEPT

Dynamic, engaging science is *not* a "stand-alone," isolated discipline focused on facts, figures, and abstract content as is sometimes perceived by parents and educators with limited science background. Rather, young children are "born" scientists, constantly preoccupied with questioning, exploring, predicting, observing, and experimenting with everything in their surroundings to find out "the way things work."

LEVEL

Primary grades. Adaptable to intermediate and higher grades.

APPLICATION

Both these units apply to a wide range of subject areas—reading, writing, mathematics, the arts, and more. Teachers can also extract and modify pieces of this unit to enhance the curriculum for gifted learners. They can also use the units as models for their own interdisciplinary learning experiences in science.

DESCRIPTION

Overview for Units 1 and 2:

When creative, hands-on science activities are integrated into mathematic, kinesthetic, and linguistic projects, students can't wait to participate!

Experience also reveals that all students, especially the highly gifted, are far more motivated and engaged when they are investigating a highly relevant topic, such as global warming.

"Exploring our sun and solar power as a new energy source" may sound like advanced topics, but when young children are artfully exposed to creative, hands-on, age-appropriate ways of demonstrating these concepts, primary students are fully capable of making these connections and applying these sophisticated insights into their daily life.

Parents of gifted students are pleasantly surprised to see their children so richly engaged by hands-on science units, especially when their children transfer this newfound confidence and expanded vocabulary to their home environment, initiating daily investigations with, "I wonder why?" "I wonder what would happen if we tried this. . . ."

On the social-emotional level, highly gifted children learn more patience in working with their peers in a creative team environment. These students learn to listen, take turns, and peacefully exchange ideas better with peers because they have participated in both group activities and individual opportunities for creatively expressing themselves (through constructing realistic models, conducting experiments, or creating drawings, diagrams, reports, graphs, and books to represent their newest scientific discoveries).

Sometimes, highly gifted students are intimidated by not having that one right answer immediately evident during scientific inquiry and are initially hesitant to participate. Each mistake in the process is viewed as an abject failure. However, as teachers consistently model creative problem-solving, the sometimes frustrating mistakes that occur during trial and error can now be perceived as positive steps to the solution. Children learn to trust that scientific inquiry and problem solving can be as fun and exciting as any video game with an even greater sense of personal accomplishment.

The following is a narration of two highly successful units on the sun and sunlight and exploring the potential of solar power as a critical energy alternative with global significance, beginning with Unit 1.

UNIT 1: SOLAR POWER AS AN ALTERNATIVE ENERGY SOLUTION TO GLOBAL WARMING

1. Identifying Types of Energy Using the Scientific Method

Explain that when scientists are confronted with a new, unknown item or event, they use the following scientific method steps of observation and record what they see. *Astronomers* are scientists that study the stars with telescopes.

Know (facts, details, vocabulary)	Understand (principles, concepts, generalizations)	Do (A demonstration of what students know and understand; for more challenge, design, task that has real-world applications.)
• What is the scientific method of inquiry? • What is energy? • What are the types of energy?	Scientists use the scientific method to Observe Ask questions Define the problem Predict an answer Use tools and equipment for investigations Record information Report conclusions • Energy is the ability to do work OR the ability to make things change. • Energy cannot disappear. It can only change into other kinds of energy; for example, *light energy* can change into *heat energy.* • Types of energy include mechanical energy, light energy and heat energy (solar), electricity, kinetic energy, and sound energy.	• Students will examine new forms and sources of energy. • By examining various objects that require one of seven types of energy to do work, students will be able to define energy by using the scientific method to identify different types of energy including light, heat, sound, kinetic, and solar energy.

2. Steps of the Scientific Method:

a. Observation—Students observe photon ball (color, size, touch, smell, sound, etc.).
b. Ask questions "Who, What, Where, When, Why?
c. Make a prediction (a guess) as to a possible answer.
d. Investigate/measure/experiment. (What enables it to do what it does?)
e. Write/draw conclusions of what they observed.

3. Introduce Large *Mystery* Object (What do you think it is?)

Hands-On Activity

a. Students go to one of four tables, handle/examine the **mystery object,** and write their observations according to the five steps in the scientific method.
b. Question: What is it? Is it alive? Is it a machine? What makes it run (batteries, on-off switch)?
c. Each table must come to a consensus as to what they think it is and record the evidence that supports their conclusion.

Journal Comment

• During the "Scientific Method" lesson, students were amused by the mystery object. Students generated good observations and questions after being given the prompts of observation, asking how to do an experiment and investigation, and needing to write down what they observed. They learned how essential it is to use the five senses (taste, touch, smell, sight, sound) and the five Ws (who, what, where, when, and why), plus, one student added, "How?" when observing.
• Sample student observations included noting that the Mystery Object is plastic, round with strange, colorful bumps (possibly antennae), makes strange noises, blinks different colored lights, vibrates (shakes), rolls across the table, stops and starts at will, bounces.

4. What Is Energy? What Are Some Types of Energy?

Hands-On Activity

• Set up one station for *each type* of energy, (i.e., light, mechanical, electric, etc. as listed above).
• Students visit each station with a clipboard and record KWL (What I Know, What I Want to Know, and What I Need to Learn) observations on the form below.

Energy Station What We Know	Where Does the Energy Come From? (Question)	How Do You Know It Has Energy? (Observations) What I Need to Learn
1 Windup toy	Mechanical/machine	Toy moves
2 Solar-powered car, fan, radio, lightbulb (items have solar cells to absorb light)	Solar energy cells absorb light and convert to energy	Car moves, radio plays, bulb lights, fan turns

(Continued)

(Continued)

Energy Station What We Know	Where Does the Energy Come From? (Question)	How Do You Know It Has Energy? (Observations) What I Need to Learn
3 Electrical object (plug-in lamp)	Plug-in lamp	Lamp lights
4 Electric blanket	Plug device into electric wall socket	Coils get warm
5 Radiometer	Housed in a glass ball, the white-and-black panels absorb light and heat at different temperatures, making the panels turn in a circle	White-and-black panels spin in circles
6 Kinetic silver balls	Silver balls suspended on nylon strings that keep colliding as they bounce off one another	Silver balls bounce against each other; perpetual energy comes from bouncing against each other
7 Sound—tuning fork, drums	Vibrates and gives off sound when struck	A humming sound; a drum rat-a-tat sound

Note: Students concluded from their explorations that there are **seven** different types of energy, plus a few students had also heard of nuclear energy plants, powered by the atom.

Journal Comments

Students had a great time examining the windup toy (mechanical), solar car, solar-powered fan, light, electric blanket, light bulb, heat element, radiometer, solar calculator, and pinwheels. Students drew wonderful diagrams of each of the types of energy. Students were amazed that someday, much of the world will be powered by solar energy to replace the need for oil. Students concluded the following:

- Energy is all around us in many forms.
- Energy is the ability to do work (move) OR the ability to make things change.
- Energy cannot disappear. It can only change into other forms of energy; for example, light energy can change into heat energy.

5. What Are Some Practical Uses for Solar Energy?

Hands-On Activity

- Using 150-watt lightbulb to shine on the cells, students at different tables experiment with using solar cells to power solar cars, solar clocks, solar calculators, solar-powered fans, lightbulbs, flashlights, radios, solar-powered heaters and ovens, and so on. Ask students how they think these items would be useful if the electricity (heat and light) in their house went out during a storm.

- The teacher shows a short video of satellites, space shuttle, Hubble Space Telescope and the International Space Station circling the Earth and sending signals to Earth and astronauts in the space shuttle.

Class Discussion After Video

- Students are asked if they have ever noticed a five-second delay when people on the television news are being interviewed and talking to each other and answering questions separated by far away cities.
- Students are reminded that some of the most recent missions accomplished by U.S. astronauts during space shuttle missions were focused on repairing or improving the solar cells that power the International Space Station and other spacecraft.
- Students are surprised to learn that they would *not* be able to watch television without the signals bouncing off these satellites in space that send pictures and sound to giant broadcasting stations in their city and then beamed to their television sets in their homes. Cell phones and radio broadcasts can be affected as well. Much of our weather forecasting to warn of tornados and hurricanes possibly developing on the Earth's surface is also accomplished by gathering photographs and other information from satellites.
- A local solar energy expert, who demonstrates how a solar energy cell is constructed and how it absorbs sunlight and converts it to solar energy power, visits the students. Solar *grids* are made of hundreds of *solar cells* to capture the most sunlight. Students examine the solar cells.
- Using a model house, the solar energy expert demonstrates how a solar heating system works first to collect solar light energy through solar cells and then to convert the energy to heat a single house or an entire building.
- As a culminating activity, students are told that they are going to get to construct a solar oven from a pizza box! After building the oven, students will get to cook food in the oven and experience how solar energy (light and heat) can be transferred to efficiently power everyday home appliances!

6. Building and Using Solar Ovens

Know (facts, details, vocabulary)	Understand (principles, concepts, generalizations)	Do (demonstration of what students know and understand: for more challenge, design task that has real world applications)
• Can we use solar energy to cook food in an oven?	• Through reflection and absorption of light from the sun, solar energy can be captured and applied to create radiant heat for cooking s'mores in a homemade cardboard oven.	• By building and exploring solar ovens, students will ask and answer questions about solar energy conversion and other applications of solar energy.

Materials for Solar Oven:

1. Thin cardboard box (pizza box)
2. Black construction paper
3. Aluminum foil
4. Clear transparency
5. Tape
6. Glue
7. Scissors
8. Exacto knife

S'mores Ingredients:

1. Two graham cracker squares per student
2. Six small marshmallows per student
3. One-third chocolate bar per student

Constructing the Solar Oven

- Students glue aluminum foil to the three-sided lid in the top of the cardboard box to reflect the sun's light toward the bottom of the cardboard box where the s'mores have been placed.
- Students cut a square hole in the top of the box.
- Students tape a piece of transparency to cover the square hole in the top of the box so that the sunlight can shine through to heat the bottom of the pizza box.
- Students glue the black construction paper to the bottom of the cardboard box to absorb the light and transform it into radiant heat to cook (melt) the s'mores.

Cooking With the Solar Ovens (Outdoor activity for a sunny day)

- Children love to eat s'mores!
- Have students assemble the s'mores by layering the marshmallows on one side of one graham square and chocolate pieces on the other graham square and place them in the solar oven.

- Have students close the oven and position it so that it receives as much sunlight as possible.
- Use the reflective lid to reflect sunlight directly into chocolate and marshmallows.
- After 15 minutes (after chocolate melts), remove both graham crackers from the oven and place the two crackers together to make the s'mores.

Journal Comments

Building on these concepts, students were shown the components: the pizza box, the aluminum foil, the clear vinyl sheets, and the black paper. They easily made the association that if we were to try to cook s'mores in the solar oven, we would need each of these parts to create the solar heat. Armed with these concepts, students were able to build the solar ovens with very little help from the teacher because they understood the purpose of each part.

Note: Additional solar energy project kits (time and budget permitting, see below) include the following:

Solar cars kits

Building solar-powered boats and submarines from plastic bottles

Building solar-powered robots

Have fun!!!

7. Resources for Unit 1

The following are some useful books, resources and Web sites on the sun and solar energy for teacher use.

1. American Science and Surplus Warehouse, Chicago, IL (solar cell kits, solar cars, solar energy books, windup toys, instruments, prisms, radiometers, kinetic silver balls on strings, etc.)

2. Constructive Playthings, Skokie, IL (Teacher Store: similar solar toys, kits, ultraviolet beads, etc.)

3. *Solar Energy.* Foss Science Series, Delta Education, Nashua, NH ISBN: 1-58356-847-6

4. www.spaceplace.NASA.gov

5. www.illinoissolar.org

6. Adler Planetarium.org and Museum store

7. *National Geographic Magazine*/August 2005

8. *Business 2.0 Magazine*/January-February 2007

9. *Championship Science Fair Projects.* Sudipta Bardhan-Quallen, p. 114 (building solar ovens), Sterling, New York, ISBN-13-978-4027-1138-1

10. *Gonzo Gizmos.* Simon Quellen Field, Chicago Review Press Chicago, IL (Older students: Build Solar Hot Dog Cookers, etc.), ISBN 1-55652-520-6

11. Solar Energy, Niles, IL www.solarserviceinc.com. Joe Gordon, speaker and supplier for renewable solar energy.

UNIT 2: EXPLORING THE SUN AND PROPERTIES OF SUNLIGHT

1. What is the "Sun and the Sun-Earth Connection"?

Teachers, be sure to share this with your students before proceeding. Background note:

"In the earlier lesson we talked about the five-step scientific method used by scientists in studying new objects. Astronomers are scientists who study the planets and the sun (Solar System) and distant stars by viewing them with large telescopes. Telescopes are instruments that astronomers point at the sky to capture the light from stars and magnify (make the far away stars and planets appear larger). Big exception: Astronomers *never* look directly at our own sun with their eyes or their telescopes because the sun's superbright light would injure (burn) their eyes."

2. Review the Scientific Method of Inquiry With Students:

a. Observation.
b. Ask questions. Who, What, Where, When, Why, and How?
c. Make prediction (a guess) as to a possible answer.
d. Investigate/measure/experiment (What enables it to do what it does?)
e. Write/draw conclusions of what was observed.

Know (facts, details, vocabulary)	Understand (principle, concepts, generalizations)	Do (demonstration of what students know and understand; for more challenge, design a task that has real-world applications.)
• What is the sun? • What is a star? • What is activity like on the sun's surface? • What are sunspots? • Where is the sun? • How far away is the sun from the Earth? • What is the Milky Way? • Why do we need the sun?	• The sun is our nearest star. You can see the sun in the daytime. • A star is a mass of exploding gases such as hydrogen that gives us light and heat energy • The sun is like a massive oven, producing light and heat through a process called *fusion*. Students were amazed at the video of the sun, to observe how it keeps exploding and regenerating heat and light • When the sun's surface has *dark* sunspots (storms), it can sometimes affect our weather on planet Earth and sometimes disrupts radio signals (crackling in radio sound) and sometimes TV, cell phone signals, etc. • The sun operates as the center of our solar system consisting of nine planets that circle the sun yearly, including planet Earth. • The sun is 93 million miles away. It takes eight minutes for the sun's light and heat to reach Earth. • The sun is only one of billions of stars in the huge galaxy, The Milky Way. Galaxies are vast clusters of stars that float in the universe. • The sun provides light and heat to planet Earth and its inhabitants (plants and animal life.) • Sun gives us night and day and the seasons and light and heat • Without the sun, life would cease to exist on Earth. There would be no weather; all plants and animals need sunlight to live and grow.	• Students watch Part 1A of a five-minute video that profiles live photography of the sun and its activities and take notes on the facts listed below for class discussion following the video. • Note: After watching *each* part of the video, students will construct a KWL chart from the notes they have taken on the nature and parts of the sun. **Note:** Photos are taken of all student demonstrations. **Hands-On Activity:** Students divide into four table groups. • **Model of the sun:** Following handout diagrams, one group constructs and paints a papier-mâché model of the sun with all parts of the sun labeled from books and the diagrams provided about the sun and presents it to the class. • Size of sun: Another group conducts classroom contest. How many Earths can fit into the sun? • In a simulation of the size of the Earth compared to the size of the sun, students guess how many marbles fit into a hollow basketball (representing the larger sun). • Students are asked to submit their best guess. • Winners get a token prize. • Students watch Part 1B of the solar video which illustrates "Night and Day," "The Reason for the Seasons," and "Solar Eclipses." • Students are provided with additional books and diagrams. • Using a globe, a flashlight (representing sunlight), and a marker

***Stress again to students to *never* look directly into the sun without special glasses or instruments from an astronomer. The sun's bright light will damage their eyes and cause blindness!!!

(Continued)

(Continued)

Know (facts, details, vocabulary)	Understand (principle, concepts, generalizations)	Do (demonstration of what students know and understand; for more challenge, design a task that has real-world applications.)
	• The sun's uneven heating of Earth's surface also creates weather and wind power and the resulting changes in planetary weather—another critical source of solar energy. • All fossil (nonrenewable) energy sources on Earth can be linked to the sun, including the formation of oil, coal, wood, and hydro-(water-) powered electricity. • Solar energy generated from the sun has demonstrated tremendous potential as an unlimited, renewable energy source.	on the classroom globe, another group of students demonstrate why we have *day and night*. • After constructing a papier-mâché model of Earth and the sun, using a flashlight (representing sunlight), a group demonstrates to the class "The Reason for the Seasons." • A third group, using papier-mâché models of the sun, Earth, and the moon, and a flashlight, demonstrated how a solar eclipse occurs. (Showing that when the moon travels between Earth and the sun, it creates a shadow on the Earth's surface, and blocks out the view of the sun). • Again, **stress** to students **to never** look directly into the sun without special glasses or instruments provided by astronomy experts—especially during a solar eclipse! • Students make a model of an indirect sun viewer. When the viewer is pointed at the sun, students are able to view the projection of the sun's image shining on a piece of paper below.

3. Solar Light: Shines Through Transparent, Translucent, and Opaque?

Know (facts, details, vocabulary)	Understand (principles, concepts, generalizations)	Do (demonstration of what students know and understand; for more challenge, design a task that has real-world applications.)
• What is the effect of sunlight when shining on different earthen objects, including us? • What causes shadows?	The sun's light shines in greater or lesser degree through different objects: • **Transparent objects** (can see sunlight shining through, like a window) • **Translucent objects** (see sunlight shines partially through) • **Opaque objects** sunlight can't shine through (creates a shadow)	Students view Part 2 of the solar video, this time learning about the sun's ability or nonability to shine through different earthen objects: One group of students demonstrated to the class how well sunlight (simulated by flashlight) shines through the following:

Know (facts, details, vocabulary)	Understand (principles, concepts, generalizations)	Do (demonstration of what students know and understand; for more challenge, design a task that has real-world applications.)
• What is the effect of sunlight when shining on different earthen objects, including us? • What causes shadows?	• **Reflective objects** (like aluminum foil) shines sunlight and heat back • **Different colored paper:** sunlight is absorbed (creates heat) differently with different colors • **When the sunlight hits an *opaque* (solid) object,** the light cannot pass through the object and a shadow is produced. • **Sundials were first made by ancient civilizations to tell time,** by watching the changes in shadows produced by the sun as it hits the arm of the sundial. (The *dial* has numbers like a clock, and the shadow touches certain numbers on the dial as the sun moves across the sky at different times of the day.) • **Review with students that a solar eclipse is one of the largest *shadows*** caused when the moon passes between the sun and the earth, casting a shadow that covers many miles across the earth.	• A sheet of plastic or glass (sunlight shines clearly) • Wax paper (cloudy light) • White paper (reflects light creates a shadow), black paper (blocks light, creates a shadow, absorbs heat) • Aluminum foil (reflects bright light and heat) • Another group of students went outside and demonstrated how to become sundials by standing in the sun and using a yardstick to measure the length of shadows that their opaque (solid) body made from noon until 3. Shadows became longer and longer from noon until 3. • Another group of students demonstrated to the class how to make a sundial to measure the time of day using cardboard and paper plates. • All students get to make and keep their own sundials and go outside to check the time by the hour.

Journal Comments

Following this lesson on sunlight's action on transparent, translucent, and opaque materials, I was especially pleased to hear a group of my students arguing at lunchtime as they held a container of orange "Jell-O" up to the sunlight.

"It's opaque!" said one student.

"No, it's *not*," said another. "I can see light shining through it. It must be transparent!"

"No," said another student, "it's translucent!"

"Why?" asked the other student.

"Well," replied the student, "it's not *totally* clear, but you can *still* see *some* of the light shining through it!"

Our *light* lesson *hit home!*

4. What Are Some *Additional* Uses for Sun Light?

- To demonstrate light waves, the teacher uses a visual prop: a labeled, multicolored Slinky" to represent how a ray of sunlight can be divided into different waves of sunlight.
- Sunlight travels in waves. Some are *visible* rays (microwave ovens), some are *x-rays* (take pictures of our bones), some are *infrared* rays (detect heat in the body), and some are ultraviolet rays (can cause sunburn at the beach—we need to protect our skin from ultraviolet rays that cause sunburn with suntan lotion).

Know (facts, details, vocabulary)	*Understand* (principles, concepts, generalizations)	*Do* (demonstration of what students know and understand; for more challenge, design a task that has real-world applications.)
• What is solar light energy? • Where does it come from? • Does light move? • How does it move? • What are these other light wavelengths called?	• Light is a form of energy that comes from the sun. • Light energy can be converted to heat energy. • Light travels in waves and in a straight line. • We can see visible light with our eyes. We can divide this light into seven colors with a crystal prism. • Some of the other sunlight wavelengths we cannot see are ultraviolet, x-rays, microwaves, infrared rays	• Students watch Part 3 of the solar video, which explains how sunlight energy travels in wavelengths. • Another student group will demonstrate to the class how to hold a glass prism in the sunlight and observe how it bends the visible light into the seven colors of the rainbow. • All students will get to *make* a rainbow with a prism. • Note: If lesson is presented during warmer weather, students can also go outside and create (view) a *rainbow* by holding the water from a sprinkler into the sun.

5. Matching Practical Uses to Light Wavelengths

Students watch Part 4 of the solar video.

Students learn that the sun's light travels in waves, and each has a different name and purpose.

Students match appropriate *use* to different light wavelengths:

Shows heat areas in body Allows us to see/colors	Shows cavities in teeth Creates a tan Used to cook food	Shows breaks in bones Creates a rainbow Causes a sunburn
Visible light	X-rays	Ultraviolet rays
Prism	Infrared Rays	Microwaves

6. Solar Light Energy and Ultraviolet Beads

Know (facts, details, vocabulary)	Understand (principles, concepts, generalizations)	Do (demonstration of what students know and understand; for more challenge, design a task that has real-world applications.)
• Does ultraviolet sunlight have a good or bad effect on our health? • How can we protect our skin against ultraviolet light? • The earth's atmosphere (the air that surrounds the earth in space) has several layers, including a protective layer of ozone. • The ozone layer protects our skin from being exposed to too much ultraviolet light, but that layer is being destroyed by air pollution.	• The ultraviolet light from the sun that makes it through our atmosphere is essential to the human body's production of Vitamin D and is good for *some* tanning of the skin. • Too much ultraviolet light from the sun can damage our skin with sunburn. • Since the ozone layer of the atmosphere is thinning due to pollution, it is now necessary for people to use some suntan lotion to protect their skin from too much ultraviolet light.	• Students will use the ultraviolet-sensitive beads to detect the presence of ultraviolet rays in their area by placing the beads in direct sunlight. • Students will apply a protective coating of suntan lotion on *some* of the ultraviolet coated beads to prevent the sunlight from reaching some of the beads. Students discover that the beads protected by the suntan lotion will not change color and the rest of the ultraviolet beads will change color.

Materials

- UV (ultraviolet-coated) beads for each student
- Pipe cleaners or elastic string to make bracelets of the beads
- A black lightbulb (in case it is a rainy day)
- Assortment of sunscreen at different SPF strengths
- Ziploc baggies
- One reporting sheet for each group

Procedure

- Give each student a small supply of ultraviolet-coated beads (they are white) and a string to make bracelets. Explain that the UV-light detecting beads contain nonharmful UV-light-sensitive indicators/chemicals that change colors when ultraviolet light is present.
- On a sunny day, have students take their UV-coated bead bracelets outside and place them in the sun full-time. Students will notice how fast the ultraviolet reacts with the sunlight and changes the color of beads.
- Students may also wish to hold their sunglasses over the beads to block out the sunlight's effect on their beads as they hold them outside or near a window.
- Since ultraviolet light is a type of light we cannot see with our naked eyes, have students discuss the benefits of wearing the bracelets. Students get to keep the ultraviolet bracelets.

Culminating Activity

- Students make and decorate their own colorful sun *masks* while learning and singing the song, "Walking on Sunshine!" Students perform a dance to the song while wearing their masks.

7. Resources for Unit 2

The following are some useful books, resources, and Web sites on the sun and solar energy for teacher use:

1. American Science and Surplus Warehouse, Chicago, IL (solar cell kits, solar cars, solar energy books, wind-up toys, and instruments (prisms, radiometers, kinetic silver balls on strings, etc.)

2. Constructive Playthings, Skokie, IL (Teacher Store: similar solar toys, kits, ultraviolet beads, etc.)

3. *Solar Energy.* Foss Science Series, Delta Education, Nashua, NH, ISBN: 1-58356-847-6

4. www.spaceplace.NASA.gov

5. www.illinoissolar.org

6. Adler Planetarium.org and Museum store

7. *National Geographic Magazine*/August 2005

8. *Business 2.0 Magazine*/January-February 2007

9. *Championship Science Fair Projects.* Sudipta Bardhan-Quallen, p. 114 (Building Solar Ovens), Sterling, New York, ISBN-13-978-4027-1138-1

10. Solar Energy, Niles, IL www.solarserviceinc.com. Joe Gordon, speaker and supplier for renewable solar energy.

11. *Gonzo Gizmos.* Simon Quellen Field, (Older students: Build Solar Hot Dog Cookers, etc.) Chicago Review Press, Chicago, IL, ISBN 1-55652-520-6

RAIN FOREST

By Rachel Whitman

MAIN CONCEPT

Young gifted learners discover the life and ecology of a rainforest by creating the environment layer by layer. This strategy allows for an explorative process that draws on inquiry, discussion, and imaginative and artistic expression.

LEVEL

Primary grades.

APPLICATION

Science, art, construction, literacy.

DESCRIPTION

This idea may seem structured but is meant only as a frame. I ask the children lots of questions and provide ample opportunity for discussion and contributions. They actually fill the frame with so many meaningful ideas and thoughts. I didn't find it necessary to indicate that over and over again in each step. I have presented the overall concept that the instructor will use to generate and encourage discussion throughout each lesson. Discussion is the basis of this project and a huge time portion of the daily lessons. Without the children's contributions, it is a meaningless project.

Focus 1: The layers of the rain forest

Focus 2: The composition of the rain forest in the various layers (i.e. animals)

Focus 1

Step 1: Book exploration builds background knowledge for all and develops knowledge even further for those already exposed to the topic. This helps everyone have a focus and at minimum, a starting point.

Begin with exploration of at least 20 or more nonfiction books for a class of 15. If there are more books than children, then, as one book is finished, another is readily available for exploration. Additionally, the books must have pictures. Book exploration can be done anywhere in the classroom. I like to take advantage of the floor. The children like to spread out and utilize various floor spaces for enjoying their book and learning.

At the end of the book exploring (a 20- to 30-minute process), we gather together to discuss what we all saw in the books. As the children tell me what they have learned or seen, I write it on a chart/poster board.

Step 2: Introduce the specific topic to be studied.

I explain that there are four layers of the rainforest. As each layer is explained, I draw a picture/symbol for it, and then I write the name. (A picture/symbol helps the nonreaders or English language learners.) We examine one of the exploration books and identify the layers as a group.

Children are at ease in this warm community environment as they contribute additional information they may know about the layers. As we leave our group (which is generally on the floor and me in a chair writing/reading/etc.), we break into smaller groups. At each small group are a pile of books broken into the forest floor, understory, canopy, and emergent layer. As the groups explore each layer, they retell what they learned, know, or are seeing in the books. After five to seven minutes, the groups switch until all layers have been explored. All over the room, connections can be seen and heard!

Step 3: Assign groups a layer.

They will know their layer based on the symbol or word I made on the chart. The picture assists the nonreaders. So they don't have to ask everyday, they look at the chart and see where their name is printed in the group.

Example of the poster:

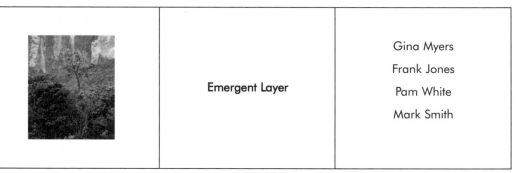

	Emergent Layer	Gina Myers Frank Jones Pam White Mark Smith

Each group is responsible for making their assigned layer of the rainforest. Typically, what works best are giant leaf templates that represent a layer. It is easy to group the kids once they are with their assigned leaves. Each group has a particular set of directions, supplies, and strategies.

I find it easiest to have all the supplies set out in the prearranged groupings. I remind them to take a minute to look at the chart and see what group they are working in. (Of course, I help them if they need it.) As we sit together on the floor, I hold up the forest floor layer and explain the area where we find it. Then, I explain the directions, how to trace the leaf, cut it out, and then paint it. I say, "If you are in this group, will you carefully stand, take these trace templates, and walk with your group." I repeat these directions for the remaining layers. Eventually, the room is buzzing, and everyone is partaking in building our rainforest.

Over the course of the next several days, I collect the layers and hang them on a tent frame. I use shipping tape to place the forest floor layers down and protect them from curious little feet. Again using shipping tape,

I attach the understory layer, the canopy, and I use sticks to elevate the emergent layer above the tent frame. Our final step is to make vines. I model to the class how to make their vines from a paper grocery bag. We cut up one narrow side and then cut away the bottom of the bag. We are left with one giant rectangle. Next, we twist the rectangle until it looks like a vine. Each child repeats this step with a second bag. Finally, we tape the bags together, to make multiple long vines. It truly is a class project.

Step 4: Similar to step one, explore books again (perhaps this time, in the rainforest). The focus is to look for animals.

After the books are explored, discuss and write on the poster board. Answer the question," What animals do we see in the emergent, canopy, understory, and forest floor?"

Step 5: If needed, explore the books again to discover and explain where animals may be living in the layers. Rotate book groups similar to step two.

Step 6: Assign groups to make particular animals for the layers. (Birds for the emergent, frogs for the forest floor, snakes for the understory, monkeys for the canopy).

This kind of process lays the foundation for gifted learners to engage in higher-level thinking and to explore topics and issues beyond their present understanding. Strategies that provide children the opportunity to build an environment—handle and examine the elements themselves—prompt questions and rouse their curiosity in ways that we can rarely predict.

IMAGINING TREES

By Joan Franklin Smutny

MAIN CONCEPT

Through identification with a tree, gifted students incorporate scientific processes of their particular species and at the same time enjoy exploring the artistic and literary responses that trees inspire. The strategy, which uses a catalyst combining art and science, enables gifted children to preserve what often becomes lost in strictly academic study—the beauty and wonder of science.

LEVEL

Primary and intermediate grades.

APPLICATION

Science, literacy, art.

DESCRIPTION

Trees are an ideal subject for creative strategies integrating science, art, and language arts. The source I have found most useful is an excellent series of prints by Thomas Locker called the *Sky Tree Portfolio*. Printed on a collection of 14 posters with text by Candace Christiansen, the portfolio has engaged countless gifted students in a creative and interdisciplinary process. Other resources I have used include: *Forest Life* by Barbara Taylor, *The Forest Has Eyes* by Elise Maclay (illus. by Bev Doolittle), *Have You Seen Trees?* By Joanne Openheim (illus. by Jean & Mou-sien Tseng), *The Great Kapok Tree: A Tale of the Amazon Rain Forest* by Lynne Cherry, and *Trees and Forests* by Scholastic.

Here is a process I have used with young gifted students.

Free Exploration

Allow the children time to think about their experiences with trees. Discuss the different parts—roots, bark, branches, leaves, and so forth. Through open questioning, discuss how each of these parts contributes to the life of the tree. As different children speak, draw into the discussion what the needs of a tree are (light, minerals, water, etc.). The more books and magazines you have for this introduction, the better, as the children will explore a greater variety of trees and learn how each has its own set of requirements—in environment and climate. Ask questions such as these: Is your tree in a forest? If so, then it lives in a shady place. If you were a tree, how would you get the light you need? The study of how light brings energy to plant life is only one aspect of trees. Here are some other areas to explore.

- The two main groups of trees, broad leaves and conifers
- Different places where trees live—the poles, temperate zones, tropical areas and how these climates affect trees (e.g., the huge barrel-shaped trunk of the Baobab tree in Africa helps the tree store water and protect it from evaporation during the dry season)
- What happens to trees in different seasons (including dry and wet for tropical climates)
- What happens to trees during the night and in the day
- Insects and animals that depend on trees and that provide nutrients for them
- People who live in the forest and depend heavily on trees

Be a Tree

After the children have had sufficient time to explore different kinds of trees, climates, and environments, have them choose a tree species and to imagine *being* that tree. Use guiding questions to spur on their own creative thinking such as the following:

- Where do you live?
- What kind of climate do you live in? Is it dry? Rainy? Cold? Warm?
- What kind of land surrounds you? Woods? Rocks? Desert? Hills? Cities?
- What kind of bark do you have? What do your leaves look like? How tall are you? How old are you?
- What kinds of animals live around you? Inside you? Who crawls or hops on you?
- What do you have that helps the animals around you?
- Are there other trees around you? How tall are they? How wide?
- What are the greatest needs of trees like you?

Children respond by drawing, writing, or discussing their ideas with each other and me. Catalysts are critical to this process. I use Thomas Locker's *Sky Tree Portfolio* because each poster is a work of art and depicts a single tree in a wide range of seasons, weather conditions, and times of day. On the back of each poster, author Candace Christiansen raises questions about each tree and provides a couple of paragraphs on some vital aspect of tree science. For example, on the back of "The Summer Tree" painting, she asks, "What does the tree do during the long summer days?" She answers that in the summer months, "The tree bathes its leaves in the light of the sun." She continues,

> The leaves also take in air. The roots are actively absorbing water and minerals from the soil. The water, air and minerals meet in the green leaves and with the help of the sunlight, the tree creates its own food: sugars. No human being or animal can create sugar out of the air, earth and water. It must be interesting to be a tree! (Locker & Christiansen, 1995)

The portfolio is an exquisite blending of science and art that invites young gifted children to enter the world of trees with both knowledge and imagination. If funds are difficult to come by, you can create your own series by collecting and laminating photographs, nature magazines, and calendar pictures and then writing some text of your own for each image.

I always offer suggestions on how students might approach their imaginative work. Here are some ideas that have worked well with young gifted children. They use whatever medium they like—writing, painting, sketching, diagrams, oral telling, silent movement, dramatization.

- If you are a very old tree (200 years, for example), tell or show a couple of the most amazing events in human history you have seen.
- Think about your most favorite season—why do you love it best? What are you doing in that time? How does it feel?
- Tell a story about how you as a tree saved a person's life. Or tell a story about a special person who stopped someone else from chopping you down.
- Express how you feel about your leaves. What do you like best about them? What do they do for you? How does the sun feel when it's beating down on them? Tell a story about your leaves.
- What would you say was the scariest moment in your life (anything that would affect the bark, roots, access to sunlight, human actions such as chopping, gashing, or spraying a chemical)? How did you survive?
- Focus on the animals that live in and on you. Who are your favorites? The squirrel family who sleep at night in the hollow on one side of your trunk? The crow family who sleep in a large nest on your highest branches? The sparrows who chirp around you all day long?

These are just ideas to get the children started. As they think about what to do, I try to keep them focused on what most interests them about trees and to point them toward media that bring out their special talents. Tell them to spend some time after school observing and touching a tree; take the class outside to a nearby tree if this is possible. Gifted students enjoy experimenting with new ways to represent and write about what they're learning. Point out that they can

- imagine and draw the *inside* of the tree;
- sketch the unique, interconnecting shapes of the bark in a close-up vision;
- create an expressive painting of the tree at a particular moment;
- create a series of images on the theme of the tree's roots (e.g., the relation of a tree's roots to people's roots).

Other children may prefer to write (stories or poems) because they find, in words, a clearer medium for their thoughts and impressions. In all the creative work we do, the children use their understanding of the actual science involved and many of them combine media to express their ideas. Examples follow below:

- A letter from a tree to humanity in combination with a chart of habitat loss and a poem

- A squirrel's story of witnessing the chopping of its favorite tree home along with a diagrammed sketch of all the animals who rely on trees to survive
- A script of an interview the child conducts with a tree that focuses on its special abilities (e.g., the baobab tree's ability to store water; the redwood's resistance to fire) and some of the amazing experiences it has had, along with a dramatization/mime to accompany a live performance of the interview

Young gifted children love learning about trees—the science, the art, the animal life in and around them. In my years of teaching, I have found that they particularly enjoy the opportunity to mix media and disciplines in order to explore the subject in far more depth and breadth. A highly gifted third grader began her study with Locker's beautifully rendered trees and a book of her own. She then composed a story of a red maple tree in her yard, which in turn, inspired more reading and research into the science and history of the maple in North America. She completed her project with a vivid watercolor and text, which documented how Native Americans first made maple sugar from the sap flowing down the bark of maple trees.

RESOURCES

Locker, T. (1995). *Sky tree portfolio* (paintings by Thomas Locker on 14 posters). Text by C. Christiansen. New York: Sky Tree Press. Available at the Center for Gifted (847–901–0173).

Smutny, J. F. & von Fremd, S.E. (2004). *Differentiating for the young child.* Thousand Oaks, CA: Corwin Press.

EXPLORING THE RAINFOREST THROUGH CONTENT-BASED FOREIGN LANGUAGE INSTRUCTION

By Kathryn P. Haydon

MAIN CONCEPT

For gifted elementary-aged children, the opportunity to learn a new system of communication early in life not only opens new avenues for self-expression but also unlocks the door to the people, environments, and customs of other worlds. Goethe said, "To acquire another language is to acquire another soul," and young gifted learners find this *soul* in an entirely new medium for exploration and self-expression. The born naturalist, with a keen appreciation for flora and fauna, is intrigued by the integration of foreign language with science projects, habitat study, and nature exploration (Smutny, Walker, & Meckstroth, 1997).

LEVEL

Early elementary.

APPLICATION

Spanish, science, reading and writing, the visual and performing arts.

DESCRIPTION

Approach: Content-Based Immersion

Numerous successful elementary foreign language programs across the country have found content-based immersion to be the most effective teaching approach, especially with gifted children. The name implies two crucial aspects: immersion and content.

Immersion

In an immersion setting, the teacher speaks only in the target language during the period designated for foreign language instruction. At first, children may respond or ask questions in English but will quickly pick up words and phrases until they are speaking in the foreign language itself. While some children focus on understanding isolated words and phrases, others will take it a step further and will pick up verb conjugations and recognize English cognates, thereby exceeding stated learning objectives. Immersion provides an optimal opportunity to differentiate for gifted children with varying learning styles.

Content

Content-based means that you integrate foreign language instruction with other content areas—in this case, science. For gifted children, learning language for language's sake (i.e., "Class, *rojo* means red in Spanish. Repeat after me, '*Rojo,* red. *Rojo,* red.'") lacks meaning and depth. It becomes an exercise in memorization rather than a creative, exciting adventure in learning. Using regular classroom curriculum content as a catalyst and framework allows you to reinforce that material and make it come alive in a different context and on a different level.

Creativity

In addition to immersion and content, the keys to a successful foreign language program are creativity, energy, gesturing, and variety. When speaking only in the target language, you'll need to have plenty of visuals as well as body movements to go along with songs and speech in order to convey the words you are saying. Although they won't know all the words at first, the teacher will speak only in Spanish, and it is the students' job to be detectives to figure out what the teacher is saying. Their drive to learn will be fueled if they associate fun with foreign language learning. Gifted children are receptive to creativity, innovation, and application. They will respond to a mixture of games, songs, stories, theater, and art projects.

Methodology

Incorporating a foreign language into your classroom curriculum is not difficult. Follow five simple steps, build a resource center over time, and foreign language will add an entirely new dimension to your classroom and to your gifted students' educational experience. You will be delighted to see how they are inspired to take their learning to new heights.

Five Steps

1. Choose the content area or regular classroom subject you'd like to reinforce. In this case, it is science.

2. Identify your target language learning objectives. Remember, the theme is the catalyst for the foreign language objective. Are you trying to teach colors, numbers, conversational phrases, or commands? Conceptual ideas such as masculine and feminine endings? Using a theme such as the rainforest, you could, for example, choose to focus on animals, actions of animals, animal habitats, food and products found in the rainforest, weather terminology, colors, numbers, and so on.

3. Identify specific concepts or ideas within the content area that you'd like to reinforce using the target language. Again, using the rainforest as an example, would you like your students to have additional work discussing animal habitats or the weather in the rainforest?

4. Design creative, theme-based activities that help meet both your language and content reinforcement objectives.

5. Be sure to structure each teaching period with a variety of activities geared toward various learning styles. Include songs, movement, a

short activity, and a main activity, not spending more than 10 minutes (in kindergarten) or 15 minutes (in Grades 1–3) on each element.

Application

Here's the scenario: You are a kindergarten teacher and have just transformed your classroom into a rainforest. Swaths of green fabric are draped from the ceiling connected to sturdy trunks woven from oversized sheets of twisted brown paper. Monkeys, lemurs, butterflies, snakes, ants, birds, and tree frogs peek from underneath the canopy, suspended from trees and hanging from the ceiling. A tiger peeks out from behind your desk. Books such as *The Great Kapok Tree* by Lynne Cherry, *Verdi* by Janell Canon, and *A Walk in the Rainforest* by Kristin Joy Pratt adorn shelves at five-year-old eye level. A tasting station full of rainforest aliments such as cocoa, sugar cane, Macadamia nuts, cinnamon, nutmeg, and ginger awaits the scrutiny of young tongues; the rhyme "Five Little Monkeys" hangs on a poster in the front of the room; and a colorful map of Brazil is positioned on an adjacent wall.

When children walk into your classroom on Monday morning, a whole new world awaits them. You have hands-on activities planned to integrate with your theme, including a basic study of South American geography; reading rainforest literature; writing about the layers of the rainforest; baking cookies full of chocolate, coconut, and various nuts to sell and raise money to save a portion of the endangered rainforest; counting the money raised in the bake sale; and patterning with rainforest animals.

This unit also marks the beginning of kindergarten Spanish language class. Since you've never incorporated your knowledge of Spanish into your regular classroom before, you're starting out small at two or three days a week for a half-an-hour each time, with the intent to expand it if all goes well. How have you decided to incorporate Spanish into the rainforest theme, and how did you do it according to the proposed five-step methodology?

1. The theme was easy to decide. Your school year is broken into monthly thematic units, so you naturally chose the one you'd be focused on next: the rainforest.

2. Your Spanish language learning objectives for the first two weeks are straightforward, as follows:
   - Children are introduced to basic greetings in Spanish and introductions (What is your name? My name is ___.).
   - Children learn to say and understand colors in Spanish: red, orange, yellow, green, blue, purple, white, brown, black.

- Children learn to say and understand the names of selected rainforest creatures in Spanish: snake, monkey, ant, tiger, butterfly, bird, frog.
- Children learn to say the colors of each animal in Spanish, that is, "The frog is green." (*La rana es verde.*)
- Children learn to count in Spanish starting with Numbers 1 through 10.

3. Using Spanish, you would also like to reinforce the mathematical concepts of patterning, seeing numerals, and counting that you will be teaching in the English portion of the rainforest unit.

4. You've designed a number of activities, geared toward various learning styles, to teach each concept. You couldn't find that *perfect* song, so you made up a little chant about going to the rainforest and the different animals that you'll see, and a couple of the art projects that you usually do in English, you've decided to conduct in Spanish this year instead.

5. Here are your class structure and activities for Day 1. Remember, you won't be spending more than 10 minutes on any one activity; ideally, it will be no more than five to seven for most activities, until you get to your art projects on the second or third day, when you might use a full 10 minutes for one activity.
   - The flight. You'll introduce the Spanish portion of the day, talking about how students have to be detectives. Then, it's time to take a flight to the rainforest in Argentina. . . . Children and teacher will hold out their arms as wings and fly, landing in *la selva tropical*.
   - Quick introduction. As you gesture around the room, you say "*¡Hola, cláse! Estamos aquí en la selva tropical.*" (Hello, class! We are here in the rainforest.) Say, "*Me llamo Señora Smith.*" (My name is Mrs. Smith) as you point to yourself. Ask, "*¿Cómo te llamas?*" (What is your name?) as you first point to a child, then gesture like you're asking a question. You may have to repeat the sentence about your own name and then ask the student again. In subsequent sessions, you might bring an item from the rainforest that you can toss around a circle, having students ask, "*¿Cómo te llamas?*" to the person they throw the object to.
   - Chant. Begin the rainforest chant that you made up. It is call and response, and begins something like this: *Estamos en la selva tropical. Vemos animales—las ranas, los monos, y los tigres.* (We are in the rainforest. We see animals—frogs, monkeys, and tigers.) You and the students act out each movement and each animal.
   - Follow the leader. You are the leader, and you ask students, in Spanish, to get in line behind you as you gesture. Walk around the

room again, pointing out the animals you'd like them to learn in Spanish—on posters, in trees, on the walls. *"Yo veo una rana."* (I see a frog.) Use this "I see" structure as an introduction to the game that you will play later. Have children return to their seats on the carpet.

- Felt animals. Use your classroom felt board and the set of rainbow-colored felt (or die-cut and laminated, with Velcro on the backs to stick) animals that you made for this unit. Only use those animals that you'd like children to learn in Spanish. Bring out each animal, place it on the felt board, and say the name in Spanish. Point to it and act it out, having the children repeat as they act it out too. This activity not only introduces the animals in a more formal way, but it provides somewhat of an introduction to the patterning activity you will do with die-cut animals in a day or two.
- I Spy. Look carefully and dramatically around the room, perhaps with your hand above your eyes as if you are trying to see something far away. Say, *"Yo veo un mono,"* (I see a monkey) as you point to your eye and gesture like a monkey. You can also refer to the felt animals that are still up on your felt board. Children have to guess which of the many monkeys around the room you are referring to. Do this with each of the animals in your target vocabulary list.
- Short song. Sing another short song, perhaps about the animals, or listen to one that you've found in Spanish about a particular animal or the rainforest.
- Back home again. Take the flight back to the United States, back to your English-speaking classroom.

Building Your Language Resource Center

Having a resource center full of music, books, posters, and materials from which you can draw will enrich your foreign language program. It is important to have these materials available and accessible so that gifted children can see and explore the language as often as they'd like. Although you are not necessarily focused on teaching the written word during your foreign language sessions, never underestimate the importance of providing children access to it. In one second-grade class, the teacher posted Spanish labels at the beginning of the year on dozens of regular classroom items such as the sink, a desk, the door, and the window.

Some basic items to have on hand, regardless of the themes you plan to teach in the foreign language, are a calendar (listing the days of the weeks and months); an English-foreign language dictionary and picture dictionary; books actually written in the foreign language ranging from very simple board books to translations of well-known chapter books such as *Charlotte's Web*; color and number posters for student reference;

foreign language labels posted around the room on regular classroom items; music in the foreign language that you can play as the children enter the classroom in the morning or during other appropriate times throughout the school day; a center with a tape recorder of you reading translations of a familiar story so children can listen along with the book; and simple games (such as bingo) presented in the foreign language.

Conclusion

Giving gifted students access to learning a second language in the early grades will open doors for them both presently and in the future. Not only is it an opportunity to challenge them academically, it will help them become well-rounded world citizens with the ability to relate to those from cultures other than their own more intimately. For students with early knowledge of a foreign language, the world will become their canvas as they explore its people and places with a more acute understanding.

It is our duty as educators to ensure that foreign language teaching in elementary schools is as creative, exciting, and substantive as the other subjects we teach. We must impart foreign language with as great a depth and sense of purpose as we do science and social studies. Better yet, why not use science and social studies to teach the foreign language itself!

REFERENCES AND RESOURCES

America 2000: An educational strategy. (1991). Washington, DC: U.S. Department of Education.

Curtain, H. A., & Pesola, C. A. (1988). *Languages and children—Making the match.* Reading, MA: Addison-Wesley.

LeLoup, J. W., & Ponterio, R. (1997). *Celebrating languages: Opening all minds!* (A. Vogely (Ed.). (pp. 43–50). NYSAFLT Annual Meeting Series 14.

Marcos, K. M. (1998, Fall). Second language learning: Everyone can benefit. *The ERIC Review, 6* (1), 2–5.

Smutny, J. F., & Walker, S. Y., & Meckstroth, E. A. (1997). *Teaching young gifted children in the regular classroom.* Minneapolis, MN: Free Spirit.

Standards for foreign language learning: Preparing for the 21st century. (1996). Lawrence, KS: Allen Press.

RESOURCES AND RECOMMENDATIONS

General Resources for Books, Music, and Videos

www.amazon.com—to search, type "children's books in Spanish"
www.bookswithoutborders.com
www.spanishtoys.com—lots of Disney and other children's movies

Recommended Music That We Use in School

Language Stars *Around the World With Language Stars*—www
.languagestars.com (click on the colorful CD on the homepage)
Dr. Jean, *Olé, Olé, Olé Dr. Jean en Español*—www.drjean.org
(click on "Secure an order form)
José Luis Orozco, *Diez Deditos* and *De Colores*—www.amazon.com

Recommended Music That Is Good to Use at Home

Maria del Rey, *Uni Verse of Song Spanish*—www.amazon.com
(English/Spanish)
Lilia Mareski, *Miss Lily's Spanish Sing-Along*—www.songsforteaching.com
(English/Spanish)
K-Rainforest
1—Los estaciones
2—El ciclo de vida de la rana/el pueblo
3—Geography and animals (habitats)

6

Mathematics Strategies

Creativity is not what one usually associates with mathematics, a subject considered by most to be a world of *hard* facts, determined by logic and reason. Thomas Gradgrind, a character in Charles Dickens's *Hard Times*, would heartily approve of this view, believing as he did, that anything else should be expunged from the classroom. " Now, what I want is, facts. Teach these boys and girls nothing but facts. Facts alone are wanted in life. Plant nothing else, and root out everything else" (p. 1). As Paul Bamberger, our first author in this chapter shows, the No Child Left Behind Act has to some extent projected a similar message, discouraging creativity in favor of a greater focus on increasing knowledge and skills, and thereby improving test scores.

In mathematics, when we talk of creativity, we are referring to active engagement in an open-ended and real-world process rather than the kind of problem solving where the steps are predetermined and the sequences formulaic. The latter involves little in-depth thinking or understanding of the concepts involved. Certainly, gifted students learn little of the implications of mathematical ideas on their interests and lives in classrooms that don't integrate more creative, out-of-the-box thinking modalities. Because they are gifted, they quickly learn the rules and formulas and content themselves with performing required tasks. Over time, they no longer remember the awe they used to feel with the intricate patterns found in a plant or a butterfly wing or the flush of excitement they experienced upon discovering a new method to add triple-digit numbers.

As shown by the authors in this chapter, the first step must be to design situations that inspire observation, reasoning, and imagination. Gifted students need lively contexts where they can explore the properties of different phenomena, seek patterns, follow clues, and devise unique formulas of their own to make mathematics a process of discovery and invention. As teachers, we need to remember that in their earliest years of life, mathematics didn't come from textbooks but from the world around us. Little children acquire a sense of patterns by rhythms they hear in music, the visual display of squares on the tile floor, the pairs of feet standing in line at the post office, and the miniscule veins threading themselves across a maple leaf. Patterns, shapes, quantities, lines, and measures surround their everyday lives.

During this time, gifted children often create strategies for solving problems intuitively. I once witnessed three young children discuss how they should split eight oatmeal-chocolate chip cookies. One child said that after each taking two, they should divide the remaining two into thirds and then each of them could take their part of the two remaining cookies. Another child thought it would be easier to split the two cookies in half then there'd just be a half cookie left over, which they could dispense with by each taking a bite. The last child had the idea of passing around the six cookies, cutting one-third off one of each of their two cookies to make an extra cookie and then pass around the three remaining cookies (one broken up into thirds). I was amazed at this interaction. All three listened intently to the different solutions and, after further discussion, agreed on the third solution as the easiest, fairest and, least messy.

With support and guidance, many gifted students can create their own solutions to problems like this. But they also need to become comfortable with a range of useful math strategies and learn when and how to apply them. Examples (Burns 1992, p. 19) include the following:

- Look for overall designs, patterns.
- Create a table.
- Make an organized list.
- Act it out.
- Draw a picture.
- Use objects.
- Guess and check.
- Work backward.
- Write an equation.
- Solve a simpler (or similar) problem.
- Create a model.

Gifted children who enjoy discovering creative connections to mathematics have a range of choices. They could do any of the following:

- Write a humorous sketch about a math problem on one sheet, and then sketch and explain how they tried to solve it.
- Explore as many different ways to solve a word problem as they can.
- Choreograph geometric patterns.
- Model problem situations through multiple modes and representations to discover solutions.

- Create geometric objects and then draw them.
- Brainstorm all the ways math appears in our daily lives (e.g., time and calendars, architecture, the math behind the building of bridges and buildings, etc.).
- Measure the ratio between an object depicted in a poster and its shadow.
- Draw three- and four-sided patterns from nature.
- Express the idea of negative numbers artistically.

If the larger purpose of math is to enable students to solve problems creatively, to reason, test, explore, and discover new solutions, we as teachers need to find many different ways for them to do this. A creative classroom varies not only the pace and level of math content (to accommodate giftedness) but also the "intelligences" involved (e.g., visual-spatial, bodily-kinesthetic, verbal-linguistic, logical-mathematical).

Opening up the subject in this way enables students who are craving for a more interdisciplinary, more varied experience to see the connections between their own interests and the rich and intricate world of mathematics. Having a keen eye for angles, lines, and patterns, for example, is invaluable if you're a botanist, a zoologist, or anyone else interested in discriminating between species in nature, as it also is if you're trying to design a home or create a map. Civil engineers depend on mathematics to construct sound bridges, tunnels, and roadways. As math teacher Paul Bamberger illustrates below, designing real contexts where students can use and explore mathematical concepts gives them much more interesting problems to solve and in far more creative ways.

REFERENCES

Burns, M. (1992). *About teaching mathematics: A K–8 resource.* Sausalito CA: Math Solutions Publications.
Dickens, C. (2007). *Hard times.* New York: Pocket.

Creativity in the Classroom

By Paul Bamberger

CREATIVITY IN GENERAL

I believe that creativity can and should be integrated into every subject area taught in our schools and at each grade level. Creativity helps students become more engaged in their own learning so that they feel a sense of ownership in the process, which ultimately leads to higher achievement scores on standardized tests. With the legislation of the No Child Left Behind Act of 2001 (NCLB), teachers often feel forced to sacrifice creative teaching strategies for memorization and drill style teaching. More often than not, the skills students acquire after long hours of repeated practice are forgotten shortly after the testing period. As educators, we all can empower students to achieve at higher levels and retain the concepts taught by integrating creativity into our daily classroom instruction.

CREATIVITY IN MATHEMATICS: SUCCESSFUL IDEA

A couple of years back, I submitted a grant idea to a local foundation for an innovative and creative idea for teaching mathematics. I titled my project "Mathematical House." Mathematical House consisted of the purchase of cardboard dollhouses and craft supplies, an innovative and creative implementation plan of its use throughout grades kindergarten through fifth, and a thorough evaluation of the progress of this project.

Mathematical House

The purpose of this project was to use an ordinary doll house to further develop mathematical thinking skills in elementary students. Mathematical House improved mathematical reasoning by situating it in a real-world context. Many students complain that math will never be used in the future because they do not see any real-world connection to what they learn. This novel project integrated interior design, art, and critical and creative thinking with mathematical reasoning. When someone tiles a floor or wallpapers a wall, math skills are utilized. Square footage is calculated, and the amount of tile or wallpaper is determined. The cost of the entire tiling or wallpapering job is calculated as well. Thus, mathematical reasoning skills come into play throughout the process as students calculate volume, surface areas, and perimeters while exploring the feasibility of different designs.

Additionally, this project enriched and exceeded the curriculum while also supporting fundamental learning goals and standards in the district. We created a curriculum binder to extend the impact of this project and enable other educators to implement its ideas in their kindergarten through fifth-grade classrooms. The gifted students clearly benefited from this project. They were able to choose their own design of the floor space, wall space, and roof. They were given materials, but they had the freedom to decide what their house would look like and how it would *feel*.

This idea is one of many that can be utilized when teaching mathematical concepts to students. The main idea here is taking their knowledge and using it in a creative and engaging manner. These students were able to take their knowledge from pen and paper and utilize it in a real world setting. Furthermore, I have seen the impact of creative teaching of mathematics on achievement tests. Students who learn in a manner similar to those in the Mathematical House project exhibit higher levels of achievement in large part because they are better able to retain the concepts taught. Not only are the benefits seen on achievement tests but also within the classroom as well. Students taught in a creative environment have more self-confidence in their abilities as well as a higher degree of enthusiasm to learn. Creative thinking is challenging, and gifted students, in particular, thrive on challenging activities.

CREATIVE TEACHING: GENERAL IDEAS

One idea I've found consistently effective for creative work in math and other subjects is the *thinking station*. A series of thinking stations in the classroom require students to use their critical and creative thinking skills to solve specific tasks or problems. Each station is slightly different, but all relate back to the main purpose and subject area. Students like the different stations because each one challenges them differently, yet each draws upon higher-level thinking modalities. The excitement students feel for the challenge and the uniqueness of the format motivate them to complete all the stations, and once they complete all stations, they usually want more!

I am a fan of activities that really immerse students in a situation and help them apply their thinking ability in new ways. To this end, I sometimes design and implement simulations that encourage team work and thoughtful analysis of the material. I have used simulations in every subject area, including mathematics. I have had students design and dramatize situations inspired by math problems as a way of finding new solutions. Dramatizations encourage students to really *get into* the material and explore concepts more creatively.

In general, I encourage my students to think outside the box in all they do. When I walk into a classroom to provide enrichment services, one will always hear me say to the students in attendance, "Think outside the box!" Students need to be encouraged to find the problems not just solve them. They need to feel free to question the world around them and think about it from different perspectives or angles. Creativity promotes links and connections between different ideas that enable students to take their thinking to higher levels. To do this though, students need to feel encouraged and free to go beyond what is expected and think about the world in novel and creative ways.

As in previous chapters, the chart that follows is offered as an aid to inspire some of your own ideas on the planning process. Seven detailed entries focus on specific areas of mathematics where creative teaching has yielded high benefits for gifted students.

Topics & Authors	Creative Strategies	Grade Level	Standards (examples)
Critical and Creative Thinking Ideas in Math *Christopher M. Freeman* P. 205	Open questioning Playing games Brainstorming Inductive reasoning Creative thinking	Elementary years, adaptable to higher grades	Instructional programs should enable all students to formulate questions that can be addressed with data and collect, organize, and display relevant data to answer them. This includes developing and evaluating inferences and predictions that are based on data.
Multiple Strategies for Encouraging Divergent Thinking in Math *Paula Koomjohn* P. 212	Divergent thinking Manipulating with numbers Exploring patterns Detecting *mystery numbers* Creating number patterns Puzzles	Intermediate and middle school years	Instructional programs should enable all students to apply and adapt a variety of appropriate strategies to solve problems. They should enable all students to make and investigate mathematical conjectures, and select and use various types of reasoning and methods of proof.
Math Is So Much More Than Two Times Four *Joyce Hammer* P. 216	Exploring geometry in art Experimenting thru different media Engineering constructions Creating patterns and designs Drawing original graphs	Primary grades	Instructional programs should enable all students to - develop and evaluate mathematical arguments and proofs, select and use various types of reasoning and methods of proof; - recognize and apply mathematics in contexts outside of mathematics; - use visualization, spatial reasoning, and geometric modeling to solve problems.
Calendar Challenge: A Creative Mathematics Activity *Carol Fisher* P. 224	Divergent thinking Creating equations Flexible reasoning Creative extensions through the use of fractions, exponents, etc.	Intermediate and middle grades and up	Instructional program should enable all students to - understand numbers, ways of representing numbers, relationships among numbers, and number systems; and - understand meanings of operations and how they relate to one another.
A Number by Any Other Name *Carol Fisher* **P. 227**	Fluency Creative reasoning Visual thinking Experimenting Translating idea to new situations	Adaptable from primary through the intermediate grades and middle school	Instructional programs should enable all students to - create and use representations to organize, record, and communicate mathematical ideas; - select, apply, and translate among mathematical representations to solve problems; and - use representations to model and interpret physical, social, and mathematical phenomena.

Topics & Authors	Creative Strategies	Grade Level	Standards (examples)
How Do YOU Count to Ten? – An Exploration of Number Bases *Carol Fisher* P. 230	Open questioning Investigating number bases Brainstorming options Examining Mayan numerals Composing counting books	Higher grades, yet there are helpful ideas for adapting this process for younger students	Instructional programs should enable all students to - understand numbers, ways of representing numbers, relationships among numbers, and number systems; - understand meanings of operations and how they relate to one another.
Math Literature Links: A Creative Approach *Carol Fisher* P. 236	Interdisciplinary learning (literature) Performing math stories Exploring interconnections between math and language arts Experimenting and improvising with math concepts in literature	All grades	Instructional programs should enable all students to - organize and consolidate their mathematical thinking through communication; - communicate their mathematical thinking coherently and clearly to peers, teachers, and others; - analyze and evaluate the mathematical thinking and strategies of others; and - use the language of mathematics to express mathematical ideas precisely.

CRITICAL AND CREATIVE THINKING IDEAS IN MATH

By Christopher M. Freeman

MAIN CONCEPT

To provide gifted students with fun, gamelike activities that promote growth in critical and creative thinking and reasoning.

LEVEL

Elementary grades.

APPLICATION

Mathematics, higher-level thinking, divergent thinking.

DESCRIPTION

Number of the Day

From the first day of school to the last, each day has a number, and every whole number is interesting. (High school students can prove that using mathematical induction, but I digress.) I begin each sixth-grade class by asking students to tell me interesting facts about the number of the day. For example, on day one, students may tell me that *one* is the only number that has the property *1 × number = number*; it is the only whole number that is neither prime nor composite (it has too *few* factors to be prime); it is *uno* in Spanish, *eins* in German, and *un* in French; it is the only number written the same way in every base; it is the title of a song from *A Chorus Line*; it was the jersey number of baseball shortstop Ozzie Smith. Every student can contribute some fact of interest, and every student can appreciate the usefulness of numbers in all fields of human endeavor.

Prime Factorizations

Every day of school, I ask for the prime factorization of the number of the day, for example, day $24 = 2^3 \times 3$. Students spend years learning to think of numbers in place value. But students need to think of numbers as products composed of factors. Why? For one thing, when they put fractions into lowest terms, they need to recognize common factors. I also ask students to list the factors of the number of the day. For example, the factors of 36 are 1, 2, 3, 4, 6, 9, 12, 18, and 36. Some good questions for students to ponder include, "Why does 36 have an odd quantity of factors?" "What kind of numbers all have an odd quantity of factors?" and "How can you predict how many factors a number will have from its prime factorization?"

Star of the Day

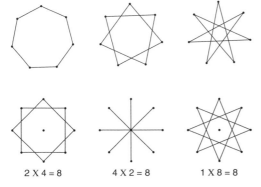

2 X 4 = 8   4 X 2 = 8   1 X 8 = 8

On the fifth day of school, I draw a five-pointed star. On the sixth day, I draw two different six-pointed stars, the Star of David and an asterisk. On the seventh day, I ask students if they have ever seen a seven-pointed star. Most say that haven't. So I draw three different seven-pointed stars. For each star, I place seven points equally spaced around a circle; when I connect them, I always count *over* the same number of points each time. These stars happen to be *continuous*, that is, each can be drawn from point to point without lifting the pencil (or chalk). However, some stars are *overlapping* copies of simpler stars. The eight-pointed stars shown nearby are composed of either two overlapping squares ($2 \times 4 = 8$) or four overlapping two-pointed segments ($4 \times 2 = 8$). But if you count *over three*, you get a continuous star.

I draw a star with the number of the points of every day up to about day 40. First, I get the right number of points in a circle—no easy feat. Then, to avoid counting, I pick an *over number* that is a factor of the number one greater or one less than the number of points. After counting a few times, it soon becomes very obvious which points to connect. Try it!

It becomes an interesting question; if you know the number of points and the *over number*, can you predict whether the star will be continuous or overlapping? For more activities on this topic, see my book *Drawing Stars and Building Polyhedra* (2005).

Number of the Day in Base 2 and Other Bases

In base 2, you count like this: 1, 10, 11, 100, 101, 110, 111, 1000, ... So day 8 is the 1,000th day of school, and day 64 is the 1,000,000th day of school. (Whew!) In base 3, you count like this: 1, 2, 10, 11, 12, 20, 21, 22, 100, ... So day 9 is the 100th day of school in base 3. In base 16, you need extra digits A for 10, B for 11, C for 12, D for 13, E for 14, and F for 15. So day 11 is the Bth day of school, day 24 is the 18th day of school, and day 161 is the A1st day of school.

Collecting Homework

Would you like your pile of homework or quizzes to be in the same order as your grade book? Would you like to collect homework or to return it in 30 seconds? Here is a system I have used for many years to collect homework. (It works for

19	20	21	22	23	24
18	17	16	15	14	13
7	8	9	10	11	12
6	5	4	3	2	1

quizzes and tests too.) I assign every seat a number. The front left desk (from the students' point of view) is *Number 1*. Count sequentially right along the front row. The next row, count sequentially to the *left* (again, from the students' point of view). The next row, count right again, and the fourth row count to the left.

When I say, "Pass down your homework," students in the desks at the right end of the room (6, 7, 18, and 19) pass their papers to their left. After that, all students in the first or third row (Number 5 and Number 17, etc.) put their papers on *top* of the pile; all students in the second or fourth row (8 and 20, etc.) put their papers on the *bottom* of the pile; then, they pass the pile to the left. Eventually, all the papers end up at the left end of the rows. I collect the piles from the back of the room, putting each new stack on top of my pile. When I'm done, I have all the homework neatly in order from Number 1 to 24. And I can return the homework in order, paper by paper, snaking around the room. This gives me the opportunity to discuss privately individual issues on the way.

Bizz-Buzz Bopp

This is a good game to teach divisibility and factoring skills. Have all the students stand up behind their chairs. Clearly define a path to follow from student to student (I use the seat number order established for collecting homework). Select a random student to begin. The first student says, "One." The next student says, "Two." The students continue in order, each saying the next whole number. But if the number is a multiple of three, the student must say, "Bizz" instead; and if the number is a multiple of 5, the student must say, "Buzz" instead. If the number is a multiple of both 3 and 5, the student must say, "Bizz-buzz" or "uzz-bizz." Students get five seconds to think. If the student says the wrong thing, he or she must sit down and no longer participates. (Such students must sit, so that others may count ahead correctly.) When there are only two students left, they are joint winners. The goal is for the class to get to 100 with three or more students still in the game. When the students get good at this game, add *bopp* for multiples of 4, *bang* for multiples of 7, and *beep* for multiples of 11. Children enjoy the odd conversations: "19," "bopp-buzz," "bizz-bang," "beep," "23," . . . and they learn to love prime numbers.

Around the World

This game practices any basic fact skill, such as adding or multiplying signed integers from –20 to 20. Follow any consistent order around the room (such as the seat number order). Select a random student to begin. That student moves to the next desk, and both students stand. I ask a random question, such as "What is -3×8?" Whoever says the correct answer first wins. But if a wrong answer is given, the other student has five seconds to say the correct answer. If both are wrong, they get a new question. If there seems to be a tie, I ask the students who are sitting to vote whether it was a tie or if someone won—this keeps everyone involved. Eventually, the loser sits, and the winner moves on to the next desk. The game is done when someone has gone *around the world* and returned to his or her own desk. Sometimes, students who don't get the best grades can really shine in this game, and everyone is practicing the skills without realizing it.

$5 \times 5 = 25$	$6 \times 4 = 24$
$8 \times 8 = 64$	$9 \times 7 = 63$
$10 \times 10 = 100$	$11 \times 9 = 99$

Integer Multiplication Near Squares

Consider the relationship of perfect squares to products of the numbers one higher and one lower. Try some other special cases. Can you write a general pattern? This is a great way to motivate practice with multiplication facts. And the algebra teacher will thank you if the students have already seen an application of the factoring formula $n^2 = (n + 1)(n - 1)$.

Exponentiation

All students know *operations* are addition, subtraction, multiplication, and division. They have more trouble thinking of exponentiation as an *operation*. One reason is that we don't use an operation symbol for it. At least, we didn't use to before calculators. Now students know that $3 \wedge 4$ is a more sensible way to write 3^4. (Teachers don't know that, but we can learn.) But another reason students don't think of exponentiation as an *operation* is that we don't usually ask students to memorize exponentiation tables. I ask my students to learn all the powers of two from $2 \wedge 0 = 1$ to $2 \wedge 10 = 1024$. (A helpful mnemonic is that $2 \wedge 6 = 64$, so the sixth and tenth powers of two start with the exponent.) Students should memorize that $3 \wedge 3 = 27$, $3 \wedge 4 = 81$, and $3 \wedge 5 = 243$. They should also memorize the third powers of 4, 5, 6, 7, and 8.

Numerator and Denominator

Do you know why the top number of a fraction is called its *numerator*? To *enumerate* means to count how many there are (like the book of "Numbers" in the Bible). And to *denominate* means to give something a name (when you *nominate* someone, you put their name on the list to consider). So the numerator counts how many, and the denominator names what you are counting.

Fractions and Repetends

It's part of our curriculum for students to memorize the fraction and decimal equivalents for denominators two, four, five, six, eight, nine, and ten. But what about 7ths? Ask students to use their calculators to find the six-digit repetends for all the fractions between 0 and 1 with denominator 7. With some prompts from the teacher, students will recognize that each repetend has the same six digits, in the same order. A similar property (with a twist) is possessed by the repetends for 13ths.

The fractions with denominator 17 all have the same 16 digits in the same order. Can you find the repetend for 17ths? Most calculators cannot display all 16 digits. But each fractions $\frac{1}{17}, \frac{2}{17}, \frac{3}{17}, \ldots$ provides a piece of the puzzle.

$$\frac{1}{7} = 0.\overline{142857}$$
$$\frac{2}{7} = \overline{0.285714}$$
$$\frac{3}{7} = \overline{0.428571}$$
$$\frac{4}{7} = \overline{0.571428}$$
$$\frac{5}{7} = \overline{0.714285}$$
$$\frac{6}{7} = \overline{0.857142}$$

Fraction Addition

We all know that, when you are adding fractions, you're not supposed to add the numerators and add the denominators. But what happens if you do? Does the answer have any meaning? Suppose in the first baseball game of the season, you get three hits for five at-bats, but the second game you get only one hit in four at-bats. What would be your overall batting average? Wouldn't it be $\frac{4}{9}$? So there *is* a use for adding fractions the "wrong" way. And the answer you get is always between the two fractions you started with.

$$\frac{3}{5} \oplus \frac{1}{4} = \frac{4}{9}$$

Fraction Division

$$\frac{8}{9} \div \frac{2}{3} = \frac{4}{3}$$

We all know that, to multiply fractions, you multiply the numerators, and multiply the denominators. Did you know you can divide fractions the same way? It always works, but it isn't always convenient.

"Random" Numbers

Ask every student to think of a random number from 1 to 10 and write it down. Then make a chart on the board for how many students chose 1, how many chose 2, and so on. It fits well into my curriculum for students to draw circle graphs of the results. But what I find most noteworthy is that, in almost every class I have asked over many years, one of the most frequently chosen numbers is either 3 or 7. Ask the students to explain why this might be so. I think that when someone tries to think of a "random" number, they shy away from extremes and from the middle, rejecting 1, 5, and 10, they arrive at 3 or 7. By the way, a commonly selected random two-digit number is 37, which shows up far more often than probable in illustrations in children's books (house numbers, train numbers, and the like). This activity demonstrates how difficult it is to select random numbers–yet we depend on lists of random numbers for many purposes in statistics. (Need I say that we do this activity on the 37th day of school?)

The 100 Game

Two people play. The first player calls out a whole number from 1 to 10. The players take turns calling out bigger and bigger numbers—never more than 10 higher than the previous number just called out. Whoever says 100 wins. Students quickly realize that if you can say 89, you will win the game, since the other player cannot say 100, but whatever number he or she does say, you can say 100. Let the students play the game several times. Soon, they will find that 78 is also a winning number. Indeed, there is a whole sequence of winning numbers, starting with 1. Once a student has found all the winning numbers, have him or her beat you in whispers. Then, swear him or her to secrecy! You don't need to use all the winning numbers—unless you are playing someone who knows them all. Otherwise, call out any random numbers you like—but be sure you say 67. Students really like keeping a secret! I have several times witnessed the following interchange:

Student A: Let's play the 100 Game.

Student B: OK, I want to go first. One.

Student A: Fine, you win. Now I want to go first. One.

Student B: OK, fine, you win.

Nim Games

A box of paper clips is all you need for your students to play these games. The basic game of Nim has five rules:

- There is one pile.
- There are 13 objects in the pile.
- There are two players.
- At each turn, a player may remove one or two objects from the pile.
- Whoever takes the last one loses.

Children enjoy playing this game, and they quickly realize that you can win the game by leaving your opponent with four objects. Gradually, students find a full winning strategy. One way to win is to let the opponent go first and always to take the opposite of what your opponent takes. Another way to think about the same strategy is always to leave your opponent in the winning numbers 1, 4, 7, 10, and 13.

For further variations, every one of the five rules may be changed. You could play with more objects in the pile (I use 15, 20, and 30). You could, "Take 1, 2, or 3." You could, "Take 1, 2, 3, or 4." You decide that whoever takes the last one *wins*. You could play with three players. You could play with two or more piles. For these and many other variations on the game of Nim, see my book, *Nim: Variations and Strategies* (2005).

The Two-Pile Game, 6 and 10

Start with two piles of 6 and 10. Two players play. At each turn, a player may remove any number of objects from one pile only, or the same number of objects from both piles. Whoever takes the last one wins.

This game is fun because you need to find winning *pairs*, not just winning numbers. The list of winning pairs begins {0,0}, {1,2}, {3,5}, . . .

How Many Squares Are There On a Chessboard?

Do you think there are 64? What about 2×2 squares? What about 3×3 squares? (There are 49 and 36 of these.) When you find all the numbers of different sizes of squares, add them all together.

A greater challenge: How many rectangles are there on a chessboard?

The 13 Coins

Here is a challenge for your best students. You have 13 coins. They all look identical. One of them is counterfeit: it weighs either more or less than a real coin. You may use a balance scale three times. Describe a sequence of steps that will locate the counterfeit coin.

Donald in Mathemagic Land

The 1959 Disney classic is now available on DVD. It's a super way to amuse students on the day before a long holiday. Every time I watch it, I find a new detail to admire. Accurate mathematics in nature, games, art, and music are displayed in winning ways.

Bad Math Jokes

What do little algebra acorns say when they grow up? "Geometry!" (Gee, I'm a tree!).

If two is company and three is a crowd, what are four and five? (Nine.)

Why were five and six scared? Because seven, eight, nine! (Seven ate nine.)

A Good Story

Once there were three brothers who grew up in New York. They decided to go west to seek their fortune, and they started a cattle ranch on the Great Plains. After several years, they grew quite successful, and they wrote home to their mother, "Mom, Mom, we've been making lots of money out west. But we don't have a name for our cattle ranch. Can you help us out?"

The mother wrote back, "Call the ranch Focus."

The boys looked at each other. They thought and thought. Finally, they wrote back, "Mom, Mom, we have no doubt that Focus would be a terrific name for our cattle ranch. But why did you think of that particular word?"

The mother wrote back, "Isn't the focus where the sun's rays meet?" (Sons raise meat.)

REFERENCE

Freeman, C. (2005). *Drawing stars & building polyhedra.* Waco, TX: Prufrock Press.
Freeman, C. (2005). *Nim: Variations and strategies.* Waco, TX: Prufrock Press.

MULTIPLE STRATEGIES FOR ENCOURAGING DIVERGENT THINKING IN MATH

By Paula Koomjohn

MAIN CONCEPT

Teachers can increase divergent thinking in solving complex math problems through multiple teaching strategies and through peer interaction.

LEVEL

Intermediate and middle school grades.

APPLICATION

Math curriculum.

DESCRIPTION

As gifted students approach the middle school years, they become more able to conceptualize mathematical topics. Gifted students in Grades 4, 5, and 6 are usually quite diverse in basic math skills. They need and actively seek more complex ideas and challenges and are ready to think more analytically and logically.

These talented individuals usually want to know *why* the math concepts are important, *why* they need to learn them, and *why* a certain process is necessary. Once they know *why*, they should be encouraged to find out *how* the problem can be solved. This can be done by providing an application problem that will further enhance the math concept.

Mathematics should be exciting, enriching, and practical. Gifted and talented students are in need of a creative teaching approach that encourages them to use divergent thinking to solve complex problems. By using homogeneous grouping, their outstanding abilities will become more pronounced. Once this type of peer interaction is encouraged, many of these students will develop multiple approaches for solving one problem. All should be rewarded and recognized.

Multiple teaching approaches should be provided for these exceptional children. Even though they are classified as gifted, they may each learn differently. It is essential, therefore, to provide these students with the opportunity to explore mathematical concepts using a variety of methods.

Mathematical Problem Solving

Gifted students thrive when given a problem-solving situation that appears "impossible" at first glance. A powerful problem is one that *cannot* be solved immediately, and the student may be required to think about it further after class. Multiple methods for solving this type of problem should be encouraged and expected. The following steps have been found to be quite successful.

Begin by allowing each student to work on the problem individually for a few minutes. Next, arrange them into small groups of three or four students. Provide appropriate materials, any extra information that will be necessary to solve the problem, and a sufficient amount of time to work on the problem.

Since all of these children enjoy sharing and solving, the teacher needs to provide a time frame for solving the problem. It is useful to remind them of the amount of time that is remaining so that they stay on task. During the group work, teachers can provide hints or clues for solving the problem, but ultimately, the students should be able to reach the solution on their own.

Finally, the entire group/class should discuss the findings. The teacher may need to facilitate and redirect the discussion if necessary.

Logical Thinking in Mathematics

These are the type of problems that require the "if–then" thinking and reasoning. Students will enjoy solving these types of problems individually, with a partner, and as a whole class. Perfect examples of these types of problems are logic grids. These are awesome tools for the visual learners in the group!

Begin by using one as an example and showing them how to solve it. After providing an example, encourage the students to work with a partner. This may lead to some interesting discussions.

Once they have mastered the skill of solving these types of problems, increase the difficulty and encourage the students to solve them individually.

Number Sense

Knowing how to manipulate with numbers to solve a problem is a critical component in mathematics. A gifted math student is already quite knowledgeable about basic math facts and needs to have further stimulation.

Some examples of these types of problems are indicated below.

All of these types of problems can easily be intertwined within the regular classroom setting to allow for differentiation.

Missing Operational Symbols

In the problem below, the student must use addition and subtraction symbols to make it a true statement.

18_23_16_29_8 = 62

This type of problem works in perfectly during lessons pertaining to order of operations.

Mystery Number Game

Students are required to ask questions that have only yes or no answers to find the mystery number. The teacher has the "mystery number," and students are allowed a limited number of questions. This is an excellent way of enhancing mathematical terminology: greater and less than, multiples, and factors.

Number Patterns

When working with these children, try to increase the difficulty level in number patterns. In the problem below, the student would need to multiply by two and then subtract two and so on.

13, 26, 24, 48, 46, 92, 90, __, __, __

Student Creation

Students are encouraged to create a number pattern or game of their own. By sharing and exchanging these with other exceptional students, divergent thinking is enhanced.

Challenging Puzzles

Many gifted and talented children are quite visual with their thinking skills. These children thrive on solving challenging puzzles. Puzzles that they can manipulate with their hands and that have more than one solution are the most powerful! Most of these are worked on individually and can be easily incorporated during quiet seat time in the classroom.

A Word of Caution

Sometimes, these exceptional children have a low threshold for frustration. For most of their education, answers have come easily and nothing was beyond them. When they are given a problem situation that cannot be solved immediately, they may feel defeated and upset. It is important to acknowledge this and teach them to overcome these obstacles. They need to learn how to step away from it and reapproach it at a later time. With this being said, many will refuse to and will insist staying on task until a solution can be found. Again, each child is an individual and the appropriate approach may differ.

Final Note

As educators, we are all aware of how important it is to incorporate Bloom's taxonomy into the lessons. Students who are mathematically talented should be required to reach the top four levels of the taxonomy: application, analysis, synthesis, and evaluation. Below are some examples.

1. Apply your knowledge about order of operations and insert parentheses into this equation to make it true.

$$17 - 4 \times 2 + 3 = 65$$

2. Analyze the problem below and explain how it is incorrect.
   15
   $\times\, 23$
   35
   $+\, 20$
   55

3. Create a logic problem of your own. Include the grid and be certain that it is solvable.

MATH IS SO MUCH MORE THAN TWO TIMES FOUR

By Joyce Hammer

MAIN CONCEPT

The purpose of using the following activities in my classroom is to guide children to begin seeing and appreciating the beauty of mathematics, which is so much more than just computation. By presenting a variety of things to learn and do, besides the necessary basic skills, children can develop a sustained interest in the subject and a lifetime love of acquiring knowledge.

LEVEL

Primary grades.

APPLICATION

Mathematics, art, hands-on learning, geography.

DESCRIPTION

The idea of numbers seems to delight even preschool children as they hold up fingers to show how old they are or tell you how far they can count. The primary grades, including kindergarten, are such important years to develop that budding interest in learning math. Bright youngsters who possess some previous knowledge of their age/grade curriculum or who can quickly grasp and retain concepts with exceptional ease, can be nurtured at a faster rate and pace and not limited to the expected grade-level curriculum.

Within the gifted range, differences in learning rate and effective learning style have existed with my pupils. It therefore seems natural to me to individualize whenever and wherever needed—with content, materials, and/or method of instruction. There is a necessary minimum standard, but no maximum level. Differentiation is still fundamental with gifted students. It does not make sense that I, the teacher, should set limits on a child's innate ability to learn. Allow children's minds to soar; results can be remarkable.

Identification

When standardized testing scores are not obtainable, there are assessment options available to help identify which young children possess the power to understand so much more than normally expected for their age.

These ideas, though probably neither original nor the only tactics to try, have been helpful to me.

- Pretest the unit. Why make students review work that has already been mastered?
- Ask the child to write and solve the hardest math problem they can. Note the speed and accuracy of the child's given answers. This gives insight into what the child perceives as his or her ability.
- Ask what games they like to play (e.g., chess or *Monopoly* or other strategy games); ask what books/stories they like to read or hear; ask what television programs they like to watch.
- Ask the parents what their child is interested in doing at home.
- Have a conversation with the child and take notes of the vocabulary and sentence structure.
- What type of questions does the child ask? Is the child seeking answers indicating a desire for more depth or for more advanced information? The exceptional child may ask the *What if* or *Why not* question rather than being satisfied with the simple *Why*.

THE ENVIRONMENT

Fostering students' interest in expanding skills and having them develop a genuine desire to learn as much as they can has always been my goal. How to attain this objective has been my intriguing task.

Whether in the role of teacher or student, I want to be in a noncompetitive classroom that supports teamwork and promotes respect and appreciation of the accomplishments of others. I endeavor to create a warm, nourishing atmosphere that encourages students to explore, create, ask questions, or request other explanations. I want students to be unafraid of making mistakes—recognizing that errors can sometimes become learning tools, and truly understanding that they will not be judged in the process. I want students to enjoy working with appropriately challenging material and ask for more.

With that in mind, my classroom is planned with the intent to stimulate minds yet be a safe harbor where children feel free to take academic risks and to enthusiastically try new things. I often like to work out the problems with the children. Why should they have all the fun? Talking about our methods can provide me with useful information about how they think.

These activities have been used with my primary students—offered by their readiness, not their age. The descriptions here are not meant to be definitive but rather to suggest ideas that can be adjusted and/or developed more fully.

Activities

Geometry and Art

The question "Who is M.C. Escher?" is written with large letters taped on a wall together with various examples of his extraordinary art. Give picture books illustrating more of Escher's works placed within easy reach of the children, allowing time to examine them. This could take place over several days. I like to choose a few of the pictures to explain why I think they are so fascinating and creative. (I have found books on Escher's art and on tessellations at bookstores and in math sections of school catalogs.) His work can also be found on his Web site at http://www.mcescher.com.

This exposure to Escher's creativity has led to student interest and subsequent lessons concerning tessellations.

- Look how a figure gradually and effectively forms into another figure.
- Notice that the figures touch each other—no space between them.
- What shapes are used?
- What shapes will not be able to fill the page this way? Let's find out.
- How do you think tessellations are made? Let's try to create some.

Pattern blocks can then be used as students make their own designs. Allow time to experiment with the different shapes and sizes. I let children work alone or in pairs—whatever they choose to do. A thin board or heavy cardboard used as a base for the blocks makes the designs easier to move to a different place if it is a work in progress. Displaying pictures of their completed efforts and/or letting students take the photos home to show others may entice some children to engage in further investigation of tessellations.

Constructing line designs from given patterns made with needle and colorful thread on card stock is another way to pique students' interests in mathematical concepts. The designs are taped on the door so that they can be seen when entering or leaving the classroom. (How can a straight line look curved?) With younger students, creating line designs using a simple pattern made with pencil and straightedge on paper is an easy task. (Line design books with illustrated patterns for simple to more intricate ones can be found in math sections of school catalogs.)

Showing pictures of designs using only a compass and a straightedge has developed my students' desire to learn more about geometry. I begin by showing various designs arising from one basic shape—the hexagon. Students then gather around and watch as I create the basic shape over and over again. They then choose which design they want me to make. Slowly, I show how the design evolves from this shape by just darkening and/or drawing some lines, erasing others, and sometimes doing a little shading. As often as needed, I repeat this method of forming the design. Each pupil has a copy of the basic shape, a sheet showing all the different ones that can be made from it, plenty of plain paper, a pencil, a straightedge, and a good eraser.

I am the one using the compass to make the circle and the six arcs, until the children know how to correctly use the instrument. At this point, my objective is to teach them how to make the designs; teaching how to work with a compass will come later and depend on their hand dexterity. As I make those arcs, I just happen to say, "Isn't it amazing that no matter what size the circle is, we can only make six equal arcs around it?" (This activity becomes a preliminary to introducing concepts such as circumference and pi.)

After students have completed several of the designs from that first basic shape, they are introduced to another one that still stems from a hexagon, but with slight differences. The same teaching method is used; new interesting designs are formed. Displaying their designs wherever space permits enhances the desire to complete more. The intent of the activity is to stimulate the ability to analyze certain designs, determine how to produce an identical figure, albeit a different sized one, and do it successfully, guided by the previous instruction. (The book I use for this has the necessary pictures and basic shapes for creating simple and more advanced designs.)

Integers

I have found using number lines ranging from -20 to $+20$ an excellent tool, even beginning in kindergarten. (Desk-sized ones are available at a teachers' store.) Students can use a pencil or their finger to move forward and backward on the line while solving integer problems—always beginning at zero, the origin. Having directional arrows over the numbers on paper or the board also helps make addition of integers a skill that can be accomplished by talented math students at an early age (e.g., $7 + -3$; $5 + 4$; $-5 + -2$; $17 + -6$; $-9 + 14 \ldots$). Good sources for these integer problems have been sheets from workbooks—sixth grade levels and up—that have pages which introduce addition of integers. The most effective ones are those that pose riddles to solve or those with solutions that form a word or phrase.

Another way to initiate the idea of how to add with negatives is by having children actually move on a line. Numbered tiles from -20 to $+20$—extending in both directions from zero to whatever distance is convenient—enable students to step from one to the other to find the answer to given problems.

Graphing pictures by using ordered pairs can start with those formed with only positive numbers. Just tell students to *crawl before they climb*. (Move first on the horizontal, or "x," axis and then on the vertical, or "y", axis). When students are successful at that stage, they can be introduced to graphing with negative numbers, thus involving the four quadrants. Finding out what the graph/picture will be when finished is a surprise and a helpful motivator. (The size of the square on the paper used—one-inch square graph paper or four squares to the inch—depends on individual needs. I keep both sizes available for use.)

When that skill is mastered, the task can be extended by giving only one number of the ordered pair; the second number can only be determined by solving a computation problem geared to the students' ability level. The children can also enjoy creating original graphs. A simple drawing using only straight lines is made on a sheet of graph paper. Points, labeled as ordered pairs that will form the picture, are listed on a separate sheet in the sequence of doing the drawing. If a line is not to be connected to the previous one, write *lift pencil* or *stop*. Then, continue with the next set of ordered pairs.

Estimating

Containers of various shapes and sizes are on a counter. Students can fill them with water or small objects to determine which shape holds more. Estimating how many pieces of different items are in those containers is fun. The student who guesses the closest to the actual amount can fill it with other objects for the next time.

A similar activity can be done with estimating weights of objects. Small items can be hidden in a paper bag. A sample of metric weights—1, 5, 10, 20, and 50 grams—is placed next to the bag. Each weight can be picked up to feel the heaviness and replaced on the table. The bag is then raised to guess its weight; the closest estimator can choose the next item. Involving students in the planning of the activity has helped strengthen interest in improving estimation skill.

Measurement and Fractions

Try having students use a set of measuring cups and spoons—filling them and pouring water from one to another, as an aid in learning fractions and measure concepts. Sample questions include the following:

- How many times did you have to fill the one-third cup to fill the one cup?
- If you filled the one-third cup six times, how many one cups can be filled?
- How many one-fourth cups are needed to fill the one-half cup or the one cup?
- How many teaspoons are needed to fill the tablespoon?
- What is one-third and one-third?
- What is one-third and one-third and one-third and one-third?

Encourage the children to see how these items are used at home. Anything that firms the connection between understanding and applying what is being taught will aid retention.

Fraction pieces—shaped as parts of a circle and/or as rectangles—are used to show how different combinations of the pieces are equal in size.

Using whole, halves, thirds, fourths, fifths, eighths, tenths, and twelfths for the pieces allow for several combinations. For example:

- Find different combinations that will exactly cover the one-half piece.
- Find different combinations that will exactly cover the one-third piece.
- Find different combinations that will exactly cover the whole piece.
- Find different combinations that will exactly cover the one-fourth piece.
- Find different combinations that will exactly cover the one-fifth piece.

Sentence strips, different colors if possible, make fraction pieces that students can create and take home. One strip is left intact and marked "one whole." Another strip is folded in half and marked ½—with the explanation that the "2" shows that the whole is divided into two parts and is called the *denominator*, while the "1" represents one part of the whole piece and is called the *numerator*. As the children are shown how to fold the strips into thirds, fourths, sixths, and eighths, keep repeating how to write the fraction and what those numbers represent.

If students have mastered the basic addition or multiplication facts, they can estimate and then measure different objects to determine their perimeter, area, or volume. Building on these skills, the lesson can be extended.

Using 24, one-inch squares—tiles or cardboard ones work well— students are asked to make rectangles with all the pieces, forming different ones each time. The task then involves finding the perimeter and the area (if multiplication is known) to determine which rectangle has the largest or smallest perimeter and area. They can also rank the shapes according to their perimeters. If students have fun with this, use 36 squares or even larger numbers.

Geometric Shapes

Figures of regular polygons and polyhedrons are on the counter. The name for each figure is used over and over again. Students make copies of some of them using toothpicks or skewers for the sides and candy dots or marshmallows for the vertices.

- Why is a tetrahedron rigid? (It does not collapse when formed.)
- Why is the octahedron rigid?
- Why are the icosahedrons rigid?
- Why is the dodecahedron not rigid? (It collapses.)
- What shape do the rigid figures have in common?
- Can you move the sides of the square or rectangle?
- Can you move the sides of the triangle?

Show pictures of bridges or other structures that illustrate how triangles are used to support them. Ask the students if they ever sat on a four-legged chair that wobbled and if they ever sat on a three-legged stool that did. Show pictures of a tripod, if an actual one is not available. Discuss where it is used and why it has only three legs. (Three points determine a plane.)

Algebra

A large-numbered balance beam is on the counter with a set of weights resting at the bottom. Students have fun finding different combinations of numbers to make each side balanced.

Extend the use of the balance beam by illustrating how it will stay balanced if the same amount is added or subtracted from each side. Let the children play with this idea until they fully understand its significance.

Solving simple equations requiring adding or subtracting numbers to keep the balance can be the next step. Explain that they are learning algebra—a word that seems to fascinate young students. (The kit *Hands-On-Equations* uses an excellent approach for teaching this topic.)

Creative Constructions

Student-designed structures made from stacks of books for height and a piece of wood or cardboard for the ramp led them to think about momentum. Toy cars go down the ramp one at a time.

- Which height makes the cars go faster? Why?
- Which height makes the cars go farther? Why?
- How can the structure be improved to make a better ramp?

Building kits for students to create marble runs are placed at the side of the room when they are in use. The children usually work in small groups trying different ways to make a better pathway for the marbles. Their feeling of success with the route depends on cooperative planning—listening to different ideas, trying them out, and continuing to look for other more spectacular ways to make the run. The construction can stay in the room for many days; building and seeing the results of their efforts is generally done for short periods and not on a daily basis. This keeps the interest and thoughtful suggestions for improvement continuing.

Puzzles

A bulletin board titled "Puzzles Galore" is completely filled with a wide variety of difficult two- and three-dimensional puzzles and strategy games—each in a separate plastic bag attached by thumb tacks, readily accessible to students after permission is asked and given—to use in the latter part of the period when assignments are completed. More puzzles, such as Nim, the Tower of Hanoi, and the Soma Cube are on the counter and often used. Students may choose to try solving them on their own or by working with others. The more challenging the puzzle, the more it appeals to these children. (The *MindWare* catalog has a good selection of puzzles.)

Geography

A large colorful world map is on one wall, and a globe is on a cart. Math activities related to geography may inspire further interest in this area. (Math is ubiquitous! It is everywhere.)

- Rank the sizes of the different continents—first by estimation, then by research.
- Rank the sizes of the different oceans—first by estimation, then by research.
- Does the earth look different when represented on a flat surface (a plane), or as a three-dimensional figure (a sphere)? Which way do you prefer? Why?

Students who complete and retain the necessary math concepts through algebra one can attend our high school's honor-level math classes. Some have been ready for that advancement at a very early age (fifth or sixth grade); others wait a little later (seventh or eighth grade). Still others enroll in the high school honor-level math classes when they graduate. The interest in studying math in the rigorous honor level classes has continued.

Over the years, there have been several examples of far reaching achievement in young children. This is just one of those examples illustrating what I have been privileged to see develop.

Several years ago, a first grader who had just entered our gifted math program, sat on the floor pulling out different level workbooks from the bookcase. As he turned the pages, he kept saying, "I want to learn this and this and this." By the end of fourth grade, this young man succeeded in mastering all math content levels through the ninth grade curriculum. At fifth grade, he happily began taking honor-level math classes at the high school with consistently excellent results. Calculus was studied in eighth grade, which culminated with his scoring the top grade of 5 on the Advanced Placement test. By giving him the opportunity to proceed at his preferred pace, he experienced the pleasure and pride of using his "gift."

Students in our gifted program, both present and past, express appreciation for having been given opportunities to maximize their potential. What better way to lay the groundwork for our brightest and youngest minds to build a better future? Reach and teach them early!

Calendar Challenge: A Creative Mathematics Activity

By Carol Fisher

MAIN CONCEPT

This strategy is designed to stimulate more creative thinking in mathematics, enabling gifted students to create their own equations. For highly able math learners, it presents unlimited possibilities, as they can use fractions, exponents, and any operations they like as long as they follow the basic framework.

LEVEL

Intermediate and middle grades and up.

APPLICATION

Highly adaptable for individual, small-group, and whole-class creative process in mathematics; it can easily be integrated into math concepts in the curriculum.

DESCRIPTION

Calendar Challenge is a numeric exercise in creative thinking. The premise is based on an idea from a National Council of Teachers of Mathematics journal from 10 or 12 years ago and is quite simple. Create equations using the number associated with a given month six times. The equation's solutions correspond to the number of days in the month. In September, students would be challenged to use six 9s to make equations with answers 1 through 30. In October, students would be challenged to use six 10s to make equations with answers 1 through 31. The framework allows students to challenge themselves or each other to devise equations that follow a specific format. This can be done as an individual, small-group, or whole-class activity. The equations, as well as the students, grow month by month as their knowledge, creativity, and algebraic thinking develops. The format can be changed to give students who typically isolate themselves an opportunity to work in a small group or whole group setting. The challenge can be competitive among students, or students can individually challenge themselves in creating equations. There is more than one solution to each part of the task, and the task builds month by month. No matter how competent a student is in computation, the challenges can continue. Any operations, negative numbers, fractions, decimals, exponents, factorial, or percentage may be used as long as the given number is the only number used, and it is used exactly six times for each equation.

In the typical school setting, this would be introduced the first week of September. It can be used in any classroom, whether heterogeneously or homogenously grouped. A whole group introduction is needed to ensure a solid foundation of understanding. Large chart paper is posted on the walls, usually three sheets, the first numbered from 1 through 10, second from 11 through 20, and third from 21 through 30. On the whiteboard (or chalkboard or chart paper), I write six 9s spaced out.

$$9 \quad 9 \quad 9 \quad 9 \quad 9 \quad 9$$

As a group, students are challenged to find a way to insert mathematical symbols to make the equation = 1. (Calculators can be used, but for most gifted students, it is a mental math challenge [with paper and pencil].) In many situations, providing parentheses to encourage grouping can be helpful.

$$(9\ 9)\ (9\ 9)\ (9\ 9)$$

(It can be solved without the parentheses, using order of operations, but it jump-starts most students' thinking.)

There are multiple solutions in this format.

$$(9 \div 9) \times (9 \div 9) \times (9 \div 9) = 1 \quad (9 + 9) - (9 + 9) + (9 / 9) = 1$$

$$(9 - 9) + (9 - 9) + (9 \div 9) = 1$$

Other formats can include using 99, 9.9, 9^9 (all of which count as two 9s).

$$99 \div 99 \times 9 \div 9 = 1 \quad 9.9 - .9 - 9 + 9 \div 9 = 1 \quad 9^9 \div 9^9 + 9 - 9 = 1$$

Once students demonstrate their understanding of the task, they are challenged to find equations for two and then three. These can easily be created by making minor operation changes in some of the above equations.

$(9 \div 9) \times (9 \div 9) \times (9 \div 9) = 1$ can be changed to $(9 \div 9) + (9 \div 9) \times (9 \div 9) = 2$

At this point in the activity, it is helpful to summarize some strategic ideas:

$$(9 - 9) = 0 \quad (9 \div 9) = 1 \quad 99 \quad 99 \div 9 = 11$$

If necessary, order of operations should be reviewed. Students are then challenged to find some of the other equations that correspond to the calendar dates. For any (or all) students who are feeling frustrated, I guide them to 16, 17, 18, 19, and 20. They can all be solved by starting with $(9 + 9)$ and the above strategic combinations.

Teachers' knowledge of the social, emotional, and academic needs of their students will help them decide the parameters of the challenge for the first month.

- Set a challenge of finding 10 of the 30 equations during the class.
- Challenge students to find *more* at home.
- Save the day's work, then continue another day.
- Challenge the class to find as many *different* solutions for a particular calendar date (or all of them).

However you decide to implement the first month, keep documentation—the student's individual work, the class chart, the amount of time, how many solutions, and so on.

During the first week of October, the challenge is resurrected. Now it's six 10s for the numbers 1 through 31. Have students refer to their work from September. Does this give them any ideas? This comparison is the springboard to creating algebraic formulas for the different numbers. (It is not a necessary part of the challenge but is usually satisfying to gifted students.)

$$(9 \div 9) \times (9 \div 9) \times (9 \div 9) = 1 \quad (10 \div 10) \times (10 \div 10) \times (10 \div 10) = 1$$

$$(a \div a) \times (a \div a) \times (a \div a) = 1$$

Wanting this to be a yearlong project suggests that only a few formulas need to be attempted each month. If there is a concept (exponents, decimals, etc.) that you wish to emphasize to correlate with your curriculum, this is an excellent way to keep the excitement going by challenging students, for example, to use an exponent in each equation.

September through December usually progress well, and then in January, many students decide it's *impossible* using only 1s to make equations for the numbers 1 through 31. This provides a wonderful opportunity for mathematical discourse as well as a new challenge. In the spring, calendar challenge usually becomes more competitive either for individual or small group solutions, or the amount of time for the whole class to solve all the equations (especially if you teach multiple classes).

In the 10 or more years I have been using this activity with both gifted and nongifted students, I have always found that students take away much more than the simple creation of mathematical equations. In terms of the NCTM standards, Representation, Connections, Communication, Reasoning and Proof, Problem Solving, Number and Operations, and Algebra are all enhanced. Social and emotional standards (ISBE—Illinois State Board of Education) such as "setting goals," "identifying personal strengths and weaknesses," "evaluating successes and failures," "advocating for others," "encouraging others," and "work cooperatively with others" can be addressed as a by-product of the monthly activities. Each group of students I have worked with has given me new insight about the depth of creativity that can be evoked by this mathematical activity.

Sample solutions for June are as follows:

$(6 \div 6) \bullet (6 \div 6) \times (6 \div 6)$	= 1	$66 \div 6 + 6 - (6 \div 6)$	= 16
$(6 \div 6) + (6 \div 6) \times (6 \div 6)$	= 2	$66 \div 6 + 6 - (6 - 6)$	= 17
$(6 \div 6) + (6 \div 6) + (6 \div 6)$	= 3	$66 \div 6 + 6 + (6 \div 6)$	= 18
$(6 + 6) \div 6 + (6 + 6) \div 6$	= 4	$6 \div .6 + 6 + 6 \times .6 - .6$	= 19
$(6 + 6 + 6 + 6 + 6) \div 6$	= 5	$6! \div (6 \bullet 6) + (6 - 6) \times 6$	= 20
$(6 \bullet 6 + 6) \div 6 - (6 \div 6)$	= 6	$(6 \bullet .6 - .6) \bullet (6 + [6 \div 6])$	= 21
$(6 \bullet 6 + 6) \div 6 - (6 - 6)$	= 7	$66 \div 6 + 66 \div 6$	= 22
$(6 \bullet 6 + 6) \div 6 + (6 \div 6)$	= 8	$6 + 6 + 6 + 6 - (6 \div 6)$	= 23
$66 \div 6 - (6 + 6) \div 6$	= 9	$6 + 6 + 6 + 6 + (6 - 6)$	= 24
$(6 + 6) - (6 \div 6) - (6 \div 6)$	= 10	$6 + 6 + 6 + 6 + (6 \div 6)$	= 25
$(6 + 6) - (6 \div 6) - (6 - 6)$	= 11	$6! \div (6 \bullet 6) + 6 + (6 - 6)$	= 26
$(6 + 6) - (6 - 6) - (6 - 6)$	= 12	$6! \div (6 \bullet 6) + 6 + (6 \div 6)$	= 27
$(6 + 6) + (6 \div 6) - (6 - 6)$	= 13	$(6 \bullet 6 - 6) - (6 + 6) \div 6$	= 28
$(6 + 6) + (6 \div 6) + (6 \div 6)$	= 14	$66 \div 6 + 6 + 6 + 6$	= 29
$(6 + 6) + (6 + 6 + 6) \div 6$	= 15	$6 \bullet 6 - 6 + (6 - 6) \bullet 6$	= 30

A NUMBER BY ANY OTHER NAME

By Carol Fisher

MAIN CONCEPT

This process allows students to explore many different ways of representing numbers, thereby enhancing individual challenge and creativity.

LEVEL

Flexible: primary, intermediate, and up.

APPLICATION

This idea integrates well into the math curriculum and reflects national standards. Students can work individually, in small groups, or as a class. There is no limit to the complexities gifted learners can create.

DESCRIPTION

The NCTM (National Council of Teachers of Mathematics) standard for Representation states that all students, Grades prekindergarten through 12 should be able to do the following:

- Create and use representations to organize, record, and communicate mathematical ideas
- Select, apply, and translate among mathematical representations to solve problems
- Use representations to model and interpret physical, social, and mathematical phenomena

Consider a standard exercise in early math education when a student is asked to list all the addition problems that have a sum of 6 (1 + 5, 2 + 4, 3 + 3, 4 + 2, and 5 + 1). There is only one solution acceptable. Now, open this up to ask students to show all the ways to "make" 6. The first time I did this with kindergarteners, I got the following fabulous answers (besides some of the expected ones):

- One hand and one finger
- Two triangles
- A nickel and a penny

From that point forward, I used this idea with students of all ages and found ways to add parameters that encouraged (or forced) advanced mathematical thinking.

In a school setting, using the number of the date is a way to structure a frequent activity. For example, on May 20th with primary students, I asked them to write five ways to make 20—using at least three terms for each answer. Some answers included the following:

- Twenty pennies
- Five squares
- $30 - 5 - 5$
- $4 \times 5 \times 1$
- $18 + 1 + 1$

On the same date, intermediate students were challenged to use only prime numbers:

- $5 + 5 + 5 + 5$
- $23 - 2$

- $2 \times 2 \times 5$
- $91 - 71$
- $2 + 3 + 5 + 7 + 11 - 5 + 3$

Challenges for older students (using 20, for example) included some geometry concepts.

Using 20° as angle X—create drawings or statements that use rules you know about angles.

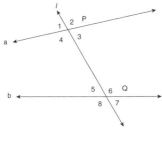

- The complement of a 70° angle
- A right triangle with a 70° angle
- A parallelogram with a 160° angle
- If Angle 5 = 20°, then Angle 3 is also 20° because of alternate interior angles (note the drawing wasn't close to a 20° angle, but the concept of the "rule" was used appropriately)

Target numbers know no bounds. They can be large; they can be different representations, such as seven! (seven factorial—$7 \times 6 \times 5 \times 4 \times 3 \times 2 \times 1 = 5,040$). They can be related to a current field of study. It is interesting how differently students approach such a challenge. Some can't wait to make as many responses as possible using a variety of approaches, while others look for the easiest way out of meeting the parameters (a skill in itself). Once, when asking students to use only decimal numbers to create 10 problems that equaled 5.23 (done on May 23) with extra credit for additional responses, a student gave me over one hundred problems following this pattern:

- 5.23 + (1.1–1.1),
- 5.23 + (2.2–2.2),
- 5.23 + (3.3–3.3), and so on.

Using fractions as target numbers can be an inventive way to have students work with both pictorial and numerical models to further fractional thinking.

Parameter: Target number is ½. Create math sentences using only fractions; each sentence must have fractions with at least two different denominators.

$$1/6 + 1/3 = 1/2$$

Having students create algebra equations with a target number can begin at an early age. At the simplest levels, equations of the form $x + a = b$ can used:

Target number 99: $x + 1 = 100$ or $x + (-15) = 84$

Equations with two variables, with a resulting graph can be required:

$$6x + 3y = 99$$

Create a t chart.

x	y
1	31
0	33
−1	35

In summary, having students look for alternative ways to represent numbers opens a world of opportunity for individual challenge and creativity. Topics can include the following:

- Whole numbers
- Operations
- Money
- Shapes
- Fractions
- Decimals
- Percentages
- Algebraic equations
- Geometric properties
- Negative numbers
- Prime numbers
- Number bases
- Factorial
- Exponents
- And many, many more, I'm sure.

How Do YOU Count to Ten?
An Exploration of Number Bases

By Carol Fisher

MAIN CONCEPT

This process introduces a creative scenario (and challenge) as a way of drawing gifted students into the world of binary numbers. It involves some prompting, and at each step as students show how they approached the challenge, they deepen their thinking significantly.

LEVEL

Middle grades and up, but adaptable to younger students.

APPLICATION

Mathematics; writing; social studies (Mayan, African). The process works best in small groups.

DESCRIPTION

I recently saw a T-shirt that said the following:

There are 10 types of people in this world.

Those who understand binary and those who don't.

Students enjoy knowing something "sneaky" that others don't, and number bases can certainly fall into this category.

My favorite way to introduce binary numbers is with a challenge. You can use learning links (available from many educational companies) or paper clips. I like to do the activity with small groups because they must discuss their thinking which deepens their thought process.

- Each group receives 63 links (in one chain or all separated) and a scenario card.
- Scenario: The Magnificent Math Maven Figure is set- ting up his next magic trick. He needs six chains of links that he can use (by showing one or more chains) to demonstrate all the numbers from 1 to 63. Can you help him?

After groups start working on the problem you may need to steer them. I usually ask them to show me the Number 1 (one link) and then the Number 2 (some will show two separate links; others will show a chain of two). Then ask them to show you the Number 3 (if they show you a link of three or three separate ones, ask them if they can do it another way— the goal is one link and a chain of two). Some groups may eventually need more prompting, but I have found that this is usually enough. The final answer should be chains of the following lengths—1, 2, 4, 8, 16, and 32— the first six place values in the binary system. Having students *show* the various numbers with their chains easily leads to setting up the place values and the notation.

Example: 57 (in base 10)

32	16	8	4	2	1
1	1	1	0	0	1

$$57 - 32 = 25 - 16 = 9 - 8 = 1$$

or

$$32 + 16 + 8 + 1 = 57$$

The next step would be to introduce the exponential representation of the place values—this sets the foundation of all other number bases for the student. I usually review base 10 first and then do binary.

100,000	10,000	1000	100	10	1
10^5	10^4	10^3	10^2	10^1	10^0

32	16	8	4	2	1
2^5	2^4	2^3	2^2	2^1	2^0

After this, continue to expand the place value chart as far as the exploration necessitates. In addition, students can explore converting from one base to another or performing operations with binary numbers.

Example: 101 + 1,101 =

	1	1	0	1	1	1		1	
		1	0	1		1	1	0	1
	1	2	0	2			1	0	1
1	0	0	1	0		0	0	1	0

Some students may need the step outlined in the dark gray boxes; others will "carry" (outlined in light gray boxes).

Some students may already know that computers use binary number system = 1 is on and 0 is off. Some may wish to explore this further. There are also several Web sites that have converters or additional activities.

Mayan Numerals (Base 20)

There are many Web sites with information about Mayan numerals. Mayans reportedly are the first (or one of the first) cultures to have a symbol to represent zero. ⬯

The Mayans used a system based on 20. A dot (one) and a bar (five), along with the zero were the only symbols they needed.

0	1	2	3	4	5	6	7	8	9
(shell)	•	••	•••	••••	—	• —	•• —	••• —	•••• —
10	11	12	13	14	15	16	17	18	19
—	• =	•• =	••• =	•••• =	≡	• ≡	•• ≡	••• ≡	•••• ≡

In base 10, we read place value from left to right. The Mayans read from top to bottom. I usually set up boxes to help students align their place values. For example:

		20	21	22
20		•	•	•
1s		(shell)	•	••

Have students construct the place value chart *vertically*! (To whatever value they wish.)

160,000	20^4
8,000	20^3
400	20^2
20	20^1
1	20^0

Students enjoy converting back and forth, with larger and larger numbers. Example:

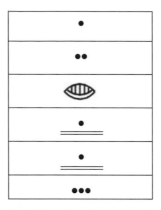

$$3,200,000 + (2 \times 160,000) + 0 + (11 \times 400) + (11 \times 20) + 3 = 3,524,623$$

There are many online resources for Mayan numerals as well as the rich Mayan history. I found a card game that has Mayan art and Mayan numerals 1 through 5 (included negative –1 through –5). In addition to the prescribed game, I have used the cards for many other types of card activities. The game is *Mayan Madness* available through the *Gamewright* Web site.

Duodecimal (Base 12)

The history of base 12 numbers is not clear, although there is some evidence of African and Asian languages using a base 12 system. Many of our measurements are based on 12—such as 12 inches in a foot and 12 items in a dozen. In fiction, Tolkien's Elvish language includes base 12 numbers. As in other bases, letters A and B are used for numbers greater than 9 (10 and 11). Other sources use T and E for 10 and 11. However, my favorite investigation into base 12 comes from *Fractals, Googols and other Mathematical Tales* (Pappas, 1993). Dr. Spacemath visits Planet Dodeka where everybody has six fingers on each hand. Each number has a symbol. When I have done this with younger students, I have made six-fingered hands for them to use (or wear) for a hands-on approach.

Hexadecimal Numbers (Base 16)

Hexadecimal numbers are also used in computer situations. Students are frequently fascinated by base 16 because it uses letters as well as numbers. Conversion and numeric operations can be explored.

1	2	3	4	5	6	7	8	9	10	11	12	13	14	15
1	2	3	4	5	6	7	8	9	A	B	C	D	E	F

The place value chart is as follows:

1,048,576	65,536	4096	256	16	1
16^5	16^4	16^3	16^2	16^1	16^0

$$2E = (2 \times 16) + 15 = 47 \text{ (base 10)}$$

$$A73C = (10 \times 4{,}096) + (7 \times 256) + (3 \times 16) + 12 = 42{,}812$$

Hexatridecimal (Base 36)

Some URLs also use a base 36 system. This is referred to as either hexatridecimal or alphadecimal. It uses the digits 0 through 9 and the 26 letters of the alphabet.

The conversion chart is as follows:

0	1	2	3	4	5	6	7	8	9	10	11	12	13	14	15	16	17
0	1	2	3	4	5	6	7	8	9	A	B	C	D	E	F	G	H

18	19	20	21	22	23	24	25	26	27	28	29	30	31	32	33	34	35
I	J	K	L	M	N	O	P	Q	R	S	T	U	V	W	X	Y	Z

The place value chart would be as follows:

60,466,176	1,679,616	46,656	1296	36	1
36^5	36^4	36^3	36^2	36^1	36^0

This can be quite confusing but an interesting challenge for some students.

Examples include the following:

$$E6 = (14 \times 36) + 6 = 510$$

$$5QI2 = (5 \times 46{,}656) + (26 \times 1296) + (18 \times 36) + 2 = 267{,}626$$

Sexigesimal—Babylonian (Base 60)

The Babylonians have the oldest known place value system. They only used two symbols:

1 𒁹 10 𒌋

They did not have a symbol for zero, so they traditionally just left a space. When more than one symbol was used, they overlapped to show a grouping. For example:

$$\text{《《 ᵛᵛᵛ} = 47$$

The rich history of the sexigesimal system—60 seconds in a minute and 360° in a circle can be explored on many different Web sites.

Other Number Bases

Bases 3, 4, 5, 6, 7, 8, and 9 are also interesting to explore. I have had many students use several different bases and create multiple conversions for challenges for other students (or their parents)!

A most interesting culminating activity is for students to create counting books in various bases. This incorporates artistic creativity with math concepts. Some students have written story books as well as incorporating math in other bases. When possible, I make several copies of the books so that copies are available in the school library for other teachers and students to use.

MATH LITERATURE LINKS: A CREATIVE APPROACH

By Carol Fisher

MAIN CONCEPT

Why should we use literature to enhance mathematics exploration? We know from Howard Gardner's writings that there are multiple intelligences. Any time we incorporate more than one of these intelligences into our instructional settings, we provide a richer environment for learning. Literature can be used to support mathematical explorations for gifted students of all ages. It can be used as a whole class adventure, or on a small-group or individual basis for exploration and creativity.

LEVEL

Ideas and materials for all grade levels.

APPLICATION

Mathematics, language arts (reading and writing), drama, visual art.

DESCRIPTION

The National Council of Teachers of Mathematics' Communication Standard states that students in Grades K through 12 should be able to

- organize and consolidate their mathematical thinking through communication;
- communicate their mathematical thinking coherently and clearly to peers, teachers, and others;
- analyze and evaluate the mathematical thinking and strategies of others;
- use the language of mathematics to express mathematical ideas precisely.

Literature is defined as "writings in which expression and form, in connection with ideas of permanent and universal interest, are characteristic or essential features as poetry, novels, history, biography, and essays" (Literature, n.d.). Mathematics is defined as "the systematic treatment of magnitude, relationships between figures and forms, and relations between quantities expressed symbolically" (Mathematics, n.d.). Literature and math support each other in their structures and in their imagination. Here are some ideas at various age levels.

Pre-Primary/Primary

The Greedy Triangle by Marilyn Burns offers an exploration into shapes. Here is an idea for a class reading of the story. Give each student a large construction paper triangle. With each change in the story have students cut off one angle—hopefully in a straight line. Have students count the sides and verify that no matter where they made the cut, or how deep the cut was, the shape will have the same number of sides (model the first one). After the decagon in the story, have students continue cutting sides until they feel they are "close" to a circle. Discuss why it is *not* a circle. Finish the story. Give the students another triangle and allow them to create a face or design. Have students find triangles in the classroom; they can write about them on the back of the triangle. Students may choose another shape, create it, and find an example in the classroom.

Many books by Mitsumasa Anno have wonderful opportunities for math, discourse, and art. *Anno's Counting Book* may seem simplistic, but it has inspired many young students to create their own book for counting. Anno's counting book has two-page spreads that illustrate months of the year, time of day, the four seasons, and a wordless story about a gradually growing town. The first number, zero, is depicted by an empty snow-covered landscape. Each page introduces a new numeral with the corresponding number of people, animals, and objects added to the scene.

Eric Carle books, with their collage art, are a visual delight, but many also offer opportunities for mathematical thinking. *The Secret Birthday Message* uses a simple code (shape symbols) to lead a child to his birthday present. Students can construct a pathway through the classroom, their home, or the playground-using shapes as a *code*. Students may also want to delve into other ciphers (codes) for alphabets. I have used this simple book as an introduction to Mayan numerals, Egyptian hieroglyphic numerals, and Roman numerals.

Tana Hoban's books all use photography to illustrate simple concepts (usually with no text). I love using these visual books with students of all ages, especially when cameras are available for students to shoot their own photos related to the concept. One example would be *Shapes, Shapes, Shapes*. Students are challenged to find shapes in their classroom, at home, or outside and to draw or photograph these shapes.

Judith Viorst's *Alexander, Who Used to Be Rich Last Sunday* provides a perfect opportunity to explore the use of money. In a very realistic manner, Alexander manages to use up the money he received *last Sunday* in a variety of interesting ways. Students create their own scenarios for getting and spending money (of any amount) and performing the necessary calculations to coordinate to the story line they unfold. This could become an illustrated book for students who want to take the project to that level.

Primary/Intermediate

Rod Clement's book *Counting on Frank* tells the story of a *nerdy* boy who knows or estimates statistics on everything around him. In the end, this skill reaps a wonderful reward. This book provides a perfect platform for estimation activities, only limited by you and your students' imagination. I like to start with Mason jars filled with various objects so students can develop their estimation strategies.

Aileen Friedman's *A Cloak for the Dreamer* weaves a folktale-like story into a study of tessellations. This provides many opportunities for discourse as well as an exploration of tessellations starting with the simple shapes in the book. This can proceed to a study of angles and how the angle measurement relates to the ability to tessellate. This exploration can proceed from regular tessellations with one shape to semi-regular tessellations with more than one shape to M. C. Escher explorations. A traditional folk tale with mathematical complexity is Demi's *One Grain of Rice*. Several countries have similar tales, and students can enjoy comparing them or writing their own modern version.

Several Mitsumasa Anno books investigate higher-level mathematical thinking, such as *Socrates and the Three Little Pigs* and the three *Anno's Math Games*, *Anno's Magic Seeds*, and *Anno's Mysterious Multiplying Jar* both provide an opportunity to explore exponential growth.

Sadako and the Thousand Paper Cranes by Eleanor Coerr provides the history of the bombing of Hiroshima while recounting the legend of making one thousand paper cranes. This is a natural lead-in to an exploration of origami (折り紙) (from *ori* meaning "folding" and *kami* meaning "paper"), the ancient Japanese art of paper folding. The goal of this art is to create a given result using geometric folds and crease patterns preferably without the use of gluing or cutting the paper medium. According to *Wikipedia,* "*Origami* refers to all types of paper folding, even those of non-Asian origin" (see http://en.wikipedia.org/wiki/Origami).

Familiar novels such as *The Phantom Tollbooth* by Norton Juster, *The Toothpaste Millionaire* by Jean Merrill, *The Borrowers* by Mary Norton, and *The Westing Game* by Ellen Raskin all provide triggers for mathematical forays.

Intermediate/Middle School

Books by David Schwartz, such as *If You Made a Million, How Much Is a Million?* and *Millions to Measure* give students "big" ideas about numbers. *If You Hopped Like a Frog* gives enthusiastic students ratios of human and animal attributes and abilities to explore. When I have used this book, we have held Olympics, created graphs, conducted experiments, and researched other animal statistics as students desired. Two other Schwartz books, although not *story* books, are great for stimulating thinking. They are *G is for Googol* and *Q is for Quark,* both reference books. My students have used them as a springboard for many discussions and explorations.

The *I Hate Mathematics! Book* by Marilyn Burns provides short explorations to intrigue students (and baffle their friends and parents). It's a great book (as most by Marilyn Burns are) for individual exploration.

Middle School/High School

Many of the books listed previously can be used successfully with older students as long as they understand this is just an introduction. I like to use *Ed Emberley's Picture Pie* by Ed Emberley for circle exploration, especially focusing on arcs. The book uses the understanding of arcs in circles for drawing techniques.

A Gebra Named Al by Wendy Isdell was written about a girl having issues with algebra; she travels through lands where math and science abound. This novel provides many links to math and science concepts students might want to explore further. Another novel students will enjoy is *The Number Devil: A Mathematical Adventure* by Hans Magnus Enzensberger.

William Sleator's *The Boy Who Reversed Himself* combines a typical teenage love triangle with science fiction in the fourth dimension. The group reading of this novel stimulates visual geometric explorations. Attempting to replicate scenes from the novel in two- or three-dimensional representations is quite challenging to students. Another *romantic* novel for older students is *Flatland* by Edwin A. Abbott and Rosemary Jann. Although originally written in 1884, it is still viable today. Its combination of philosophy, mathematics, literature, fantasy, and reality engage readers who wish to be challenged. Other recommendations for older students include *Coincidences, Chaos and All That Math Jazz* by Edward Burger and Michael Starbird; *Do The Math: Secrets; Lies and Algebra* by Wendy Lichtman; and *In Code: A Mathematical Journey* by Sarah and David Flannery. *The Adventures of Penrose the Mathematical Cat* by Theoni Pappas is a great way for motivating students on individual or group explorations on a variety of topics, including magic squares, fractals, and the golden rectangle.

There are endless books and endless ways to use literature to facilitate math exploration. I have spent many years using books with students of all ages and have developed an extensive annotated bibliography of books to use to inspire mathematical thinking. I am happy to share this information with any interested persons.

Additional Recommended Books

Several books are available as professional resources for math literature. I recommend resources by Marilyn Burns such as *Math and Literature, Grades K–1* or *Living and Learning Mathematics: Stories and Strategies for Supporting Mathematical Learning* by David Whitin.

Fascinating Fibonaccis: Mystery and Magic in Numbers by Trudi Hammel Garland explores the sequence in nature, art, architecture, music, poetry, science, and technology.

Frank Lloyd Wright for Kids: His Life and Ideas, 21 Activities by Kathleen Thorne-Thomsen already has 21 activities that incorporate the mathematics of his architecture.

There are several books by Theoni Pappas that offer a cornucopia of math concepts to explore. They include *Math Stuff; Math Talk,* which provides poetic dialogues to be read aloud by two people; *Mathematical Scandals;* and *Fractals, Googols and other Mathematical Tales.*

Blue Balliet is writing books about a group of students who use math to help solve artistic mysteries. My favorite, *Wright 3* includes the use of pentominoes as a problem solving device throughout the adventure.

The title alone interests many students in this book, written by the actress Danica McKellar—*Math Doesn't Suck: How to Survive Middle School Math Without Losing Your Mind or Breaking a Nail.* Another with an interesting title is *Do the Math: Secrets, Lies and Algebra* by Wendy Lichtman.

Paul Giganti has many books to offer, also. I use *Each Orange Had 8 Slices* for multiplication and subsets. Students enjoy finding their own examples and illustrating them.

For those who enjoy *Numb3rs* on TV, they may also enjoy *The Numbers Behind Numb3rs: Solving Crime with Mathematics* by Keith Devlin and Gary

Lorden. Texas Instruments also provides free lessons and activities to coordinate with each show—check online.

The Lemonade War by Jacqueline Davies combines economics and social issues in an interesting book.

Steve Jenkins has a number of books with interesting concepts for younger students, such as *Actual Size* and *What Do You Do With a Tail Like This?*

Jerry Pallotta has many, many books with mathematical links. Some relate to candy products, some to animals. One of my favorites is the *Icky Bug Counting Book* because it provides great scientific information about the bugs that can lead to many activities. Another prolific author is Robert Wells with books such as *What's Smaller Than a Pygmy Shrew? How Do You Lift a Lion?* and *Can You Count to a Googol?*

An interesting set of books are all set in medieval times with *punny* story lines to explore geometry concepts are offered by Cindy Neuschwander. These books are fun to use on *pi day*—March 14. They include *Sir Cumference and the First Round Table, Sir Cumference and the Sword in the Cone,* and *Sir Cumference and the Dragon of Pi.*

Elinor Pinczes has several books of interest for younger children looking at divisibility and other topics. My students have enjoyed using these books as a basis for creating their own stories with different (or more complex) numbers. These include *One Hundred Hungry Ants, Remainder of One,* and *Inchworm and a Hal.*

RESOURCES

Abbott, E. (2005). *Flatland.* New York: Penguin Group.

Anno, M. (1986). *Anno's counting book.* New York: HarperCollins Children's Books.

Anno, M. (1986). *Socrates and the three little pigs.* New York: Penguin Young Readers Group.

Anno, M. (1987). *Anno's math games.* New York: Penguin Young Readers Group.

Anno, M. (1999). *Anno's magic seeds.* New York: Penguin Young Readers Group.

Anno, M. (1999). *Anno's mysterious multiplying jar.* New York: Penguin Young Readers Group.

Balliet, B. (2007). *Wright 3.* New York: Scholastic.

Burger, E. & Starbird, M. (2006). *Coincidences, chaos and all that math jazz.* New York: W. W. Norton.

Burns, M. (1975). *The I hate mathematics! book.* London: Little, Brown.

Burns, M. (1995). *The greedy triangle.* New York: Scholastic Bookshelf.

Burns, M. (2004). *Math and literature, Grades K–1.* Sausalito, CA: Math Solutions.

Carle, E. (1986). *The secret birthday message.* New York: HarperCollins Children's Books.

Clement, R. (2006). *Counting on Frank.* Boston: Houghton Mifflin.

Coerr, E. (1999). *Sadako and the thousand paper cranes.* New York: Penguin Young Readers Group.

Davies, J. (2007). *The lemonade war.* Boston: Houghton Mifflin.

Demi, H. (1997). *One grain of rice: A mathematical folk tale.* New York: Scholastic.

Devlin, K. & Lorden, G. (2007). *The numbers behind* Numb3rs: *Solving crime with mathematics.* New York: Penguin Group.

Emberley, E. (2006). *Ed Emberley's picture pie.* London: Little, Brown.

Enzensberger, H. (1998). *The number devil: A mathematical adventure.* New York: Henry Holt.

Flannery, S. & Flannery, D. (2003). *In code: A math journey.* Chapel Hill, NC: Algonquin Books of Chapel Hill.

Friedman, A. (1995). *A cloak for the dreamer.* New York: Scholastic.

Gardner, H. (2000). *Intelligence reframed: Multiple intelligences for the 21st century.* New York: Basic.

Garland, T. (1987). *Fascinating fibonaccis: Mystery and magic in numbers.* Lebanon, IN: Dale Seymour.

Giganti, P. (1999). *Each orange had 8 slices.* New York: HarperCollins.

Hoban, T. (1986). *Shapes, shapes, shapes.* New York: Greenwillow Books.

Isdell, W. (1993). *A gebra named Al.* Minneapolis, MN: Free Spirit.

Jenkins, S. (2003). *What do you do with a tail like this?* Boston: Houghton Mifflin.

Jenkins, S. (2004). *Actual size.* Boston: Houghton Mifflin.

Juster, N. (1988). *The phantom toolbooth.* New York: Random House.

Lichtman, W. (2007). *Do the math: Secrets, lies and algebra.* New York: HarperCollins.

Literature. (n.d.). In *Dictionary.com Unabridged* (v.1.1). Retrieved February 12, 2008, from http://dictionary.reference.com/browse/literature

Mathematics. (n.d.). In *Dictionary.com Unabridged* (v.1.1). Retrieved February 12, 2008, from http://dictionary.reference.com/browse/literature

McKellar, D. (2007). *Math doesn't suck: How to survive middle school math without losing your mind or breaking a nail.* New York: Penguin Group.

Merrill, J. (2006). *The toothpaste millionaire.* Boston: Houghton Mifflin.

National Council of Teachers of Mathematics (NCTM). (2006). *Principles and standards for school mathematics.* Retrieved July 30, 2008, from http://standards.nctm.org

Neuschwander, C. (1999). *Sir Cumference and the dragon of pi.* Watertown, MA: Charlesbridge.

Neuschwander, C. (2002). *Sir Cumference and the first round table.* Watertown, MA: Charlesbridge.

Neuschwander, C. (2003). *Sir Cumference and the sword in the cone.* Watertown, MA: Charlesbridge.

Norton, M. (2003). *The borrowers.* New York: Harcourt Children's Books.

Pallotta, J. (1991). *Icky bug counting book.* Watertown, MA: Charlesbridge.

Pappas, T. (1993). *Fractals, googols and other mathematical tales.* San Francisco, CA: Wide World/Tetra.

Pappas, T. (1993). *Math talk.* San Francisco, CA: Wide World.

Pappas, T. (1997). *The adventures of penrose the mathematical cat.* San Francisco, CA: Wide World.

Pappas, T. (1997). *Mathematical scandals.* San Francisco, CA: Wide World.

Pappas, T. (2002). *Math stuff.* San Francisco, CA: Wide World.

Pinczes, E. (1999). *One hundred hungry ants.* Boston: Houghton Mifflin.

Pinczes, E. (2002). *Remainder of one.* Boston: Houghton Mifflin.

Pinczes, E. (2003). *Inchworm and a half.* Boston: Houghton Mifflin.

Raskin, E. (2004). *The westing game.* New York: Penguin Young Readers Books.

Schwartz, D. (1994). *If you made a million.* New York: HarperCollins.

Schwartz, D. (1997). *How much is a million?* New York: HarperCollins.

Schwartz, D. (1998). *G is for googol.* New York: HarperCollins.

Schwartz, D. (1999). *If you hopped like a frog.* New York: HarperCollins.

Schwartz, D. (2001). *Q is for quark.* New York: HarperCollins.

Schwartz, D. (2006). *Millions to measure.* New York: HarperCollins.

Sleator, W. (1998). *The boy who reversed himself.* New York: Penguin Young Readers Group.

Thorne-Thompson, K. (1994). *Frank Lloyd Wright for kids: His life and ideas, 21 activities.* Chicago: Chicago Review Press.

Viorst, J. (1978). *Alexander, who used to be rich last Sunday.* New York: Simon & Schuster.

Wells, R. (1995). *What's smaller than a pygmy shrew?* Morton Grove, IL: Albert Whitman.

Wells, R. (1996). *How do you lift a lion?* Morton Grove, IL: Albert Whitman.

Wells, R. (2000). *Can you count to a googol?* Morton Grove, IL: Albert Whitman.

Whitin, D. (1991). *Living and learning mathematics: Stories and strategies for supporting mathematical learning.* Portsmouth, NH: Heinemann.

7

Strategies in the Arts

From the primary level on, gifted learners come alive in classrooms that draw upon the visual and performing arts as bridges to the curriculum. I have witnessed too many of them revive through the simple offering of an arts activity not to know that for a large number of these promising students, learning without artistry, beauty, imagination, and feeling holds little enticement. Who can deny that dramatizing history or analyzing the light quality in a painting can sometimes inspire more advanced thinking than taking notes or reading a text? The arts are serious work. Goertz (2003) envisions art instruction as the "fourth R" in education and argues that it increases the skills of observation, abstract thinking, and problem analysis.

> The artist visualizes and sets goals to find and define the problem, chooses techniques to collect data, and then evaluates and revises the problem solution with imagination to create. . . . The artist, in his or her creative process, requires a higher-order thought process. (p. 460)

The artistic domain offers a creative bounty for the classroom that teachers would be hard pressed to find anywhere else. Not only do students frequently discover new talents in the process of art making, but those with strong leanings toward the visual, the kinesthetic, or the auditory also find their learning styles embraced—some for the first time. The arts also bring unanticipated outcomes. The sudden, imaginative leap or improvisational moment; the unexpected role reversal; the inspired, multimedia composition never before attempted—all are signs of gifted learners awakening to thoughts, meanings, and sensibilities rarely experienced in classrooms that do not offer the arts.

By extension, the arts also provide new access points to other disciplines in the curriculum. Units that place the visual or performing arts at the heart of the learning process naturally lead students to more complex thinking and enable them to make significant and lasting discoveries in various subject areas (Smutny, Walker, & Meckstroth, 1997). Many teachers, such as those in this chapter, have witnessed the versatile nature of the arts as bridges to the curriculum. The chart below demonstrates this.

Art Processes That Apply to the Curriculum

Music: sensing patterns; embodying whole, half, quarter, and eighth notes; measuring beats, steps, durations of sound; evoking moods or atmospheres; composing, synthesizing sounds, rhythms, themes; feeling; shaping; creating story in sound.

Mathematics, language arts, social studies

Dance: measuring lines; following angles; creating circles; telling stories kinetically; expressing and exploring force and gravity; interpreting music, poems, sounds; choreographing planetary movements, animal species, weather changes; grouping together/falling apart; exploring animate/inanimate, static/dynamic; sculpting.

Mathematics, science, language arts, social studies

Theater: stepping into histories, geographies, cultures; assuming identities of leaders, pioneers, inventors, creators; performing political and social satire; reporting; staging debates; exploring fashion styles/gestures/tastes; improvising; dramatizing stories; miming poems; imitating objects, flora, fauna.

Social studies, language arts, science

Visual arts: imagining other worlds; exploring images; sensing; feeling; reasoning spatially; exploring perspective and dimension; analyzing compositional elements—shape, proportion, light, color, movement; measuring distance, ratios (e.g., an object to its shadow); interpreting meanings, moods, textures.

Mathematics, science, language arts, social studies

The teacher-authors that follow present a wide range of creative ideas and processes in both the visual and performing arts. Since the arts are inherently creative, this collection can be applied to the other subjects (language arts, social studies, science, and math) as well as to other arts classes. As in previous chapters, here is a chart to aid in the planning process.

Topic	Level of Challenge	Applications
Creative Arts & Words: Creative Approach to Reading, Writing, and Arts for Young Elementary Students *Pat Hollingsworth* P. 246	Primary grades	Integration of drawing, writing, reading, and movement Practicing fine motor skills in creative art projects that link to emerging writing
First Start in Art *J. Christine Gould & Valerie Weeks* P. 252	Primary grades	Visual arts processes Integrations with art history (meet the artist) Cultural explorations (African design)
Looking at Art With a Critical Eye *Jeanie Goertz & Keith Arney* P. 256	Applicable to all grades, with adjustment	Visual art critiques Integration of Bloom's taxonomy to explore artist's work, style, life
Teaching Gifted Children to Use Creative Imagination and Imagery to Produce Pictures in Verbal and Visual Art Forms *Joe Khatena & Nelly Khatena* P. 262	Level is flexible, and these strategies can adjust to the experience and talent levels of individual students.	Imagination as a means to create verbal and visual pictures Integration of language and visual arts Focus on creative thinking strategies— synthesis, destructuring, restructuring, and analogies
Music Improvisation and Composition: Essential Strategies for Developing Musicianship and Engaging the Creative Minds of Children in the Music Education Classroom *Lois Veenhoven Guderian* P. 270	The ideas presented can be adjusted to different levels depending on experience and background. This is for music teachers or for those with a solid background in music and composition.	Improvisation and composition in music Strategies for integrating the creative element in music education, and thus extending the curriculum and reaching the needs of gifted learners for creative expression in music
Strategies for Practical Acting Workshops: "Creating an Ensemble" *Scott T. Barsotti* P. 279	Adaptable to all grades	Self-expression in theater Ice-breakers to engage imagination and free students from self-consciousness Strategies that reinforce confidence, problem solving, and improvisational abilities Becoming an ensemble
Creative Art Strategies for the Gifted *Marian McNair* P. 286	Middle grades, but adaptable	Interdisciplinary: social studies City planning Multimedia arts Research
Musical Theater Experience *Leah Novak* P. 288	All grades	Performance experience Kinetic learning processes Theatrical production Design and construction (sets, costumes, props)

REFERENCES

Goertz, J. (2003). Searching for talent through the visual arts. In J. F. Smutny (Ed.), *Underserved gifted populations: Responding to their needs and abilities* (pp. 459–467). Cresskill, NJ: Hampton Press.

Smutny, J. F., Walker, S. Y., & Meckstroth, E. A. (1997). *Teaching young gifted children in the regular classroom: Identifying, nurturing, and challenging ages 4-9.* Minneapolis, MN: Free Spirit.

CREATIVE ARTS AND WORDS: CREATIVE APPROACH TO READING, WRITING, AND ARTS FOR YOUNG ELEMENTARY STUDENTS

By Pat Hollingsworth

MAIN CONCEPT

The "Creative Arts and Words" approach builds upon whatever the present reading skills of young students are. It develops the fine motor skills needed for handwriting and drawing which are often lacking in young gifted learners. Further, this approach allows gifted students to *create* their own reading and writing content. Gifted students become more willing to learn handwriting and drawing because they are focusing on the imagination rather than on skill acquisition.

LEVEL

Primary.

APPLICATION

Art, literacy; creative movement; social studies.

DESCRIPTION

In "Creative Arts and Words," the strands of writing, drawing, reading, and movement are woven together to provide students with productive work that will help them develop their gifts and talents. This method, which I have used for 25 years, is based on the work of Sylvia Ashton-Warner and Katie Johnson.

Even if students are already good readers, have them give you single words and then trace these words. Remind them that this is a special writing style that you want them to learn. This method helps students develop strong fine motor skills and the confidence that leads to writing and drawing fluidly.

Daily Movement Time

For about 10 minutes each day, have your whole class participate in a movement activity. This activity is particularly good after students have been working diligently for a good length of time. Have all children stand with space between them so that their arms will not touch. There can be many types of movements that you teach the children while they are standing in place, such as bending, stretching, running in place, jumping, dancing, and robotic moves. Use your imagination and have the students silently follow your movements. After you have been the leader for a while, begin selecting students to be the daily "movement leader."

Daily Drawing: Portraits—Step 1

The teacher demonstrates on the board.

Face, Neck, Shoulders

Have students get a partner and sit facing each other. Have them look at each other's face as you talk with them. Ask students to describe the shape of a human face. Draw that shape on the board for students to see. Ask them to notice that our necks have two sides. Add a neck to the oval you drew on the board. Next, have them notice that their shoulders are wider than their heads. On the board, draw a half-rainbow shape attached to each side of the neck for shoulders. Next, draw a simple U-shaped or V-shaped collar.

Eyes, Nose, Mouth, Ears

Talk with your students about the location of the eyes on the face. Have them look at their partner. Eyes are about halfway between the top of the head and the chin. Have the students use their figures to make an approximate measure. On your drawing on the board, draw two rainbow shapes in the middle of the face. Then draw a straight line for the bottom of the eye. Inside this semicircle eye shape is the round baseball shape of the iris and pupil. Have the students look at each other's eyes. Have them notice how the round baseball shape of the iris and pupil fill the semicircle. Then have them look for a small reflection light on the iris and pupil. On the board, draw in the iris and pupil very dark except for one little reflection light. Then, have students look at their partner's eyebrows and eyelashes.

Tell them that the nose is hard to draw, but it can be made with an L. The mouth can just be a U-shape or a slice of watermelon shape. If ears show, draw them by making one a small C shape and the other a backward C. Add all of these parts to your drawing on the board as you are having the students observe their partners.

Hair

Have students notice how many different kinds and colors of hairstyles that students have. On the board, draw some hair on the face. You can show how to draw straight, wavy, and curly hair.

Daily Drawing: Portraits—Step 2

Materials needed include the following:

White paper

Pens, pencils, or markers

Whiteboard or chalkboard for the teacher to demonstrate as student's draw

This time you will tell the students that they are going to draw pictures of some of the people on their word cards. The teacher will draw on the board while they each draw on paper. Students will have one piece of paper. If they do not like the drawing on one side, turn it over and use the other. They are not to wad up paper and throw it away. Tell the students that what may look like a mistake is all part of learning.

Tell students to draw along with you as you draw on the board. Go over exactly the same procedure that you did the prior day. In other words, you will talk and draw just as you did the day before. For this process to become internalized, you will need to verbalize the exact steps that you went through in Step 1.

Ask them to draw an oval on their paper at the same time you are drawing it on the board. Then, talk about the neck, shoulder, and collar just as you did before. Move on to the location and shape of the eyes, the L-shaped nose, and the watermelon-shaped mouth. Remember, this is just like teaching anything else; it takes time for the process to become internalized.

Use any excuse for the students to practice drawing their face, neck, and shoulder portraits. Whatever you are studying can become your subject matter. Draw pictures of families, teachers, friends, Marie Curie, Abraham Lincoln, Maria Tallchief, George Washington, Betsy Ross, Martin Luther King, or whomever you wish. Just be sure that you walk them through the drawings in the same way each time.

Daily Drawing: Full-Body Portraits—Step 3

You may start the full-body drawings at any time after doing the portraits for a week or two. Remind the students that you have talked about body proportions during *movement time*. Tell students whether their paper should be turned in "Portrait" or "Landscape" direction. If drawing more than one person, *landscape* direction is usually best. Ask all students to write their names in the bottom right-hand corner of their page. Pens, marker, or pencils may be used. Pens and marker have the advantage of not being able to be erased. Some gifted children are such perfectionists that they spend most of their drawing time erasing.

Start With the Head and Neck

Begin by drawing a head on the board and ask students to do likewise. Ask them about where eyes should be. Then draw them on the board as they are drawing on their paper. Ask them what kind of nose they will use and continue with the same script you have used previously.

Drawing the Body

Ask students to draw a rectangle for the top part of the body. Then ask students to decide whether to have their person wear long pants, short pants, long skirt, or short skirt. Draw those four alternatives on the board and tell the students to pick one. Remind students to draw shoes. Draw flat oval shapes for shoes for the person you are drawing on the board. Students may then wish to decorate the shoes and the clothes.

Do not be at all concerned if the lesson does not "take" at first. Just continue to talk through the head and body parts and get the students to observe. It takes almost a whole year for the approach to be internalized by some students. This approach does not at all hinder creativity; it only enhances it.

Daily Reading and Writing

Materials needed include the following:

500–600 blank 5 in. × 8 in. cards

Pocket folders for each child with individual names on each folder

Cheap, thin 8.5 in. × 11 in. white copy paper

Sets of large-size colored markers (teacher will use the black marker take out yellow markers because they do show up well on white paper all other colors are for the students)

Phase 1: Words on Day One

Step 1

Each day write the name of each child in the class (in the upper left-hand corner) on a separate card. Due to its flowing nature, D'Nealian style works well, but any handwriting method will work. You can work with as many as six children at a time, or you may work individually with one child at a time while others are working in centers.

Step 2

When children come to you for the first time, ask each of them to tell you the name of someone they love. If Sarah comes to you first, use the card with her name on it. In the middle of Sarah's card write the name of her loved one. Ask Sarah to read the name to you. Tell her the card will stay at school in her pocket folder.

Step 3

Show Sarah how she may trace the loved one's name on the white copy paper using one of the large, colored markers. Show her how to put the thin, white paper over the 5×8 card, and then ask her to trace her name and that of her loved one. Have Sarah trace her own name at the top of the paper (portrait direction) and then trace the name of her loved one under her name. Since this is Sarah's first card, ask her to trace the name several times. Later, when Sarah has many word cards, she will usually trace each word only once. Sarah's first tracing page might look like this:

Sarah

Mom

Mom

Mom

Mom

Mom

Step 4

Show Sarah how to put the 5×8 card in the pocket folder and where it will be kept in the classroom. The folder and the 5×8 cards will stay in the classroom. The copy paper will go home each day with the student.

Phase 1: Words on Day Two

Step 1: Students bring folders to the teacher.

Students will get their folders from their designated location and bring them to the work table.

Step 2: Students read words to teacher.

Ask students to open their folders, get out their 5×8 cards, and read the words on their cards to you.

Step 3: Teacher writes students' names on 5×8 cards.

As they come to you, you will write each student's name in the upper left-hand corner of a 5×8 card.

Step 4: Students give new words; teacher writes words on 5 × 8 cards.

Next ask students for names of people whom they love (continue this for about a week). Try to get the names of the important family members who will most likely also include the names of pets. This is a wonderful way for you to get to know the names of people who are important to the student. Some students will want more than one word a day. This is fine as long as the students are learning to read the words as they go along.

Step 5: Students trace words from 5 × 8 cards onto white copy paper.

Always have the students begin with their own names. After they have traced a whole page of words, another word may be given. The students take home the page of traced words and return the folder to its proper storage location for use the next day. If on Day 2 Sarah now has three words on 5 × 8 cards, her tracing paper might look like this:

Sarah

Mom

Dad

Grandma

Mom

Dad

Grandma

Step 6: Students return folders and take home their tracing pages.

Phase 1: Writing Ideas for Following Days

Group Building Direction

Next, if you wish to help build group rapport, ask students to give you the name of someone in the class. Continue until everyone in the class has every name and can read every name. The next step after everyone has all the class names is for students to write compliments to each other. A form that can be used is like the following:

Date_____

Dear _____,

I want to compliment you for_____.

Your friend, _____

Even though some students can write their own compliment, it is important to have a list from which to choose, for example, being nice to me, being kind, playing with me, do good work, and so on.

Student-Led Direction

You could just continue with asking for a word each day without giving any directions. Sometimes that is very powerful for students. Be sure that they write a whole page of words each day. Also be sure that the students can read the words they have requested. By the end of the semester, students will be requesting and reading their own sentences, which means they are ready for Phase 2.

Phase 2: Sentences and Paragraphs

By second semester and sometimes sooner, all students are ready to write their own sentences and paragraphs. They may use the words from their folders to write sentences, or they may create their own.

Story paper with an area for a drawing at the top is ideal. By this time, your students will be comfortable both with writing and drawing. Tell your students that their homework every night is to think of sentences to write the next day.

Encourage students to use "sound spelling" when they are doing their first drafts. They can always go back and make corrections.

While the "Creative Arts and Words" approach may benefit all students, it particularly benefits young, gifted students. By combining movement, drawing, and writing, teachers are able to build on their natural strengths and interests while at the same time developing good fine motor skills for writing and drawing. As mentioned, the imaginative dimension of this work engages the interests of gifted children, enabling them to invent their own reading and writing material.

FIRST START IN ART

By J. Christine Gould and Valerie Weeks

Every child is an artist. The problem is how to remain an artist once he grows up.

—Pablo Picasso

MAIN CONCEPT

The keen art interests of young, gifted children is the impetus behind a program that uses the study of artists and art history as a vehicle for reflecting on and developing their ideas about art as well as discovering their own artistic styles. Focusing on the life and times of artists creates a rich, interdisciplinary dimension to the program.

LEVEL

Primary grades.

APPLICATION

The ideas presented here apply to history, geography, reading, writing, and the study of culture.

DESCRIPTION

The First Start in Art program utilizes arts-based activities to introduce kindergarten children to art history, along with personal artistic expression. The developmental level remains matched to kindergarten students while the complexity level is raised.

The First Start in Art program is divided into three sections:

1. Meet the Artist

2. I'm an Artist

3. The Finishing Touch

The first two sections of the program are designed to be taught in two-and-a-half-hour sessions per week for six months. The third section is designed to be taught in one hour-long session per week for three months. Depending on the nature of the Finishing Touch project that has been selected, more time may be needed for this part of the program.

Because art evolves, First Start in Art is not a static program. It grows and changes with the interests of the children each year. This program description follows the activities of First Start in Art for one year.

1. Meet the Artist

Ms. Weeks seats 20 five-year-olds around her and places the *art trunk* in front of her. She tells the children that they are about to meet an artist. Excitement fills the room. The art trunk contains essential materials about the artist who is about to be brought to life. On this day, it is the abstractionist Jackson Pollock. After Ms. Weeks opens the art trunk, she begins to draw items out that visually explain who the artist is. The first item drawn from the art trunk is a book about the artist. It is followed by samples of the artist's work. The children are introduced to the key vocabulary words about the artist: *abstract expressionism*, *spatter painting*, *movement*, and *balance*. They discuss the meaning of the key vocabulary words as they relate to samples of the artist's work.

The discussion always begins with introducing the artist as a child. What was the person like? What brought about his or her interest in art? How was the artist like or different from the children in the room? The discussion continues and includes the artist's life, important works, and any artistic stages that may be pertinent. Through this discussion, the artist becomes almost real—almost like one of the excited children sitting in the classroom.

2. I'm an Artist

Each school year is divided into several units of study. This year's units included African Design, Twittering Machines, Concrete and Abstract, and the Personal Collage. Each unit begins with the introduction of the key vocabulary words and a discussion utilizing the context/interest questions to create background knowledge.

African Design

Key vocabulary words: *symbols, meanings, culture, belief system*

Context/interest questions: Where do you think Africa is? How large do you think Africa is? What is a culture? What is a belief system? What is a symbol?

To create a contextual background for understanding African art, the unit begins by discussing African history, geography, belief systems, and cultures. Once background knowledge has been established, the children are introduced to art forms that developed specifically within African cultures. They learn about African symbols and their meanings. They then learn to use dye to create colors and designs that are distinctively African. Next, the children create stamps of African symbols and stamp them onto paper bags. The unit finishes with the creation of a burlap bag costume the children can wear. They cut holes for arms and necks out of burlap bags and decorate them with African symbols.

Twittering Machines

Key vocabulary words: *twittering machine, line, shape, color, imaginary*

Context/interest questions: What is a machine? What does twittering mean? How would someone make a machine? What kind of music do you think the *Twittering Machines* played? Why did the artist Paul Klee love color?

This unit is based on the photographs of *Twittering Machines* created by the artist, Paul Klee. Copies of his drawings of *Twittering Machines* are made in black and white. Students are introduced to the watercolor medium which they then use to color in the machines as the artist, Paul Klee, might have done. As a second part of the unit, students make a twittering machine of their own based on Paul Klee's designs but use their own imaginations.

Personal Collage

Key vocabulary words: *texture, rhythm, pattern, overlapping, weave, combination, 3D, repetition*

Interest/context questions: What does overlapping mean? What does texture mean? How can you create texture or a 3-D effect with objects?

Unlike collages that express characteristics of an individual's personality, this collage focuses on differences in texture of materials. Children are given a poster board on which to create their collages and are encouraged to put together items of varied textures. Items that might be included are fabrics with different patterns and textures, metal pieces, wire, flat objects, pieces of toys, string, wallpaper pieces, and objects that have depth, creating a 3-D effect.

While creating this project, the children practice the texture techniques of tearing and cutting paper. They also experiment with overlapping items onto each other. The children are encouraged to combine the various textures of the materials on their personal collage.

Concrete and Abstract

Key vocabulary words: *Rose Period, Blue Period, cubism, abstract, concrete emotions*

Context/interest Questions: Have you heard the name Pablo Picasso before? What is Cubism? How can an artist make something flat look like it is floating in the air? What is a 3-D effect?

Pablo Picasso is used as the vehicle for studying the differences between abstract ideas and concrete ones. The first project introduces children to the idea of making something flat on a paper look as though it is floating in air. Black and white copies of the *Old Guitarist* by Picasso are made. The children use the medium of colored pencils to add color and details to the painting. The second project is a creation of students' own cubist paintings.

3. The Finishing Touch

This year's finishing touch project was a sculpture of the Twin Towers that were tragically destroyed on September 11, 2001. A local artist, Jennie Becker, agreed to work with the children in creating their own group sculpture of the Twin Towers. After studying about the Twin Towers, the children were invited to the artist's studio. She placed squares of porcelain clay about the studio—one piece for each child. After students painted their personal impression of the Twin Towers, the clay tiles were fired in a kiln. A local construction company volunteered to build a concrete facsimile of the Twin Towers on which the tiles were set into place. One of the city's universities donated space for the children's sculpture. It stands on the grounds of Wichita State University today as an honor to those who died.

Benefits to Gifted Children

For anyone, the study of art promotes creativity. For gifted children, it may help to uncover advanced ideas waiting for an opportunity for expression. The study of artists and art history helps gifted children develop opinions and reflect on their own ideas.

After finishing the Concrete and Abstract Unit, an emotional five-year-old girl rushed to Ms. Weeks and burst out, "I hope I never have a Blue Period like Pablo Picasso." Ms. Weeks answered, "I hope you never have a Blue Period, either." She knows that now, at five years old, this young girl is an artist. Will she be able to remain one?

REFERENCES

Evans, J., & Skelton, T. (2001). *How to teach art to children*. Monterey, CA: Evan-Moor Educational.
Micklethwait, L. (1996). *A child's book of play in art*. London: Dorling Kindersley.
Venezia, M. (1991). *Getting to know the world's greatest artists* (set). Chicago: Children's Press.

LIST OF ARTISTS FOR STUDY

Pablo Picasso (1881–1973)

Mary Cassatt (1844–1926)

Georgia O'Keefe (1887–1986)

Claude Monet (1840–1926)

Paul Klee (1879–1940)

Jackson Pollock (1912–1956)

LOOKING AT ART WITH A CRITICAL EYE

By Jeanie Goertz and Keith Arney

MAIN CONCEPT

In this process, gifted children use both critical and creative thinking to respond to and evaluate a work of art. This includes developing the skill to provide a rationale for their responses by specific aspects of a composition. Bloom's taxonomy can aid this process and can act as a tool for analyzing, interpreting, and judging art.

LEVEL

This process can be used at almost any grade level with some adaptation.

APPLICATION

These activities can apply to arts, social studies, and language arts topics as well as to any learning situation that requires critical and creative thinking opportunities for advanced students.

DESCRIPTION

There is only one way to learn about criticism of a work of art and that is to use creative and critical reasoning skills to determine if you like a piece of art work and why or why not. Students need to learn to cite their proof and support for their reasons for liking or disliking a piece of art. Gallagher and Gallagher (1994) suggest that many gifted children never learn to give reasons to support their arguments and may use their advanced language skills to camouflage what they don't understand correctly or well. Consider the intellectual aspects of art study and practice presented in increasing levels of difficulty using Bloom's taxonomy as a framework for looking at art with a critical eye.

Knowledge

- Ability to recall separate bits of art information such as terminology, names, dates, things, materials, processes
- Ability to recall how the information is organized into sets, methods, sequences, and customary procedures
- Ability to be knowledgeable about art principles, abstractions, and theories

Comprehension

Ability to understand to do the following:

- Translate art into other terms or symbols including words
- Interpret art to show meanings of works
- Make predictions and show implications

Application

Ability to use art knowledge and understandings in producing art, in criticizing art and in talking about it historically.

Analysis

Ability to break down artistic communications clearly into smaller constituent parts:

- To show the relation between these parts
- To show how they are organized by structure or principles to make wholes

Synthesis

Ability to do the following:

- Put together parts and elements to produce a new and unique artistic or theoretical whole
- Produce a plan on a proposed set of artistic operations
- Develop a set of abstract relations within the whole theory or artwork

Evaluation

Ability to make considered judgments about value of ideas, solutions, methods, and materials by consideration of internal evidence and external criteria (J. Moody, personal communication, August 10, 1986).

Bloom's taxonomy is the framework for the next activity. The focus of each section is to allow the student to progress through the stages of Bloom's.

THE ACTIVITY USING BLOOM'S TAXONOMY

Study of an Artist

Each student will select an artist's print and select one or more task cards prepared by the teacher from different levels of Bloom's taxonomy to complete these topics: the artist, the artist's style, and people in the artist's life. Print one question on each card or shape you design from the list below. Each student has one or more artists' prints. The student selects one or more task cards and answers the questions using the prints.

Topic: The Artist

- Find out who the artists are and the titles of their paintings. (knowledge)
- Identify the historical and the artistic period in which the artists painted. (knowledge)
- Find five other paintings by each artist. (knowledge)
- Write a brief description about two or more of the paintings and information about the artist's message. (application)
- Decide which painting you like the best. Why? (analysis and evaluation)

Topic: The Artist's Style

Each artist has a particular painting style; some examples of styles are impressionistic, surrealistic, cubistic, and classical.

- Examine the painting(s) and determine the artist's painting style. (knowledge)
- Examine one style and report your findings. (knowledge, comprehensive, analysis, and synthesis)
- Based on your research, tell the importance of an artist's style. (Evaluation)

Topic: People in the Artist's Life

Other people, especially friends, teachers, and mentors, influence artists.

- Read about the life of two or more artists and then tell what people made a difference in their lives. (knowledge and analysis) Why do you feel these people made a difference in the artist's lives? (evaluation)
- Compare the two artists you read about for likenesses and differences in their lives and paintings. (knowledge and analysis)

With respect to creativity, divergent thinking, and problem solving, Dunn and Griggs (1985), in their extensive study of the learning preferences of academically and intellectually gifted students, concluded that they are often uncomfortable taking risks or dealing with ambiguity and open-ended problems. According to Rogers (2002), this can lead to "sloppy thinking habits." Consider the activity of writing a critique as a starting point to help the student think critically and creatively in describing, analyzing, interpreting, and judging a work of art.

To prepare for this lesson, "The Art Critic," have a variety of copies of well-known paintings by da Vinci, Picasso, Rembrandt, van Gogh, Degas, Gainsborough, and Gauguin. Then have each student select a painting and proceed using the directions below. Another method would be to prepare individual packets with the set of questions and a painting.

The Activity: The Art Critic

Description

Have students look at the painting or artwork of their choice. Have them record the size and medium and try to imagine the actual size of the artwork.

Now, have them study the artwork carefully and list everything they see. Have them be objective. Tell them not to make guesses or let their feelings about the work influence them. Have them write down every fact that they observe.

When they finish describing the work, read through the following questions. These questions will help them recognize the types of details they may have noticed.

- What appears to be the focal object of the work of art?
- What appear to be the other (subordinate) objects of importance?
- Where or what appears to be the setting?
- What appears to be in the far background?
- What are some of the details found in the focal and subordinate objects?
- What "facts" can be found in the work of art?
- Did the artist use the same color, shape, or item more than once in the composition?
- How much of the composition is filled with "positive spaces?"
- Did the artist include any "minute" detail in the composition?
- What can be found in this composition that you have seen in other works of art?
- Are the colors real?
- Can you tell the materials that things are made from—wood, metal, fabric, and so on?
- Can you identify things from nature?
- Can you determine a light source?
- What condition are the "things" in?

Tell students to try not to make suggestions or guesses, and save their clues.

Analysis

The elements of art are as follows:

- **Line**: Movement between two points, either graphically or spatially drawn, such as gradual change in states of one line element or by repetition of line elements. The quality of line changes from thin to fat, to rough, to wavy, to short, to swift, and tall.
- **Texture**: Changing quality or character or surface from soft, smooth, glossy, waxy, rough, and grained or of a line from dots or short lines.
- **Shape**: A line enlarged to become an area or an area defined by a line that assumes the geometric proportions of a rectangle, circle, triangle, or polygon.
- **Form**: Shapes and planes joined to become areas. Forms are often called the *three-dimensional* shapes.
- **Color**: Property of things seen such as red, yellow, or blue. Studies developed through relationships such as opposites and complementary, by attributes such as value, intensity, tint, and shade or in contextual units such as high value, cool hue; low value, warm hue.
- **Space**: The area that appears not to be in use. Often, we do not consider space when we create a work of art. Artists use space to create interest in their work.
- **Value:** This refers to the lightness or darkness of a color. It also refers to how artists use elements of art to create a sense of light or dark.

Now in this phase, analysis, students make statements about the elements of art: line, color, value, texture, space, form, and texture. Again, this step is factual, and no interpretation or emotion is involved. Students should include in their analysis evidence of perspective in the composition (formal, informal, overlapping, diminishing value, etc.).

Interpretation

Students review the clues they have collected. Ask them what do they think the artist is telling them about the relationship(s) in the work of art? These relationships can include the environment. Some questions to help include the following:

- What do you think is happening in the work?
- What do you interpret from the clues that you collected in step-one description?
- What do you think the colors mean?
- Why do you think the composition was arranged in the manner it was?
- Do you see any special feelings?
- What do you think the artist is saying about being a part of things, life, and so on? Other than the title, can you draw conclusions that lead you to feeling the way you do about the composition?

The students can try to go beyond the events that appear to be taking place in the artwork. Have them seek the general idea or theme that they believe the artist is trying to express. If they put together the facts and their own ideas about the world, they will probably discover the meaning of the artwork for them.

Judgment

Finally, students are ready to decide if they like the work of art. As they judge the work, they need to be ready to give their reasons for liking or disliking it.

Questions to consider in judging artwork include the following:

- Do you like the way the artist imitated reality? Why? Why not?
- Do you like the way the artist used and organized the elements? Why? Why not?
- Do you think the artist has been successful in expressing feelings and ideas? Why? Why not?
- Does the work of art make you think? Give the reason for your answer.
- Would you like the work of art displayed in you home? Where? Give your reasons.

REFERENCES

Bloom, B. S. (1956). Taxonomy of educational objectives, handbook 1: The cognitive domain. New York: David McKay Co. Inc.

Dunn R., & Griggs, S. (1985). Teaching and counseling gifted students with their learning style preferences: Two case studies. *Gifted Child Today*, 41, 40–43.

Gallagher, J. J., & Gallagher, S. (1994). *Teaching the gifted child*. Boston: Allyn & Bacon.

Rogers, K. B. (2002). *Reforming gifted education: Matching the program to the child*. Scottsdale, AZ: Great Potential Press.

TEACHING GIFTED CHILDREN TO USE CREATIVE IMAGINATION AND IMAGERY TO PRODUCE PICTURES IN VERBAL AND VISUAL ART FORMS

By Joe Khatena and Nelly Khatena

MAIN CONCEPT

To teach gifted children to be creative in verbal and visual art forms, teachers need to become familiar with creative imagination and imagery, and their application to verbal and visual art forms. They also need to provide students with sufficient opportunity to practice creative thinking strategies (e.g., synthesis, destructuring, restructuring, and analogies).

LEVEL

Adaptable to a wide range of grade levels.

APPLICATION

These activities apply to any hands-on arts experiences. They are also valuable as a means for developing higher-level and creative thinking.

DESCRIPTION

Creative Imagination

Creative imagination consists of two dimensions. One related to producing something from what has not existed before. This lies in the province of the divine or cosmic, responsible for the creation of earth, sky, ocean, sun, planets, human beings, and the many creatures of the universe. Samuel T. Coleridge, an English poet of the 19th century, called this creative activity the operation of the "primary imagination." The creativity of human beings he calls the "secondary imagination." That is to say, human beings can simulate in small the activity of the divine by using what already exists but freshly perceived and manipulated to give birth to the new. It is this dimension of creative imagination that lies in the province of human creativity. By becoming knowledgeable in what constitutes the processes of creative imagination, we begin to be in a position to instruct children how to become creative.

Imagery

Creative imagination, as used by human beings, involves imagery. Information derived from the world around us is stored in our brain first as images, later symbolized in one language form or another. In the non-language form, images may be primarily visual and auditory, although to a lesser extent, they may be in other sensory dimensions. Language forms of images may be verbal, mathematical, musical, and related symbolic forms. To recall these images, we may be stimulated to do so by the visual and hearing alphabet or by the symbols of mathematical or musical notation. Sometimes, we have called imagery "the language of discovery" since it is directly connected with the creative imagination.

Instructional Use of Imagery and the Creative Imagination

The purpose of this contribution is to suggest to teachers that gifted children can be taught to use imagery and creative imagination in the production of the original. This can be done by teaching children at first to use several creative thinking strategies among which are synthesis, destructuring, and restructuring, as well as analogies. Students need to be given practice in the use of these strategies. To this end, we have designed a number of exercises to stimulate creativity generally. Similar strategies using visual art content will be dealt with in the second half of the paper. Teachers may refer to two of our books on the subject for more complete information (Khatena, 2000; Khatena & Khatena, 1999).

EXERCISES

Synthesis-Destructuring-Restructuring

Synthesis requires the creative imagination to combine a number of elements to make something unique. You may give students a number of elements for this operation. They have the freedom to use imagination to acquire other elements to assist them in the process.

Example

Construct a black flannel board (8 × 12 in.) and have three geometric shapes—a square, triangle and semicircle—cut out from a bright colored vanguard sheet. Beginning with a one-inch square that can be divided into four equal strips, cut across diagonally to make two equal triangles and circles cut into two semicircles. In all, have 10 pieces of each shape placed in a small plastic bag. These materials will be used for the operations of destructuring and restructuring as well. Hand out these materials to your students.

Exercise 1

The geometric shapes can be combined in various ways to produce interesting pictures. Each of the pieces may be used more than once. You should demonstrate that one possibility would be to create two children on a seesaw. Then have children make other interesting pictures with the shapes, each time encouraging them to close their eyes and image what they will construct (Figure 7.1).

Destructuring and restructuring require pupils to take apart, for instance, the shapes combined to make two children on a seesaw and recombine them into another interesting picture on the flannel board to be recombined or restructured into another picture. Demonstrate how a car can be constructed using the same number of shapes. Then, tell pupils to construct other interesting pictures using additional pieces from the bag as needed (Figure 7.1).

So far, we have used figural or nonverbal materials for the purpose. The same thing can be done with verbal materials. For instance, give students a pool of words as illustrated. They can then extract a number of them to be put together into an interesting and unusual expression. The teacher can demonstrate this.

Pool of Words

*dog mouse fish
rock door tree flower
star ruby snow sun
wind moon earth*

Students can then put these words back in the pool and select these and other words to make other interesting and unusual expressions, each time imaging them before producing them on paper.

Analogy

This involves comparison of similarities of two unlike things in the context of familiar experience to aid understanding. The simplest kind

Figure 7.1   Restructuring Man to Car

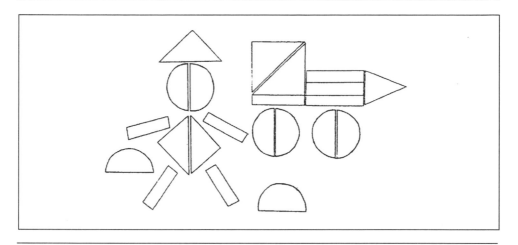

From *The Creatively Gifted Child: Suggestions for Parents and Teachers* (p. 34) by J. Khatena, New York: Vantage Press. Copyright © 1978 by J. Khatena. Reprinted by permission.

of analogy is found in the simile where some element in one object is found to resemble another, while each one remains different. For instance, in the simile "The man is as thin as a stick," both the man and stick have "thinness" in common while remaining a man and a stick. The metaphor is another comparison form where elements in two unlike objects are made similar. For instance, should the above comparison be "The man is a thin stick," we are saying that the man and stick are identical. In these ways, we can help others understand more easily what we think about the world around us. Although the above examples are verbal, analogies can be made using sound and sight: laughter as a rippling stream, or the wave motif seen as the body of a worm, leaf, or curly hair.

Analogies are images organized as comparisons. Students may be encouraged to imagine the comparisons when they make them. They can do this with their eyes open or closed.

Give your students activities in constructing similes and metaphors that are both verbal and nonverbal. Here are a few for their practice.

Verbal

(a) Complete the following similes:

Cunning as _____

Bright as _____

_____as a balloon

_____as an ox

(b) Make a metaphor with each of these words.

Flower_____.

Ice_____.

Train_____.

Wild_____.

Nonverbal

    (a) Record a few sounds and play them to your pupils. Let them guess what they are. Get them to communicate these by using comparison. They can verbalize their responses on a piece of paper or make drawings of the images they experience. The teacher may use the sounds recorded for the measure of originality called *Sounds and Images* for this purpose (Khatena & Torrance, 1998).

    (b) Present them with a few figures like the straight line, circle, and wave. Demonstrate a few analogies that can be made with them like a leaf, flower, snake, and shell. Then encourage your pupils to try making their own analogies. They may image the comparisons with eyes closed or open before they draw them.

CREATIVE IMAGINATION AND IMAGERY APPLIED TO VISUAL ART

Introduction

We now come to the second half of this contribution which will deal with the use of similar creative thinking strategies that stimulate the creative imagination described above with visual art as content. These are synthesis, destructuring, and restructuring as well as analogy.

Let us first begin by saying something about the language of visual art whose alphabet is drawn from nature in terms of seven generic motifs. These are the *spiral, circle, half-circle, two half-circles, wavy line, zigzag,* and *straight line.* These shapes seen by the human eye in nature include the whirlpool, wave, mountain, sun, fish, animal, plant life, fire, and human shape and form (Figure 7.2).

The teacher can encourage students to identify these forms in various natural objects and happenings around them. This activity may also be given to students with the purpose of getting them to derive the seven generic forms by their observations.

Figure 7.2   Seven Generic Motifs Drawn From Nature

Synthesis-Destructuring-Restructuring

Generic motifs can be used as basic materials to be synthesized into pictures. Take, for instance, several generic motifs that are combined to make pictures in the oval (Figure 7.3).

These motifs that make the pictures can be pulled apart, as it were, and put together to make other pictures. We call this process destructuring and restructuring.

Students can be given practice in these operations to make various pictures using the same generic motifs. These activities can be the precursor of creative art much like *Reptile Walk* done by Nelly Khatena (Figure 7.4).

Figure 7.3   Generic Motifs in Stylized Drawing

Figure 7.4   Reptile Walk

Analogy in Visual Art

As described above, analogy involves comparison of similarities of two unlike things in the context of familiar experiences to help understanding. In visual art, we may use generic motifs to form visual analogies. Take, for instance, the wave motif acted upon by creative imagination to produce a rope, caterpillar, leaf, and shell (Figure 7.5).

Teachers can give students practice in using any one or more of the generic motifs to make visual analogies. This can serve as preparation for the creation of more complex visual analogies, illustrated in Nelly Khatena's artwork entitled *Ginko* (Figure 7.6).

REFERENCES

Khatena, J. (2000). *Enhancing creativity of gifted children: A guide for parents and teachers.* Cresskill, NJ: Hampton Press.

Khatena, J., & Khatena, N. (1999). *Developing creative talent in art.* Stamford, CT: Ablex.

Khatena, J., & Torrance, E. P. (1998). *Thinking creatively with sounds and words.* Bensenville, IL: Scholastic Testing Service.

Figure 7.5   Analogous Relationships of Wave Motif

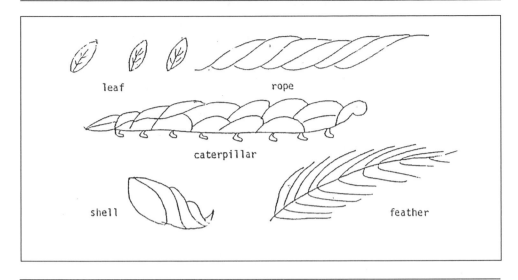

Figure 7.6   Ginko

MUSIC IMPROVISATION AND COMPOSITION: ESSENTIAL STRATEGIES FOR DEVELOPING MUSICIANSHIP AND ENGAGING THE CREATIVE MINDS OF CHILDREN IN THE MUSIC EDUCATION CLASSROOM

By Lois Veenhoven Guderian

MAIN CONCEPT

Music educators have the difficult task of helping students develop the skills and understanding necessary to support creative work while at the same time nurturing creative thinking for students' original work. This task requires balance in activities in the classroom that help students to acquire domain knowledge and those that develop students' capacity to put their knowledge to use in creative ways. In music class, creative thinking can be ongoing when opportunities for creative problem solving in music, such as music improvisation and composition, are embedded into the curriculum.

LEVEL

Intermediate to upper grades; however, the ideas presented here can be adapted to lower grades as well.

APPLICATION

Music, history, language arts; any process that requires creative thinking and improvisational ability.

DESCRIPTION

Introduction

All human beings have creative potential and a need for creative expression. It is possible that in gifted children and people, the need for creative expression and challenge is more acute. While some individuals have innate propensities for creative thinking, creative thinking can be nurtured in all students. Performing and creating music on complex levels requires many years of dedicated practice and the study of music. However, there are many ways to engage students in satisfying musical experience and creative thinking along the journey of developing musicianship. With opportunities to apply learning through explorations in sound and experimentations with musical ideas (improvisation), children gain in musical skills and understanding and are motivated to continue their learning.

Nurturing Musical and Creative Ability
in the General Music Classroom

Human beings must have opportunities to express their thoughts and feelings in creative ways. Creating sound structures—compositions—is one way. In the music classroom, the experimental processes of improvisation and the applied thinking processes of composing help children learn to think in sound and to develop in musical understanding. Children's efforts to notate their original work in either traditional or nontraditional systems of notation—including students' self-devised notational systems—strengthens musical understanding and allows children to construct their own knowledge in music. Exposing children to many musical sounds and styles of music and providing opportunities to extend their learning through creative problem solving and expression can fulfill the demand for a sequential, comprehensive course of music study and at the same time nurture creative thinking in music.

On a very elementary level, one example like this, in support of curricular goals, might involve students learning how to play a piece on soprano recorder using only three notes (such as G, A, and B) in the musical values of quarter and half notes. When the students have facility in playing the piece, they can create their own piece (i.e., students can use what they have learned to improvise or experiment with the pitched notes and note values and compose a piece for their class to play). Under the framework of the assignment, suggested length could be four to eight measures but should be open-ended for students who want to compose longer pieces. Some children will have had more experience outside of class and will want to compose more complex pieces.

Differentiated suggestions are as follows: (1) Create one piece that fulfills the assignment so all fellow classmates can play it; create a second piece that you or an advanced performer can play; (2) create a countermelody, rhythmic parts or harmony for the piece; (3) create a piece for soprano recorder and perhaps additional instruments. On a middle elementary level, to reinforce the acquisition to the musical ear of a newly learned rhythmic pattern, an assignment might resemble the following: Assign the composing of a new melody for a particular song that the children have learned as part of their curriculum and that contains the pattern under study, in this case the dotted eighth- and sixteenth-note rhythm pattern. "Improvise or create a new melody for the song *Battle Hymn of the Republic*. Retain the same lyrics and rhythm. Notate your work." In this example, the dotted eighth- and sixteenth-note rhythm pattern is reinforced in a creative way.

As follow-up, listening for the pattern in a variety of examples that contain it, as well as singing and playing examples—including the students' assigned original compositions—helps to place the rhythmic pattern in musical context, thus deepening students' understanding and reinforcing their facility in sight reading and playing skills. Again, flexibility is important. Students will come up with many creative ideas as variations to the assignment such as, "Can we change the lyrics, too?" and "Can we add a long ending to the piece?" To suggestions like these, I almost always say, "Yes! What a great idea! If you want to put in the extra time to expand the assignment in this way, that would be wonderful. Just remember, it is possible that not everyone in the class will be able to play or sing your piece with these additions. If you want to share your piece with the class, make sure you find people who can perform your piece." Gifted children are enterprising and ingenious. If they cannot find someone in class to perform their piece, they will find students from other classes or adults to assist in this way.

Preparation. For older elementary children, fifth- or sixth-graders who have had more experience in music and perhaps in composition in various major, minor, and pentatonic tonalities, assigned improvisations and compositions in different sound systems can be exciting assignments for nurturing musicianship and creative thinking. Preparation experiences in listening to pieces created in these systems, analyzing works, whole-class and small-group experimentations, improvisations, and exercises with a particular scale or system can follow listening experiences and studies of modern works and can precede a composing task.

The following preparation example for such studies, especially to develop understanding of serial music, is useful. Hand out a chromatic octave of 12 melody bells to students, in random order for chance creations of tone rows, and allow students to scramble their order to create additional tone rows. Give students opportunities to apply various composition strategies such as inversion, retrograde, augmentation, and diminution to shorter, student-composed rows or to traditional, well-known tonal melodies. This not only helps to develop creative thinking in music but also to enlighten students' understanding when engaged in guided listening experiences and analyses of modern works. In this way, students *experience* music; they learn *in* music rather than learning *about* it.

While general music classes are not designed to teach music composition exclusively, when improvisation and composition assignments are an outgrowth of curriculum content, both domain knowledge and skills can be acquired and creative thinking in music nurtured. Designing specific assignments depends on both the music curriculum and whether a school includes interdisciplinary or integrated curricula. With careful planning, assignments in improvisation and composition can support both the music curriculum and other areas as well.

Children and the Composing Process

Many researchers have offered opinions on whether or not children are truly composing music if they cannot hear the sounds in their heads before they attempt experimentation and exploration in sound and notation (Wiggins, 2007). From my experience as a child and adult composer as well as years of nurturing improvisation and composition in children, I believe that there are many ways to engage children in developing their creative abilities in music—that all children have "Songs in Their Heads" (Campbell, 1998). Innate abilities are varied. Learning to hear music in one's mind, to listen for it, and to think in sound and sound systems can be nurtured like any other learned human activity. Children with large amounts of this kind of innate ability will compose whether or not the opportunity is available to them in school. However, a comprehensive music program that offers opportunities to develop skill, understanding, and creative potential as well as emotional support from teachers and the community may be the critical elements that make it possible for a young composers to realize their abilities as adults.

Regardless of innate ability, all children require a comprehensive music program to realize and develop creative potential. Those who have less innate talent to hear or *audiate* (to hear and comprehend music without the presence of physical sound, like thinking in a language) music in their minds, and have had less exposure to musical styles and experience in working in sound, might begin their explorations for improvising and composing on an instrument rather than by thinking in sound. As they experiment with sounds and develop musical ideas, they construct knowledge, teaching themselves how to think in sound and how to think in musical ideas. Giving children a variety of structured and semistructured assignments that are, for the most part, open-ended and flexible, helps them to gain more confidence in their ability to improvise and compose music. For many children, an assignment serves as a starting point for their creative ideas.

While it is true that professional composers often begin a piece with an idea that is formulated in their minds or seems to come (and perhaps it does) unexpectedly from some unknown place, composers also create commissioned works where the initial idea comes from someone else—an idea that is most likely not expressed in sound. It is then up to the composer to explore the sound possibilities of that idea whether those explorations are completely in their head, made on an instrument, or a combination of the two. The resulting product is most often a beautiful composition that fits the bill so to speak. Giving children opportunities to experiment with and explore musical ideas on instruments or giving them prompts and semistructured assignments as points of departure and frameworks for their ideas are often helpful—not a hindrance.

The Importance of Nurturing Creative Thinking in Music Education

Already in the 1950s, Guilford and later Torrance in the 1960s, realized that the survival of an anticipated technological society lay in the development of creative potential and creative thinking more than simply the diligent acquisition of knowledge. It was learning how to use knowledge in applied, creative ways that would ultimately have an effect on the quality of human life (Torrance, 1963). "Children can be taught to use creative thinking abilities in acquiring even traditional learnings" (p. 7).

Similarly, Sternberg believes that school achievement can be better accomplished by teaching for *successful intelligence.* Sternberg found that teaching students for *successful intelligence*—according to his *triarchic* theory of teaching and learning that involves analytical, creative, and applied practical aspects of thinking—raised students' levels of achievement (Sternberg, 2006; Sternberg, Torff, & Grigorenko, 1998a). In my own work and research with students in music composition for many years, I have found this to be true. The process of composing involves analytical, creative, and practical kinds of thinking as well as a synthesis of all of these. Each composition is a learning experience. Students' former knowledge and ideas blend with explorations and applications in newly learned content. The result is not only a product (composition) but also a new level of understanding and knowledge.

As applied to music education, the underlying assumption here is that it is possible to develop domain knowledge in music and creative thinking in students for the most part simultaneously when students are given opportunities to apply curriculum content—what they are learning—in creative ways. Furthermore, an approach to teaching and learning that is balanced in this way is more effective in developing students' conceptual understandings in music than a traditional approach that requires memory, drill, and practice without creative application.

Many music educators and researchers support an approach to curriculum that maintains a balance between, on one hand, teaching and learning skills, concepts, and musical understanding (convergent) and, on the other, teaching for creative thinking (divergent). Webster (1990, 1991, 1992) recommends the teaching of convergent content as a starting point for divergent thinking to achieve optimal conditions for creative work, learning, and motivation. Priest (2002) expounds on the necessity of creative work in balance with the more structured aspects of learning, rehearsing and performing music. Ainsworth (1970) believes that the process of creative work involves informed decisions, suggesting a learning framework as a prerequisite to composing. Eaton (1992) points out the importance of developing creative thinking skills in the arts and providing a balance between instruction and discovery in pursuit of creative tasks. In an archive-based study that looked at the results of the Music Education for the Under-Twelves Committee, Cox (1999) found that music teaching practices in the United Kingdom were out of balance. Drill-oriented instruction outweighed those that nurtured creativity and creative expression. The committee determined the need for a balance between instruction and freedom for potential creative work. Reimer (1989) urges teachers to foster creativity in students in the early stages of music learning beginning with composition in the first class or lesson.

Convergent and Divergent Thinking in Music Education

Much of the literature surrounding the study of creative thinking in music emphasizes the importance of the interplay between convergent thinking and divergent thinking, that is, "the importance of divergency of thought and imagination in context with the more convergent thinking that often involves just plain hard work" (Webster, 1990, p. 23). Webster believes creative thinking to be a "dynamic process of alternation between convergent and divergent thinking, moving in stages over time, enabled by certain skills, both innate and learned, and by certain conditions, all resulting in final product" (p. 26). Enabling conditions are various conditions in the environment such as the teacher's scaffolding techniques, motivation for a particular task, and innate propensities to certain personality traits (Webster, 1990).

Similarly, in her *Componential Theory of Creativity*, Amabile (1996) uses different language in expressing the importance of the interplay between innate abilities, and learned knowledge that she calls domain relevant skills and creative tendencies and abilities termed as creativity relevant skills (i.e., those that require divergent thinking such as flexibility, fluency, originality, and motivation [task motivation]). Amabile also conveys the importance of learned knowledge, or domain relevant skills, as necessary in all levels of creative endeavors within a domain. "Clearly, it is only possible to be creative in nuclear physics if one knows something (and probably a great deal) about nuclear physics" (p. 86). According to Amabile, products are creative as so deemed by the consensus of experts in a domain. It is in the task motivation stage of Amabile's model of creativity, as applied to music education that social influences and task parameters become crucial issues in regard to children's ability to find meaning through music composition. Social interactions with peers and teachers and the way tasks are designed have a large effect on students' learning. Learning facts or doing assigned tasks within strict guidelines may restrict creativity and global understandings of music and creative work, while learning in the context of large principles and assignments that are more open-ended may be better for most individuals and effect both the learning and the meaning making of students (Amabile, 1996; Hickey, 2003; Kennedy, 2004; Strand, 2006).

In a chapter on teaching music composition, Barrett (2003) points out the inadequacies in approaches to teaching music composition that offer learning opportunities in either extreme—too much freedom or too much structure—that is, one that requires no guidelines or structure, no technical mastery or parameters, and one that dictates by rule and model in step-by-step processes as parameters for creative work (p. 6). Too much emphasis on self-expression gives students little in technical skills and understanding to create work that has meaning within the context of a domain, while the other approach can result in the stifling of students' creativity. Creative works must be deemed both novel and useful within the accepted under-standing of a domain (Amabile, 1996; Barrett, 2003; Hickey, 2001, 2002).

Children's creative work reflects the kind of musical exposure and formal training they have had since they were little. Barrett (2003) inter-viewed two children who had received the same introductory lesson pre-ceding an assigned compositional task. The lesson included guidelines from the teacher as well as a listening example of an orchestral piece for ideas in form, dynamics, musical gestures, and instrumentation. These served as a point of departure for divergent thinking. However, the children used their past-learned convergent knowledge—the knowledge of the instruments and the music theory they had learned thus far—in synthesis with these preparations to fulfill the composition assignment. One child used her knowledge of flute playing and the treble clef to com-plete the composing task, and the other child used his knowledge of chords and guitar playing learned at his private lessons. These examples suggest that students need to acquire domain knowledge to realize their creative work. For many children, the school is the only place they will have that opportunity.

Vygotsky's (1986) principles of cognitive development and schema theory are important to keep in mind when assigning individual and group compositions. As in Webster (1990, 1991, 1992, 2002) and Amabile (1996), in Vygotsky's (1986) theory, the social interactions with knowl-edgeable others at the child's level of learning readiness are very impor-tant and require teacher scaffolding and peer interactions to guide the child toward higher levels of understanding.

Conclusion

Children draw on their convergent knowledge in realizing creative and expressive intent. Teaching for curriculum substance and giving students opportunities to apply their knowledge in creative ways helps them to discover the creative possibilities that might exist in their learning and to develop their innate creative potential.

Students can develop musical thinking, creative thinking, musical skills, and knowledge by engagement in applied creative work. In the long run, these engagements in the classroom may lead toward a more cre-atively fulfilled society of individuals who can experience the joys of improvising and creating music as well as toward the discovery of excep-tional composers who will create the world masterpieces of the future.

Although creative work should be an outgrowth of the curriculum, a few general suggestions are given below that can be modified according to curriculum content and subject matter.

- **Reinforce concepts, notation, theory, sight-reading, and playing by giving students opportunities for creative application.** Music composition, improvisation, and creative activities embedded into the curriculum can be ongoing from the very first day of class so that creative thinking in music is a normal and natural outgrowth of class studies. Even at elementary levels, explorations in durations of sounds on recorders, xylophones, and other classroom instruments and notated in either traditional (such as quarter and half notes) or nontraditional ways can be exciting for children and can reinforce concepts learned in class.

- **Improvisation.** Explorations in the pentatonic scale provide a nonthreatening and enjoyable way to engage students in creative improvisation. These improvisations can be linked to curricular goals and concepts in melody, rhythm, harmony, and meter. An example follows: Improvisations on the black keys of the piano and the F pentatonic scale, prepared on barred instruments by removing scale degrees four (B) and seven (E), are wonderful means to engage children in improvising. Little to no dissonance is created when improvising in pentatonic, and this sometimes makes children feel confident in their composing. It is usually easy to sing the melodies that are created, too, and to compose accompanying ostinati. Of course, other scales—whole-tone, 12-tone—modes, and other systems are recommended so students have the opportunity to explore many tonal systems.

- **Creative application: Students as teachers.** As follow-up to learning in music theory, have students compose sight-reading examples and pieces for themselves and their class from new rhythmic and scale notation learned.

- **Allow students to notate in original and nontraditional ways.** Exposing students to a variety of ways to notate helps develop creative thinking in sound and facility in notating. Nontraditional notation can free the child for creative expression. Use of graphs, charts, pictures, and symbols as well as student-created notation systems often make possible the realization of complex musical compositions that the child may be able to compose but not notate in traditional notation. There are many computer programs for composing in traditional and nontraditional notation that students find especially exciting.

- **The power of suggestion: Prompts and models.** To create background music for stories or dramatic productions, the study of *program music* as models for ideas is helpful (*Sorcerer's Apprentice*, *Peter and the Wolf*, etc.). Stories, poems, or pictures as prompts can serve as springboards for creative work in music.

- **Musical forms as frameworks for creative work.** Use standard forms such as twelve-bar blues, rondo, theme, and variation as frameworks for improvisation and composition. Give listening examples in these forms as prompts to generate ideas and understanding. Choose examples of forms from different periods and styles.

- **Song writing.** Give students the opportunity to "listen to their heads" for music and melodies that express the text of a poem or their original poetry or lyrics. They can sing these and notate the contour of the phrase before exploring the particulars of pitch in written form. The speaking of the text with expressive emphasis gives some students ideas in the direction of the melody (i.e., the rise and fall of the voice in reading a poem). Speaking the text helps to determine the use of meter as well. Again, listening to a variety of song styles; analyzing folk, pop, art songs; and so on is a good place to start in generating ideas for songs.
- **Harmonization.** Knowledge and understanding of harmonization for compositions can be taught and nurtured (students can come up with beautiful, original-sounding harmonies as well) through analysis of songs and pieces and through explorations in sound on classroom instruments. Again, allow students to notate harmonies in nontraditional and self-devised ways.
- **Scaffolding and editing.** Through editing students' efforts in notation, students can learn many things about music and the notating of their creative work. To address solutions for students' creative work, use inquiry as part of scaffolding techniques. "Have you thought about the possibility of extending your composition?" "What are some ways you could do this?" "Could you extend it by repeating it in a varied form?" "By adding a special ending?" "By adding a contrasting section?" "By changing the form from AA to ABA and so on?" and "Is your piece all one dynamic level or are there places you would like played soft or loud?"
- **Peer and self-examinations, portfolios, and rubrics.** To engage students in reflection and self-evaluation of their creative products use methods of inquiry rubrics, and one-on-one discussions with the teacher in examining work stored in student portfolios. Simply, "Tell me about your piece" can be a good opener.

REFERENCES AND RESOURCES

Ainsworth, J. (1970). Research project in creativity in music education. *Bulletin of the Council for Research in Music Education, 22,* 43–48.

Amabile, T. M. (1996). *Creativity in context: Update to the social psychology of creativity.* Boulder, CO: Westview Press.

Barrett, M. S. (2003). Freedoms and constraints: Constructing musical worlds through the dialogue of composition. In M. Hickey (Ed.), *Why and how to teach music composition: A new horizon for music education* (pp. 3–30). Reston, VA: National Association for Music Education.

Campbell, P. S. (1998). *Songs in their heads.* New York: Oxford University Press.

Cox, G. (1999). The development of creative music in schools: Some perspectives from the history of musical education of the under-twelves (MEUT) 1949–1983. *Bulletin of the Council for Research in Music Education, 141,* 32–35.

Eaton, M. (1992). Teaching through puzzles. In B. Reimer & R. Smith (Eds.), *The Arts, Education, and Aesthetic Knowing* (pp. 151–168). Chicago: University of Chicago Press.

Hickey, M. (2001). An application of Amabile's consensual assessment technique for rating the creativity of children's musical compositions. *Journal of Research in Music Education, 49,* 234–245.

Hickey, M. (2002). Creativity research in music, visual art, theater and dance. In R. Colwell & C. Richardson (Eds.), *The new handbook of research on music teaching and learning* (pp. 398–415). New York: Oxford University Press.

Hickey, M. (2003). Creative thinking in the context of music composition. In M. Hickey (Ed.), *Why and how to teach music composition: A new horizon for music education* (pp. 31–54). Reston, VA: National Association for Music Education.

Kennedy, M. A. (2004). Opening the doors to creativity: A pre-service teacher experiment. *Research Studies in Music Education, 23,* 32–41.

Priest, T. (2002). Creative thinking in instrumental classes. *Music Educator's Journal, 88*(4), 47–51, 58.

Reimer, B. (1989). *A philosophy of music education.* Englewood Cliffs, NJ: Prentice Hall.

Sternberg, R. J. (2006). Creating a vision of creativity: The first 25 years. *Psychology of Aesthetics, Special Volume* (1), 2–12.

Sternberg, R. J., & Torff, B. & Grigorgenko, E. (1998). Teaching for successful intelligence raises school achievement. *Phi Delta Kappan, 79*(9), 667–670.

Strand, K. (2006). Survey of Indiana music teachers on using composition in the classroom. *Journal of Research in Music Education*, 54, 154–167.

Torrance, E. P. (1963). *Education and the creative potential.* Minneapolis: University of Minnesota Press.

Vygotsky, L. (1986). *Thought and language.* In A. Kozulin (Ed. & Trans.) from the 1934 edition of the author's work by the same title. Cambridge, MA: MIT Press.

Webster, P. R. (1990). Creativity as creative thinking. *Music Educator's Journal, 76*(9), 22–28.

Webster, P. R. (1991). The preschool child and creative thinking. *The American Music Teacher, 40*(6), 18–19.

Webster, P. R. (1992). Research on creative thinking in music: The assessment literature. In R. Colewell (Ed.), Handbook of research in music teaching and learning (pp. 266–280). New York: Schirmer Books.

Webster, P. R. (2002). Creative thinking in music: Advancing a model. In T. Sullivan & L. Willingham (Eds.), *Creativity and music education* (pp. 16–34). Thousand Oakes, CA: Sage.

Wiggins, J. (2007). Compositional process in music. In L. Bresler (Ed.), *International handbook of research in arts education* (pp. 453–469). Dordrecht, the Netherlands: Springer.

STRATEGIES FOR PRACTICAL ACTING WORKSHOPS: "CREATING AN ENSEMBLE"

By Scott T. Barsotti

MAIN CONCEPT

Dramatic performance is not and should not be considered an esoteric art form reserved for students who are specifically interested in acting and theater; rather, performance is a creative mode of self-expression that enforces confidence, problem-solving skills, and an ensemble-driven collaborative mind. The careful and studied preparation of a role, followed by the contribution and execution of that role in rehearsals and live performance, is no easy task. It requires poise, concentration, and flexibility—all attributes that can improve public speaking and classroom production from students. Acting as a creative form teaches students how to use their own bodies and voices as well as react to others, and in doing so, it fosters the ability to improvise and work with others, while at the same time encouraging and recognizing individual commitment.

LEVEL

Intermediate to middle school grades and up; however, theater work can always be adapted, to some extent, to the elementary level as well.

APPLICATION

Performing arts. Focus on the theater process—from ice-breaking exercises to role preparation and rehearsals—makes the activities here highly useful for any subject where dramatization or simulation may be useful.

DESCRIPTION

Perhaps the biggest obstacle facing an acting class is the icy self-consciousness that hangs in the air like fog the first couple of class periods. Especially in the case of students who have no acting experience prior to workshop, the doubts they have on day one would likely sound something like, "Am I going to be any good at this?" or "This is going to be embarrassing," or "I'm going to look silly onstage." Creating a supportive environment is crucial to the ensemble experience and to each student's growth. To build this environment, an acting workshop can employ ensemble games and warm-ups that lower inhibitions and break the ice. These games aren't just for students but are used regularly by theater professionals; they are straightforward and simple but can generate creative discussion and inquiry, as well as loosen things up.

Ductball

For this game, it's important to have open space. If you are in a classroom, move all of the desks and chairs out of the way, leaving room to move. In fact, most if not all of a practical acting workshop should be done in an open space, preferably with high ceilings; if such a space is not available, clear out as much room as you can before each class. The company I work with in Chicago—Curious Theatre Branch—plays Ductball before every rehearsal and performance. A ball the size of a grapefruit is formed from soft materials (traditionally, newspaper and plastic bags) and wrapped in tape (typically duct tape, hence the name of the game). The ball is constructed this way for safety reasons but also because its light weight is more conducive to the game. Standing in a circle, the ensemble shares the responsibility of keeping the ball in the air with their hands. The basic physical aspect of the game serves as a warm-up for the body and mind, especially for morning classes. Ductball is as simple as a game gets, but what it can teach an ensemble is depthless. Personalities emerge in a real way once a ball is in the air; we learn who is shy and who is boisterous, who needs a hand and who can lend it. When the ball floats into the space between two students, who will get it? Nonverbal cues become very important; students learn how to read the body language of those around them and be mindful of the shared task. The fact that there are countless ways to keep a ball in the air is a source for creative debate, and students can be encouraged to suggest new strategies to achieve higher team scores. Ductball is a perfect example of how creativity and learning are not always buried in big ideas, but finding solutions to simple problems—and doing it as a team—is just as valuable to an ensemble.

Name Gestures

This game serves three main purposes. First, it requires some abstract thinking and following of impulse; second, it requires focus and use of the body for expression; and last, but certainly not least, it serves as a helpful tool for learning everyone's names in workshops where students don't know each other. Standing in a circle, students put a gesture to their name that reflects their personality or mood. Students interpret this in a number of ways. Some students will simply wave or shrug their shoulders and say their names quietly. Others will perform a complex series of gestures or even dance moves. Others will perform an action from a sport they play or a hobby they have. The idea is that they do something that not only represents them but that can also be duplicated and mimicked by the class. This exercise requires that students really pay attention and manipulate their bodies and voices to mimic what they see. Going around the circle, each student says his or her name and performs the gesture simultaneously, which then the entire class imitates in unison.

Compositions

Compositions are an introduction to staging. The exercise begins with one student striking a pose in front of the class. Then, one at a time, other students join the "picture," making one point of contact with one of the other students in the picture (i.e., a hand on the shoulder, a finger on the nose, a foot on a foot) and freezing in position. All students in the picture should be silent and as still as possible. Once there are four or five students in the picture, pause and have the rest of the class reflect on what they see.

Ask questions about the picture: What's happening? What are the relationships? Who is doing what to whom? Who are friends; who are enemies? If this were a scene from a play, what might that play be called? Then resume; have more people join the picture, creating more dynamics and relationships. Encourage the students to explore levels. It can be a revelatory moment when students realize what a difference is made in the scene if one person changes position, crouches, lies down, turns his or her back, or breaks contact. Have volunteers who are not in the picture enter the picture and change the position of one actor. Have someone else change two actors or three. In addition to improvisation and creative/adaptive thinking, this exercise requires a director's mind to shape and customize the scene, and it shows students how to shift focus, imply status, and create entire environments and conflicts with only their bodies as tools.

Precious Objects

Objects tell a story all their own, which is why a performer's interaction with a prop can be used to such great effect. For this exercise, students are asked to bring in an inanimate object from home that is somehow special to them. The level of sentimentality is up to the students, and the objects can range from swimming medals to dolls to iPods. Sitting in a circle, each student holds the object in front of him or her and inspects it. They are asked to remember when it was that they got this object and how they got it. Was it a gift from a loved one? Did they buy it with hard-earned money? Did they find it in the attic? They consider the shape of the object, the texture, the weight, they close their eyes and really explore the object's attributes. Then, they pass their objects down the circle, say two or three spaces. Now, they have a new object, a foreign object. They repeat the same process, considering the object's attributes and imagining the story behind it. Then, they pass this object down the circle, again two or three spaces. Now, with this third object, they spend the most time. Give them several minutes to really think about what this object's story is and then have each student share with the class the story of the object they hold. This should be done as a first-person monologue, so not "This guitar belonged to Eric Clapton," but rather, "I got this guitar from Eric Clapton when I met him backstage at a concert on my birthday." The story is completely imagined and improvised (indeed, they *have* to be) and the more detailed the better—inventive details make the story more convincing. This exercise gives actors the chance to essentially create a character, channeled through the object before them, and experiment with impromptu storytelling.

Character Sketch

Cries of "I can't draw" fill the room during this exercise, but the skillfulness of the drawing is not what's important. Using pencil and paper, students break up into pairs and draw their partner's face. Give them 5 to 10 minutes to do this, and advise them to not put any names on the papers. Then, have them bring their drawings back to the group and pass them two or three spaces down the circle. With this new drawing, students look at the face in front of them and give that person a made-up name. Then, the drawings with the fake names are passed two or three spaces down the circle again, leaving each student with a face they haven't seen and a name they haven't heard. Give the students 10 to 15 minutes to write a monologue for this character on the back of the page. When an actor gets a role, they typically aren't told everything there is to know about that character: Where are they from? What are their interests? What makes them tick? The actor has to create the character by defining a back-story. When time is up, have students read their character's monologue while affecting a voice that is not their own (i.e., a high-pitched voice; a deep, gruff voice; a British accent, etc). Besides the fact that it can be really funny, this exercise illustrates the many facets of the actor's role in character creation, requires several levels of creative thinking, and strengthens vocal exploration.

Games. These are only a few of the games and exercises that an acting workshop can use. In any workshop, regular vocal warm-ups are important as well, as they prepare students to enunciate and project their voices, as well as get the blood flowing. Warm-ups take many different forms: Many actors like the consonant warm-up, where each consonant in the alphabet is pronounced clearly in a series of utterances (Ba ba ba ba . . . Da da da da . . . Za za za za . . . etc); others enjoy spins on tongue twisters ("Unique New York/New York's unique/You know you need/Unique New York"; or "A big black bug bit a big black bear, and the big black bear bled blood"). In any case, vocal warm-ups should be done as a group as well as physical warm-ups (stretching is always good). Games such as these show students that acting is not embarrassing and elusive but really fun and highly creative both for the individual performer and for the entire ensemble. Breaking down personal barriers and getting the students to appreciate each others' impulses and talents facilitates smooth and productive rehearsal time, which ultimately elevates the final performance as well as each student's ensemble experience.

Rehearsal. When moving to rehearsal, let it happen naturally. Once the ensemble is built over time through games and group warm-ups, introduce text. Do what any theater company would do and read the play or play a section or scene that the class will be performing out loud. Once you've read it, talk about it, switch roles, and read it again. This is called "table reading." It is a place for students to discuss what they see in the play, how they relate to it, how they see it in their minds. Once the ensemble is familiar with the play, casting is the next natural step. Have a discussion about each character, how they fit in, and what their motivations are, and have students choose roles rather than any form of auditioning that has connotations of skill level. It may be necessary, therefore, to use a ranking system for the students' choices and make certain casting choices yourself based on what you've seen and would like to see from each individual.

Role sharing. To give students some semblance of equal stage time, it is worth considering the method of role-sharing. For example, if you have 16 students, choose a play or scene from a play that features four strong roles, and have 4 students share each role. If the scene is 20 minutes, have each student perform for 5 minutes and then switch out. Role-sharing generates team discussion, necessitating that each *character group* define their character and decide together how they want to portray the character. Do they each want to play the character differently, or do they want to have something in common (a costume piece, a prop, a mannerism) to which they each add their own interpretation? This method of casting is also effective in that it keeps students engaged during rehearsal when they are not onstage. Rather than sitting idle, they watch their character partners rehearse and take notes. They can help direct each other and make new discoveries.

Once rehearsal begins, keep it simple. Let the students improvise physically while reading the lines from the page and watch for choices that work and don't work. Actors of all ages and experience levels should be treated with respect, but be sure to give clear and specific guidance to students as they create the scene. Rather than giving orders, ask questions about why they chose what they did. This stage should be playful, but focused. Soon enough, the play will begin to take physical shape (it can happen pretty quickly, depending on the group), and the ensemble can make decisions about set, costumes, props, and so on together as the process moves forward.

Memorization. Something that is a stressor for many performers is memorization. While at-home study of lines is helpful to some, the most tried-and-true method of memorization is *repetition, repetition, repetition.* Have students meet with their scene partners before rehearsal in a catch-as-catch-can fashion and speed through each of their scenes three or four times in quick succession. In rehearsal, start and stop as you go. If you like a choice or want to suggest a change, stop the scene, give the note, and then, rather than have them pick up where they left off, tell them to go back a dozen lines and start from there. Memorization should happen beat-to-beat (that is, moment-to-moment) rather than line-to-line. It's easier for most actors to learn a chunk of lines as an emotional beat as opposed to learning individual lines letter by letter and reciting them in order. By memorizing in beats rather than by lines, students prepare themselves to improvise if need be, say if their scene partner drops a line. Also, memorizing beats will reinforce listening to their scene partner and reacting accordingly by knowing where they need to get to in the scene.

Take, for example, a section of dialogue like this:

A: How's your brother?

B: Bill? He's good.

A: Working again?

B: Yep, at the mall.

It would be better for students to understand the intentions of the lines rather than obsess about the lines themselves. Let us say the first actor accidentally says, "How's your sister?" It wouldn't make sense for the second to respond, "Bill? He's good." But by understanding where the scene needs to go instead of being hung up on the mistake, something like this can happen:

A: How's your sister?

B: I don't have a sister; I have a brother, Bill, and he's good.

A: Oh, right. He's working again?

B: Yep, at the mall.

Set an "off-book" deadline that is at least one week before the performance. Encourage students to attempt to rehearse without scripts in hand as early as possible; if they get lost, have them stay in the scene and just say, "Line . . ." and then feed them the beginning of their next line. Be sure to conduct projection drills (this is when it's good to have high ceilings) so that students can work on making themselves heard in a room full of people. This is especially helpful for quieter actors, but it's beneficial for even the most seasoned performers.

If at all possible, arrange for a test audience to watch one of the last rehearsals. Even though students are enrolled in an acting workshop, it may still take them by surprise that they are going to perform this role they've created in front of a large audience. All of those eyes can cause some serious nerves, and it's a good idea to break them in with a test audience.

Nothing requires people to work together quite like theater, and an effective, practical acting workshop can be a positive learning experience for any age group. An ensemble works best when each of its members is comfortable, focused, and ready to explore the stage. An atmosphere of trust and respect is crucial, and above all, it should be fun. Acting differs from other classroom activities and artistic forms and requires its own level of sensitivity because it employs students' most basic and personal tools—their body and voice—in a highly visible forum. Keep them thinking, laughing, and working together, and the workshop will take shape in no time.

CREATIVE ART STRATEGIES FOR THE GIFTED

By Marian McNair

MAIN CONCEPT

While the creative process is unique for all children, gifted students especially need creativity to express the wide range of abilities that are inherent in this population. Problem solving is one way gifted learners can give of their unique gifts as they delve more deeply into themselves to discover the richness within.

Working in visual arts with painting and sculpture can be a catalyst for social studies. The integration process is vast and offers gifted learners a chance to see connections between visual arts and social studies by creating a city in the classroom.

LEVEL

Intermediate and middle grades.

APPLICATION

Visual art classes, social studies.

DESCRIPTION

This unit is for Grades 4 through 6, depending on the students involved and the depth that is undertaken. Research needs to be done by the students to understand how a city is run. Will there be a mayor, a city planner, a police commissioner? Who decides the governing body? Are there parks and public transportation? What kinds of populations are represented in this city? Planning requires a great deal of problem solving and discussion. It also involves a comprehensive understanding of how a city works. The gifted learners have an opportunity to expand their knowledge and understanding of this complex issue, offer valuable input to whole group learning, and begin to delve into areas of special interest either independently or with small peer groups.

The room needs to be large enough to accommodate a growing city. I begin by getting some colored paper that is available to teachers in rolled form. Students decide what color works best for the ground, maybe green or brown. Once the form has been put down in a corner, then the space can be planned and the fun begins! At this point, group interests can decide in which area they will work. Are there enough students to work on transportation ideas? Where will the roads and sidewalks be? Some students might like to be involved planning the city zoo or natural habitat.

I always give each student a soy milk container for designing a building. It is one of the requirements of the unit. It doesn't have to be a soymilk container, but something like it would work. They can cut it up in any way or add extra, flexible cardboard (like cereal box cardboard) to their design. They can also bring in other recyclables that help them complete their vision. It is fun to see different possibilities as new work is added and more work is joined together. When the group is connected to the creative process, many exciting things take place. Input from group members is valuable and teaches students how to work together cooperatively.

Buildings can be covered with construction paper and glued. If there is a theme for row houses, then they will be decorated accordingly. I always offer plenty of supplies so that the students are free to explore different materials and media. Paints, glue, glue guns, pom-poms, foam, craft sticks, aluminum foil, and yarn are available. I have a gluing area covered with newspaper. It helps to visualize the flow of traffic in the room and set it up for maximum work spaces. Also, I leave the city set up so that students can see the work in progress. Gifted learners especially like to spend time visualizing and creating new ideas. I find this helps the creative process as well. I encourage them to write down ideas when they are fresh in mind. These ideas can be brought up in class meetings the following day, and help everyone remember where they were and what they were doing. It also helps to begin class reviewing these notes so misunderstandings won't happen. Group work can be exciting and frustrating, depending on the participants. By offering a collective forum for communication, there can be tremendous growth and cohesion among students and teachers.

Another activity to add to the city project is puppet making. Generally, felt works the best for sewing. Patterns for puppets are made and puppets are cut and sewn (great for fine motor skills). Decorations are added (as needed) for their character in the city. The same gluing area can be used for attaching yarn and pom-poms to their puppets. Scrap fabric can be applied and sewn to alter the puppet into a character in the city. The puppets seem to take on a life of their own with the help of their creators! The more the students play with their puppets and interact with each other's puppets informally, the more comfortable they are creating character interactions. After all puppets are completed, more brainstorming is needed to facilitate a group dialogue with the outcome of a class puppet show. Maybe the mayor is involved with passing an ordinance in a city council meeting, or an owner of a restaurant can't find supplies because of transportation problems. The students will determine their puppet characters, and the teacher will guide dialogues relating to important components of a city.

The characters lead back to the main concept of creating a city and support the various aspects of its functions. Who is in the city? Why? Some new element of history can be created. Maybe there is an ethnic neighborhood that has changed. Research may be done to understand when the migrations of peoples in the specific neighborhood first appeared for example. The class may decide to add elements of ideas that will alter the initial concept of the city. Because the city has democracy in its roots, majority voting will to be taken into account. Students will have plenty of ideas to add. Each time the city is completed, there will be new dynamics that keep it exciting and fresh, just like a real city. One group might want the fantasy of dinosaurs invading, while another group may have unique waterways, bridges, and shipyards.

After the characters are in place, then the script can be written. A small group of gifted learners are helpful in outlining, organizing, and creating the script. Class meetings are held to determine if everyone is being represented and other valuable input. This is an opportunity for the gifted student who has leadership qualities and feels a sense of responsibility for the creation of the script. Group divisions are vital for the outcome of the project, and groups may have informal meetings to see the direction other groups are taking. I have found this to be a very valuable process in the classroom, and if time allows, the puppet show can be videotaped and used for evaluation.

It is an advantage for students to take responsibility for themselves and their group as well as for the teacher to see partnerships form and problem solving and higher-level thinking take place. Gifted students offer the general education classroom valuable responses and problem solving not often seen. Because the city unit is an open-ended study, all students can gain insights not normally offered with direct instruction methods, but it really allows gifted students a chance to achieve new heights in their unique skills and creativity.

To teach an open-ended unit, the teacher must be able to let go of a certain element of control to let the beauty of the process grow and evolve. It is through the balance of questioning, limits, and creativity that this process can impact student's learning and alter lives in the process. That is the aim of this method. Can students create and nurture with the right guidance? What kind of city will be created? Where does our future reside? What acts alter our destiny? Give it to the students. Let them understand and impart themselves in the process. Miracles can happen.

MUSICAL THEATER EXPERIENCE

By Leah Novak

MAIN CONCEPT

All gifted students should have the opportunity to participate in a musical theater "workshop" or class, as it provides an organized structure for them to break loose and have fun. Gifted students frequently get caught up in mental, academic challenges and rarely have an opportunity to explore less academic, more creative activity. Musical theater experiences provide a structure for creative growth that evolves through kinesthetic processes not prevalent in academic settings.

LEVEL

This contribution provides information that applies to all different grade levels.

APPLICATION

Performing arts (music, dance, drama) and language arts.

DESCRIPTION

When preparing a musical theater experience, the age of the students is important. First, find a musical with a big cast or an integral ensemble that can be expanded. For example, *Mame* is difficult because the number of characters is limited, and it is hard to expand. *Peter Pan* is great because you can have an infinite number of lost boys and pirates, and you can make all of those characters important with speaking roles, musical solos, fight scenes, and so on. Musicals set in schools are also good choices, such as *Bye-Bye Birdie*; *Grease*; *You're a Good Man, Charlie Brown*; *Sound of Music*; and *Annie*.

In first through fourth grade, avoid musicals with obvious love stories. Shows with lots of action are better, such as *Cats* or *Peter Pan*. With older students, you can choose musicals with romantic couples, but the students will appreciate "brushing over" the love scenes and romantic duets.

For auditions, choose a big production number that everyone will eventually perform in the play. You only need about 64 counts. Teach this as the audition piece that you will use to gauge the students. Let them perform in small groups and take vigorous notes: who's a good dancer, who's a good singer, who hams it up, who can sing *and* dance, who is shy, who can't sing, who is confident, and so on. Ideally, this process takes four or five sessions, but if you are doing a minicourse such as a two-week summer program, it can be done in one session.

After choosing roles and parts, write the script. Focus on songs—singing and dancing is the fun part. Acting is important but just not as much fun for younger students. Pick enough production numbers while considering story line, performance time constraints, and how much rehearsal time you have. Generally gifted students learn a song and dance in one session with about 60% retention. Songs with choruses where the choreography also repeats are terrific when you have time constraints.

When staging production numbers, make sure that every single student gets a time to sing by themselves somewhere in the play. For example, in *The Wizard of Oz*, the majority of "If I Only Had A Brain" might be sung by the Scarecrow, but the crows can sing a verse. In "The

Wonderful Wizard of Oz," munchkins can have solos and then everybody sings the chorus together. Note, in Broadway productions, ensemble members take on several roles. In one scene, an ensemble member may be a maid. In the next, they could be a townsperson. In this experience, students have their own special roles; they are a munchkin, or a winged monkey, or a crow, but not all three. This gives their role more individual importance and students won't feel that they've been cast as an "extra."

Write 45- to 60-second scenes to transition between songs. This is used to outline the plot. It's also a great place for weaker or less confident singers; they get to highlight a speaking role. Make sure you communicate to parents and any others who might be involved that you are *not* doing an actual show; you are creating a musical theater experience based on a known musical. This will avoid the "you know, in the *actual* show . . ." conversation.

Teach the play in order. Assign parts, then read the script through. I photocopy a script for each student. For younger students, I highlight their individual parts; with older students, I expect them to do it themselves. (Don't forget that with younger students, there will be a greater discrepancy in their reading ability. You may need to address this issue beforehand with the class so students are allowed to proceed at their own level.) I usually call students by their character names throughout the class. The students like it, and it helps the younger students remember their character. When you get to the songs, read the lyrics first then play the song for them (from a Broadway recording).

Once this is done, go through scene by scene. Block the scene, and repeat it once. If you repeat the scene more than twice in a given session, the students become restless. Do the transitions and songs the same way. Time things carefully so that you can run through everything you have learned from the beginning of the play, one time straight through before the end of class. Do this everyday! The repetition creates a strong foundation.

Note: By the end of the first song and first scene, everyone should be involved. The only exception might be for someone who has a *big* part that occurs later in the script. Sometimes, students are not comfortable with their assigned roles. You can enlarge the part for those you underestimated, or talk to the student who isn't handling the part and find out what the issue is; then turn it into a duet or whatever will help the student be more comfortable.

Once the play is learned, begin talking about costumes, props, and scenery. It is easiest to use classroom furniture for set furniture. We discuss props when we are running the play. Questions such as, "What could be in our hands?" help students brainstorm. They are usually creative about props. This is also a great opportunity for cooperation; one student might have an idea, and another student says he or she has that item and will bring it in to use. Avoid situations where one or two students promise to bring everything. Parents are usually supportive about letting the students use a few items from home but might not be willing to donate their entire china set.

Costume guidelines are basic and simple. Again, students brainstorm. In *Cats*, are they real cats? Yes. So, what colors might they use? Black, brown, tan, white, gray. Ask parents to discuss costuming with their child. I usually send home a note that says, "Your child has chosen to be a _____ cat. Please help him or her put his or her costume together. For some, it might just be a top and bottom of the same color. Others may add stripes or a tail. In class, we make some costume piece that unifies the characters, such as cat tails or ears or noses so everyone has something special.

Another few run-throughs and it's time to put it all together. Students and others enjoy the performance. We should never dismiss the value of participation for gifted students. They get so much out of this class because it offers them a completely different experience from those they are used to as "gifted students."

8

Discovering Your Own Creativity

For some of us, creativity seems to belong exclusively to an artistic elite. We classify members of this elite as rarities on the basis of what they accomplish in contrast to the rest of us. They hold a certain mystique—conjuring unusual creations from nowhere, stumbling upon brilliant ideas in odd places, and ferreting out original solutions with an ease that can be both maddening and admirable. Most research studies on the creative adult or child do what we do—look to the production of visible results to validate that something creative actually happened.

Yet, Maslow (1968) saw creativity as *a way of being,* which he called "self-actualization." Self-actualized human beings live lives of spontaneity and freedom. Unhampered by a concern over others' opinions or censorship, they give themselves the license to be original in all that they do. Self-actualized human beings distinguish themselves not by membership in an artistic elite, but by their lack of stale stereotypes and clichés. They have an acute "sense of wonder" about many things (Carson, 1965). Puzzling paradoxes intrigue rather than frighten them. They would rather seek the unknown than settle into familiar answers because of some nagging need for security. Their "peak experiences" (Maslow, 1968) or "encounters" (May, 1975) imply a creative way of being as distinct from either talent or training.

May (1975), Maslow (1968), Carson (1965), and Rogers (1954) noticed several primary characteristics of imaginative people:

- Total immersion in the moment (experiencing a temporary suspension of time, past and present)
- Openness to experience as an original event (leaving the past behind and treating the present as new)
- Complete self-acceptance (judging oneself independently of others and validating one's own individuality without reservation).

We can see an example of this kind of freedom in the child's simple encounter with nature (Carson, 1965). Creating a new relationship with nature every day, the clear-eyed child transcends the level of the adult, who values knowledge over feeling and tries to identify each plant and bird correctly. The child, through imaginative response, often learns more than the classifying adult.

Maslow (1968) distinguished raw, creative behavior, which he termed the "primary processes," from technique, which he called the "secondary processes." The two are often confused. The finest artists, of course, have both originality and technique. Yet, many acquire a technical brilliance that can masquerade as creativity (i.e., good training is mistaken for creative talent) (May, 1975). Impressive imitations can sway even the most critical of us, simply because they involve a technical mastery of unmistakable achievement, whereas highly original works can sometimes jolt us where we least like it. Skill has more status than originality in our society, and what is more, skill can often compensate for a lack of creativity. Hence, raw creativity has become, unfortunately, the servant of superficial judgments.

Yet, if every scientist, artist, and performer preserved the unassuming child spirit (the creative self) within, his or her work would become more original, spontaneous, and imaginative. Even valuing creativity as a natural outcome of imaginative thinking rather than of hard academic labor would bring a healthy new impetus to various fields. Creative self-expression in its most basic element determines how life is experienced, how problems are perceived, how duties are performed, how instruments are played, and how visions are realized. It demands openness and spontaneity, as well as the courage to fend off the unreceptive responses of hard-nosed or narrow-minded thinking. Albert Einstein saw creativity in this light:

The important thing is not to stop questioning. Curiosity has its own reason for existing. One cannot help but be in awe when he contemplates the mysteries of eternity, of life, of the marvelous structure of reality. It is enough if one tries merely to comprehend a little of this mystery every day. Never lose a holy curiosity. (*Albert Einstein Quotes on Spirituality*, n.d.)

(See more quotes by Einstein at www.simpletoremember.com/vitals/einstein.htm)

Three author-teachers conclude this book. All of them address the subject of discovering and nurturing the creative spirit not only for our role as teachers but as a way of being. All provide rich food for the spirit— a way of keeping our private flames alight as we continue to share, uplift, inspire, and ignite the creative fire within our students.

Winged to Fly

By Pamela Walker Hart

When once you have tasted flight, you will forever walk the earth with your eyes turned skyward, for there you have been and there you will always long to return.

—Leonardo da Vinci

On a windy, wintry day in March, a friend ventured outside to remove accumulated snow from the walkways. When my friend finished, he returned to the garage and discovered a small black-capped chickadee flapping and flailing about. The little bird was throwing itself against a glass windowpane trying to escape the confines of the garage. The two large garage doors and a small door were quickly opened wide to serve as escape routes. But the frustrated bird just kept trying to fly through the closed window.

Finally, my friend slowly approached the confused, frightened chick- adee. As he did, the bird become very alert, still, and quiet. Gently, the tiny bird was lifted up with gloved hands, carried out to an open area, and released toward the sky. My friend watched with delight as the small bird spread it wings wide and began to fly aloft.

As teachers, we endeavor to emulate the helping hands in this black- capped chickadee happening when working with gifted learners. How gratified we are for the many who let our helping hands lift them and cheer them on their ways. But what about the ones we encounter who won't let us help? How do we connect with children suspiciously perched just beyond the reach of our helping hands fearfully flapping and flailing about?

Scholastic boredom and difficulty with making friends frequently cause gifted learners to manifest their frustration in disturbing social behavior. What do we do when we realize our teaching methods no longer meet the needs of a gifted child? How do we gently guide ones who are tenaciously determined to do their own thing in their own way? What is our response to the silent—or not so silent—screams from others who have moved beyond the help we are offering?

CREATIVITY

The challenge of developing the multifaceted, artistic talents of our gifted learners—as well as their exceptional scholastic abilities—can indeed be daunting. An understanding of creativity processing enables our cultivation of innovative teaching approaches and appropriate—out-of-the-box thinking and doing—responses that will move us and our gifted learners out of restrictive "garage-type" confines.

Comprehension about *how* creativity works facilitates our structuring classroom experiences that will show gifted children how to prepare their own peak performance flight plans. Through an enlarged appreciation for the continuous, cyclical nature of creative choosing, we recognize when to employ the spectator applauding-hands mode and when to implement the facilitator helping-hands approach. We become perceptive guides for our gifted learners as they build and maintain their own flight launchpads, their own creative happening spaces through acknowledging, accessing, and releasing their own inherent wisdom.

Cherished Individualism

The first choice creative, innovative people make is to embrace their difference and aspire to accomplish their own unique, innovative achievement. They choose to do their own thing—not someone else's, not to merely follow or copy something another has done. However, many gifted children are not comfortable with being considered different. They would prefer to be like their peers, to fit in and be popular. Trouble is, they intuitively know it doesn't work for them. It is not who they really are. Praising their difference and reassuring them that the difference they see as themselves is *not* less than their peers' position will fortify their confidence.

Our steadfast conviction about their ultimate success helps them side step the fear of embarrassment and failure. We can convey to them that unknowns are a necessary prelude to creative breakthrough. We can help them see themselves as a doing-it-now creative who knows making mistakes is just *doing discovery*. We can encourage them to trust their intuition and to press on—through the ambiguity—until the right ideas come together and are ready to emerge as something new.

Doing-It-Now Creatives

As doing-it-now creatives, we encourage breakthrough happenings to occur by turning the focus of our attention and thought away from the outside, in-the-world events. We take our outside, in-the-world observation inside to own thought and process it. We churn those outside, in-the-world observations around with our inside, felt-and-seen happenings in order to transform them into a something that becomes uniquely our own.

We search deep within our own thought as we consider the many facets of our project from our own unique perspective. The goal is to transform our idea and then gift it back to the world as a new, innovative whatever. Traveling the road of invention and originality requires courage. As we explore our inner mental landscape, we keep reminding our self *not* to choose the more familiar and frequently traveled path of replicating what another created.

We learn to thrive in a territory of unknowns. We remind ourselves not to panic. We learn to trust the creative process. Trust that more ideas will come if we just keep on working, keep on listening to our own thoughts. We learn to ignore the fears of failure or of being considered "different" by another or others.

Whole-istic Thinking

When considering creative processes, let's *not* get stuck believing or debating that one mode of thought is more successful during a particular creativity stage than another. The bottom line is that innovative endeavors thrive best when individuals employ *all* the means at their disposal to accomplish their creative *whatevers*. Doing-it-now creatives discover the most successful approach is to choose *whole-istic* thought processing when trying to transform an in-the-head idea into an in-the-world actuality.

Creative, imaginative, innovating thinking fully involves *both* left-mode and right-mode means of contemplation. *Both* the verbal and the visual realms of realization come into play as creative thought shifts to wherever a solution may possibly be discovered. The conscious and subconscious, the logical and intuitive, the planned and spontaneous are all potential contributors and need to be invited to take part in the voyage of creativity. Comprehension of the continuous, cyclical nature of creative processing gives us insight as to the thinking-doing environment of innovative doing-it-now creatives.

STAGES OF CREATIVITY

Great things are not done by impulse, but by a series of small things brought together.

—Vincent Van Gogh

The choice to be creative is *not* a onetime decision. The decision to create involves signing on to a process of making many different choices. When trying to simplify, describe, and understand what happens when a person creates, researchers often refer to the process involved. The thinking-doing stages of creativity include intention, immersion, incubation, illumination, verification, revision, communication, and validation.

Obviously, it is not possible to actually separate one creativity stage from another because of the concurrent, continuous nature of the multiple choices and decisions being made both consciously and subconsciously. However, an understanding of the creativity stages model is beneficial to both experienced and nonexperienced creatives because it informs us what is likely to happen during a flight of creativity.

While the stages of creativity are listed as sequential events and presented as a set of consecutive actions, the process of creativity is not a stair step circumstance. In practice, involvement in the creative process is more cyclical than sequential. Making a decision generates multiple creative choices for the creator to engage in. An abundance of ideas is generated with each one traveling its own unique path in and around the focus area. To discover what is taking place during this creative experience event, let's look a bit closer at the eight creativity stages of intention, immersion, incubation, illumination, verification, revision, communication, and validation.

FIRST STAGE: INTENTION

One's mind, once stretched by a new idea, never regains its original dimensions.

—Oliver Wendell Holmes

During the *intention* stage, we choose an idea. We can encourage original ideas by scheduling quiet times to pay attention to our thoughts within. As we listen, we just duck and dodge the destructive, distracting stuff that would intrude upon our thought. The noise of negativity wants to keep us from becoming enthused and inspired. We push the negative noise out by focusing our attention—our listening—on affirming, constructive words we hear as our own thought. Inspiring ideas are all around us ripe for us to catch and claim when we are receptive and make room for them.

Whether we are aware of it or not, we are surrounded by a reservoir of ideas constantly coming to us. As this happens, each of us mentally chooses to grab this idea—or that one—and hold it in thought even as we opt to let other ideas fly right by us.

We experience life simultaneously in two distinct landscapes. Our everyday existence is a combination of our unique outside-inside simulcast. Each lives both as a seen-and-felt, in-the-world event *and* a felt-and-seen, in-the-head happening. We simultaneously deal with both.

Because our physical survival depends on it, most of us already know how to process the onslaught of seen-and-felt, in-the-world information that comes at us. We mindfully respond or mindlessly react to a wide variety of outside, in-the-world stuff—what to say, what to do, where to go, etc.

Fewer are tuned in to the inner landscape. When we change the focus of our attention from the outside world to our internal thoughts, we uncover a mental world as vibrant and exciting as any out there experience. Learning to listen to the thoughts within is best done in times of quiet, and quiet times are hard to come by, unless we specifically plan or schedule them. However, when we take the time to listen and investigate our mental landscape, we discover a scene filled with enormous action and diversity.

Catching an Idea

Catching an idea—or selecting a thought—is *not* rare or unusual. It is the normal state of our existence. In our mental landscape, we repeatedly grasp bits and pieces of ideas that flow through our mental vista. We decide—consciously or subconsciously—where to focus our attention. We select this mental morsel to taste or opt to send another bite on its way as not fit for our consumption.

The process of selecting thoughts—ideas or mental images—is similar to taking photographs.

To photograph an in-the-world landscape scene, the following steps can help:

- *Employ* a camera.
- *Use* the viewfinder to see and search the physical landscape.
- *Select* something of interest.
- *Focus* our view on that something.
- *Click* the picture that will be *developed* later.

To capture an in-the-head landscape image, the following steps can help:

- *Employ* our own thoughts.
- *Use* quiet moments to listen and search our mental landscape.
- *Select* something of interest.
- *Focus* our attention on that something.
- *Hold* the image in thought—for further *development*.

It is relatively easy to use a camera to photograph an in-the-world picture. What is not so easy is getting great—or even good—pictures. How we direct the what-when-where-how focus choices for the camera's viewfinder largely determines if the resulting picture will be bad, mediocre, better, or wonderful.

Selecting an internal image presents similar challenges. For the best results, we need to choose a desirable, appropriate focus for the attention of our thought. Doing-it-now creatives routinely achieve success by making a concerted effort to carefully choose which ideas to catch, claim, and contemplate as their own—and which thoughts to duck, dodge, and let fly by.

When we have selected an idea of interest and meaning to ourselves, then our enthusiasm and energy begin to heighten with our desire to get on with it. Now, we become even more focused. We have a general sense of where we want to go. Our time and effort now turn to preparing flight plans and building launch pads.

SECOND STAGE: IMMERSION

You have to have an idea of what you are going to do, but it should be a vague idea.

—Pablo Picasso

The *immersion* stage is where we involve our conscious and subconscious thoughts together, in, and around our chosen area of focus. We prepare our creativity flight plans, do the research, learn related skills, and practice techniques. We begin the work of bringing our idea to actuality, of transforming our thought into something seen.

Unfortunately, lots of well-intentioned folks find their names falling off the directory of doing-it-now creatives right about this time. Rather than choosing to commence, they let themselves fall prey to the "all-talk-no-action" affliction. They cite any number of different reasons or delay mechanisms. But the fundamental cause is usually fear of making mistakes and fear of embarrassment.

By refusing to commence, these all-talk-no-action folks turn themselves into noncreatives. They fall prey to the misconception that mistakes are bad and mean failures. They decide that the absolutely only certain way to avoid ever making a mistake is to never actually do or create anything. No doubt about it, we can't fail if we don't try. We can exist and vegetate this way. But we cannot live a truly productive-constructive life if we never actually do or create anything.

The use of open-ended art projects is an extremely effective means for commencing imagination flows and immersing participants in the *doing* processes of creativity. When structured as vehicles for *doing discovery*—rather than for display or competition purposes—art projects will be welcomed not only by children with recognized artistic talents but also by gifted learners in other curriculum areas who have not yet revealed their inner artist.

Doing Discovery Visual Arts Experiences

- Thinking and seeing

Excellent drawing exercises—devised to expand *intuitive* ways of thinking and *spatial* ways of seeing—are included in Betty Edwards's (1999) book, *The New Drawing on the Right Side of the Brain.*

- Media materials
  - **Draw:** pencils, colored pencils, crayons, pastels, NuPastels, pens, markers, bamboo, twigs, and other items
  - **Paint:** tempera, watercolor, acrylic, water-based inks, chalk-tinted sand to glue onto cardboard background
  - **Monoprint**: Plexiglas plates—painted with tempera; linoleum and Styrofoam plates—incised and painted
  - **Stamp:** Potatoes cut, incised and painted; other found objects—rock shards, leaves, pieces of metal, costume jewelry, plastic fittings, toys, buttons, doilies, and the like
  - **Sculpt:** wire, clay, papier-mâché, natural and man made found objects, fabric and stitchery

- Subject matter ideas
  - Work in a *series* to interpret

  1. A *single* model or *subject*: animal, insect, plant, fish, bird, or building
     - in a variety of media: pencil, paint, print, clay, wire
     - on differently sized format grounds: rectangle, square, oval, round, triangle
     - from different perspectives: close-up, bird's-eye, worm's view, multiple views
     - *in the style of* established artists: Leonardo, Holbein, Cezanne, Van Gogh, Miro, Kandinsky, Mary Cassatt, Picasso, Georgia O'Keefe, Frida Kahlo, Helen Frankenthaler, Paul Klee, Jackson Pollock, Lee Krasner, Charles Burchfield, Susan Rothenberg, Manuel Neri, and others

  2. *Multiple* models or *subjects*: a friend, pet, hiding place, private space
     - to emphasize a specific design element: line, shape/space, value, texture, color

- to emphasize a particular design principle: unity, balance, contrast, repetition, emphasis, pattern, movement, rhythm, pattern, proportion
- to emphasize a specific feeling: joy, anger, sadness, confusion, fear
  - **Record a *remembered* experience:** Recall something or someplace: a trip, park, seeing a sunrise, sunset, waterfall, ocean, lake, or being in a rainstorm.
  - **Envision an *imagined* place:** Create a fantasy environment.
- Use a photographic reference: Create something with it and then use *the first something* as the inspiration to create *a second something;* next, use *the second something* to create *a third something,* and so on.
  - **Make an *experimental* work:** Pour paints, blow through a straw, or paint and draw with found twigs
  - **Work *on location*:** At home or school, draw and paint what you know best.

Making mistakes and failing are integral parts of the creative process. As doing-it-now creatives, we are just *doing discovery.* Mistakes are routine occurrences whenever we are doing new and innovative things. As doing-it-now creatives, we learn to take mistakes and temporary failures in stride. We learn from each mistake and we take our new found knowledge with us as we begin again.

THIRD STAGE: INCUBATION AND FOURTH STAGE: ILLUMINATION

While in the process of executing an idea, creativity happens not with one brilliant flash but in a chain reaction of many tiny sparks.

—R. Keith Sawyer

Incubation—the most mysterious stage in the creative cycle—occurs when we engage our intuitive thoughts in the process of immersing ourselves in something. It involves a conscious and subconscious inquiring of the self, "What if . . .?" We also ask, "Why?" when something unusual or unexpected arrives at the door of our minds. Incubation is a primed patience that lets things brew on the back burner of thought—and remembering to schedule quiet times to mentally watch that back burner brew. Unexpected support comes through night dreams, daydreams, spontaneous happenings, and serendipitous findings that strengthen something we are contemplating or doing in our focus area.

Illumination is that split second when the light comes on and the pieces of the puzzle suddenly seem to come together. Up to the illumination moment, we know lots—and keep learning more—about what is *not* the answer to our searching. But we are also becoming increasingly confident we will have no difficulty in identifying our special something—when it appears. The precise arrival time of illumination is *not* predictable. But the "Aha" realizations and "Eureka" moments come with regularity when we consciously invite them and prepare for their arrival with our flight plans and our launchpads. These illumination moments occur as a result of what we choose to actively pursue and relentlessly put into practice.

Several years ago, I committed to write an essay. I completed the research and made decisions on what to include in the article. But I kept bumping into a block when it came to *how* to put the parts together so the piece would work well as a whole. Thoughts about this writing project consumed me. I totally immersed myself in writing the individual parts. I began experimenting with a variety of ways to assemble the piece. Nothing seemed to work, and I remained perplexed. I kept at it, expecting a solution to pop into thought any moment.

Instead, I began to mentally hum and sing the words of an old song. I couldn't get this song that I had not thought about in years to leave me. The words of this song were foremost in my thought at this time in spite of my efforts to push them away. Finally, I began to wonder why. Why would these words come to me now? I began to listen to the words more closely. Then, I realized one verse in that song offered a wonderful way for me to package the parts of my essay. I found my solution of how to make this writing work as a whole. Illumination came when I listened and followed the guidance of my inner wisdom to an unexpected place of an old song. Who would have guessed?

FIFTH STAGE: VERIFICATION AND SIXTH STAGE: REVISION

The problem solving work of verification and revision actually occurs concurrently with the earlier stages of intention, preparation, incubation, and illumination. During *verification*, we make certain our creative something is progressing as intended. Success during the *revision* stage requires the ability to return to the work—often numerous times—with a renewed spirit of adventure, fearlessness, and persistence. It is a willingness to continue taking part in a creative conversation with the work in progress.

For instance, an artist routinely steps back to contemplate the work, view it from a different perspective—upside down, sideways, or as a reverse mirror image—in verification of its progress. Then, revision activities of changing and editing are employed by the artist to improve the work in progress. As the piece moves closer to completion, the artist verifies again—placing it in a mat or frame, hiding it away to be viewed later with fresh eyes, soliciting input from a supportive friend, or requesting a critique from a respected artist or mentor. Should the artist conclude that more work is necessary, the revision stage is revisited again.

Not infrequently, major revision or monotonous editing is required to make something work well as a whole. Our innate wisdom helps us solve these problems creatively. As we attentively listen to the artist within, we become totally immersed in the decision-making zone of our creativity, in the rapid cycles of creative choosing that occur during the verification and revision stages. Our inner wisdom enables us to move beyond seeming failures—the mundane and ordinary—to find that something that is entirely new. The something that is truly our own!

SEVENTH STAGE: COMMUNICATION AND EIGHTH STAGE: VALIDATION

When we finally push through the obstacles and failures and discover we have done something really special—honest and wholly our own—what do we do next? What do we do when we find ourselves at the communication and validation stages? We know that the answer—in our heart if not in our head—is, "Now we must choose to share our creative something." When we stop short of sharing, as far as the world at large is concerned, our creative something was never even done. Unfortunately, this happens all too often.

Frequently, folks justify this stopping-before-sharing by announcing it is "all about the process." Perhaps a more accurate assessment would reveal this decision to be "all about the self"—a self that is fearful about stepping outside of the safety zone of personal preferences. It is so sad when an insight of something special is not allowed to be seen by the world at large, never shown to the few—or many—that may be receptive.

Teachers can encourage their young creatives to stretch beyond trepidation by explaining that communicating and validating are an integral part of the creative process. These stages prepare and motivate doing-it-now creatives to release this special something, thus freeing them to begin anew. The *communication* stage is when doing-it-now creatives gift their special something to the world. Receptive, ready receivers for what has been created will welcome it warmly in *validation*—or confirmation. Their gratitude adds joy to the creator's own feelings of self-validation which remain primary. This indescribable joy combines with intuitions from our innate wisdom to energize and motivate us for our return to the fun as we prepare our new creativity flight plan and customize our creativity launch pad.

And what about the noise of naysayers? We check out their works of creativity to determine whether they are genuine, doing-it-now creatives or simply envious wannabees. When comments come from envious wannabees, we politely smile and pay no attention. When a respected, doing-it-now creative gives negative input, we decide whether the remark will help us become better at doing what is meaningful to us and at going where we want to go. If so, we grow by taking note and graciously giving thanks! If not, we politely smile and pay no attention.

CONCLUSION

> *You have only your own pair of wings and the pathless sky.*
>
> *Bird, Oh my bird, listen to me.*
>
> *Do not fold your wings.*
>
> —John M. Tutt

When we find our gifted learners or ourselves paralyzed by fear, frustration, and failure, innate creativity is ready to come to the rescue. Our understanding of the creative process calms and reassures us as we change the focus of thought to the wisdom within. We remind ourselves that our innate creativity can maneuver us through the confusion and panic and help us regain the freedom to fly.

As we stop flailing and flapping about and become still, quiet, and attentive, we can hear the whispering voice within. Then, we are lifted away from the fixation on destructive thoughts and failed efforts. We perceive things from a different perspective when we focus on constructive ideas. Our innate creativity gently guides us as we greet each new circumstance ready to move forward—ready to fearlessly embrace this happening-now moment as a welcomed *doing discovery* adventure.

When we learn to trust the creative process, we turn off suggestions of fear and failure and turn on our spirit of adventure with its joy of wonder and discovery. Then, we discover we never really lose our freedom to fly. We can always do some small—or not so small—bit of our own special something and gift it to the world today. Soon, we find ourselves soaring as we transform our ideas into actualities one-by-one and step-by-step. Indeed, each of us is always winged to fly!

RESOURCES

Cameron, J. (1992). *The artist's way: A spiritual path to higher creativity.* Los Angeles: Jeremy P. Tarcher/Putnam.

Cameron, J. (2002). *Walking in this world.* New York: Jeremy P. Tarcher/Penguin.

Edwards, B. (1986). *Drawing on the artist within.* New York: Simon & Shuster.

Edwards, B. (1999). *The new drawing on the right side of the brain.* New York: Jeremy P. Tarcher.

Henri, R. (1984). *The art spirit.* New York: Harper & Row.

Ten Actions for Finding the Song, Dance, Hope, Art, and Magic of Creativity

By Susan Scheibel

Genius without education is like silver in the mine.

—Benjamin Franklin

Magic, excitement, energy, the art of connection and the beauty and joy of learning seldom are the songs we hear or sing in 21st-century education. The rhetoric of the day has the melody of data, accountability, and evidence-based practice raising the bar for learners. Have we thrown out the classical, forgotten the genius, and focused on the rap of the day? Our gifted and talented learners deserve more!

As we create for our children, students, ourselves, and our environments, let us continue to raise our paintbrushes, feet, voices, and our energy. Let us solidly focus on finding the art, the dance, the songs, the magic and the creativity of math, language arts, science, social studies, the arts and ourselves as we mine the silver of our world. Let's turn our dedication and the art to the creative magic of the task at hand!

First, let's solidly pretest, utilize ability grouping, modify the pace, differentiate, become experts of advanced curricula and materials, use the data, allow for independent work opportunities, hold students responsible for achievement, ask higher-level questions, compact and telescope, teach concepts, encourage thoughtful discussion, and raise the bar for gifted learners because we are solidly grounded in evidence-based practices and accountability. Then, with meaningful action and energized hope, let's also find the art, dance, songs, and the magic of creating unique "silver" for the future!

The melody of creativity begins when we act, glean hope, and take the first step. Pick and choose for yourself. Begin at 10 and work toward 1. Create your own path. Start in the middle or with a favorite, as the choice is yours. Please move to take that first step since there is no right or wrong. Move now to take action and keep the hope alive. Find your fit!

I. CHANGE YOUR ENVIRONMENT

Familiarity breeds contempt.

—Mark Twain

If you have been working in the same space, make a change. Look around. Consider new options. Do something different. Start small or go large. Move your desk or paint the walls. Rearrange the room. Look around for inspirational quotes, posters, or art. Redecorate. Change the color or change your room. Work outside. Allow others to help or go it alone. Work in the library, at the zoo, under a tree, or on the back porch. Quietly observe others at work and learn from them. Try something new to change your environment! Be brave because change is good, and the sky's the limit!

II. EXPERIMENT

The difference between the impossible and the possible lies in a person's determination.

—Tommy Lasorda

Do something completely new today. Greet everyone at the door. Smile all of the time. Wink at a colleague. Write a note to say thanks or good work. Start with a quote. Set greater expectations. Change the way you look at a child, a student, or an administrator. Try a new book for yourself or with others. Read a different genre and talk about it. Have a class seminar. Quicken the pace and allow for more questions at the end. Make more connections. Bring treats. Tell them how much you care. Reread and explain it a different way. Be open and positive to everyone. Regroup and rethink. Find more challenging material. Defend a child or student. Give the hardest test and help them prepare. Sing all the way home. This is the time to seek the impossible, so be determined!

III. GET ORGANIZED

It's what you learn after you know it all that counts.

—John Wooden

Hours, days, weeks, months, and years speed through our lives. The world will never slow and the pace will never be perfect. There is never time for it all, but don't allow yourself to become exhausted or frustrated. Really. Stop today. Sit down and make a list of what is really important today, this month, and this year. Distinguish between what you need to do and what you want to do. There is a difference, and that difference can allow you great opportunities and creativity. Make a plan. Write it all on paper and keep it handy. Begin with your plan each day and end with it each day. After the first week, the first month, and the first year, look at what you have accomplished, smile, and be proud. It's okay to also celebrate! Allow yourself to stay focused and organized. Say yes to what needs to be done. Say no when it's prudent. Organize your time first, then your space. Make time to organize your thoughts and enjoy the time that you earn. Keep it going each day, week, month, and year. Reflect. Make the change and live an organized life. Appreciate your new energy and your time for creativity. Organization is the gift we give ourselves!

IV. LISTEN TO MUSIC

When I hear music, I fear no danger.

—Henry David Thoreau

Music to my ears is true, but music is also healthy for our mind, body, and spirit. Today, we read about creative musical energy for healthy living. It's natural and comfortable to have music as we wake, on our way to school or work, in the elevators, while we shop, study, exercise, compute, and even socialize. Research we read tells us about the internal rhythms that mirror the alpha waves of our brain and are associated with creative thought and actions. We see our children with their iPods and radios, boom boxes, and hear music blaring from their cars. We all have our favorite artists, composers, and tunes that help us relax. Music is an effective tool to consciously manage our mind, body, and mood when used appropriately. Music appeals to our emotions, can calm and center, aids concentration, and eliminates interfering brain clutter. Try it today, tomorrow, and often. Put on great music, different music, and create the mood; listen to songs that will improve your state of mind, and let yourself find that positive place of quiet, relaxation, and comfort. And, when you're ready use fun, exciting, new music to raise your spirits and your energy. Let yourself be caught by the music and creative energy! Sing! Dance! Celebrate! Create!

V. TAKE A CLASS

To be able to be caught up into the world of thought—that is educated.

—Edith Hamilton

Be a lifelong learner and model that excitement of learning for those around you! Look for opportunities to expand your knowledge, stay engaged, and seek new experiences and learning. Find a friend or colleague to join you or go it alone and meet new people who are interested in similar topics. The more we learn, the more we think and can share with others. Begin a book club, learn from each other, start a Socratic café group to feed your mind and spirit. Or consider professional classes on teaching strategies to enhance your instruction. What are the newest evidence-based best practices for gifted and talented learners? Pull together colleagues, talk through a new publication, and support each other with implementation and encouragement. Build a new instructional team or energize existing ones with creativity. What insightful and rewarding learning opportunities are waiting for you? Allow yourself to be caught in the world and magic of new learning, ideas, and thought!

VI. GET CLOSE TO NATURE

The richness I achieve comes from Nature, the source of my inspiration.

—Claude Monet

Take a hike; learn about the flora and fauna in our world. Learn to walk regularly and appreciate the nature around you. Find the beauty. Smell the flowers. Climb the mountains. Take on a new sport that gets you outside and connected with the beauty that abounds. Sunrise, animals, birds, parks, rivers, water lilies, and your backyard will freshen and revive your senses and your spirit. We can never have enough of the nature that surrounds us! Appreciate and learn from the clouds in the sky, ladybug behaviors, natural flock migration, the pattern of oceans, or the aroma and variety of roses. Spend time with the wonders of science and enjoy the creativity of Mother Nature and yourself! Allow yourself to be inspired and share that magic with children, students, and friends!

VII. QUESTION

Some men see things as they are and say, "Why?"

I dream of things that never were and say, "Why not?"

—George Bernard Shaw

Take and make time to ponder, to wonder, and to question! Consider the whys and the why nots around you and in our world. Allow yourself to question! Keep a notebook of your thoughts, your ideas, your inspirations for they are possibilities for the future. Look for the logical and illogical. Consider convergent and divergent ideas. Juxtapose thoughts, questions, ideas, and hopes. They are windows to your mind and doors to open when the time is right. Work through the difficult and the exhausting times to find the beauty and the magic of children. Their questions are pure and hopeful as they mirror wonder, magic, and dreams. Explore. Creativity abounds!

VIII. RECONSIDER YOUR GOALS

The greatest danger for most of us is not that our aim is too high and we miss it, but that it is too low and we reach it.

—Michelangelo

What are your life goals? What are your personal goals and professional goals? What's really important to you now and in the future? Sit down and contemplate the possibilities as you jot it all down. Allow yourself time to continue the process for days or years, but, at some point stop to read, ponder, modify, and organize what you have created. Allow yourself to spend time on the process as it will take you great places! Become the master of your fate. Be the composer, the sculptor, the architect, the director of your future! What are your priorities and when should they be accomplished? Develop and create the plan for your life. Feel fine with adjusting as no one will know. Right now it's all about you and your magic for the future. Aim high and set your course! The time is right when you take the first step and begin to reach!

IX. MAKE TIME TO THINK AND REFLECT

The people who get on in this world are the people who get up and look for the circumstances they want, and if they can't find them, make them.

—George Bernard Shaw

In today's world, our minds are constantly engaged, our senses are assaulted, our pace is grueling, and time is a top commodity. Brainstorm, accomplish, activate, generate, problem solve, direct, coordinate, plan, prepare, clean, cook, pick up or deliver, schedule, be responsible, monitor, organize, orchestrate, and the list goes on and on and on until the day that we make time to think and take time to reflect. A favorite strategy for me on both personal and professional levels is to go slow to go fast. Stop now! Make time in your day and week and schedule time to think and to reflect. Become your own guide and manage the map. Be creative with yourself, your children, your students, your family, and your friends. Take time to think and to reflect and to model it in your life for those around you. Talk to others about your thoughts and reflections. Think, reflect, pair, and share in your family, school, neighborhood, community, city, state, nation, and world. Ideas, creativity, and possibilities will spill out for us all to contemplate. Get up and look for the circumstances that you want, and if you can't find them, feel free to make them for yourself, your children, your students, and our world!

X. FORCE IT

Action may not always bring happiness, but there is no happiness without action.

—Benjamin Disraeli

Believe in what you believe. Stand for positive action. Move when the time is right. Know what is really best. Do what is right! Make it happen repeatedly! Find your vision for today and make it happen tomorrow! Believe, stand, move, know, and focus on our gifted and talented children and the learners. Concentrate your energy. Ignite the flame in yourself and others. Let creativity guide your work and your song to capture the essence. Allow your subconscious to take over. Pay attention to the results and work each day. Be patient but maintain the focus. Allow yourself to be awed by gifted and talented children, learners, colleagues, ideas, yourself, and your work. Relish the unexpected and the magic! Maintain the vision for today and tomorrow because all children will benefit. Talk about it, be proud, write about it, and share it with everyone! We need to know!

XI. CREATE YOUR OWN . . .

Cherish your visions and your dreams, as they are the children of your soul and the blueprints of your ultimate achievements.

—Napoleon Hill

Never underestimate possibilities! Search out opportunities! Connect with amazing children, students, friends, parents, and teachers everywhere! You have taken the first step; now climb the hill, the mountain, and ford the stream! Ignite your creativity and that of those around you each day, each week, each month, and each year. Take care of yourself and others. Relax and rest when you must. Be the architect of your future with creativity, dreams, and vision as your blueprint. Change the picture and the melody! Dance to the music! Work hard, make it good, make it great, and celebrate in private and with everyone! Ignite your passion! Creativity is magic, excitement, energy, the art of connection and the beauty and joy of learning and the song that we sing for and with our gifted and talented!

We can improve the rhetoric of the day and allow the classical, never forget the genius, and focus on the best as we act and sing for the future!

You hold all of our futures in your hands. So you better make it good.

—Jodie Foster

A likely impossibility is always preferable to an unconvincing possibility. We are what we repeatedly do. Excellence, then, is not an act but a habit.

—Aristotle

RESOURCES

Davis, G. (1999). *Creativity is forever.* Dubuque, IA: Kendall/Hunt.
Van Tassel-Baska, J. (2006). A content analysis of evaluation findings across 20 gifted programs: A clarion call for enhanced gifted program development. *Gifted Child Quarterly, 50,* 199–215.

Suggested Readings

Csikszentmihalyi, H. (1996). *Creativity.* New York: HarperCollins.
Koch, L., & Lobser, M., (1997). *Oops-a-daisy.* Littleton, CO: OOPS Creativity Machine.
May, R. (1975). *The courage to create.* New York: W. W. Norton.
Steinbart, A. (1999). *Creating brilliant ideas.* Winnipeg, Canada: Gildner-Reynolds.

You Teach What You Are: Self-Care for Educators

By Elizabeth A. Meckstroth

When you walk into a school, you walk into a system. How do you fuse yourself into that system? What reflection do you hold up to others to show how you see them? How do you envision yourself? What nurturing supports do you use to bring your bright self into your school culture? What obstacles and challenges impede bringing your fine and full self into your school? Since you are all you have to give and to receive, let's explore how you can choose your options wisely. What aspects of yourself do you want to enhance and what do you choose to diminish?

As you nurture your students and colleagues, they tend to cooperate with you and support you. One of the best things you can do for yourself is to enhance your relationships with your students and school staff.

Smile. This gesture works inside and out! As you smile, your own attitude is enhanced to being happier, more receptive.

Show empathy. This is a critical element of teaching, and it has a boomerang effect. When students feel that their teachers have high empathy for them, some significant benefits ensue. Academic achievement, positive self-concept, and positive peer relationships can improve in your classroom. Perhaps a spin-off of your expressed empathy for someone in a difficult situation is just as valuable to you. With acute listening, as you acknowledge a child or colleague's feelings, attitude, and viewpoint, you will likely become more compassionate and intimate in your relationship.

To glean their cooperation and support, your students and colleagues need to experience that you are right there with them understanding their point of view.

Here are some ways to express empathy and convey your interest in another's situation.

Employ clear body language. Look into their eyes. Crouch or sit so that you have the same eye level. Listen with your entire body, mind, and spirit as if nothing else at that moment matters as much as their thoughts and feelings. Listen as if the child has something important to give to you. Reflect essential bits of the other's thoughts and feelings. Repeat and paraphrase what you hear. Do not add your own ideas. Be careful to use the person's own words rather than interpret.

Ask for clarification and amplification. "I'd like to know how you felt about that." "What were some of the ways you were feeling when he said that?" "What are your thoughts now?"

Allow them to own their thoughts and feelings. "I get it that you're furious having such a short lunch period." Feelings and thoughts do not mean doing or being something. This is the process of making constructive decisions about choosing behaviors. Accepting and understanding do not mean agreeing.

Invest a few seconds in recognizing and appreciating a colleague or student as he or she arrives or leaves your classroom. Greetings and leavings convey a lot about a relationship.

Empathy is not just a nice idea, it is a real force! In each encounter, we have the power to give life or death to another's ideas, feelings, self-value. Every time someone receives an empathetic response from you, you have enhanced your relationship with that person and bestowed a moment of loving kindness to your *self*.

Tame your brain! One of the kindest customs you can adopt for yourself is to tame your thinking modes. Attitude greatly determines how you enjoy success, health, and relationships. The force and effects of your attitudes are crucial, especially in relating to astute, intense gifted children who tend to be more aware and emotionally sensitive than most. Maybe your ultimate power is your power to make choices about how you think. How much mental cruelty do you inflict upon yourself? Check the quality of your thinking: Are your thoughts working for you or against you? Replace a stress-producing thought with a calming one. Just like you select television programs, you can switch channels!

Pay attention to your intention! There are plenty of reminders in the media and popular books to impress us how effective our intentions are. Burdening yourself with dread, resentment, or remorse drains your energy and erodes your presence appeal. Some of us are convinced that essentially, what we think is what we get. You can self-check and do occasional attitude scans. Be your own GPS and determine if your thoughts are directing you to a place of gratitude, competence, and enjoyment or resentment and dread.

To soothe your relationships with your students and colleagues, a valuable gift to yourself is to use your mind to focus your time and energy investment in solutions and contributions. As long as you're thinking, you might as well make your thoughts work for you rather than against you! The next time you are tempted to think, "I *have* to do something," you might assert, "I choose to . . ." or "I've decided to . . ." Sometimes, we deplete our time and mental energy in trying to resolve issues that are out of our responsibility range.

Find understanding and support. One of the most nurturing practices you can do for yourself is to develop supportive relationships and maintain balance in your life. Give time to initiate and develop close, encouraging, inspiring friendships. Consider what you want from others. *Being that quality with them can generate a reciprocal response.*

- If you do not have enough fun and play in your life, explore what is going on in your community; invite someone to share some intriguing venture.
- Do you wonder who you might count on for help if you get sick? You can plan to start your support team: When someone you know is home sick, you can be the one who calls and offers to do an errand on your way home or to pick up and deliver some chicken soup.
- Are you a little too bored? Step out to a bookstore signing or to a study group or lecture that is interesting to you and schmooze a little to rev up new life for your life. You get the idea!

I often hear kind, sensitive, intelligent, interesting adults concede that they feel invisible. They really don't feel heard, understood, or appreciated. Perhaps your empathetic listening skills will be a key to some gratifying social relationships for you.

Be a solution finder; work in resolutions. Refuse to invest in affirming how awful circumstances are. You can shed light on situations by inviting, "How are we going to work this out?"

Scrutinize which old rules no longer apply. Just reflect on a historical perspective and surprise yourself about what used to be proper and true and what options are now open to you. Evaluate the "shoulds" in your life. How much effort is invested in outgrown habits and lifestyles?

Guard time for your creative self-expression. This could be through creating art, music, dance, or any medium that gives you control and expression of your ideas, feelings, meanings—an audible or visual metaphor of what your think, feel, and are.

Exercise for more energy! Try it and decide for yourself.

Breathe. Conscious breathing is instantly accessible to amend your mind and body. Breath is life. For amazing calming and focus, use these simple transformative breathing practices:

- Sit up straight. Exhale completely through your mouth.
- Breathe in through your nose slowly:
  o Start by expanding your belly.
  o Slowly, draw your breath up through your ribs and feel them expand.
  o Continue to inhale up to your collarbone level.
  o Briefly hold your breath for four counts.

- Exhale slowly to the count to four:
  o First, release the air by your collarbone.
  o Continue to exhale down through your rib cage area.
  o Keep on exhaling, drawing in your belly.

- Breathe normally.

Habitually, we are shallow breathers. The more stale air you exhale, the more oxygenated air you can inhale. A quicker calmer is to take a deep breath through your nose. Hold while you count to 10. Exhale. Smile. Your smile somewhat programs your psyche that you're OK!

Listen to your body. What does shoulder pain, tiredness, or headache tell you? Your body doesn't lie.

Acknowledge and accommodate your personality type and different personality preferences of your colleagues and students. If you haven't already done so, investing in taking and interpreting a personality-type indicator, or at least learning about different personality types is a valuable asset for yourself, students, and school faculty and staff. Personality type doesn't go away! You introverts need alone time to regain your energy! You're not being antisocial; you are nurturing your abilities to be amicable! The Platinum Rule: There is often more benefit to all involved to treat other people how they would like to be treated rather than impose what you would prefer.

Have your own dreams. Set small, attainable goals. Do something every day toward achieving satisfaction in your own life. Again, you teach what you are.

Letter to My Fifth-Grade Teacher

Dear Miss Lorenz:

I'm writing because I was remembering you today,
how soft and kind your voice was and how your eyes
sparkled with laughter and light

which is why I wanted to impress you
and why I was so afraid of spelling
where I knew you would discover
I was just another stupid kid.

And so, on the day of the Big Spelling Test,
I made that tiny piece of paper
and when we put our books away,
I cupped it in my hand for use
only when absolutely necessary.

And you moved up and down
the rows of our desks
pronouncing words until
you stopped next to me,
called out a word and,
when everyone was writing,
reached into my clenched fist,
took the paper and then
walked on.

You never made an example of me,
never spoke to my parents about it,
or even mentioned it to me.
And you never treated me differently either,
just went on as though nothing had happened.

But, of course, something did:
I never cheated again, Miss Lorenz.
I never stole another candy bar
or money from my mother's purse
or the top of my father's dresser.

And I am writing to thank you
for treating me with dignity
even as you caught me,
red-handed in sin.

It was as close to Grace as I have ever been.
Perhaps some day I'll know it once again.

Glaser

With grateful permission of the author
Michael S. Glaser

REFERENCES

Albert Einstein's quotes on spirituality. (n.d.). Retrieved February 12, 2008, from http://www.simpletoremember.com/vitals/Einstein.htm

Carson, R. (1965). *A sense of wonder.* New York: Harper & Row.

Maslow, A. H. (1968). *Toward a psychology of being* (2nd ed.). New York: D. Van Nostrand.

May, R. (1975). *The courage to create.* New York: W. W. Norton.

Rogers, C. (1954). Towards a theory of creativity. In P. E. Vernon (Ed.), *Creativity: Selected readings.* Suffolk: Richard Clay.

Index

CORWIN PRESS

The Corwin Press logo—a raven striding across an open book—represents the union of courage and learning. Corwin Press is committed to improving education for all learners by publishing books and other professional development resources for those serving the field of PreK–12 education. By providing practical, hands-on materials, Corwin Press continues to carry out the promise of its motto: **"Helping Educators Do Their Work Better."**